Managing with Altiris 6.x

Stephen Byrne Publications

Notice

First published in the UK by Stephen Byrne Publications

ISBN: 0-9548070-1-4

Printed and bound in the UK by Tandem Press – *www.tandempress.com*

Contents

Preface

Welcome to Managing with Altiris 6.x Second Edition. Whether you are an experienced Altiris Administrator or just learning this product, you are going to be impressed with the new features, increased flexibility and expanded management capabilities.

The development team at Altiris have done an outstanding job of continuing the Altiris tradition of offering superior and well integrated management software.

Audience

Managing with Altiris is designed to walk you through the process of designing, implementing and administering an Altiris infrastructure. The book has been written for:

- Those who are already managing with Altiris but require a better understanding of the how's, why's, do's and don'ts.
- Those who are not familiar with managing with Altiris and require a comprehensive, step by step guide to designing, implementing and administering an Altiris infrastructure.

Software Versions

The following software version and build numbers have been used in this book:

- Notification Server v 6.0.5287 (SP2)
- Inventory Solution for Windows v 6.1.1044
- Software Delivery Solution v 6.1.1023
- Application Metering for Windows v 6.0.1024
- Carbon Copy Solution v 6.1.2003
- Patch Management Solution v6.1.1395
- Deployment Solution v6.1.393

Managing with Altiris at a glance

Chapter 1 – An Introduction to the Altiris Infrastructure, introduces the components that make up an Altiris Infrastructure as well as providing and an overview of some of the solutions developed by Altiris to help manage your enterprise.

Chapter 2 – Designing an Altiris Infrastructure, provides an introduction to designing an Altiris infrastructure.

Chapter 3 – Installing Notification Server, provides detailed information on the installation of Notification Server.

Chapter 4 – Administration Part I, introduces the components that make up the Notification Server Web Console, guides you through navigating within the console and performing basic administrative tasks.

Chapter 5 – Configuring Notification Server guides you through important post installation configuration tasks.

Chapter 6 – The Directory Connector, guides you through installing and configuring the Altiris Directory Connector.

Chapter 7 – The Altiris Agent, covers all aspects of the Altiris Agent, including installation, configuration and administration.

Chapter 8 – Administration Part II, introduces more administrative tasks that all Altiris Administrators should be familiar with.

Chapter 9 – Package Servers, comprehensively covers all aspects of Package Servers, including installation, configuration and administration.

Chapter 10 – Inventory Solution for Windows, guides you through installing, configuring and customizing Inventory Solution for Windows.

Chapter 11 – Software Delivery Solution for Windows, introduces installing, configuring and using Altiris Software Delivery Solution.

Chapter 12 – Software Portal, guides you through configuring and using Software Portal.

Chapter 13 – Application Metering will guide you through the use of Application Metering Solution, which is used to monitor application usage.

Chapter 14 – Carbon Copy Solution looks at deploying, configuring and using Altiris Carbon Copy solution to remotely control and manage remote clients.

Chapter 15 – Patch Management Solution introduces Altiris Patch Management Solution which is used to rollout Microsoft Security patches to desktops and servers.

Chapter 16 – Reporting, guides you through using, creating, modifying and cloning reports.

Chapter 17 – Inventory Forwarding introduces the process of configuring Inventory Forwarding from one Notification Server to another.

Chapter 18 – Upgrading from Notification Server 5.5, provides step by step instructions on upgrading an existing Altiris 5.5x infrastructure to version 6.x.

Chapter 19 – An Introduction to Deployment Solution, provides a design overview as well as step by step instructions on installing Deployment Solution and Server. The chapter also covers configuring Deployment Server and PXE, basic console usage and an introduction to using DS Replication, PCT and RapidInstall.

Appendix – Includes a sample case study, Minimum security permissions for NS, XP SP2 Configuration, SQL best practices and troubleshooting custom inventory scans.

Feedback

I have done my best to make this book as accurate and complete as a single volume reference can be. However, because the topics covered in this book are complex, I'm sure that alert readers will find omissions and possibly some errors - although I hope that there aren't too many of those! If you have suggestions, corrections or comments, please e-mail me at feedback@managingwithaltiris.com or use the web site forum (www.managingwithaltiris.com). I genuinely appreciate hearing from you and sincerely hope that you find Managing with Altiris 6.x Second Edition to be enjoyable and helpful.

1

An Introduction to the Altiris Infrastructure

New Features of Altiris Notification Server 6.x

For those of you who are new to Altiris, skip this section and go to the section 'An Overview of Altiris Suites'. If you are familiar with Notification Server 5.x, read on. For information on upgrading your existing infrastructure, see the chapter 'Upgrading Notification Server' later in this book.

Old Term	*New Term*
Resource Explorer	Resource Manager
Advertisement	Software delivery task
NS Client	Altiris Agent
Notification Server Web Console	Altiris Web Console

New Notification Server Features

Has better support for Terminal Services.

Visual settings, such as the position and size of windows, are retained for each user using the Web Console.

Microsoft Messaging Queue is no longer supported as Altiris now implement their own improved queue.

SQL 7 or MSDE 7 and below are no longer supported.

An overall increase in speed when processing data.

Security Roles to secure the Console.

A new addition to Notification Server 6.x is the 'Reports Builder', which is a wizard-based application used to create reports.

New Package Server Features

Package Servers now support HTTPS. When a certificate is installed on the Package Server it will automatically publish HTTPS URLs instead of HTTP URLs.

Package Servers no longer require IIS to be installed. If IIS is not installed, the Package Server will publish UNC share paths to the packages.

When the Package Server Agent is installed on a computer running Windows 2003 Server it will automatically enable the execution of ASP scripts.

New Altiris Agent Features

The Agent is a single process using fewer system resources.

Power management allows you to wake a machine up, force a machine to request a configuration update or request a basic inventory.

Compress event data over a certain threshold.

Does not depend on Internet Explorer for HTTP communications although Internet Explorer is still required for XML support.

Basic inventory now reports connectivity data for computers - this indicates the percentage of time the computer is not connected to a network, is connected via a LAN, and is connected via a WAN.

No longer restricted to using port 80 for HTTP communication. Client communications can be configured to use a different port number. This is a global setting and applies to all clients.

Localized into seventeen languages with context sensitive help for five languages.

The client Agent can download from UNC sources with bandwidth throttling and checkpoint recovery.

Advertisements are considered disabled once they are no longer active.

When the event queue on the client is full the oldest events are discarded, saving the most recently generated inventory data.

Enhanced agent utility program (AeXAgentUtil.exe).

The Agent now supports multicast package delivery.

New Carbon Copy Features

Support for multiple agent configuration allowing you to target different machine collections with specific Carbon Copy client configuration settings.

Add CCWin32.ini configuration settings through the Web Console instead of editing the file directly.

Localized into eight languages.

Integrates with the new role based security.

New Software Delivery Solution for Windows Features

Includes Software Portal which allows users to manually install and request software through a web interface.

A software delivery wizard.

Ability to send a software package to a client immediately.

Wake a computer up to deliver a package.

Configure the client to run a software package from the source instead of downloading it if over a set threshold.

Removal of a software package from the client if unused for a set threshold.

Customize success and failure codes.

Multicasting Package Delivery is now supported.

Customize the name and description as it appears in the Altiris Agent interface.

New Reporting Features

A reports builder wizard to guide you through setting up simple and complex reports.

Dashboards to show a Solution summary.

The ability to create a collection from the SQL of a report or from the results of a report.

An Overview of Altiris Software Suites

Altiris produces great software to help you manage servers, desktops, laptops and handhelds. Other vendors provide management tools but only Altiris provides total depth of coverage and seamless integration.

Client Management Suite

Client Management Suite is a comprehensive systems management solution for desktops and notebooks. Client Management Suite includes:

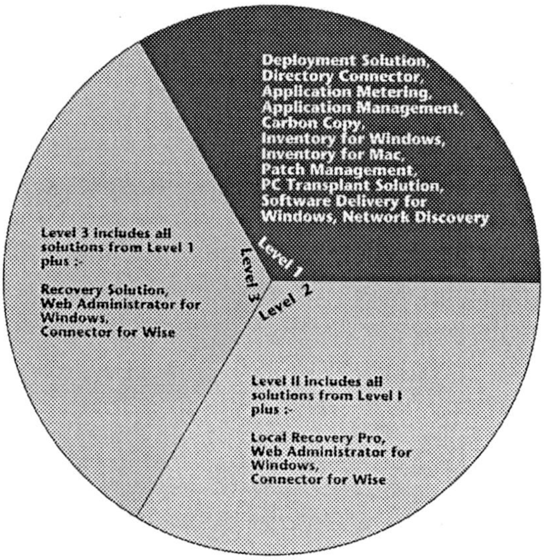

Server Management Suite

Server Management Suite is a comprehensive systems management solution for servers. Server Management Suite includes:

Asset Management Suite

Asset Management Suite is a comprehensive suite used to actively manage your entire asset lifecycle. Asset Management Suite includes:

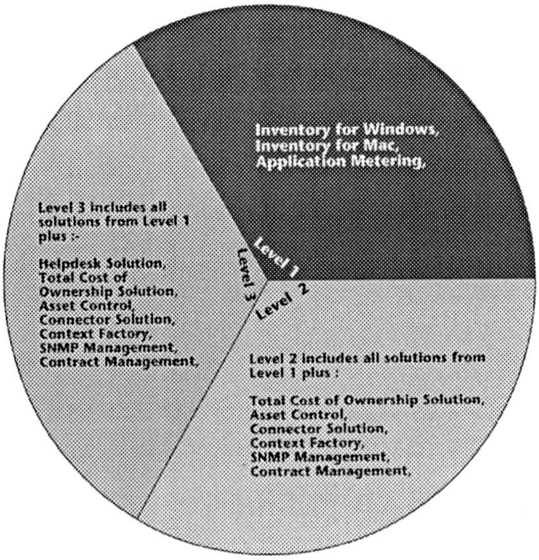

Handheld Management Suite

Handheld Management Suite is a comprehensive systems management solution for Pocket PC, Palm and RIM handhelds. Handheld Management Suite includes:

Visit the Altiris web site at http://www.altiris.com/products for up to date product information.

Altiris Solutions

Inventory Solution for Windows

Inventory Solution for Windows comprehensively and accurately reports hardware and software information to a central repository. The data gathered can be used for tasks such as reporting and software delivery.

Carbon Copy Solution

Carbon Copy Solution is primarily a web based remote control tool but also includes the ability to transfer files, initiate a chat session, remotely print and access a remote clipboard. Carbon Copy Solution is fast, secure, can be centrally managed and is ideal for LAN or WAN environments.

Software Delivery Solution for Windows

Software Delivery Solution for Windows provides a mechanism to deliver and install Windows applications to managed clients from a central web based console. The Solution is easy to use, easily configured and is suitable for LAN, WAN, mobile and remote client environments.

Deployment Solution

Deployment Solution provides image capture and deployment, scripted operating system deployment, user settings migration and LAN based remote control and software delivery.

Patch Management Solution

Patch Management Solution allows you to manage Microsoft software updates and patches. The Solution allows you to configure client analysis and reporting of vulnerabilities as well as providing a flexible mechanism for delivering patches to managed clients.

Application Metering

Application Metering Solution is used to monitor and discover applications used by managed clients. The Solution is easy to use and provides a detailed analysis of specific or all applications used by specific users in your enterprise.

Application Management

Application Management Solution provides a mechanism to manage MSI installed applications and analyze and report changes to a client machine using local registry and file scans. The scheduled scans provide an accurate way of detecting non-standard configurations on managed clients.

Recovery Solution Enterprise

Altiris Recovery Solution provides an automated solution for protecting Windows servers, laptops and desktops. Backup schedules are configured for the entire estate through a central console and offer the capability of backing-up to a central scalable recovery solution server or to local storage.

Local Recovery & Local Recovery Pro

Altiris Local Recovery and Local Recovery Pro provide an automated solution for protecting Windows laptops and desktops. Recovery offers the capability of backing-up to local storage, (local hard disk). Recovery Pro offers the same functionality as Local but also supports open and locked files, Aggregate and individual status reporting and more comprehensive hardware support.

Helpdesk

Altiris Helpdesk Solution is an incident management tool that is built on the Notification Server architecture and is fully integrated with Altiris components such as asset management and remote control tools.

Connector Solution

Altiris Connector Solution allows you to transfer data to and from the Notification Server database. The solution supports ODBC, OLE, LDAP, XML and CSV data formats.

Connector Packs

As well as the generic connector provided in Connector Solution, Altiris also provide connectors for HP OpenView, HP SIM, Remedy, Wise and Microsoft SMS.

Please visit the Altiris web site for a complete and up to date listing of available Altiris Solutions. (http://www.altiris.com/products/)

Altiris Infrastructure components

The basic framework of an Altiris infrastructure consists of a server running Notification Server and all clients that need to be managed, run client software called the Altiris Agent. Package Servers can be used to provide a local package source when delivering software packages to managed clients.

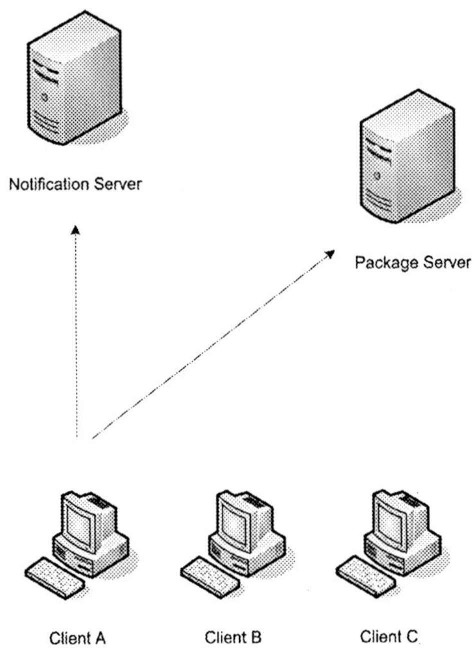

Notification Server

Notification Server is the framework used for Altiris Solutions. On its own, it's just the framework, solutions such as Inventory solution need to be added to make it useful. The infrastructure is modular, meaning that you can start with one or two solutions and grow from there, with each solution adding more functionality. The administrative interface to the Notification Server is web based and can be accessed from any compliant browser, providing the person connecting has the correct permissions.

Solutions

Solutions make Notification Server useful. Each Altiris solution added to the Notification Server framework provides its own specific set of management functions. For example adding a Solution, such as Altiris Inventory Solution for Windows, will allow gathering of inventory data from managed clients.

Altiris Agent

The Altiris Agent runs on the client and provides communication with the Notification Server. At a basic level the client will send basic inventory periodically (Name, Domain, IP information etc), check for new configuration updates, manage bandwidth throttling and checkpoint recovery. As Solutions are added to the Notification Server an agent specific to the new Solution may be added to the Altiris Agent.

Package Servers (Optional)

A Package Server (PS) is used to provide scalability when delivering software and patch packages to clients. Clients receive configuration settings and advertisements from the Notification Server but download software packages from a PS.
The addition of multicasting now allows a client machine to act temporarily as a PS to other clients. Allowing clients to act as a Package Server has two advantages; Firstly it will take some of the load off the dedicated Package Servers and secondly, in a small remote office a dedicated Package Server will not be required because an existing client can be used instead.

Reporting Server

A Reporting Server is a Notification Server that is configured to receive forwarded inventory from one or more Notification Servers. This server is used only for creating, scheduling and viewing reports. Clients report to their assigned Notification Server, data is then forwarded from the clients NS to the reporting Notification Server.

Deployment Server

A "Deployment Server" provides imaging, software delivery, and other real-time tasks for a local area network. Deployment Servers can be located locally on sites and managed centrally.

Deployment Agent

The Deployment Agent also known as the Aclient runs on the client and provides communication with the Deployment Server.

Concepts

Collections

Groups of computers based on defined criteria such as, all Windows XP workstations or all computers running Microsoft Office XP. The Notification Server installation creates many predefined collections to get you started. You can find collections in the Resources tab of the Web Console.

Packages

A package defines the files, command-line and instructions for distributing software. For example a Software Delivery package could include a single file or multiple files which are sent to a client and then executed. Packages can be found in the Resources tab as well as the Configuration tab of the Web Console.

Task

In the context of Software Delivery, a Task notifies a collection of computers that a program is available to run.

Policies

There are two types of policies, Notification Policies and Solution Policies. Notification Policies consists of a set of instructions designed to automate an administrative function. For example, a Notification Server policy can instruct the Notification Server to e-mail a monthly hardware inventory report to a specific user. A Solution Policy is used to configure Solution Agent settings and perform tasks such as software package advertisement. Most policies can be found in the Configuration tab of the Web Console.

Reports

Reports are used to view data in the Notification Server database. All reports can be found in the Reports tab of the Web Console.

Summary

This chapter introduced the new features of Altiris 6.x, the suites provided by Altiris, and the basic components that make up an Altiris infrastructure.

Altiris 6.x has had a major interface overhaul as well as a large number of small changes to framework and solutions. This has helped to improve the overall functionality and speed of the product.

In this chapter we also saw that the Altiris infrastructure components include, the Notification Server, the client and the Package Server. The Notification Server is the framework, Package Servers provide clients with a local package download source and clients are clients.

The next chapter, 'Designing an Altiris Infrastructure', provides an overview of the requirements, considerations and steps necessary to design an Altiris infrastructure.

2

Designing an Altiris Infrastructure

Introduction

This chapter provides an introduction to designing an Altiris CMS infrastructure. The design considerations detailed in the chapter along with the examples should help you get a better understanding of the typical requirements and considerations.
Use this chapter to get a basic understanding of the design considerations but consult with a qualified Altiris Design consultant prior to implementation.

Outline of the Design Process

Asset Discovery – Asset Discovery provides you with an accurate and complete view of the technological assets in an organization. Having an accurate and complete view of the assets is the first step toward effectively determining how to design the Altiris infrastructure. Use this phase to determine the number of physical sites, the number of machines per site, WAN links, Operating System levels etc.

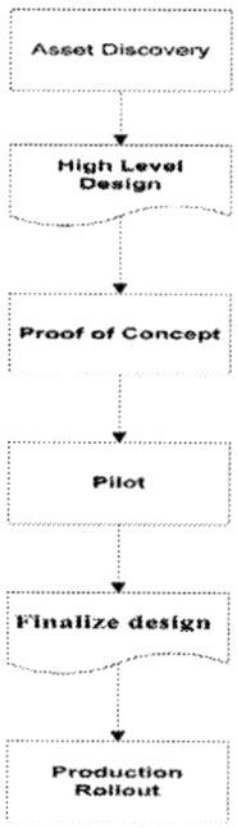

Initial or High Level Design - A High-Level Altiris infrastructure Design presents a non-technical view of the different infrastructure components, how they work, how they interact with each other and how they will be implemented. Use this phase to provide an overview of where the Altiris infrastructure components will sit within the infrastructure. Remember this is a high level phase so don't worry if it has to be changed in the final design.

Proof of Concept – A Proof of Concept (POC) is used to validate product functionality normally prior to full product purchase. Specific scenarios unique to your organization can be tested, validated and documented during this phase. The POC will also allow provide you with an understanding of the basic components and functionality and enable you to develop a pilot test plan for deployment to your environment.

Pilot – A Pilot is used to validate the high-level design and should only exist within a limited-scope of the production environment. During this phase, significant time will be spent customizing the Altiris infrastructure and settings as well as further validating process and procedures. This phase can also be used to introduce internal staff to the Altiris toolset.

Finalize the design – The Pilot phase may flag the need to alter the initial design. Use this phase to document the detailed design and produce a production rollout plan.

Begin Rollout – Begin the Altiris Infrastructure rollout followed by the client agent rollout as per your production rollout plan.

Design Objective

The objective of a design is to define the number and placement of Notification and Packages Servers.

To determine the number and placement of a Notification Server(s) you will need to consider;

- The network Topology including the bandwidth availability between sites.
- The business model.
- The total number of clients that will be managed.
- The desired administrative model.
- Which Altiris Solutions are used and how each Solution and the associated Solution Agent will be configured.

To determine the number and placement of Package Servers you will need to consider;

- The number of physical sites and the number of clients per site.
- The Solutions that will be used.
- The bandwidth availability between sites.

The following pages will discuss these considerations and outline typical design scenarios.

The number of Notification Servers

One of the first design considerations, after you have performed an asset discovery, is to determine the number of Notification Servers required to support the management of your estate. Altiris have tested one Notification Server installed with Client Management Suite Level 1 and 50k clients. In theory this means that up to 50K clients can use one Notification Server. In practice, the number of clients that can use one Notification Server will depend on factors including the number of clients, the solutions used, the hardware specification of the server, agent configuration, the network infrastructure and the administrative model.

The number of Clients

A typical installation of Client Management Suite will use Inventory, Carbon Copy, Software Delivery and Patch Management. In this instance allow one Notification for every 15k-20k clients. One Notification Server can handle more clients if fewer solutions are used or if the solution agents are configured to communicate with the Notification Server less frequently.

The Solutions

Adding a solution to a Notification Server will typically add to the load on that server. The addition of the solution does not in itself add load but the related components such as a solution agent will. Don't install a solution until you intend to use it.

Agent Configuration

Managed clients use the **Altiris Agent** to communicate with the Notification Server. Clients periodically send Basic Inventory and check the Notification Server for configuration updates. If these tasks are performed frequently, clients will be more up to date but the load on the Notification Server and the amount of network traffic will be increased. If the load on the NS becomes too high over a sustained period then consider either reconfiguring the agent to communicate less frequently or add another Notification Server.

Each solution will typically have one or more solution agents which plug-in to the Altiris Agent. A solution agent such as the Inventory agent will periodically report hardware and software inventory to the Notification Server. If this agent is configured to report inventory frequently then the inventory for the client will be more up to date but the load on the Notification Server and the amount of network traffic will increase.

If there is a need to have frequent collection of inventory for a large number of clients, the load may become too great and a second NS may be required. Before adding another NS, consider configuring clients to report inventory at different times.

Network Infrastructure

The network infrastructure will heavily influence the design of an Altiris infrastructure. With respect to the number of Notification Servers, the primary consideration will be the total number of clients and the physical network infrastructure. In a multiple site infrastructure, sites with a large number of users and a heavily utilized or slow connection to the other sites may warrant a separate Notification Server for each site. See the examples in the following pages.

Administrative Model

The IT Administrative model will influence the number of Notification Servers. For example, in a worldwide organization where IT support staff are located in different geographical regions each region may warrant its own Notification Server.

Using one Notification Server.

In a one Notification Server infrastructure all managed clients are configured from that Notification Server. Administrative functions such as software delivery and patch management are all executed from one Notification Server. Clients report too and receive their configuration from one Notification Server.

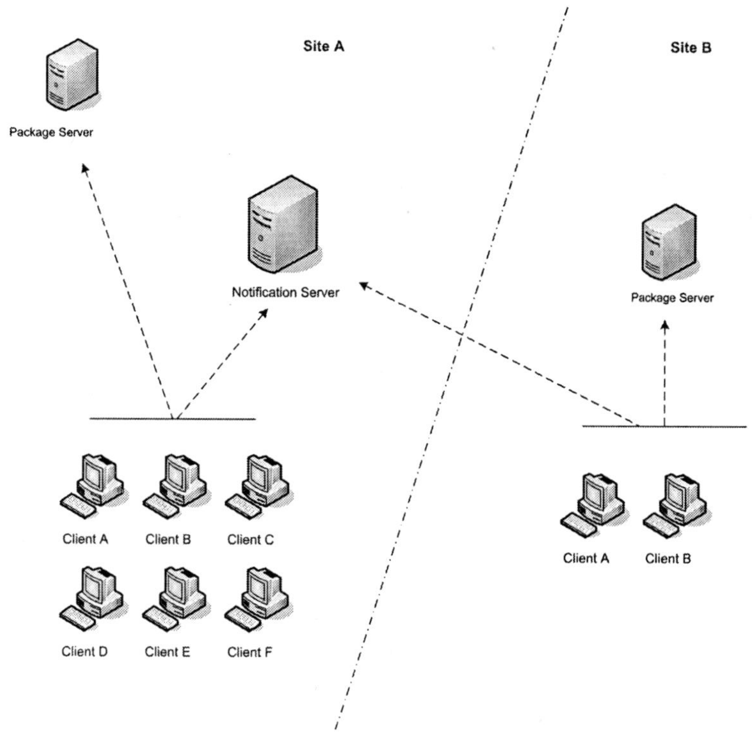

Advantages

All clients can be easily managed from one Notification Server.

Disadvantages

In a geographically dispersed infrastructure all clients will receive configuration updates and upload inventory data across the WAN.

Using multiple Notification Servers

Multiple Notification Servers can be used to scale the Altiris Infrastructure as well as decentralize administration. In the diagram below each region has a Notification Server. All clients pass Inventory data and receive their configuration and software/patch advertisements from their regional Notification Server. Inventory data is then forwarded from each regional Notification Server to a central Notification. Once forwarding is complete, the central Notification Server contains the Inventory data for all clients in all regions.

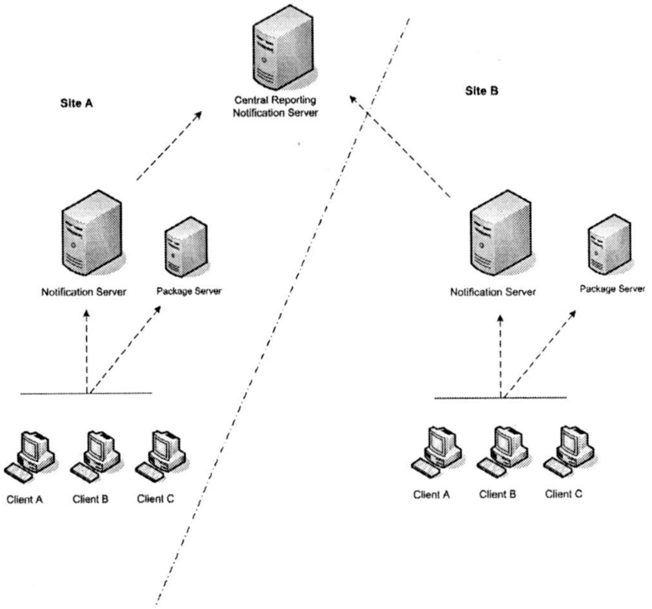

Altiris Notification Server 6.0 does not currently support passing data from the parent to child sites. Data only flows up to parent sites. For this reason a Notification Server Administrator can not manage child sites from the central site. An Administrator must connect to the Notification Server of the child site in order to manage tasks such as software and patch delivery.

Advantages

Provides a more scalable solution and a means of decentralizing administration.

Disadvantages

All clients can not be managed from one Notification Server. (Even if Inventory forwarding is used.) For example to roll out a patch to all clients, the patch package definition and task must be created separately on each Notification Server.

Notification Server location

All managed clients need to be able to talk directly with the Notification Server to request configuration updates as well as report inventory data, application metering data and status events. For this reason it is important that the Notification Server is placed in the site with a network connection that has enough available bandwidth to accommodate the network traffic from managed clients in its own site and in other sites.

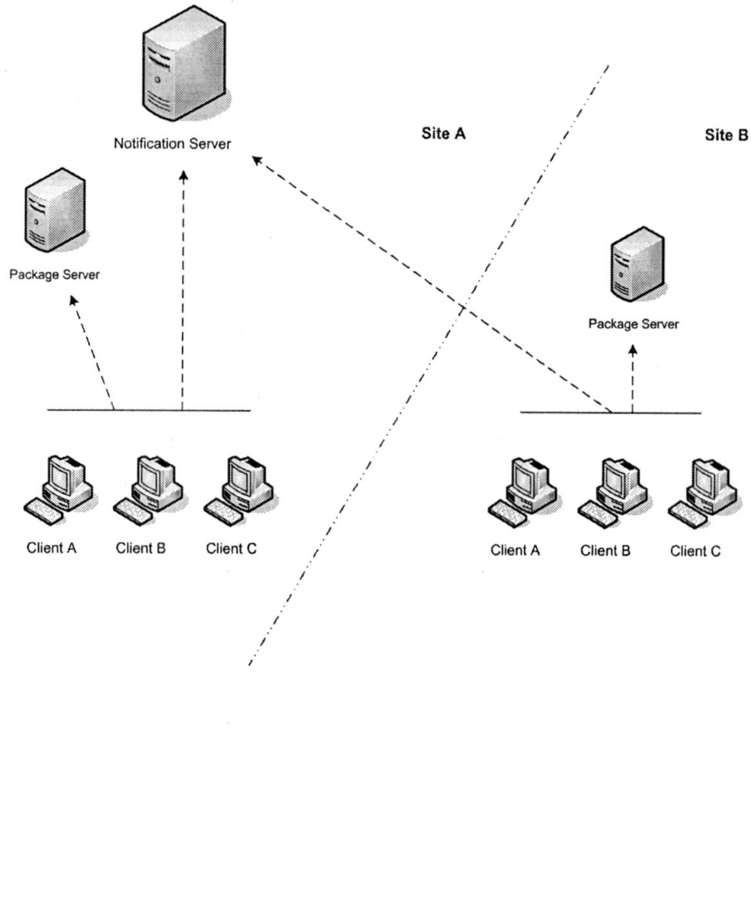

The number and placement of Package Servers

Package Servers are optional but are recommended in an infrastructure where Software Delivery Solution or Patch Management Solution is used. Clients download advertised software packages and patches from the Notification Server or from a Package Server. If no Package Servers exist in an Altiris Infrastructure then clients can only download packages from one source, the Notification Server. When Package Servers are used, clients can be configured to download packages from a closer package source instead of a remote package source.

Number and location of Package Server

The number of physical sites and the number of managed users per site provides a good indicator of the number of Package Servers required in an Altiris infrastructure. Plan for one Package Server for every 1,000 managed clients in a location. Use multiple Package Servers in locations with more than 1,000 managed clients. Use the design examples later in this chapter for some ideas.

Multicast Distribution

The addition of multicast distribution allows a managed client to act temporarily as a Package Server to other clients. Allowing clients to act as a Package Server has two advantages; Firstly it will take some of the load off the dedicated Package Servers and secondly, in a small remote office a dedicated Package Server will not be required because an existing client can be used instead.

To use this new feature, multicasting must be enabled on all network switches in your infrastructure and the Altiris Agent must be configured to use multicasting. *For more information on multicasting see chapter 7, The Altiris Agent.*

Altiris Infrastructure Design Examples

One Site Design

The figure below shows an infrastructure with one physical site. Clients request configuration information from the Notification Server and can download packages from the Package Server or the Notification Server.

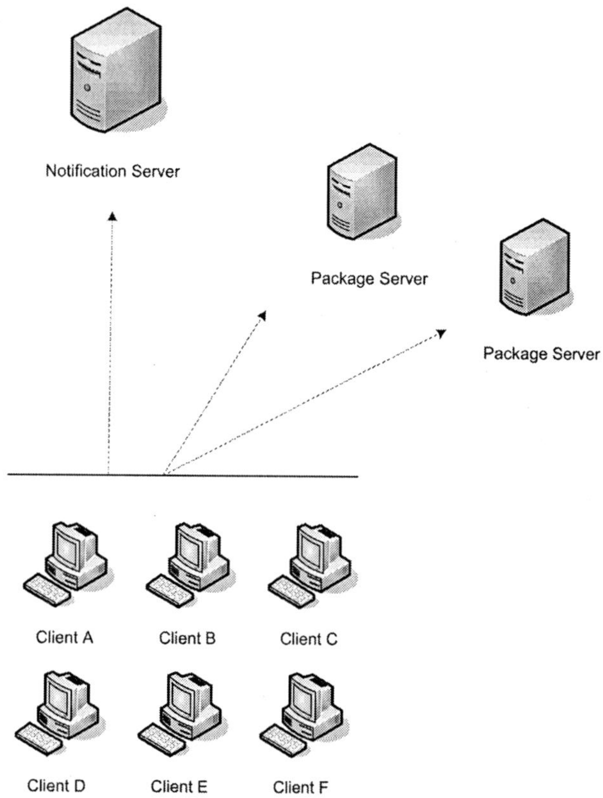

Packages are downloaded from the Package Server or the Notification Server. Inventory data as well as event data are always sent directly to the Notification Server.

Two-Site Design with centralized Administration

The figure below shows an infrastructure with two physical sites. Package Servers have been used in both sites.

Clients in Site A will request configuration information from the local Notification Server and will download packages from the local Package Server in Site A.

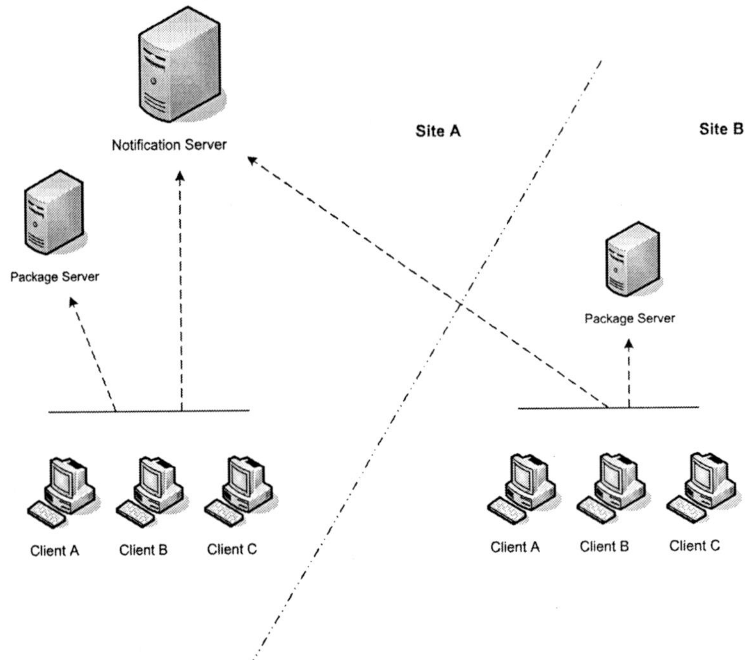

Clients in Site B will request configuration information (2-5K) from the Notification Server across the WAN but will download packages from the local Package Server in Site B. All clients are managed using the Notification Server in Site A.
Inventory data as well as event data are always sent directly to the Notification Server.

Two-Site Design with decentralized Administration

The figure below shows an infrastructure with two physical sites. Each site has it's own IT staff and will manage their own Altiris infrastructure.

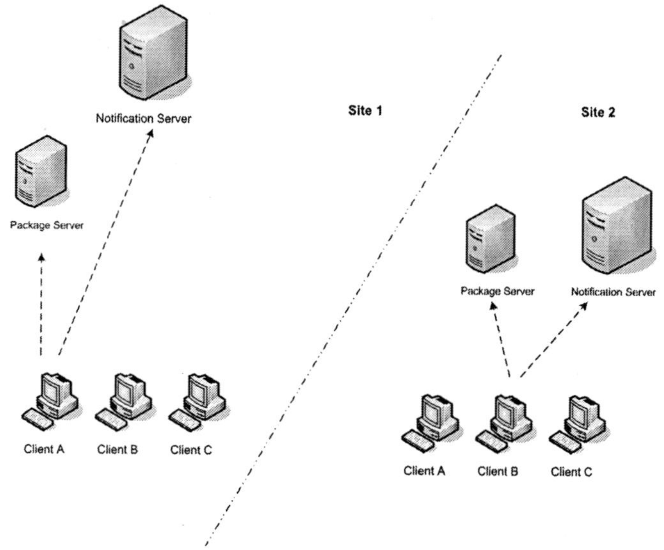

In the figure above clients in Site 1 only communicate with the Notification Server and Package Server in Site 1. Clients in Site 2 only communicate with the Notification Server and Package Server in Site 2.

Two-Site Design with decentralized Administration and Inventory Forwarding

Inventory forwarding is used to consolidate the inventory data from multiple Notification Servers.

In the design below inventory is forwarded from both Notification Servers to a central Notification Server in Site A. The central Notification Server does not have any clients and is only used for reporting purposes.

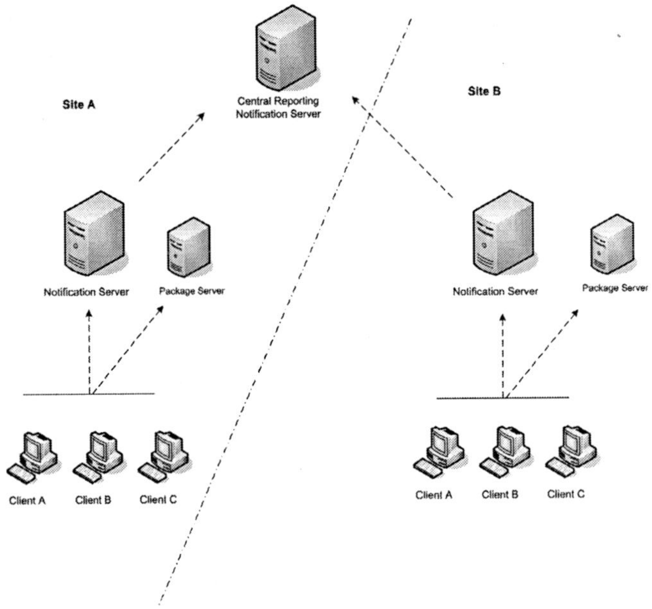

IT staff in Site A manage clients in Site A. IT staff in Site B manage clients in Site B. An authorized user can run reports from the central Notification Server using the data forwarded from both Notification Servers.

Hardware & Software Suggestions

Notification Server

A Notification Server has similar hardware requirements to an Application Server. The number of managed clients that can be supported by one Notification Server will largely depend on the Solutions used, the Server specification and the configuration of Solutions and associated agents. The more frequently clients talk to and send data to the Notification Server, the busier it will be. More RAM and processors will allow the Notification Server to handle more clients.

Other NS Considerations

Notification Server uses Microsoft SQL to store all data. The database can reside on the same server as the Notification Server or on another server. Having SQL on another server will free resources on the Notification Server and may improve performance but make sure that there is at least a 100 Mb connection from NS to the SQL box.

Package Server

One Package Server for every 1,000 managed clients is recommended. The Package Server itself has similar hardware requirements to a File & Print Server. A fast hard disk preferably RAID and a good network card is the key. The Package Server Agent that runs on the Package Server has little impact or overhead on the server.

Summary

This chapter provided an introduction to designing an Altiris infrastructure. The primary components of the infrastructure are the Notification Server, the Package Server and the client. The role of each of the components were discussed and sample designs and scenarios were provided to help you understand where each component sits within the infrastructure.

The next chapter 'Installing the Notification Server Framework' guides you through installing Notification Server step by step.

3

Installing the Notification Server Framework

Introduction

The Notification Server installation is segmented in to two parts, the Windows GUI phase and the Web phase. The initial Windows GUI phase unpacks the Notification Server install files and creates the folder and web structure. The second phase, the Web Phase, asks configuration questions, then creates the Notification Server database, completes the configuration and launches the Altiris Web Console.

Notification Server System Requirements

Minimum	*Recommended Minimum*
Win2k Server SP2 or above	Win2k Server SP4 or Windows 2003
IIS running on NTFS	IIS running on NTFS
MSDE 2000 SP3 or above	SQL 2000 SP3 or above
Pentium III 800 MHz	Pentium IV 2.8 MHz
1 GB Ram	2 GB RAM
HDD 150MB plus of free space	HDD 1GB plus of free space
MDAC 2.7, .Net 1.1 & IE 6.0	MDAC 2.7, .Net 1.1 & IE 6.0

The Packages and patches you may wish to deploy now and in the future can be stored on the Notification Server or on another server. Ensure that you have enough free space available for such storage.

Installing Notification Server Step by Step

Step 1 – Install the Prerequisite Software

Install either MSDE 2000 SP3 (Testing only) or SQL 2000 SP3 or above on either the server that will be your Notification Server or a remote server. For instructions on installing SQL see your Microsoft documentation. For recommendations on the SQL configuration and some general pointers see the appendix at the end of this book.

Install the software prerequisites such as MDAC and the .Net framework on the machine that will be the Notification Server. All of the components can be downloaded from the Microsoft web site and some operating systems such as Windows 2003 include .Net framework. Reboot the server after the prerequisite software has been installed.

Step 2 – Create an Application Identity account

Create a Domain User account in Active Directory. Make the account a member of the local Administrators group on the server where Notification Server will be installed and also an administrator on the machine hosting the SQL server. The account should be a member of Domain Users so that you can browse Active Directory resources within the console and should be a local Administrator so that it has full access to the system.

This account will be used as the application identity account for Notification Server and is used to move data within NS, IIS and to the SQL database. Always ensure that you logon with the Application Identity account, when installing Notification Server and any add-on solutions. Use a complex password and ensure it is configured to never expire.

Step 3 – Logon using the Application Identity account

Once you have created the Application Identity account, login using the new account on the server that will host Notification Server.

Step 4 – Download and start the Install Helper

Using the Install Helper to install Notification Server is the recommended method of installation. The helper will check your server for prerequisites and prompt for any applications that need to be installed prior to installing Notification Server.

Go to http://www.solutionsam.com/solutions/6_0/ and download the install helper files.

Once downloaded, double click the file to launch the helper. (Unpack if necessary)

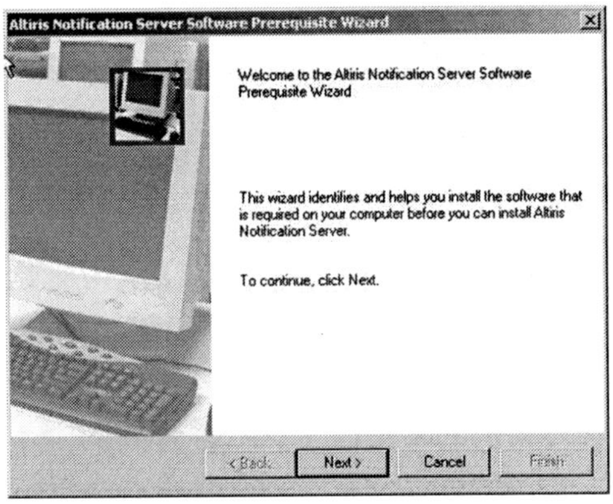

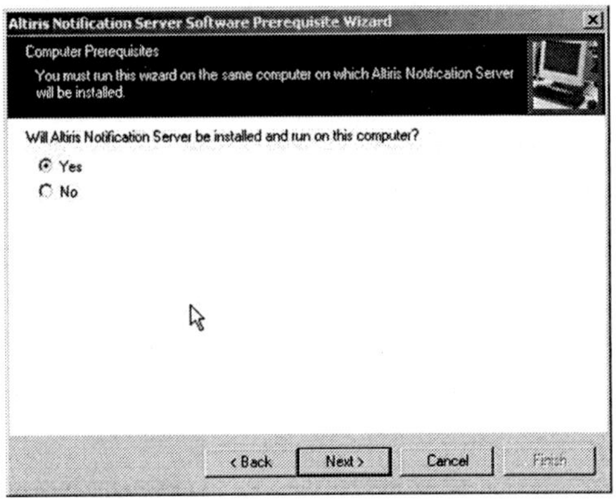

Once the Helper is launched use the **'Next'** and **'Back'** buttons to navigate the wizard. Any prerequisites that have not been met will be displayed in the Install Helper screen. Ignore MDAC, ASP and .Net if you will allow the Notification Server installation to install these components.

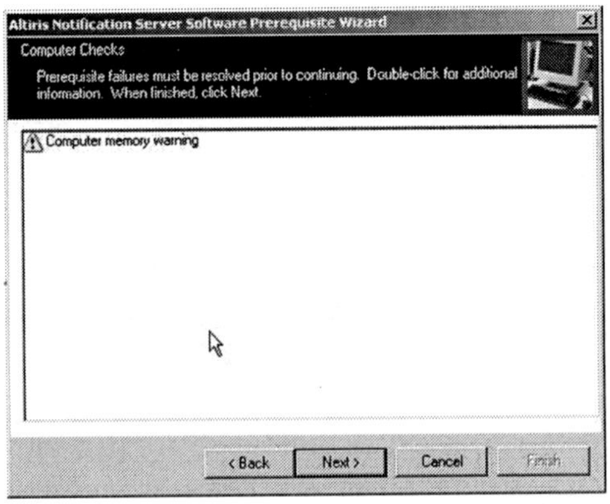

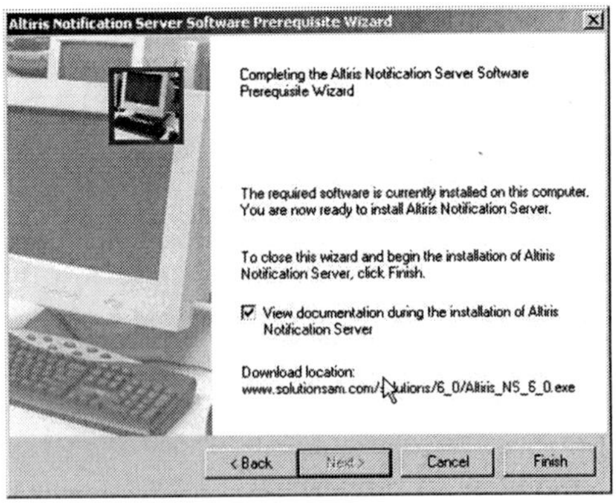

At the end of the Install Helper, when all prerequisites have been met, the Helper will connect to the Altiris web site and download the Notification Server install file.

Click 'Open' when prompted to download the Notification Server install file.

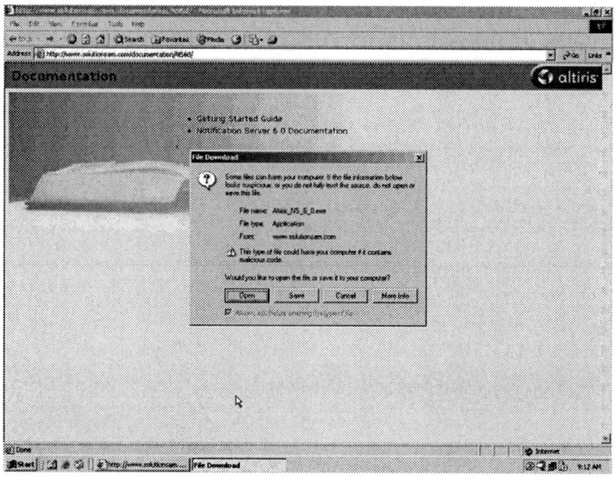

Note If the server does not have Internet access, then the Install Helper will be unable to automatically download the file. In this case, cancel the Helper once prerequisites have been met then go to http://www.solutionsam.com/solutions/6_0/ and manually download the Notification Server source file. Once the file has been downloaded, start the Server installation by double clicking the downloaded file.

Step 5 – Starting the installation

Once the installation file has been downloaded, the setup application will unpack the downloaded file and begin the installation.

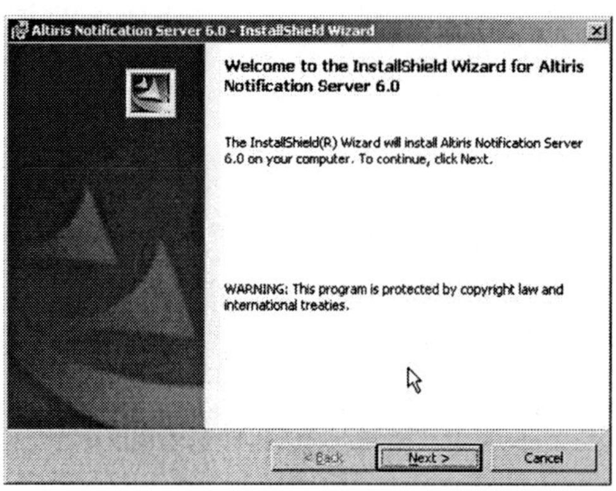

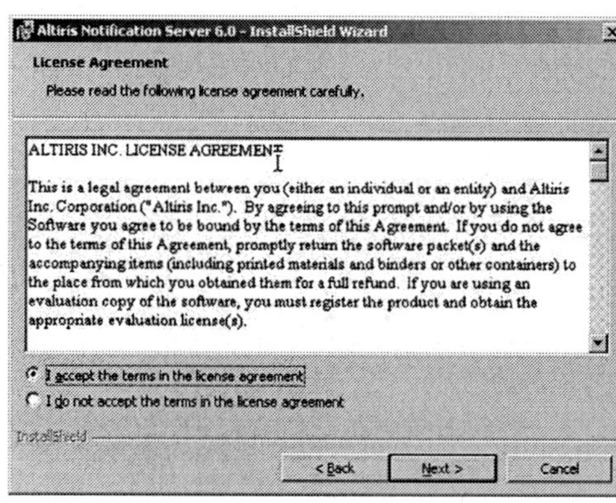

Read and agree any licensing agreements and use **'Next'** and **'Back'** buttons to navigate. (This step also applies if you manually started the install) After you have accepted licensing, enter the user and organization name then click **Next**.

Step 6 – Choose a Custom or Complete installation method

The only difference between a Custom or Complete install is that the Custom install will allow you to change the installation drive and path. Use the **'Next'** button to continue through the install wizard.

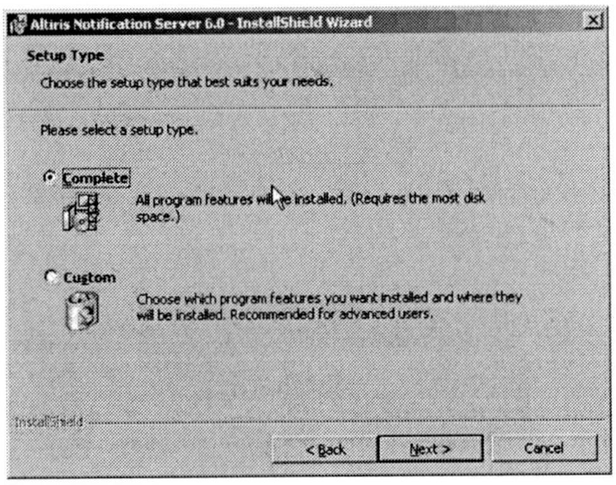

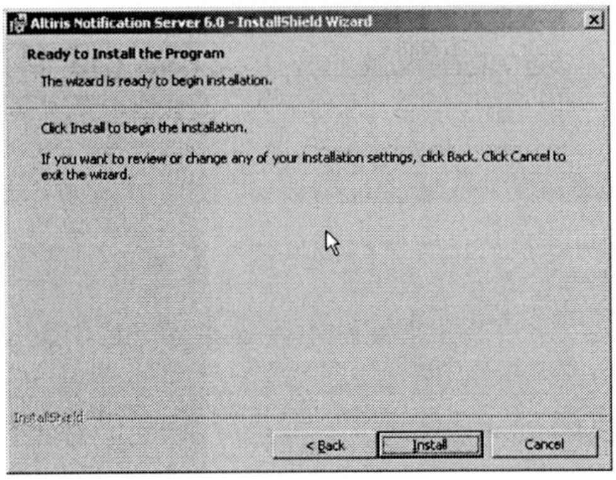

The installation files will now be unpacked to a temporary location. Use the **Finish** button to end the first phase of the installation.

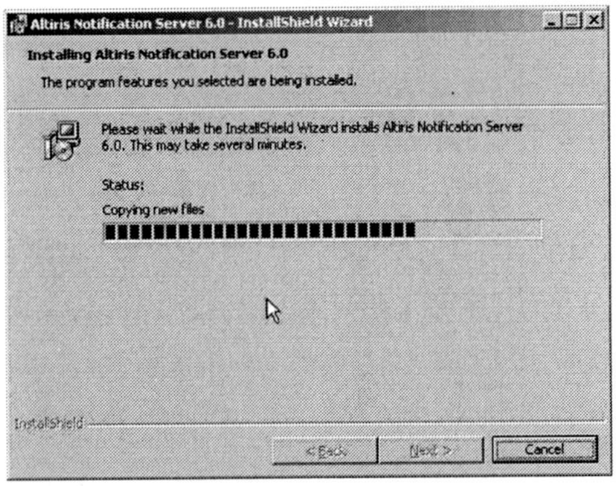

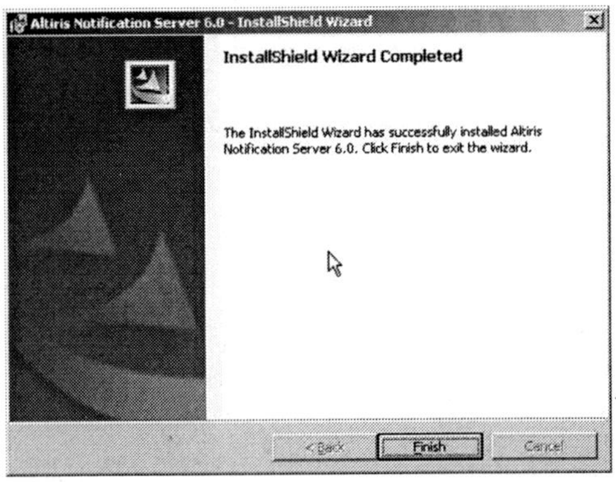

After **Finish** is selected, applets such as the Helpdesk Proxy and AppWeaver are installed. Once the applets have been successfully installed, a browser window is displayed and the second phase of the installation begins.

Step 7 – User Identity Settings

This is the first step in the second phase of the installation, the web phase. In this dialog you must provide the name and password of the account that will be used by Notification Server to move data and run services on the server. This account is called the Application Identity account and as mentioned previously must be a local Administrator on the Notification Server and must be able to logon to the SQL server. The name must be input in the form, Domain\User Name or ServerName\User Name. Input the Application Identity account details created earlier.

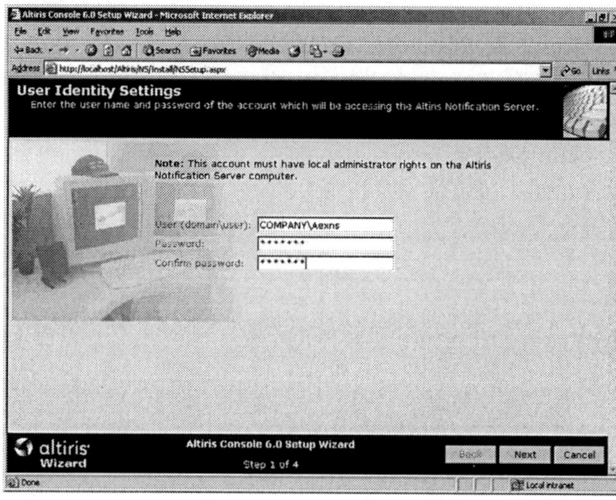

Step 8 – E-Mail Settings

Notification Server can be configured to send an e-mail alert when a predefined condition is met. Enter the name of an SMTP server and a username and password if required. This dialog is optional.

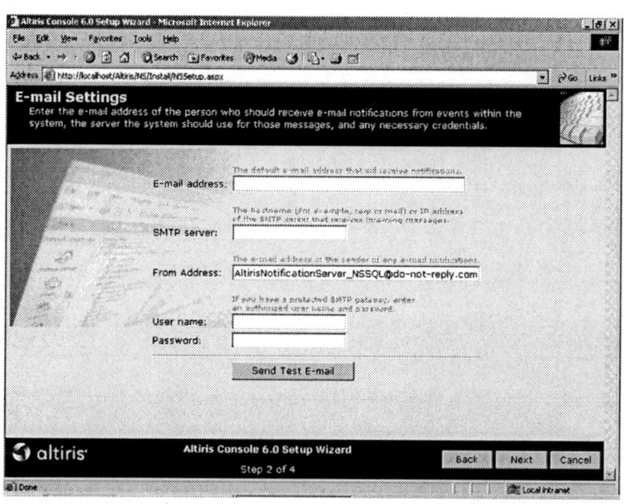

Step 9 – Database Settings

This step is used to configure the name of the SQL server, the database name, timeouts and SQL application credentials.

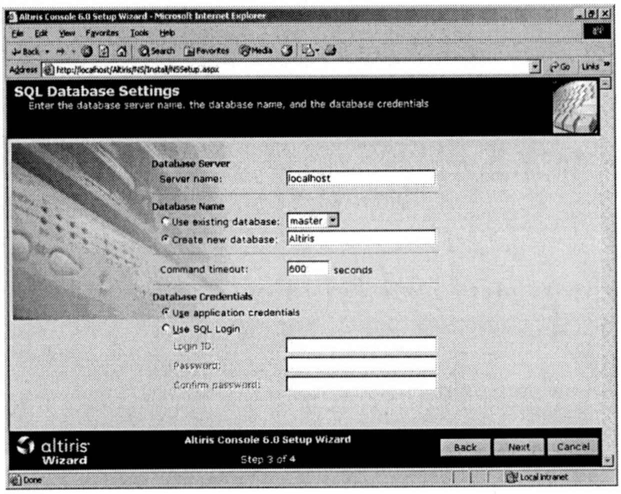

Enter the name of the server where SQL has been installed. Use **'Localhost'** if the SQL server is on the same server as the Notification Server. Use the application credentials to access the SQL server and leave the timeout as default. See the appendix for SQL Server configuration and best practices.

Step 10 – Configures the Database and Services

This step displays a summary of the options chosen during installation. If you want to change any of the options use the 'Back' button to go back. All of the options chosen can be changed later using the Altiris Web Console. Use **Finish** to continue.

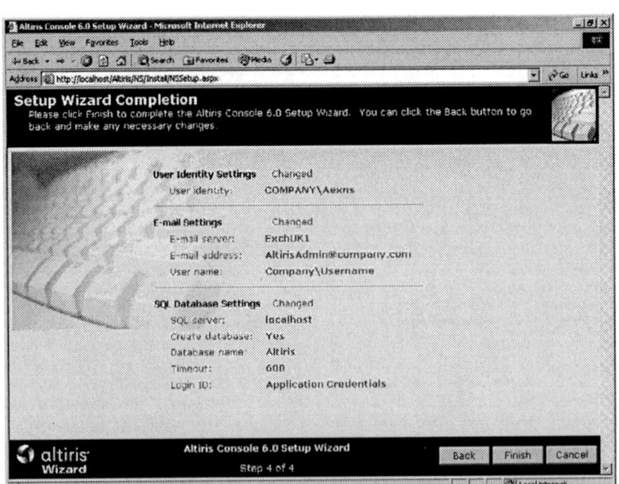

The final part of the installation creates services, the database and folder structure. This step can take approximately 20 to 30 minutes depending on the server specification.

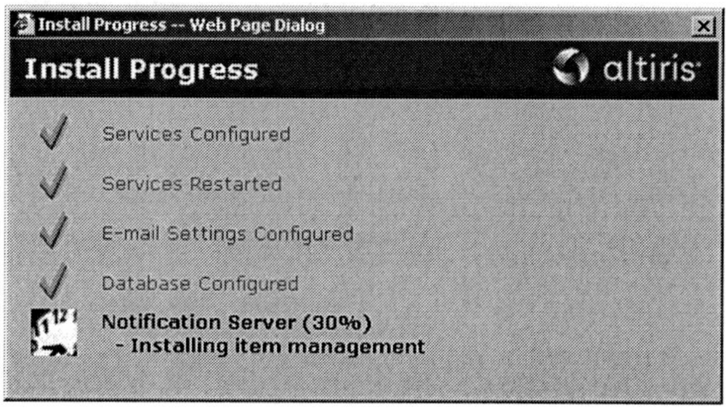

Step 11 – Launches the Altiris Web Console

Once the installation is complete a web browser is launched displaying the Altiris Web Console.

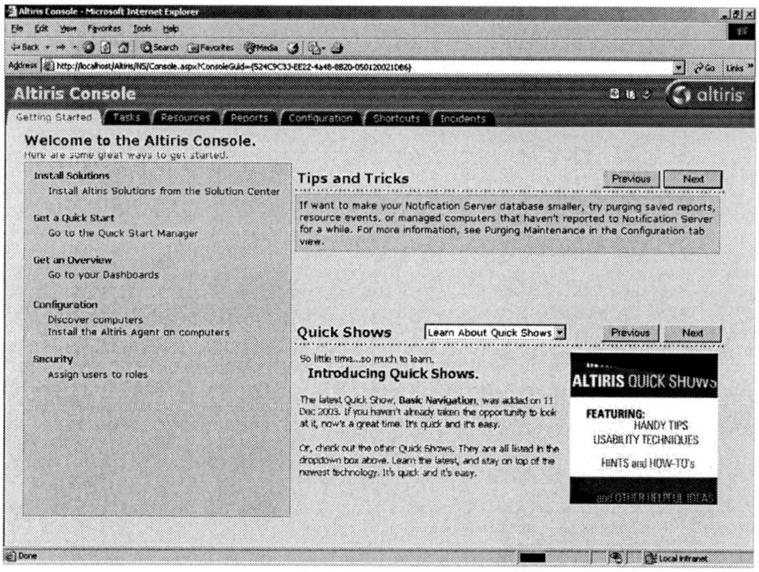

The installation of Notification Server is complete when the Web Console is launched.

Summary

This chapter described the requirements and the process of installing Notification Server framework step by step.
The installation had two phases, the Windows GUI and the Web phase. In the Windows GUI phase the Install Helper was used to check prerequisites then download the Notification Server software from the Altiris web site and start the installation. When the GUI phase of the installation was finished the Web phase began and asked for configuration information before completing the installation and launching the Web Console.

The next chapter 'Administration Part I' guides you through using the Web Console and performing common administrative tasks.

4

Administration (Part I)

The Web Console

The Web Console is the interface to Notification Server and is used to access and configure the Server as well as administer managed clients. The console can be accessed locally at the server or from a workstation with Windows NT and IE 6.x or above.

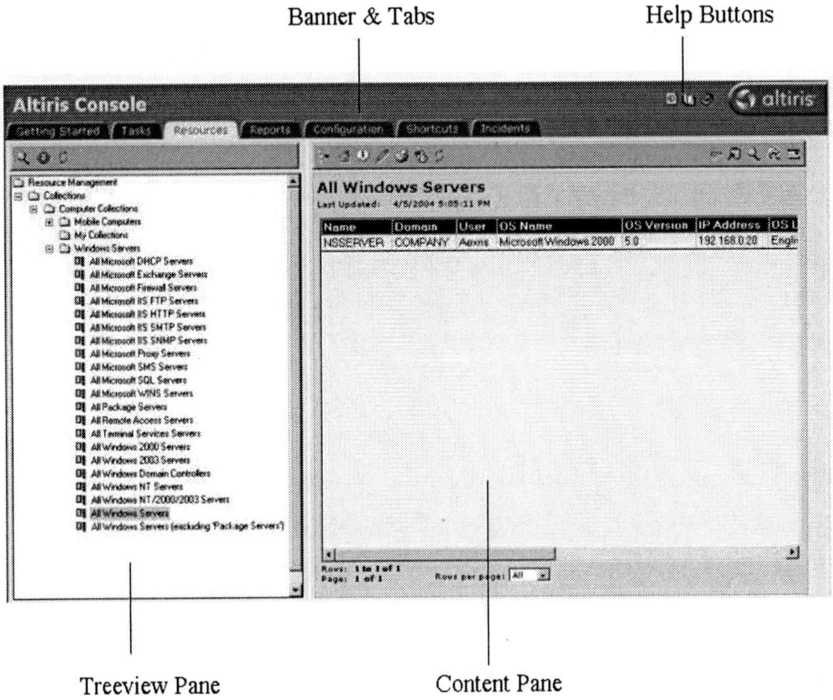

The Web Console shown above consists of a Banner, Tabs, a Treeview pane and a Content pane.

Ports used to access the Console

If the Web Console is accessed from a remote browser RPC, HTTP and DCOM are used during communications.

The following ports are used:
HTTP port 80, DCOM ports 135, RPC 135, 1500 and 2500, SQL ports 53, 135, 137, 139, 1433.

Accessing the Console

Use this URL when accessing remotely

http://NSServer/Altiris/NS/Console.aspx

(Where NSServer is the name of your Notification Server.)

The first time you connect to the Web Console from a machine, local administrative privileges are required to install Web Console ActiveX controls. A user without local administrative rights must either be given local admin rights or the ActiveX controls must be installed with elevated permissions.

Note Security Roles can be defined to control what can be seen in the Console. See the security section of the chapter 'Configuring Notification Server' for more information.

Common Web Console Toolbar Buttons

The Web Console toolbars are context sensitive meaning that the toolbar set that is displayed in the console will depend on what Tab you are viewing and what object is currently selected.

 **Help Index**

 **Help for the current page**

 **Copy Right**

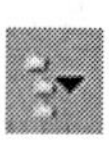 **Right Click Toolbar**

 **Copy**

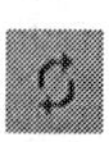 **Refresh**

 **Expand All**

 **Find**

 **Find Again**

Getting Started Tab

This section of the web console is used by first time users of the console and provides access to frequently used configuration and security tasks.

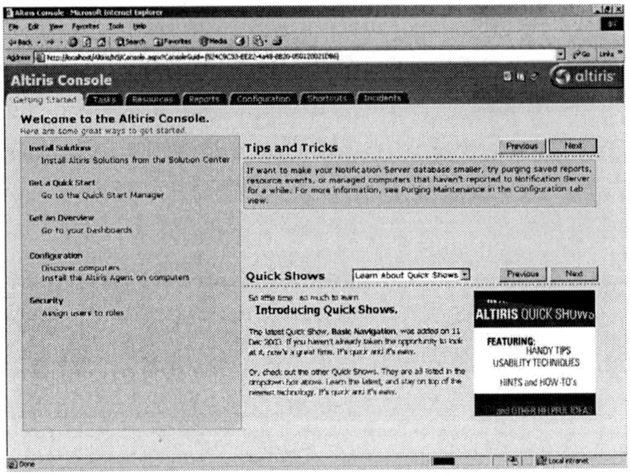

The Tasks Tab

The Tasks tab is where you perform tasks such as deliver a software package, remote control a client, define applications to meter and capture a user's computer profile. Specific solutions are required to provide this functionality. This section is displayed in a tree and folder structure as shown below.

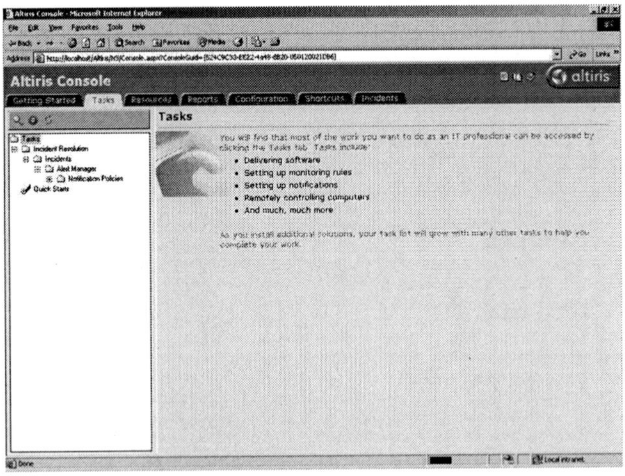

The Resources Tab

The Resources tab provides access to the assets, software packages and computers in your enterprise. This section is displayed in a tree and folder structure as shown below.

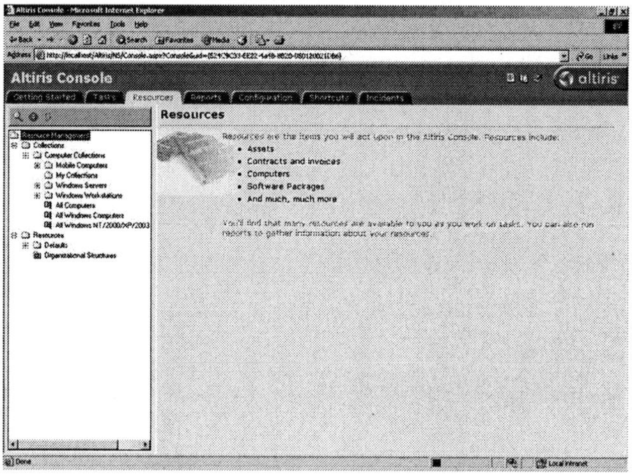

Folders within the tree structure include:

Collections folder – Notification Server creates default collections when installed. Computer collections such as 'All Windows Workstations' contain all machines that are running a Windows operating system and are workstations, not servers. Collection membership is based on predefined collection criteria and is dynamic, machines may move in and out of collections based on that criterion. An administrator can create customized collections based on the data in the Altiris database.
As solutions are added to Notification Server, solution Specific collections may be added to Notification Server by that solution.

Resources folder – Provides access to imported active directory objects (Directory connector required) as well as software packages (Software Delivery Solution required) and internal resource objects used by Notification Server..

The Reports Tab

The Reports tab provides access to the many predefined web based reports provided by Altiris. As solutions are added to the Notification Server framework, solution specific folders containing reports pertaining to that solution are added. A new addition to Notification Server 6.x is the 'Reports Builder', which is a wizard based application used to create reports. The reports tab is displayed in a tree and folder structure as shown below.

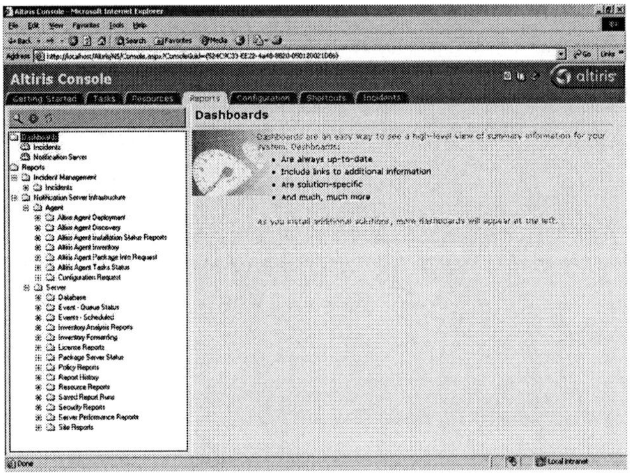

Folders within the tree structure include:

Dashboards – Dashboards provide an overview of important aspects of your system. Dashboards summarize the activity of a solution. For example if Software Delivery Solution is installed, then a Software Delivery Dashboard will display package download and execution summary information.

Reports folder – The reports that are available depend on the Solutions installed. Each solution installed will add its own list of web Reports.

The Configuration Tab

The configuration tab is where most of the Notification Server configuration tasks are performed. This section is displayed in a tree and folder structure as shown below.

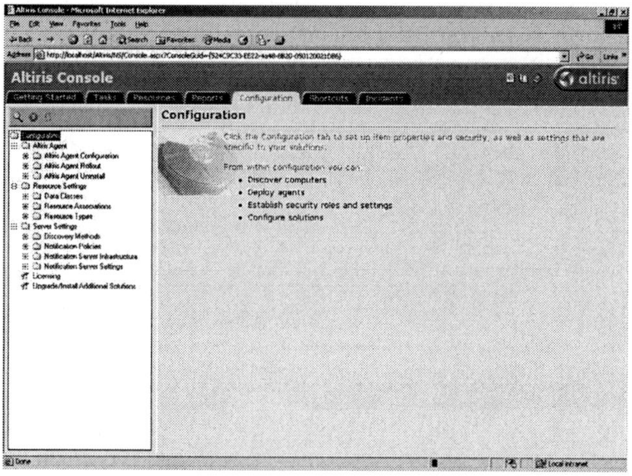

Folders within the tree structure include:

Altiris Agent folder – Includes options to Install, Uninstall, Configure and Upgrade the Altiris Agent

Resource Settings – Provides access to Data Classes and Resource Types

Server Settings – Includes Discovery Methods, Package Server Agent install and uninstall, Inventory Forwarding and Notifications configuration.

Solutions Settings – Provides access to Solution Configuration. This folder is populated once solutions have been added to Notification Server.
The root of the tree structure includes access to Solution Installation and Licensing.

The Shortcuts Tab

The Shortcuts Tab is used to store shortcuts to objects that reside in other parts of the Web Console. Any object in the Altiris Web Console can be added to the shortcuts tab apart from another shortcut. A tree folder structure should be created in the Shortcuts Tab prior to adding shortcuts to the Tab.

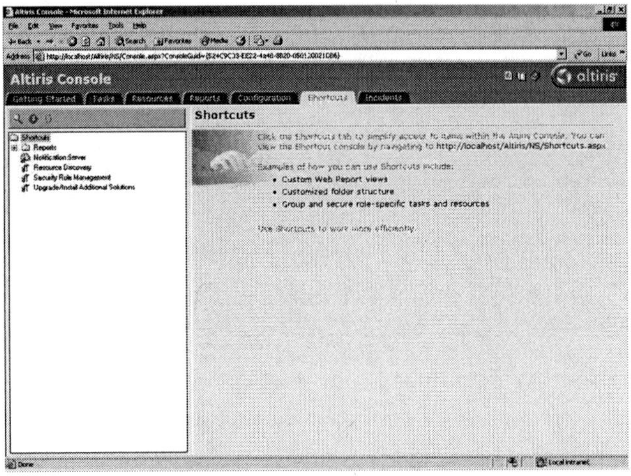

To create a new folder in shortcuts

Open the Web Console and select the **Shortcuts** Tab.

Right click the root of the folder structure and from the shortcut menu choose **New > Folder.**

Name the folder and click **Apply**.

To create a shortcut

Open the Web Console and select the Tasks, Resources, Reports or Configuration Tab.

Right click any object and from the shortcut menu choose **New > Shortcut**.

In the Create Shortcut dialog select where to store the shortcut and click **OK**.

To Move a Shortcut

Open the Web Console and select the Shortcuts Tab.

Right click a shortcut and choose **Move**.

In the Move Item dialog select where the shortcut is to be moved and click OK.

The Incidents Tab

The Incidents Tab is used to view Incident Manager. The first time you enter this tab you must enter your name and contact details.

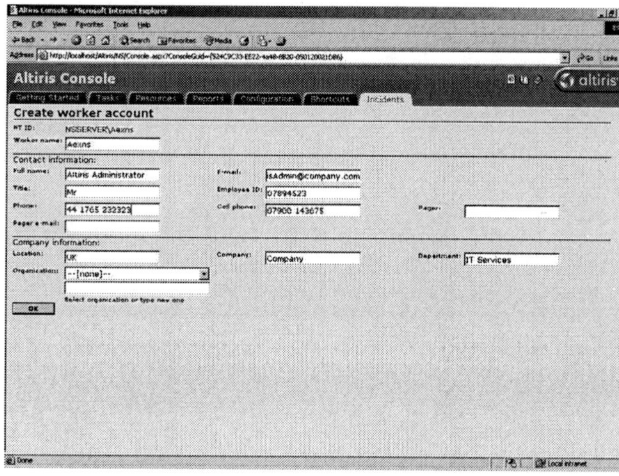

Enter the name and contact details for the Application Identity account.

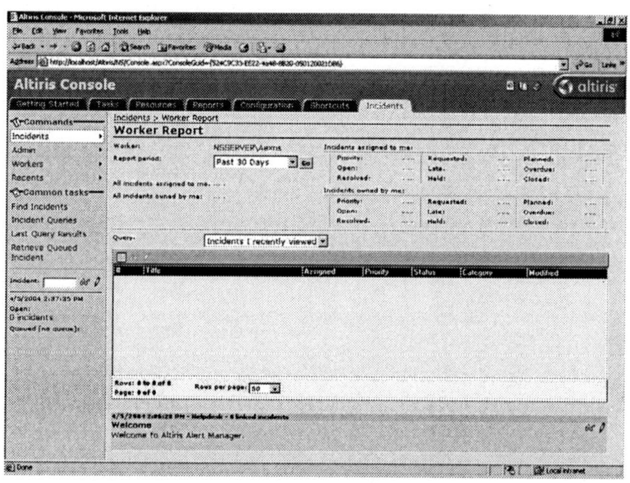

The Incident Worker Report is the default page in the Incident Manager and displays incidents that have been assigned to the currently logged on user (Application Identity account).

Cloning, deleting and moving objects

Cloning an Item

Cloning is effectively copying.

Select the item to copy in the Treeview pane.

Right click the item and choose **Clone**.

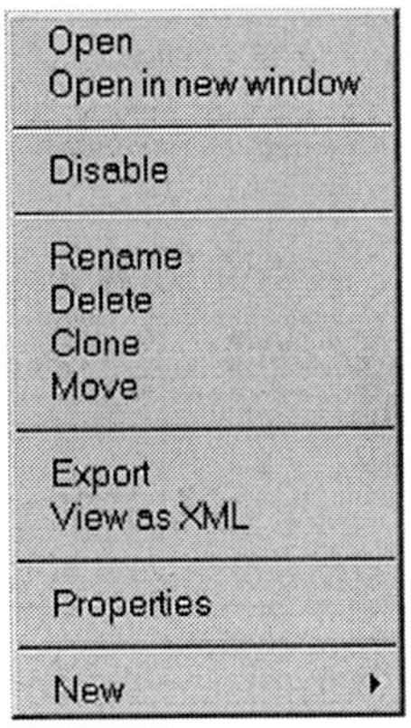

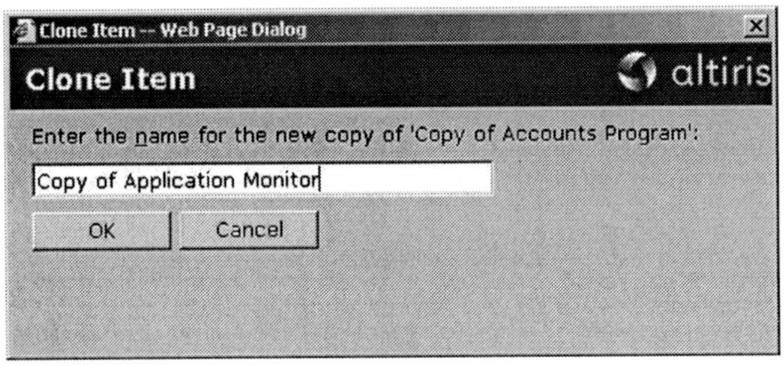

The Clone Item dialog is displayed.

Enter a unique name for the cloned item and click **OK**.

Deleting an Item

Select the item in the Treeview pane.

Right click the item and choose **Delete**.

The Delete Item dialog is displayed.

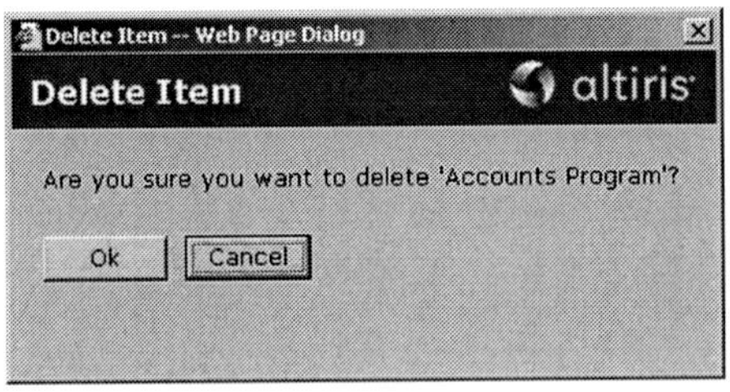

To confirm the deletion click **OK.**

Moving an Item

Select the item in the Treeview pane.

Right click the item and choose **Move**.

The Move Item dialog is displayed.

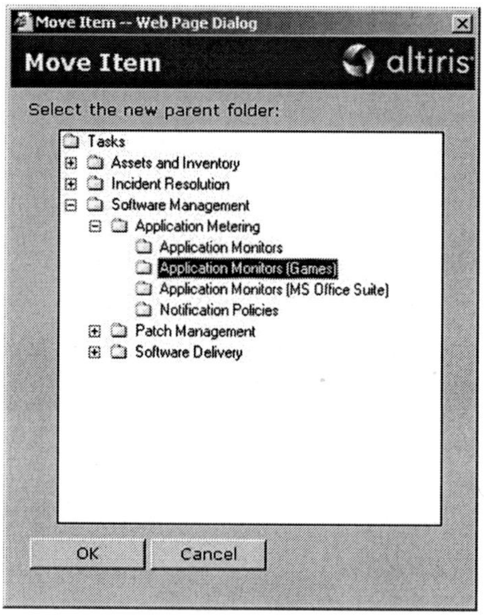

Navigate to and select the parent folder where you want to move the selected item.

Click **OK**.

Introduction to Collections

Collections are groups of related objects. The Notification Server installation installs default collections. Subsequent installation of Solutions may also add solution specific collections.

Viewing Collections

From the Resources tab of the Web Console expand Collections. Navigate to a collection and select it.

The details pane will display machines that are a member of the selected collection.

Secured Collections v Non Secured Collections

There are two different types of collections, Secured and not secured. Secured Collections are used to limit the resources a user can use when creating a new collection. There are two collection creation privileges, Create Collections and Create Secured Collections. Both roles are granted to users through membership of security roles.

A user with the Create collections permission can create a collection containing any other collection(s) in the database.

A user with the Create Secured Collection privilege can only create collections using collection resources that have the 'Use for Secured Collection' permission.

Introduction to Reports

Altiris Solutions come with an excellent range of built-in reports. Each solution installed will add its own set of reports. Reports are located in the Reports tab of the Web Console.

To view a report, open the web console select the **Reports** tab then navigate to the category of report you wish to view. Drill down through the folders until you find the report you want.

Once a report is selected, the details pane displays the options to run the report in the same window or in a new window.

Select the link to 'Run the report in a new Window'. 

Some reports will run and display the results immediately while others will offer options to further specify what is to be returned in the selected report. If you are prompted for parameters, configure them, then click the **run** button. 

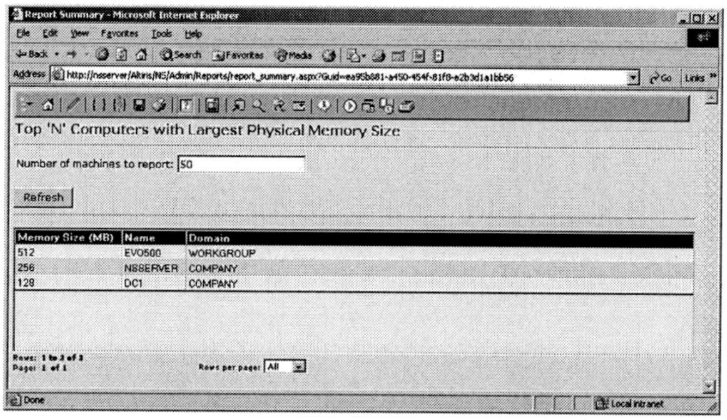

Installing Altiris Solutions

Solutions can be installed manually or using the Solution Centre (recommended). The Solution Centre may require configuration before it can be used in your environment. Go to the section 'The Solution Centre' in the next chapter 'Configuring Notification Server' for more information.

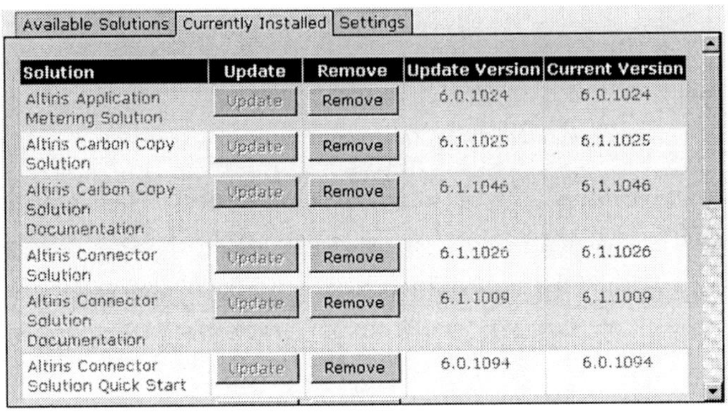

Tip **When you install a Solution always make sure that you are logged on to the Notification Server using the Application Identity account credentials. Some Solutions such as Patch Management Solution should be installed at the Notification Server and not through Terminal Services (See the relevant solution documentation for details).**

Install one solution at a time, allowing time between each Solution installation to rollout the associated Solution Agent to clients. Use built-in reports to confirm that clients have the new Solution Agent and that everything is working okay before you start rolling out another Solution. I recommend rolling out Inventory Solution before any other.

Installing Solutions using the Solution Centre

From the Web Console select the Configuration tab and navigate to **Upgrade/Install Additional Solutions**.
Under the Available Solutions tab click the **Solutions** button.
Select the required Solution link to start the installation.
A progress dialog is displayed. Click the **Start** button within the dialog to begin the download and installation.
See the associated chapter for specifics and recommendations when installing solutions. (A copy of the solution installation file will be saved to InstallPath\Altiris\Setup Files)

Warning If your network uses a Proxy Server to access the Internet, ensure that you have configured the Proxy Server name and credentials in the Proxy Configuration page under Notification Server settings. See the chapter 'Configuring Notification Server' for more details.

Manually installing a solution

Go to the web link *http://www.solutionsam.com/solutions/6_0/* and download the required solution to your local hard disk.
Once the Solution has been downloaded, double click the install file to launch the installation and follow the on-screen instructions.

Removing a Solution

If you don't intend to use the Solution again, uninstall the Solution agent from clients before removing the Solution from NS.
Always use **Add/Remove Programs** in Control Panel to remove Solutions. Using the Solution Centre to remove Solutions will cause issues.
When a Solution is removed from the NS framework, the data for that Solution is not removed from the database but will not be viewable through built-in reports.

Upgrading a Solution

From the Web Console select the Configuration tab and navigate to **Upgrade/Install Additional Solutions**.
Select the Currently Installed Tab.
An **'Upgrade'** button is provided for Solutions when the currently installed version is older than the version available from Altiris.
Click the **Upgrade** button beside the desired Solution to begin the upgrade.
Follow the on-screen prompts.
A Solution upgrade may upgrade the agent for that solution. Always check for an agent upgrade policy in the Configuration tab of the Web Console after you have upgraded a Solution.

Applying Hotfixes

Occasionally Altiris release will release a solution hotfix. Hotfixes can be installed through the Solution Centre interface or can be manually downloaded from the updates section of the Altiris website (Altiris.com/support/updates).

To apply a hotfix using the Solution Centre

From the Web Console select the Configuration tab and navigate to **Upgrade/Install Additional Solutions**.
Click the Segments button in the Available Solutions tab.
Scroll down and expand the Solution Hotfixes section.
Select the hotfix to apply and follow the on screen instructions.

(Always use Add/Remove Programs in Control Panel to remove Solution Hotfixes.)

Licensing Altiris Solutions

Most solutions come with a built-in 7-day license. Longer trial licenses can be obtained from Altiris by going to http://www.altiris.com/eval. Notification Servers in a production environment must use a full license which can be obtained from Altiris.

Viewing the License Status

From the Web Console select the Configuration tab and navigate to Licensing.
Select the **License Status** tab if not already selected
View the license and AUP (Automatic Upgrade Protection) status

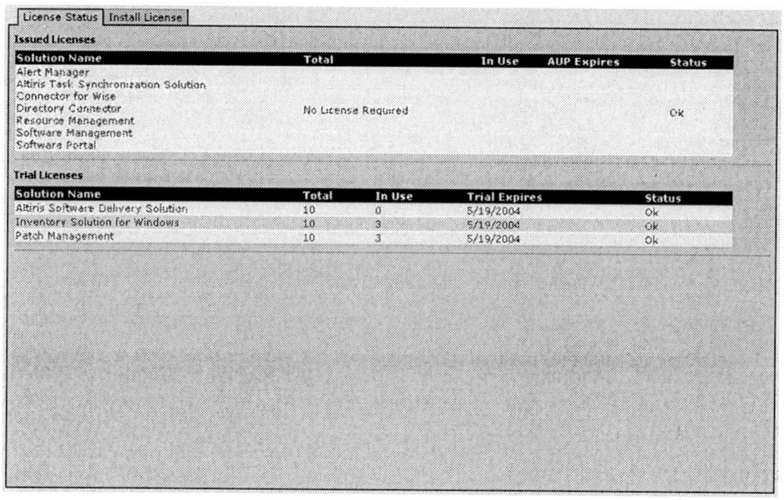

Applying a Solution License

Licenses come in a .txt file format from Altiris. If the file is zipped then unzip it.

Put the .txt file(s) into a folder.

Open the Web Console, go to Configuration Tab and select Licensing.

Choose the Install license tab

Browse to the folder containing the license(s).

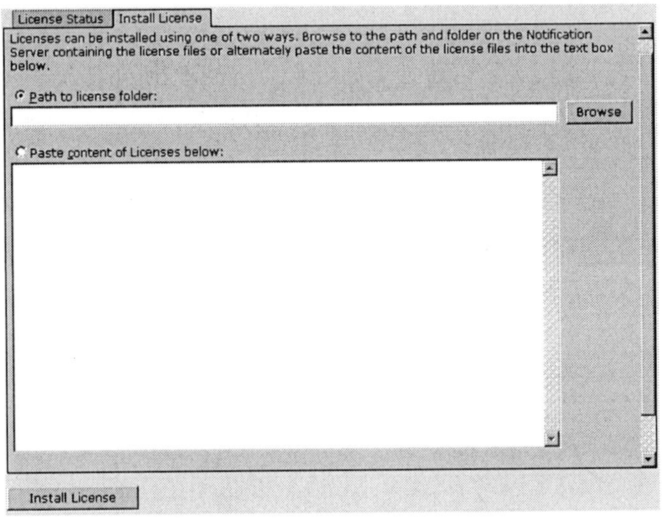

Click **OK** to return to the Install license page.

Click the **Install License** button.

Return to the License Status page and click **Refresh**.

Note The license count is updated automatically by the license refresh schedule (Every 30 minutes) or it can be manually updated by clicking the **Refresh** button in the license Status page in the Notification Server Web Console.

Summary

This chapter introduced some of the basics required to administer a Notification Server, including navigating the Web Console, viewing collections and reports and installing and licensing Altiris Solutions.

The next chapter 'Configuring Notification Server' will guide you through important post installation configuration tasks.

5

Configuring Notification Server

Security Role Management

Security is new to NS 6.x and allows an Administrator to configure access to the Notification Server Web Console and features within the console. Like NTFS permissions, console privileges are cumulative meaning that a user gets all privileges from the roles he or she is a member of.

There are five roles created during the Notification Server installation. Extra security roles can be added and existing roles can be modified. As Solutions are added to Notification Server extra roles and privileges may be added. Each security role corresponds to a local group on the Notification Server. The default roles that are created during the installation are;

Altiris Administrators

Members of the Altiris Administrators role by default have full control, no restrictions in the Web Console. It is advisable that only a very small number of people are added to this role.

Guests

Guests can access the Reports tab. What reports Guests have access to within the Reports tab will depend on the security that has been configured on individual and groups of reports.

Level 1 Workers

This role is meant for helpdesk type people who can view all tabs but do not have permission to create or edit anything except an incident.

Level 2 Workers

This role is the same as a Level 1 Worker but also has all of the 'Altiris Management' privileges such as create collections and reports.

Supervisors

This role would typically be given to a helpdesk supervisor or third level support person. The Role has all the permissions of an Altiris Administrator except 'Administer Incidents' or change the 'System Privileges'.

To View Security Roles and Privileges

Select the Configuration Tab in the Web Console and navigate to **Server Settings > Notification Server Settings > Security Role Management**.
Select a Role then view the privileges in the privileges window below.

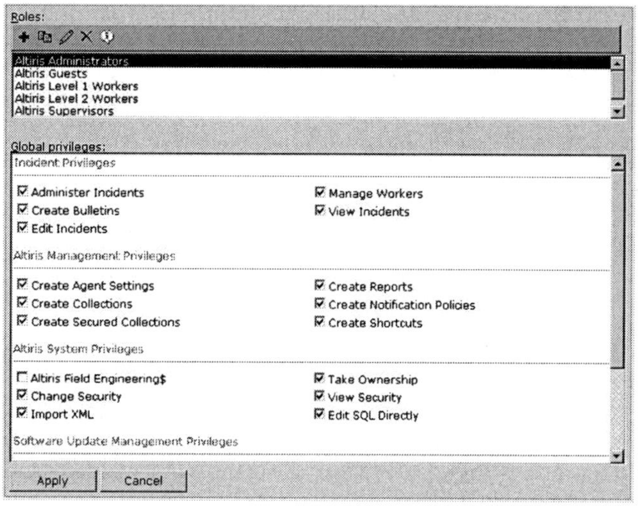

To Edit Security Role Privileges

Select the Configuration Tab and navigate to **Server Settings > Notification Server Settings > Security Role Management**.
Select the Role to edit in the Security Role Management interface and check or uncheck privileges as appropriate.
Click **Apply** to save the changes.

To Create a Security Role

Select the Configuration Tab in the Web Console and navigate to **Server Settings > Notification Server Settings > Security Role Management**.
Within the Security Role Management interface click the **'Add Role'** button.
Type a Role name and Description.
Use the **Add** button to add users from the local Notification Server accounts database or Users and Groups from a trusted Domain.
Click **Save** when finished.

To Edit Security Role Membership

Select the Configuration Tab and navigate to **Server Settings** > **Notification Server Settings** > **Security Role Management**.

Select the Role to edit in the Security Role Management interface and click the *Edit the Selected Role button.* (The Pencil)

Click the Add button to display the Select Users and Groups dialog.

Search for the users and groups in the local accounts or the Domain database to be added to the role.

Once found, select the users or groups and click **OK**.

Click **Save**.

Advanced Security

Altiris Security Roles provide users with access to specific tabs and the ability to perform certain tasks within the web console. It is important to note that if a user is given permission to access a tab within the console, it does not necessarily mean that they can access anything within that tab.

To allow and enforce more granular security, permissions are configured on individual objects within the console. For example, users that are members of the Level 1 Workers role can access the Reports tab. You may not want them to have access to all of the reports within the tab. Permissions can be used on individual folders and reports or groups of reports to control access.

Each folder or item in the web console can be secured using permissions.

Settings permissions on objects

Right click on the folder or item and choose **Properties**.

When the Properties of the objects appear, click the Security Tab to view, modify and grant permissions.

Note Creating a new role will create a new local group on the Notification Server. The local policy of some companies prevents the unauthorised creation of local groups on servers. If this is the case within your own organization, ensure that you let them know before creating a new Altiris Security role.

Computer Discovery

Discovering machines does not provide any management functionality, but it is a requirement if you want to push the Altiris Agent to client machines. The discovery process is used to populate the Notification Server database with a list of machines on the network. This list can then be used to push the Altiris Agent remotely to Windows NT/W2K/XP/2003 machines from the Web Console.

(The Altiris Agent can not be pushed to Windows 9.x machines. To install the Altiris Agent on a Windows 9.x machine you can either, manually install it or use a Login script. See the chapter 'The Altiris Agent' for more details.)

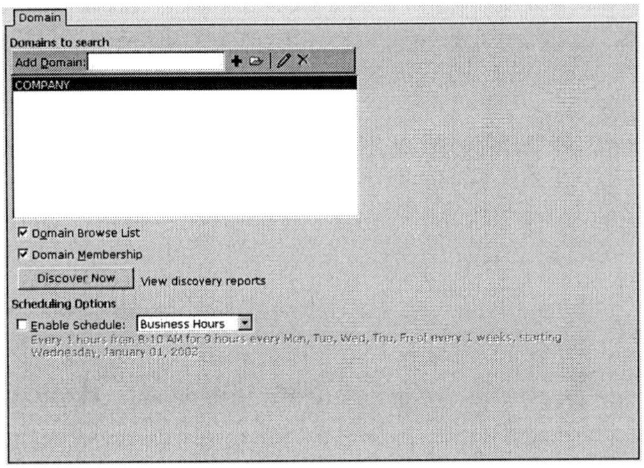

Viewing Discovery Settings

From the Web Console select the Configuration tab and navigate to **Server Settings > Discovery Methods > Resource Discovery**.

Resource Discovery options and configuration are discussed on the following pages.

Configuring Discovery

From the Web Console select the Configuration tab and navigate to **Server Settings > Discovery Methods > Resource Discovery**.

Type a Domain name and click the **'Add Domain'** button on the toolbar.

This will add the Domain name to the list of Domains to search. By default the Application Credentials are used to connect to a DC of the Domain specified. If the Application Credentials is a local account and does not have rights to read Active Directory then different account credentials must be used for Discovery. Select the Domain name and use the Edit button to change the credentials used.

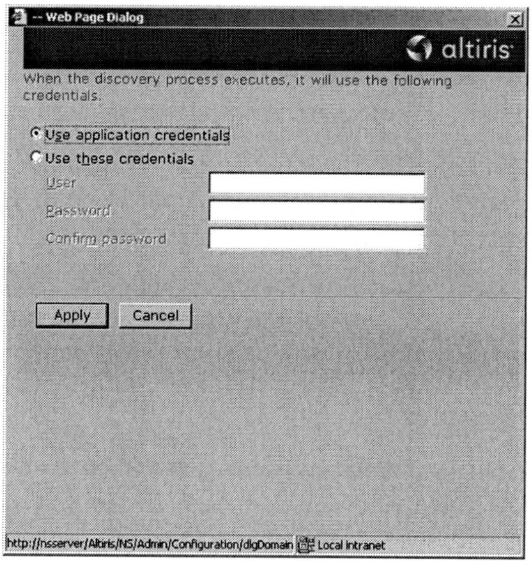

Repeat the process to add more than one Domain.

Select the **method(s) of Discovery**.

Domain Membership Discovery will query a Domain Controller in each Domain specified for a list of Windows NT/2000/XP/2003 machine accounts. In a large environment if Domain Membership is used to discover machines, the initial discovery should be done out of hours as it is quite a hit on the local Domain Controller. Scheduling can be used to control when discovery is initiated.

Tip Clear out unused computer accounts from Active Directory before enabling Domain Membership discovery.

The Domain Browse List discovery method will query the local browse list for machines listed in the Domain(s) specified. This operation will have no impact on the network. This type of discovery will find NT/2000/XP/2003 machines running messaging service as well as 9.x machines with sharing enabled.

Select the **desired discovery schedule** from the drop down list. A reoccurring schedule will ensure that after the initial discovery, any new machines will also be discovered. (Click **Discover Now** to begin discovery immediately.)
Enable Scheduling using the Enable Schedule check box.
Click **Apply** to finish.

Viewing the list of discovered machines

Once the discovery schedule has run, the discovered machines can be viewed by either viewing one of the reports in **Reports tab > Notification Server Infrastructure > Agent > Altiris Agent Discovery** or from within the Web Console. To view the discovered machines within the console select, the Configuration tab and navigate to **Altiris Agent > Altiris Agent Rollout > Altiris Agent Installation**.
From the drop down, select the option 'Discovered Computers Sorted by Date' from the drop down box and wait until the list is displayed.
Cancel the dialog using the **'Cancel'** button.

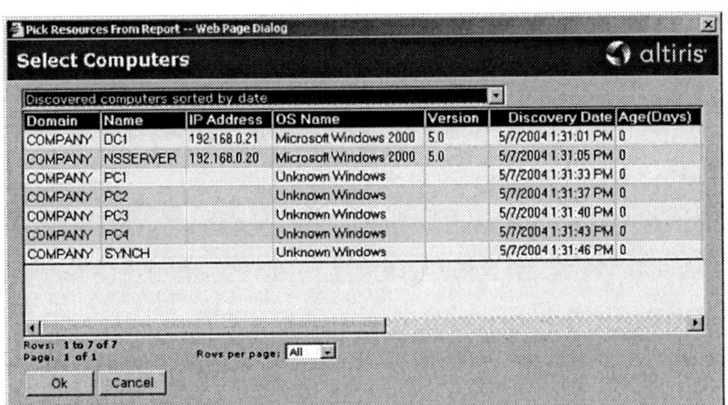
Pick Resources From Report -- Web Page Dialog
Select Computers
altiris
Discovered computers sorted by date

Domain	Name	IP Address	OS Name	Version	Discovery Date	Age(Days)
COMPANY	DC1	192.168.0.21	Microsoft Windows 2000	5.0	5/7/2004 1:31:01 PM	0
COMPANY	NSSERVER	192.168.0.20	Microsoft Windows 2000	5.0	5/7/2004 1:31:05 PM	0
COMPANY	PC1		Unknown Windows		5/7/2004 1:31:33 PM	0
COMPANY	PC2		Unknown Windows		5/7/2004 1:31:37 PM	0
COMPANY	PC3		Unknown Windows		5/7/2004 1:31:40 PM	0
COMPANY	PC4		Unknown Windows		5/7/2004 1:31:43 PM	0
COMPANY	SYNCH		Unknown Windows		5/7/2004 1:31:46 PM	0

Rows: 1 to 7 of 7
Page: 1 of 1
Rows per page: All
Ok
Cancel

What else is the list of discovered machines used for?

The list of discovered machines is also used to report on what machines on your network don't have the Altiris Agent. Notification Server will compare the list of discovered machines against the list of machines with the Altiris Agent installed.

Proxy Configuration

The Solution Centre which is used to install and upgrade solutions will, by default, connect to the Internet to display the available upgrade/solution list. Solutions such as Patch Management will also connect to the Internet to download patches, bulletins and utilities. If a Proxy Server is used in your environment then Notification Server will require the URL as well as credentials with permission to access the Internet through that proxy server.

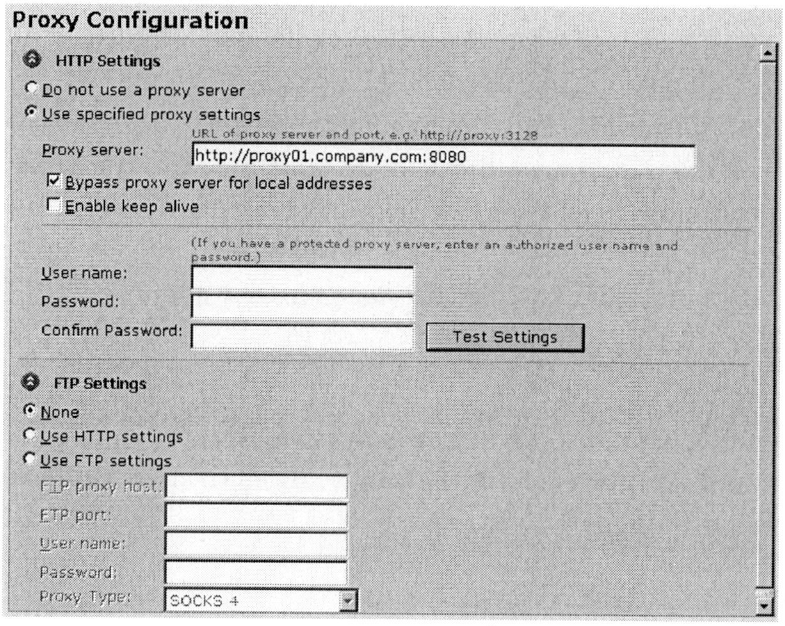

To configure HTTP and FTP Proxy Settings

Select the Configuration Tab in the Web Console and navigate to **Server Settings > Notification Server Settings > Proxy Configuration**.

Under HTTP Settings select the option **Use specified proxy settings**.

Enter the URL for the proxy server.

Enable or disable **Bypass proxy server for local addresses**

Enter user credentials with permission to access the internet through the proxy.

Repeat the process for FTP Settings is required then click **Apply**.

Tip If a Proxy Server is used in your network, make sure that Internet Explorer on the Notification Server is configured to use that Proxy.

The Solution Centre

The Solution Centre is used to install and upgrade solutions. The Solution Centre can be configured to download solutions from one of three locations, a local CD on the Notification Server, the Altiris web site or another location such as a share on another server.

How does it work?

When you access the Solution Centre, a list of available solutions are displayed. Available solutions are read from a file called solutions.xml. By default, the Solution Centre reads the solutions.xml from the Altiris web site, http://www.solutionsam.com/solutions/6_0/solutions.xml. Configuring the Solution Centre to get the list of available applications from the Altiris web site will ensure that the latest versions of the solutions are always available to download and install.

The Solution Centre can also be configured to read solutions.xml from a local CD drive or from another location. See below for further information on creating a Solution Centre CD or local repository.

Viewing available Solutions

From the Configuration tab of the Web Console select **Upgrade/Install Additional Components**.

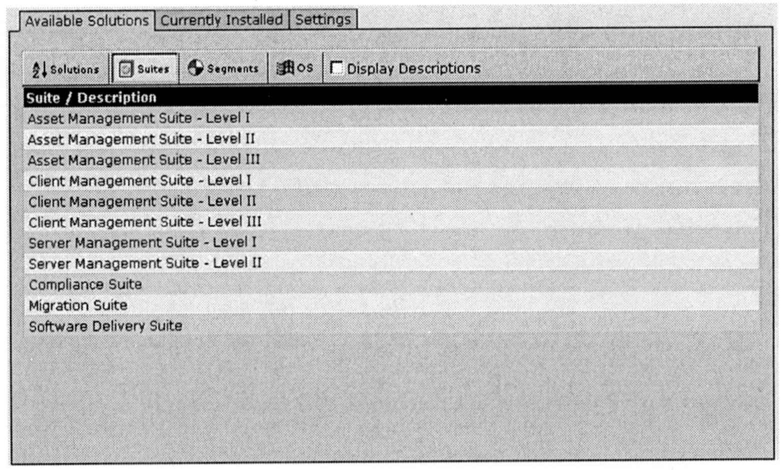

Four buttons allow you to change how solutions are displayed. The Solutions button will display the list of solutions for all operating systems. The Suites button (Default) will display Solutions grouped by suite. The Segments button will group solutions by category and the OS button will group by operating system.

Viewing installed Solutions

From the Configuration tab in the Web Console select **Upgrade/Install Additional Solutions.**

Select the **Currently Installed** tab to view the Solutions installed on your Notification Server.

Configuring the Solution Centre

From the Configuration tab in the Web Console select **Upgrade/Install Additional Solutions.**

Select the **Settings** tab.

Options within this dialog allow you to configure the Notification Server to point at the Altiris web site, a local CD or another location for Solution Centre data.

Creating a Solutions CD

To create a CD with solutions, download the required solutions, the solutionCenter.dtd and the solutions.xml from http://www.solutionsam.com/solutions/6_0/ and burn to CD.

Creating a Solution Repository

Create and share a folder on a server. Download the solutions, the solutionCenter.dtd and the solutions.xml from http://www.solutionsam.com/solutions/6_0/ and save them to the shared folder. Configure the Solution Centre to point to the shared folder path on the server.

Note In a multiple Notification Server environment with multiple administrators it is important to ensure that all NS servers run the same version of a solution. To control this, download the solutions used to a shared folder on a server(s). Also download the solutions.xml file and solutioncenter.dtd from the same location to the shared folder. Configure the Solution Centre on all Notification Servers to point to the same UNC path.

Database Settings

Notification Server stores data in an SQL database (SQL 2000 or MSDE 2000). This dialog lets you specify the name of the server running SQL, the name of the database on that server and the credentials used to connect to the database. The default is that, during installation, Notification Server will create a database named Altiris on the local machine and use the credentials of the application identity account. Use this dialog to change the options made during the installation.

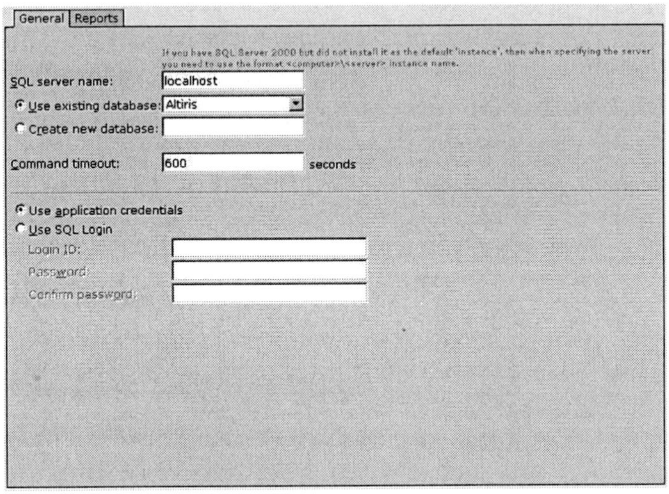

To view Database Settings

From the Altiris Web Console select the Configuration Tab and navigate to **Server Settings > Notification Server Settings**.

Select **Database Settings**.

Options in Database settings are rarely changed. The options available allow you to change and create the database used by the Notification Server as well as to modify the account used to access the database.

Advanced Settings

Some Solution policies and packages have Event status options as part of their configuration. Options in this dialog allow you to decide what status events, if any, should not be sent by clients. By default none of the events are discarded.

To change event settings

Uncheck the Event name and click **Apply**.

If an Event is unchecked but a client is not yet aware that the Event is not to be sent, the client will send the Event to the Notification Server but the Notification Server will discarded it.

Once clients have requested an update configuration, they will see and apply the new configuration and stop sending the unchecked Event from that point on.

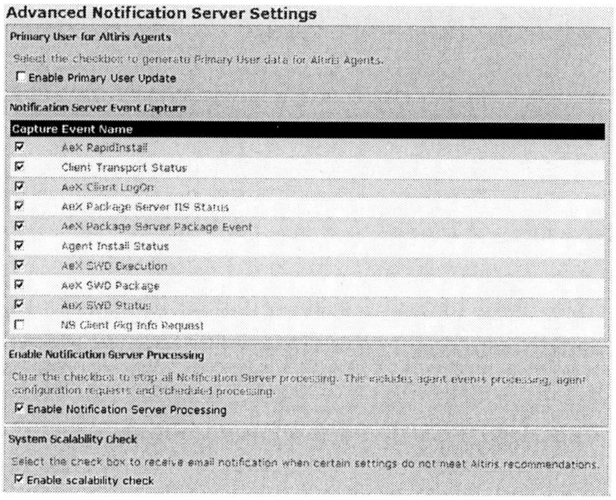

To View Advanced Settings

From the Altiris Web Console select the Configuration Tab and navigate to **Server Settings > Notification Server Settings**.

Select **Advanced Settings**.

Primary User Settings

Primary user data lets you know who the primary user is of a machine. Use this dialog to enable or disable primary user data generation. The Altiris Agent 6.x generates the primary user information in three ways, when Basic Inventory is sent to the Notification Server, when a Machine Inventory is run or by the Altiris Agent when the user logs on/off. When Primary User Data generation is enabled, it is enabled for all machines in all collections.

To Enable Primary User Settings

From the Altiris Web Console select the Configuration Tab and navigate to **Server Settings > Notification Server Settings > Advanced Settings**.

Select Enable Primary User Update.

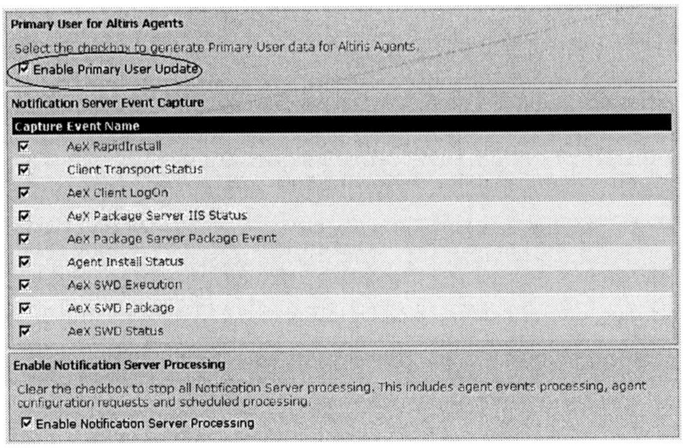

To view Primary User information for a client

From the Altiris Web Console select the Resources Tab and navigate to **Collections > Computer Collections**.

Open the collection containing the target computer.

In the details pane, right click any computer and choose **'Resource Manager'**.

A new window is displayed.

Click the Inventory Tab and select **AeX AC Primary User**.

(If the AeX AC Primary User class does not appear check to ensure that Primary User Data generation is enabled.)

Notification Server Processing

Disabling this option will stop the Notification Server processing data sent from clients. Any data sent by clients during this time will be queued in the EvtQueue folder on the Notification Server folder structure.

Shared Schedules

The Shared Schedules are a set of common schedules that can be used and shared by solutions installed on the Notification Server. The default schedules are shown in the figure below.

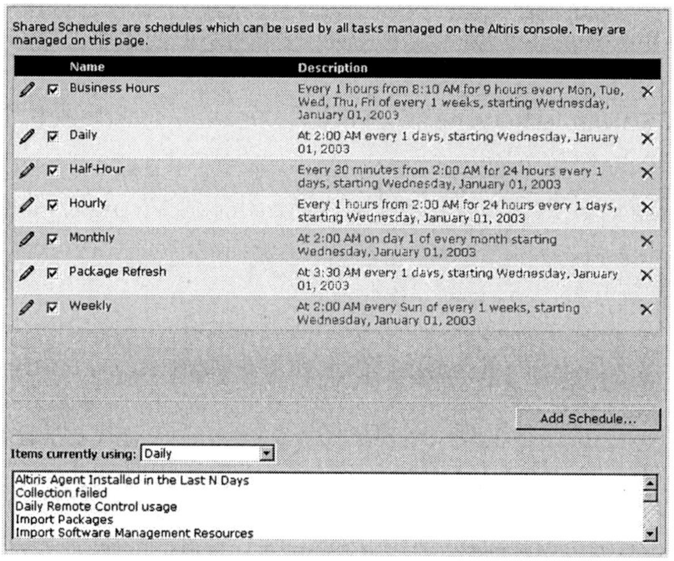

To View Shared Schedules

From the Altiris Web Console select the Configuration Tab and navigate to **Server Settings > Notification Server Settings**.
Select **Shared Schedules**.

To Add a Shared Schedule

In the shared schedules dialog select the **'Add Schedule'** button.
In the Schedule Editor dialog, enter a unique name for the new schedule.
Configure the schedule and click **OK**

To View items using a specific Schedule

In the shared schedules dialog select a schedule from the 'Items currently using' drop down.
The item box below will display any items using the selected schedule.

Error Logging

Notification Server uses log files to log status messages. Notification Server stores its log files in InstallPath\Altiris\Notification Server\Logs. Each log file is approximately 200 kb in size and named a.log, a1.log, a2.log, a3.log etc. Messages within the logs are broken in to four categories, Errors, Warnings, Information and Trace with all logging options on by default except Trace. The Trace option will add status messages that occur at a thread level. Turning on trace will create large amounts of data and is primarily used for troubleshooting.

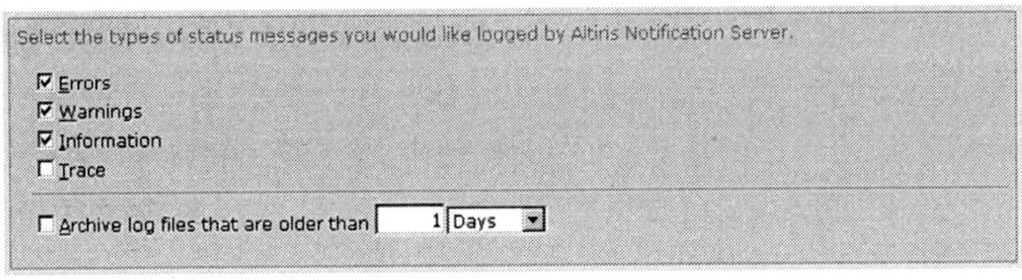

Configuring Notification Server logging

From the Altiris Web Console select the Configuration Tab and navigate to **Server Settings > Notification Server Settings**.

Select **Error Logging**.

Options within this dialog allow you enable or disable any of the four message categories as well as decide how often information in the log files should be archived to the Notification Server database. (Logs are archived to a table named Evt_NS_Log).

Viewing Event Logs

Click the 'View status messages' button in the Error Logging configuration page

or

Open a browser and navigate to http://nsservername/Altiris/NS/Logview.asp

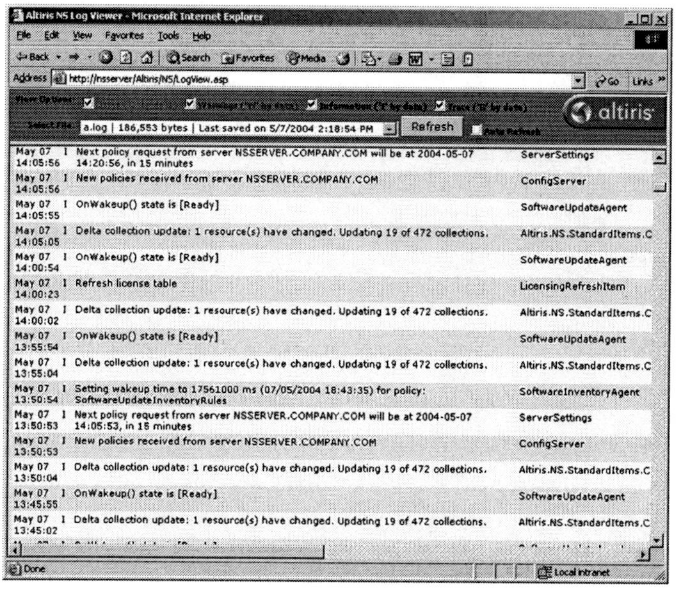

Note Log file settings such as file names and size can be customized using a registry editor. Settings are stored in HKEY_LOCAL_MACHINE\Software\Altiris\Express\Event Logging.

Security Note

Anyone who is a member of the 'Everyone' or the 'Administrators' group can view the Notification Server logs. Use NTFS permissions on the logs folder on the Notification Server folder structure to increase security.

E-mail Settings

Some Altiris Solution Notification Policies can be configured to send an email when Notification Server receives certain data. The Notification Server needs the name of the SMTP server in order to forward these e-mails. Options within E-Mail Configuration include:

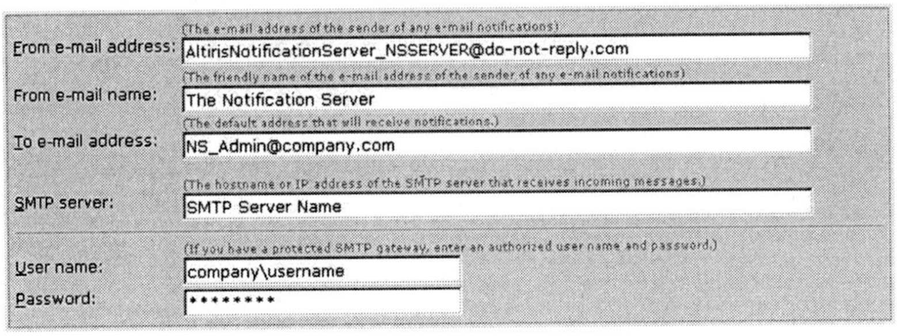

From e-mail address – Indicates the e-mail address of the sender.

From e-mail name – Indicates the name of the person who sent the e-mail.

To e-mail address – The default address e-mails are sent to. Each configurable policy can override this default address.

SMTP Server Name – The SMTP server name.

Username – If you have a protected SMTP gateway a username and password may be required.

Password – The password.

Viewing E-mail configuration

From the Altiris Web Console select the Configuration Tab and navigate to **Server Settings > Notification Server Settings**.

Select **E-mail configuration**.

Application Identity

The Application Identity, is the account that is configured during the installation of Notification Server. This account must have local admin rights on the Notification Server, have read access to Active Directory and must be able to logon to the SQL server where the Notification Server database resides.

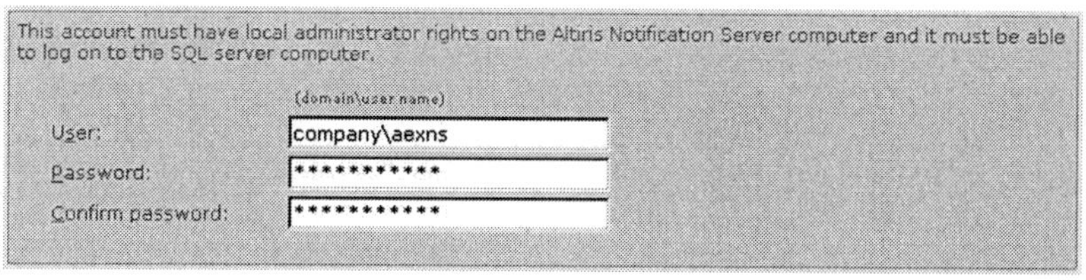

Viewing Application Identity settings

From the Altiris Web Console select the Configuration Tab and navigate to **Server Settings > Notification Server Settings**.
Select **Application Identity**.

Options in this dialog include:

User – Should be in the format Domain\Username or Machinename\Username
Password – The password
Confirm Password – The password again!

Note In version 5.x of Notification Server the Application Identity account was also the account used to push the NS client to a remote workstation. That meant that the application identity account also needed administrative privileges on all clients. In Notification Server 6.x you do not have to use the Application Identity account when pushing out the Altiris Agent. When the agent is being pushed, you can define the account used.

Purging Maintenance

Purging Maintenance is used to clean out old data and reports periodically from the Notification Server database.

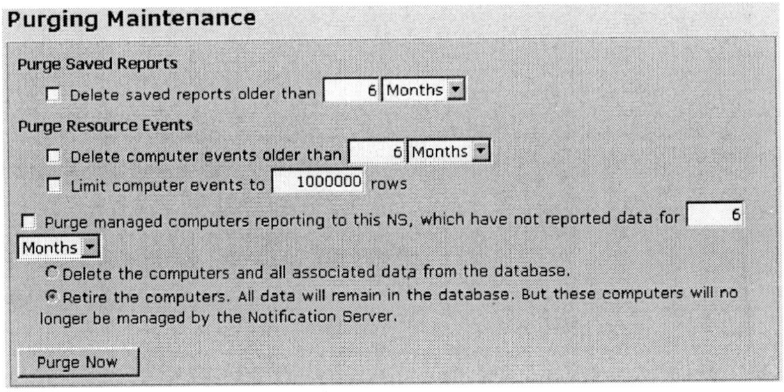

Viewing Purging Maintenance Settings

From the Altiris Web Console select the Configuration Tab and navigate to **Server Settings > Notification Server Settings**.

Select **Purging Maintenance**.

Before enabling any of these options decide how long you want to keep old machines, events and reports. I would suggest enabling the reports and events options at a minimum and using the default values as a good starting point (6 months).

Resource Data History

The Resource Data History configuration page allows you to configure whether Notification Server keeps a history of resource data and if so, for how long.

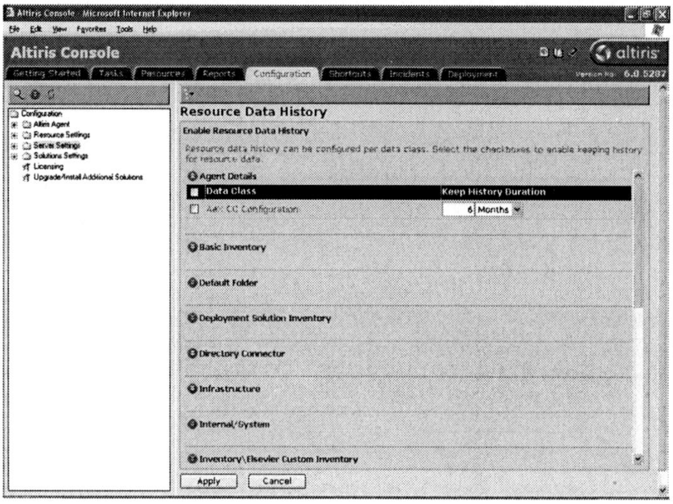

Viewing Resource Data History Settings

From the Altiris Web Console select the Configuration Tab and navigate to **Server Settings > Notification Server Settings**.

Select **Resource Data History**.

In the treeview pane, expand each Data Class to view the configuration.

Configuring Resource Data History Settings

From the Altiris Web Console select the Configuration Tab and navigate to **Server Settings > Notification Server Settings**.

Select **Resource Data History**.

In the treeview pane, expand each Data Class to view the configuration.

To enable history to be kept, select a whole Data Class or individual check boxes within a data class.

Configure the time period for each selected item.

Click **Apply** to save the changes.

Incident Settings

The Incident Settings page lets you configure the name of the Incident database as well as the credentials used to connect to it. The incident database is very similar to Altiris Helpdesk Solution but with limited functionality.

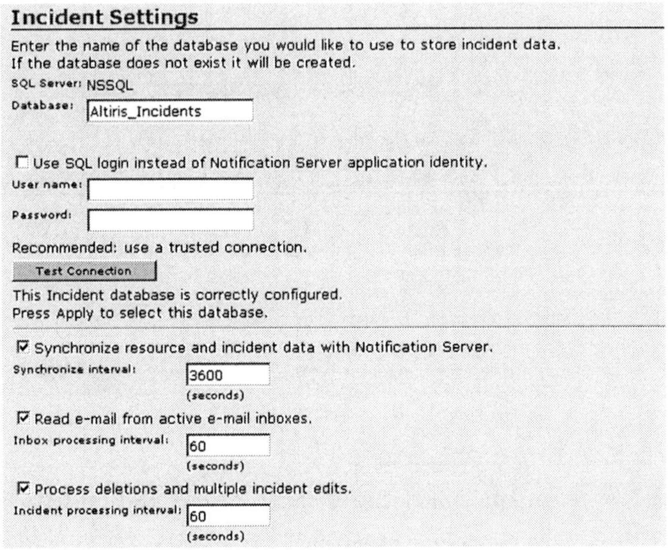

Viewing Incident Settings

From the Altiris Web Console select the Configuration Tab and navigate to **Server Settings > Notification Server Settings**.
Select **Incident Settings**.

Automatic Collection Updating

Computers are grouped in to collections by default based on their operating system version and hardware type. For example default collections such as 'All Windows 2003 Servers' contain all machines running Windows 2003 Server. When a new machine is configured with the Altiris Agent it reports basic inventory that includes its operating system version, it is then added to the appropriate collection based on this information.

The Notification Server must periodically update collection membership to ensure that machines are in the correct collections. Collections are only updated based on the configured collection update schedules, however this schedule can be overridden by using the 'Update all collections now' button in the Collection Updating configuration page.

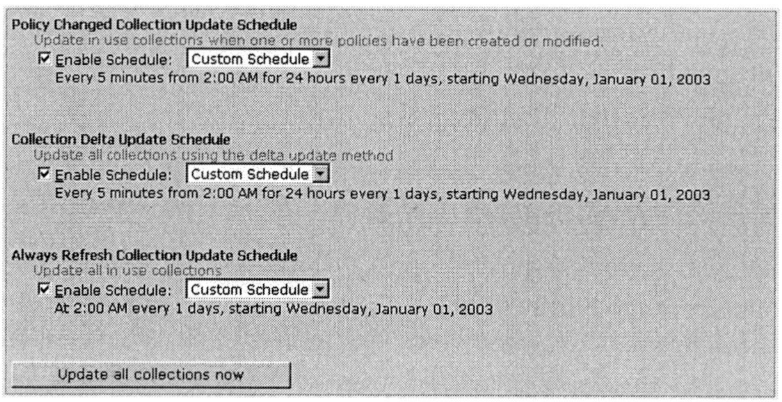

Viewing the collection update schedule

Open the Web Console and select the Configuration tab then navigate to **Server Settings > Notification Server Settings > Automatic Collection Updating**.

Manually updating all collections

Open the web console and select the Configuration tab and navigate to **Server Settings > Notification Server Settings > Automatic Collection Updating**. Click the 'Update all collections now' button at the bottom of the configuration page. This button can be useful in a lab or Proof of Concept situation when you want don't want to wait for the automatic collection membership update.

Configuring the collection update schedule

Select the Configuration tab in the Web Console and navigate to **Server Settings > Notification Server Settings > Automatic Collection Updating**.

Modify the three policy schedules as appropriate.

Click **Apply** when finished.

Three policies exist to allow you to configure automatic collection updating:

Policy Changed Collection Update Schedule

This policy will update the collections targeted by a new or changed policy. This policy is not very processor intensive and is enabled and scheduled to run every five minutes by default.

Collection Delta Update Schedule

This policy updates all collections with new or changed inventory since the last collection update. This policy is not very processor intensive and is enabled and scheduled to run every five minutes by default.

Always Refresh Collection Update Schedule

This policy schedule updates all collections regardless of the two previous settings. This policy is very processor intensive and is enabled and scheduled to run every day at 2 am by default.

Note The default policies are good for most environments. Consider changing the **'Always refresh collection Update Schedule'** if other processes must be run at 2 am on the Notification Server.

Summary

This chapter introduced the majority of the configuration tasks required immediately after Notification Server has been installed. I tend to configure Security Roles first, followed by Discovery and then the rest of the configuration tasks mentioned in this chapter.

The next chapter 'Installing & Configuring the Altiris Agent' looks closely at all aspects of the Altiris Agent, including installation, configuration and administration.

6

Directory Connector

Introduction

The Altiris Directory Connector allows you to import objects from a Standalone Windows Server or from Active Directory. Objects such as Users, Network Printers, Computers and Subnets can be imported manually or on a schedule using pre-defined and custom rules. An import can either be a 'Full Import' or an 'Update Import'. Once objects are imported they can be used for tasks including configuring Package Server Subnet mappings and targeting organizational units with software packages.

Importing an object such as a computer from Active Directory does not enable the computer to be managed by Altiris, the Altiris Agent must first be install on the client.

Installing Directory Connector

From the Configuration Tab in the Web Console select **Install/Upgrade Additional Solutions**.

Select the Segments button if it is not already selected.

Select Components and then the Altiris Directory Connector link.

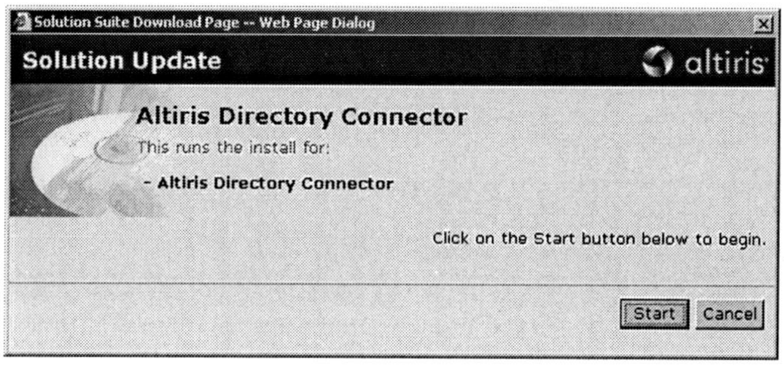

Click **Start** and follow the on screen prompts.

This solution does not require an Altiris license.

Directory Connector Toolbar

 Create a new import rule.

 Delete the selected import rule.

 Run the selected import rule now (Full import).

 Run the selected import rule now (Update import).

 Stop the selected rule.

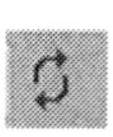 Refresh the import rules.

Viewing Import Rules

From the Web Console select the **Configuration Tab** and navigate to **Server Settings > Notification Server Infrastructure > Active Directory Import**.
A list of rules is displayed in the details pane.
The default rules can be configured and enabled to import objects on a schedule or manually.

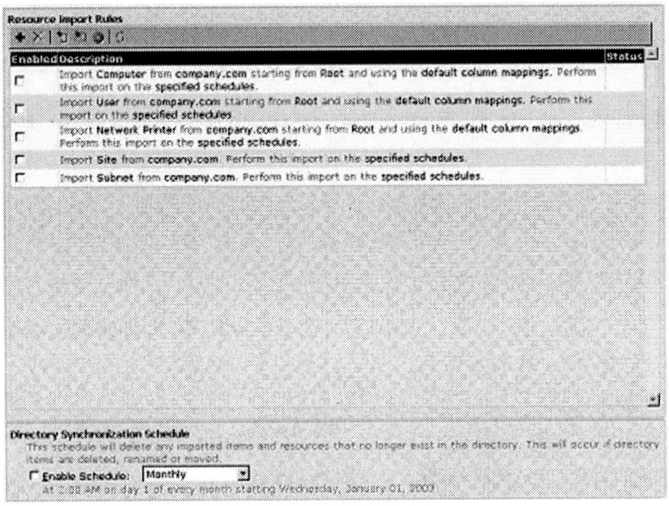

Creating a New Import Rule

From the Altiris web console select the **Configuration Tab** and navigate to **Server Settings > Notification Server Infrastructure > Active Directory Import**.

Click the **'Create a new import rule' b**utton. 
A new rule is created and added to the bottom of the existing list of rules.

Once the rule has been created, configure it using the instructions in the following pages.

Configuring an Import Rule

The Directory connector provides the ability to import objects manually or using a schedule. Using schedules is the most common method.

During the connector installation, five default rules are created to import Computers, Users, Printers, Sites and Subnets. Each of these rules can be configured to import their respective objects on a schedule using a full or partial import. A combination of importing and synchronization is normally required to keep imported data up to date.

Select the Configuration tab from the web console and navigate to **Server Settings > Notification Server Infrastructure > Active Directory Import**.

Select an import rule. For example the Import Computer rule. Once the rule is selected it will change colour.

Each rule has multiple links to allow you to configure what, when and the type of import. Select the first link **'Computer'** to launch the dialog shown below.

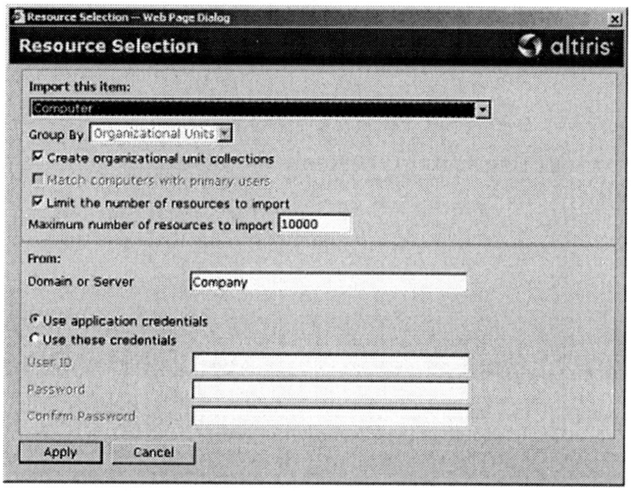

This dialog allows you to select the object type as well as specify the Domain/Server and application credentials used during the import.

Options contained within the dialog will vary depending on the object chosen but generally the available options are:

Import this item –
Use to select what object to import. A drop down list shows the available objects.

Group By –
Group the imported objects.

Create organizational unit collections –
This option will create a collection for each organizational unit imported from AD.

Limit the number of resources to import –
Default maximum is 10,000.

From –
Enter a Domain name. Pointing to a Domain will allow import from an NT/W2K/2003 Domain.

Credentials –
Use the Application identity account or use specific account credentials. The account specified must have at least read access to Active Directory.

Once you have configured all of the options in the **Resource** Selection dialog, click **Apply**.

The dialog will close and return you to the rules page. The next item to configure is where in Active Directory to begin the import.

Configure where in AD to start the import

Click the root link in the selected rule to display the **Organizational Unit Selection** dialog.

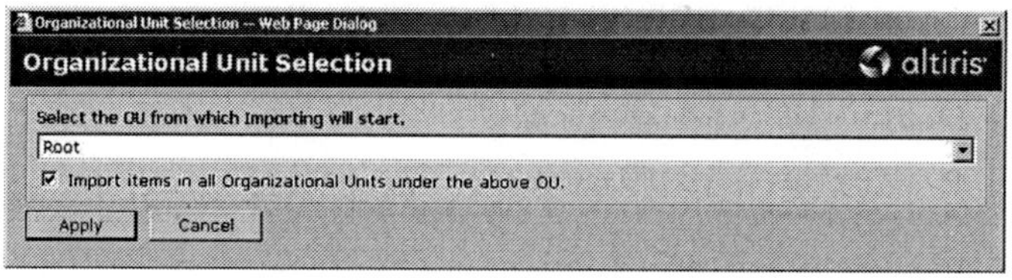

Use the drop down dialog to select where in Active Directory you want to start the import. The root is the default.

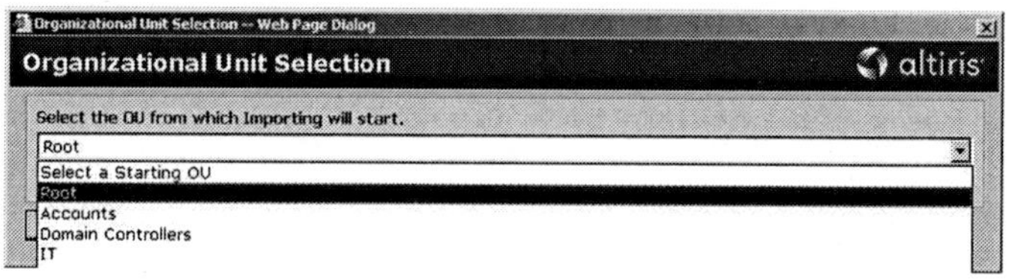

When you have chosen the OU to start the import from, click Apply to close the dialog and return to the selected rule.

Configuring Column Mappings

The default column mappings are sufficient for importing users and computers from Active Directory. The column mappings dialog is primarily used when importing new custom objects in to the Notification Server database.

Scheduling an Import Rule

From the Altiris Web Console select the **Configuration Tab** and navigate to **Server Settings > Notification Server Infrastructure > Active Directory Import**.

Click the 'specified schedules' link for the rule to configure.

In the Rule Scheduling dialog choose a **Full** and or an **Update** Import and configure the associated schedules.

Click **Apply** when finished to return to the rules page.

The full import will import all of the specified objects and the update import will import any new or modified objects since the last import.

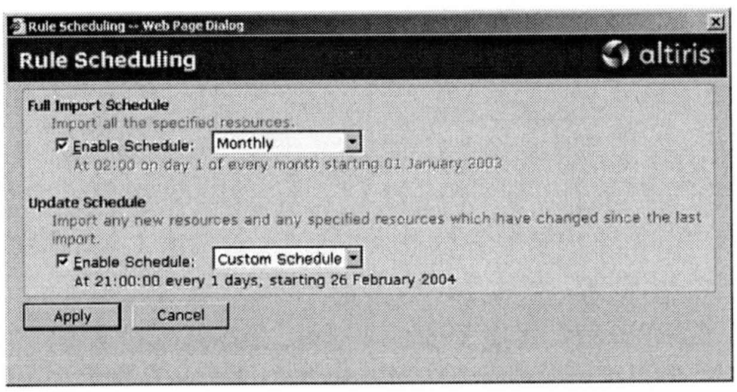

Once all configuration options for the rule have been completed, **enable** the rule by checking the enable check box.

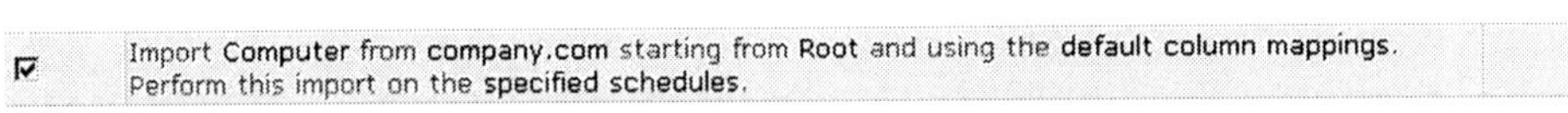

Once the rule has been configured and enabled it will import the selected objects from Active Directory, based on the **Full** and **Update** schedules.

Configuring Synchronization

Unlike a Directory Import, synchronization will not import any new objects from Active Directory. Synchronization is used to synchronize objects previously imported from AD. For example if a computer is moved in AD from one OU to another, or a Computer is deleted from AD, synchronization will synchronize the imported objects previously imported from AD.

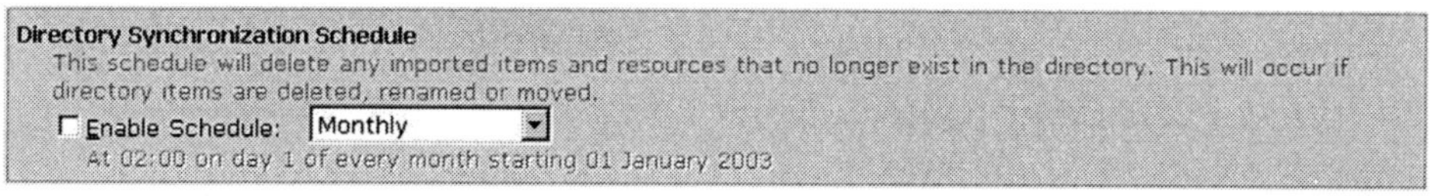

The synchronization schedule applies to all previously imported objects imported by the Active Directory connector.

Choose a shared schedule or select and configure the custom schedule.

Enable the schedule then click **Apply**.

Manually Starting an Import

From the Altiris web console select the **Configuration Tab** and navigate to **Server Settings > Notification Server Infrastructure > Active Directory Import**. Select the Import Rule by clicking just right of the Enable/Disable check box. The rule will be automatically highlighted.

Click either the 'Run the selected import rule now (Update Import)' 

Or

Click the 'Run the selected import rule now (Full Import)'. 

The import will begin immediately.

Full Import

A full import will import all resources specified in the import rule regardless of whether the object has previously been imported.

Update Import

An update import will import all new and objects that have changed since the last import. If an object has moved to another OU or been deleted, the import will not import this change. Use synchronization to reflect this type of change.

Viewing imported objects

From the Web Console select the Resources tab and navigate to **collections**

Select **Directory collections**

Drill down to the desired collection and view the membership of the selected collection in the details pane.

Useful Directory Connector Reports

To view the following reports open the Web Console, select the Reports Tab then navigate to **Software Management > Server > Active Directory folder**.

Directory Import in the Last 'N Days

This report details how long each Directory import took over the last N days.

Directory Import Rule Task Runs

This report will list all the resources that were created and updated during each import rule run.

Directory Resources by Container

This report will list Directory containers by category (user, computer, etc.)

Resources Imported per Import Rule

This report will list the resources that were imported for each import rule configured in the directory connector.

Windows Computers Not Found in Directory

This report lists Windows computers that are NS clients but are not found in Active Directory.

Summary

In this chapter we examined how to install and configure the Altiris Directory Connector. The connector is used to schedule a partial or full import of specific objects from a directory source such as Active Directory. Rules are used to define what and when objects are imported. Import will only import new or changed objects, synchronization must also be used to synchronize object deletion and movement within AD.

The next chapter 'Installing and configuring the Altiris Agent', covers all aspects of the Altiris Agent, including installation, configuration and administration.

7

Installing & Configuring the Altiris Agent

Introduction

Machines that will be managed by the Notification Server must run the Altiris Agent. The Agent runs on the client and is configured to periodically send basic inventory, manage bandwidth throttling, checkpoint recovery and check with the Notification Server for configuration updates. In short, the client allows communication with the Notification Server. What other communication occurs largely depends on the agents that are embedded in the client. Most solutions installed on the Notification Server will add a solution specific agent to the Altiris Agent. The Altiris Agent must be installed on a client prior to adding solution agents.

Altiris Agent Prerequisites

Internet Explorer 5.5 or higher.
5MB free Hard disk space.
64 MB RAM.
Windows 9.x or higher.

Ports used by the Altiris Agent

During a push installation

UDP 138, TCP 445, TCP 80 & ICMP Type 8

After installation

Clients download packages using HTTP or SMB depending on whether the Package Servers run IIS or not.
Default TCP port 80 for HTTP.
SMB uses Microsoft NETBIOS UDP 135, 137, 139 & TCP 135, 139.
SMB over TCP uses UDP & TCP 445.
Tickle/Power Management uses 52028 and 52029 for multicast
Package Multicast uses 52030

Altiris Agent standard communications

Update Configuration

On a schedule, which is set by the Notification Server Administrator, the Agent requests a configuration update from the Notification Server. The request is used to find out if the client has any new configuration settings or software packages to download or update.

Basic Inventory

On a schedule, which is set by the Notification Server Administrator, the Agent sends Basic Inventory data to the Notification Server. Basic Inventory includes information such as IP address, computer name and OS.

Status Events

Status Events can be enabled for policies, packages and tasks. For example if the package download status is enabled for a package, the client downloading the package will report the download status to the Notification Server. If the package task status is enabled for a task, the client will report execution status to the Notification Server.

Communications

HTTP Port 80 is used by clients to communicate with the Notification Server. The port can be changed by modifying the Advanced settings in the Agent communications policy on the Notification Server.

Files used by the Altiris Agent

CreateResource.asp – Located on the Notification Server. This file is used by newly installed clients to request a unique client GUID.

GetClientPolicies.asp – Located on the Notification Server and used by the clients to request configuration information.

NotificationServerName.XML – (Where NotificationServerName is the actual name of your Notification Server.) This file contains the configuration settings for the Altiris Agent. The file is located locally on the client in the Client Policies folder under the Altiris Agent folder structure.

AeXSWDInstSvc.exe – Used to setup the Agent installation service. The service checks to see if the Agent is already installed. If the Agent is not installed, the service will check the Agent perquisites and if prerequisites are met, connect to the Notification Server, download the AexNSC.exe to the NT folder (Admin$) and install the Agent. This install service and the AexNSC.exe are removed once the Agent is installed. If the installation service finds that the Altiris Agent is already installed then the installation will abort.

AeXNSC.Log – Located on client (%WINDIR%\System32 folder), used to detail the Agent install, what dll's are registered, if there were successful or unsuccessful installations etc.

AeXUserMonitorLog.xml – This file is located locally in the root of the Altiris Agent folder on the client and stores user logon information for the machine.

AeXConnectionMonitorLog.xml – Records the connection times to the Notification Server and whether it was a LAN, WAN or an internal communication.

Agent.log – Altiris Agent log file located locally in the Logs folder of the Altiris Agent folder structure. The log details client Agent communications with the Notification Server. Each logfile is approximately 100 KB by default. Subsequent logs are named Agent1.log, Agent2.log etc.

Agent installation files – The Altiris Agent installation files are located on the Notification Server in "Install Path\Altiris\Notification Server\NSCap\Bin\Win32\X86\NS Client Package\". There is also an MSI version of the Agent install program in "Install Path\Altiris\Notification Server\NSCap\Bin\Win32\X86\NS Client Installation\"

GetPackageInfo.aspx – Used by the client to get information on which Package Servers have a specific package.

Note The MSI version of the installation file should only be used if you intend rollout out the Agent using Group Policy. The Altiris Agent upgrade policy within the Notification Server console cannot be used to automatically upgrade Agents that have been installed using the MSI version of the install program.

Installing the Altiris Agent

Every machine that will be managed by the Notification Server requires the Altiris Agent. There are several ways to install the Agent including, Push, Pull, Manual, Group Policy and Login script.

Performing a Push installation

The Altiris Agent can be pushed to machines running Windows NT4 SP4 or higher. From the Web Console select the Configuration Tab and expand the Altiris Agent folder, then the **Altiris Agent Rollout > Altiris Agent Installation**.

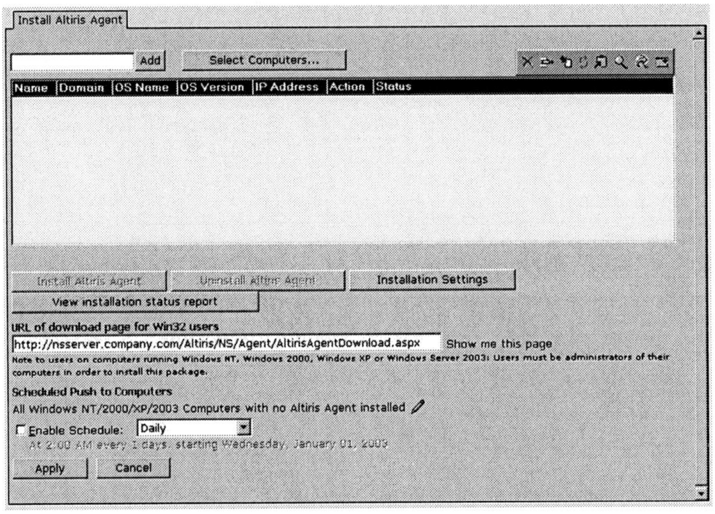

Use the **'Select machines'** button to display the list of discovered machines. If the **'Select Machines'** button is greyed out, that means you have not configured Discovery. Go to the chapter 'Configuring Notification Server' for more details on computer discovery.

In the Select Computers dialog, select the computers that you want to push the Agent too and click OK.

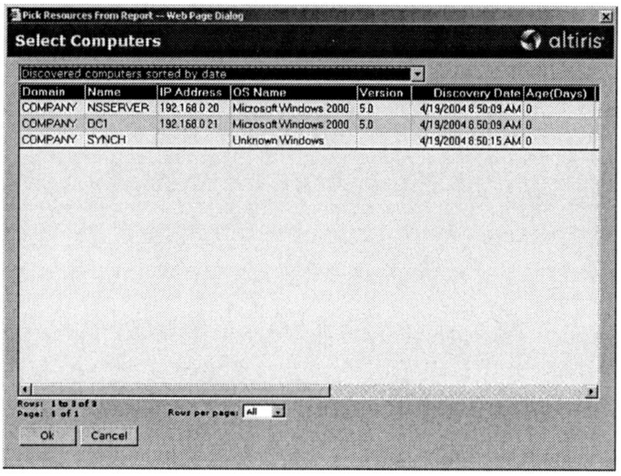

The selected computers will now be listed in the Altiris Agent Installation dialog. Select the target computers and click the Install Altiris Agent button.
The Agent Installation Options dialog allows you to override the default installation settings.

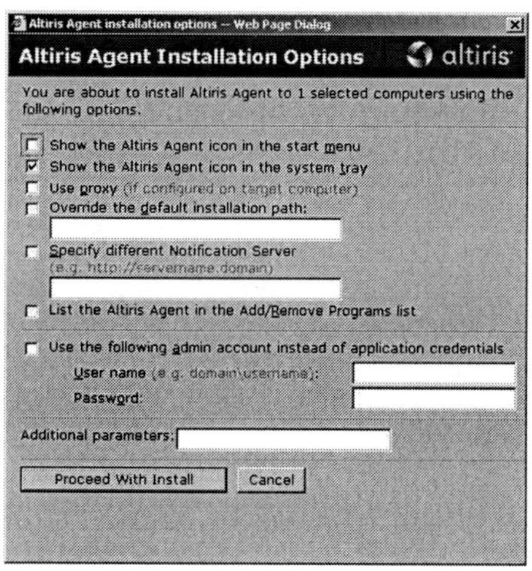

Note If the Application Identity account does not have administrative rights on the target machine(s) you must specify an account in this dialog that does.

Once you have chosen your desired options click the **'Proceed with Install'** button. The Action and Status columns in the Agent Installation screen will tell you how the install is proceeding.
Use the **'Refresh'** button to keep the status updated. 

Performing a Pull installation

Connect to the web address below and follow the instructions given
http://YourNotificationServerName/Altiris/NS/Agent/AltirisAgentDownload.asp

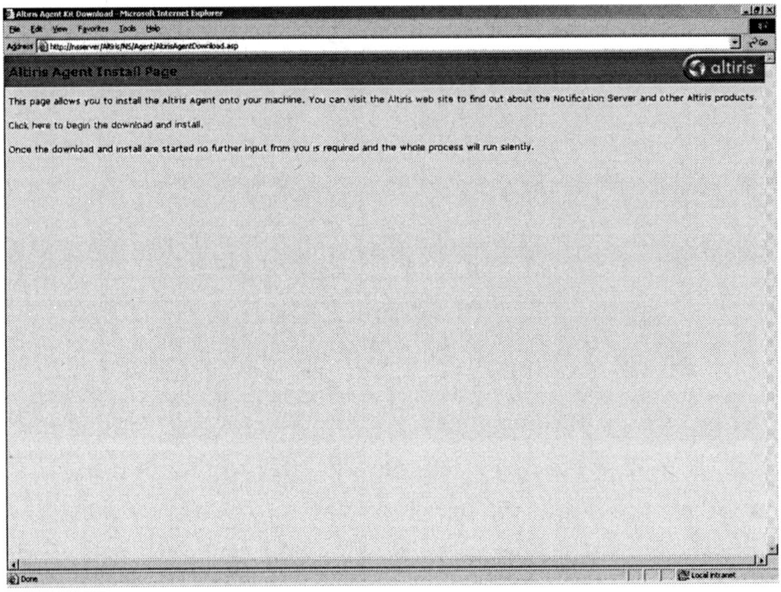

A Pull installation is a silent install and will automatically configure the client to talk to the Notification Server the Agent was installed from.

Manually installing the Altiris Agent

A manual installation by default is not a silent install you will be required to provide the name of the Notification Server during the installation.

Connect to the **NSCAP** share on the Notification Server and run the executable AexNSC.exe from the subfolder *\bin\win32\x86\NS Client Package*.

The installation can be customized using the following switches.

-s	Silent Package Extraction
/NoLogging	Disables client logging
-a	To pass arguments
ns= "NotificationServer"	Name of the Notification Server
nsweb="NotificationServerWeb"	Name of the Notification Server Web page
path=InstallationPath	Overrides the default install path
NOSTARTMENU	Don't include link to Agent on the Start Menu
NOTRAYICON	Don't include link to Agent on the System Tray
OKTOREBOOT	Prompt for a reboot after Agent installation
/remove	Silent uninstall of Agent
/NOADDREMOVE	Don't add a link in Add/Remove Programs
/s	Silent Install
/Regdiag	Very useful addition, adds a log viewer as well as many useful diagnostic additions to the Altiris Agent shortcut menu.

Example

AexNsc.exe -s -a ns="Server10.Domain.com" nsweb="http://Server10.Domain.com /Aexns" NOSTARTMENU /s

Note Deployment Server Jobs can be used to rollout the Altiris Agent. Create a Job with two tasks, one task to copy the AexNSC.exe to a local folder on the client and the other task to kick off the install using the switches above.

Using Group Policy to install Altiris Agent

Altiris provides an MSI type installation file for deploying the client from a Group Policy.

The MSI package can be found on the Notification Server in the '*InstallPath*\Notification Server\Nscap\Bin\win32\X86\NS Client Installation' folder, which is under the 'nscap' share.

See Microsoft documentation for details on deploying applications using Group Policy.

Using a Login Script to install the Altiris Agent

Copy the 'Client Installation Package' folder ('Install Path\Altiris\Notification Server\NSCap\Bin\Win32\X86\NS Client Package\') from the Notification Server to a shared folder on a server. Create a batch file, as shown below, and configure the login script properties for users to run the batch file.

```
If not exist C:\Program Files\Altiris\Altiris Agent\AeXNSAgent.exe
goto Install
:Install
Net Use K: \\YourServerName\ShareName
K:\AeXNSC.exe -a ns=" YourNotificationServerName"
nsweb="http://YourNServerName/AeXNS" /s
Net use k: /delete
:end
exit
```

Including the Altiris Agent in an image

Stop the Altiris Agent Service on the machine that you will create an image from. Use Regedit to delete the following MachineGuid values:

HKLM\Software\Altiris\Altiris Agent\MachineGuid
HKLM\SOFTWARE\Altiris\eXpress\MachineGuid
HKLM\SOFTWARE\Altiris\eXpress\NS Client\MachineGuid

Close the Registry editor.
Delete the file *NSSERVER*.xml under install path\Altiris\Altiris Agent\Client Policies. (*Where NSServer* is the name of your Notification Server.)
Delete the install path\Altiris\Altiris Agent\Software Delivery\Software Packages folder and all subfolders.
Under the Install path \Altiris\Altiris Agent folder, delete all *.nsi, *.nse and *.tmp files.
Shut down the computer and image it.

Note There are three instances of the MachineGuid. Each instance has a purpose.

HKLM\Software\Altiris\Altiris Agent\MachineGuid is used by the Altiris Agent to identify itself as a Notification Server Managed Resource.
HKLM\SOFTWARE\Altiris\eXpress\MachineGuid is used by the Deployment Server Agent, in order to relate a Deployment Server Managed Resource with a Notification Server Managed Resource, when the Deployment Server is being synchronized with Deployment Solution.
HKLM\SOFTWARE\Altiris\eXpress\NS Client\MachineGuid is used by the Altiris Agent for backwards compatibility with 5.5 Notification Servers.

Agent Rollout tip

Rollout the Altiris Agent site by site. The size of the client is approximately 5MB. (Each solution enabled will, more that likely add an agent to the Altiris Agent on the client, size varies. It is important to ensure that solution agent rollout policies are disabled before rolling out the Altiris Agent. You don't want to install your 5MB client and then have it pull down X MB of solution agents straight after!)

Data Flow for a Newly Installed Altiris Agent

- A request is made to the Notification Server, by the new client, for a GUID.
- Notification Server generates and sends GUID to new client.
- New client sends basic inventory. Basic inventory includes the IP address, OS version, domain name and computer name, etc.
- Notification Server updates its collections and adds the new client to collections based on the Basic Inventory.
- The Client requests configuration information. The Notification Server will evaluate its policies and see what policies apply to the collection(s) the Agent is a member of. Based on this evaluation, the Notification Server will send a client policy to the requesting Agent. These settings are contained in a XML formatted policy file in the Client Policies folder in the Altiris Agent folder structure. The file is given the name of the Notification Server e.g. Server10.XML

Agent Folder Structure

A new Agent installation creates the folder structure shown in the picture below.

Altiris Agent folder – This is the root folder containing the core Altiris agent files.

Client Policies folder – Contains one XML file containing the policy configuration for that client. The file is named NSserver.xml where NSServer is the name of your Notification Server.

Languages folder – Contains different language versions of the client interface.

Logs folder – Contains the logs files for the Altiris Agent.

Queue folder – Contains a sub-folder with the same name as your Notification Server. Inventory and events are queued there before being sent to the Notifications Server. This folder should be empty unless there is a communications issue.

Software Delivery folder – This folder is used to store software, patch and agent packages downloaded by the client.

Tasks – Used as a temporary folder for the Task Scheduler.

Express – Contains a sub-folder named Inventory where Inventory data is stored. This folder only exists if the Inventory Agent has been installed on the client.

Note If the Altiris agent has been upgraded from version 5.5x, the Altiris Agent folder will be named 'NS Client'.

Also When installing the Altiris Agent on to a machine that will later become a Package Server, it is advisable to install the Agent on to a partition with enough space to accommodate future packages. This is because by default, packages sent to a Package Server are stored under the Altiris Agent folder structure.

The Altiris Agent Interface

The Altiris Agent interface, shown in the picture below, is used to view the download and execution status of internal and scheduled tasks on a client. The interface comprises of a Tasks pane and a details pane. If an item is selected in the details pane, that change will be reflected in the Tasks pane.

To view the Agent interface

Right click the Altiris Agent icon on the taskbar of the client and choose **Altiris Agent** from the shortcut menu.

If the Altiris Agent configuration policy has removed the icon from the Taskbar then run the file AeXAgentActivate.exe from the root of the Altiris Agent folder.

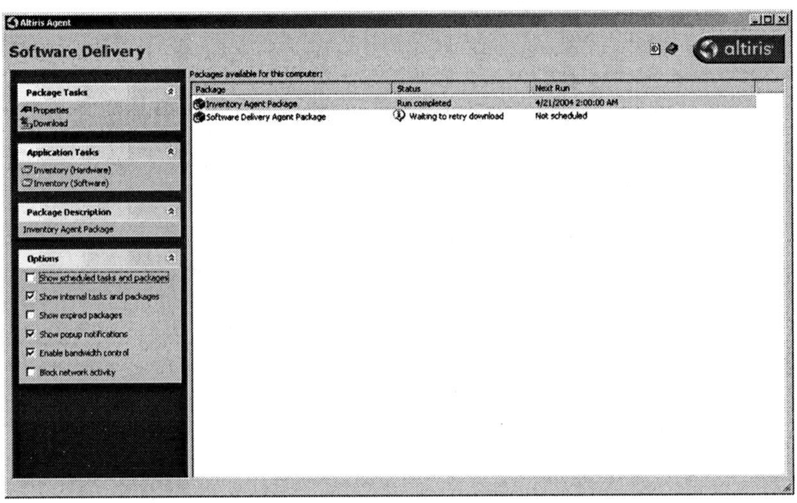

The Task pane contains the four sections; Package, Application, Description and Options.

Package Tasks Section

This section contains two options; Download and Properties.

The download option forces the client to download the package selected in the details pane even if has been previously downloaded.

The Properties option lets you view the properties of the package selected in the details pane. Properties include useful information such as the run and download history, as well as detailed information on the Tasks associated with the package selected. The dialogs below show the properties of the package and tasks for the Inventory Package. As you can see there are several tasks associated with this package, each of which can be selected from within the dialogs.

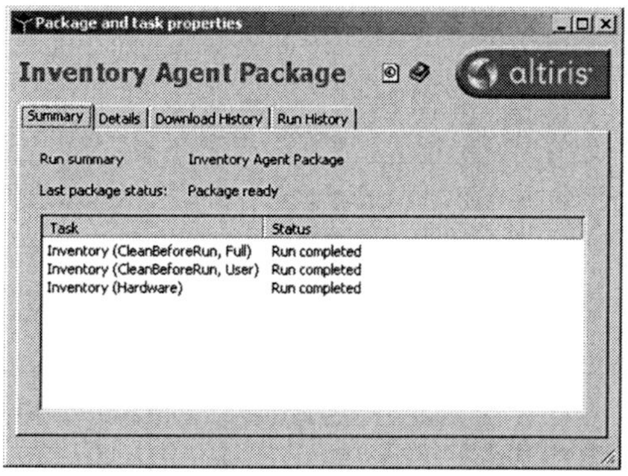

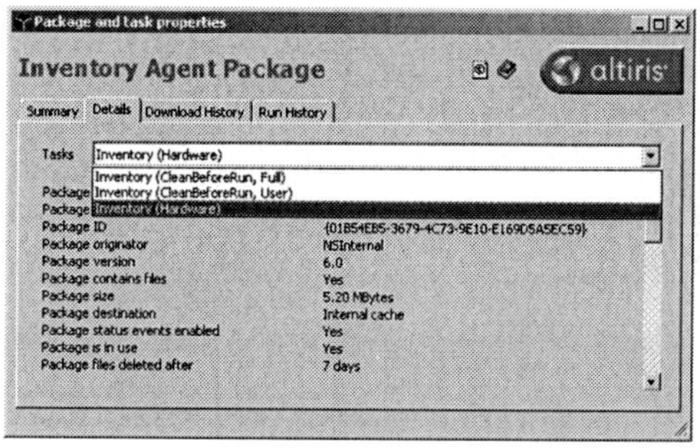

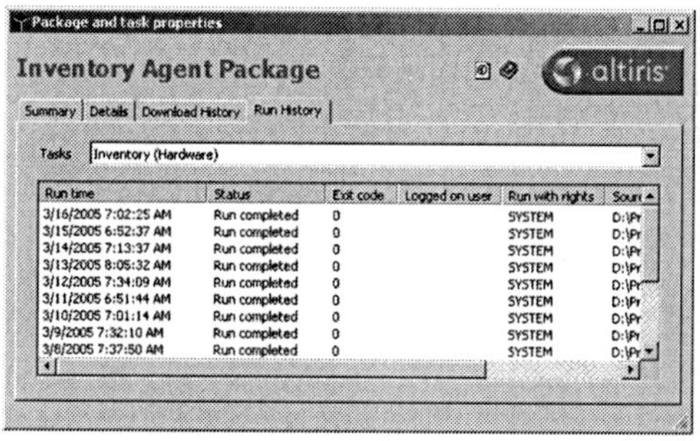

Application Tasks Section

This option lets you displays the list of Tasks (Programs) available for a Package. Select a Package in the details pane to view the available Tasks.

To run a task, click the required task link in the Application Tasks section. This will cause the selected task to run immediately.

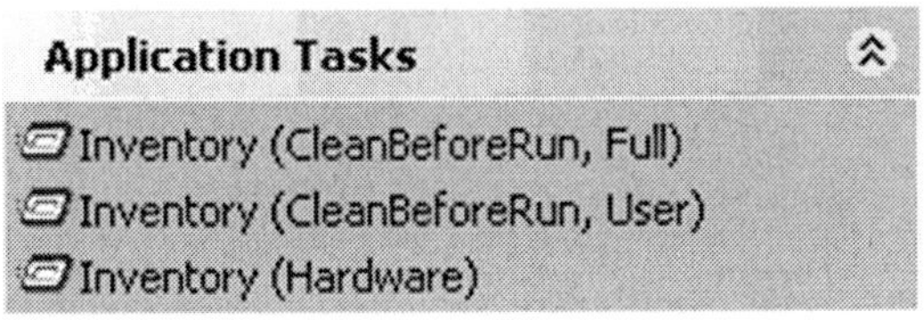

Package Description Section

This section simply displays the description of the selected package.

Options Section

This section allows you to control what is seen in the Agent interface as well as how bandwidth throttling and blockout are configured. The ability to view the options section is controlled through the Altiris Agent configuration policies. Allowing users access to this section will give them the ability to override throttling and blockout settings. I would suggest not allowing users to view this section.

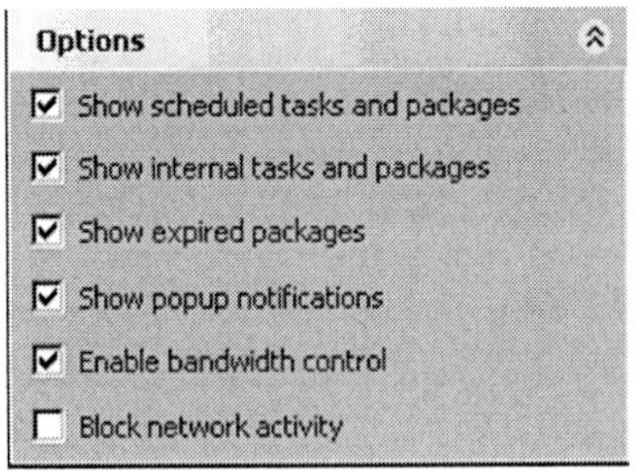

See configuring the Altiris Agent later in this chapter for more information on configuring access to this section.

Accessing help and about

Two buttons are available in the Altiris Agent interface to access 'Agent Help' and 'About'.

Agent **Help** button  gives you access to help surprisingly enough.

The Agent **About** button  gives you access to licensing, Agent version, Solution Agent status, Last Configuration information and when Basic Inventory was last sent as well as buttons to manually request a configuration update and send basic inventory.

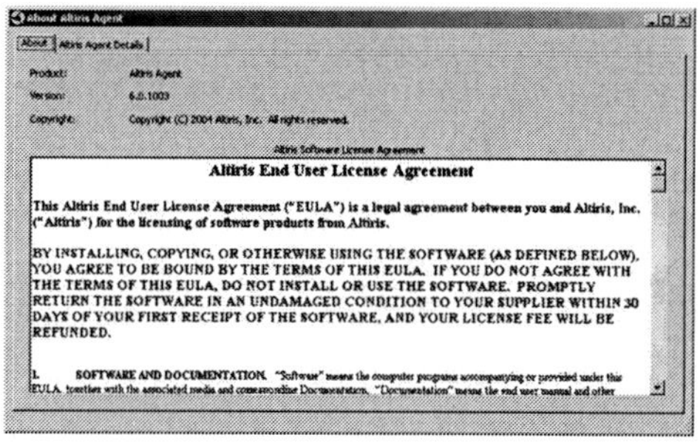

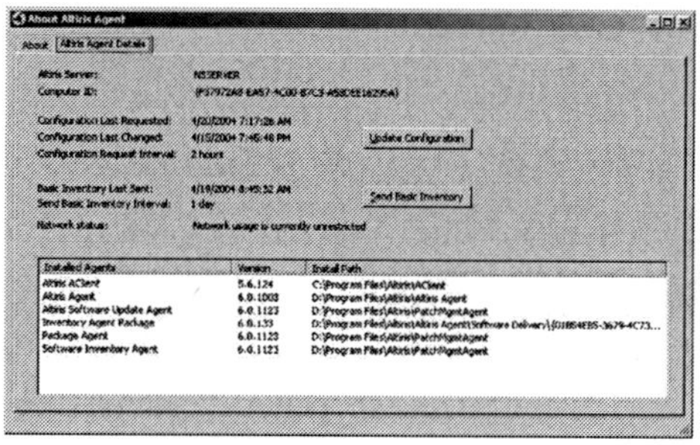

The Altiris Agent Details show useful information such as which agents are installed, when the agent last updated its configuration and when basic inventory was last sent.

Manually requesting a Configuration update

Manually requesting an update is useful if you don't want to wait for the configured update cycle.

On the client machine right click the Altiris Agent icon on the task bar and choose **Altiris Agent Details** from the shortcut menu.

Click the **Update Configuration** button.

Manually sending Basic Inventory

On the client machine right click the Altiris Agent icon on the task bar and choose **Altiris Agent Details** from the shortcut menu.

Click the **Send Basic Inventory** button.

Altiris Agent Configuration

The Notification Server installation creates five policies, which are used to define the Altiris Agent communication settings. There are four collection specific policies and one global policy.

The collection specific policies are All Desktop Computers (Excluding Package Servers), All Windows Servers (excluding Package Servers), All Package Servers and All Windows Mobile. Each policy provides the same options but each can be configured differently.

Using multiple agent configuration policies allows different settings for different types of machines, which in turn allows you to be more granular when configuring client communications.

The Global Altiris Agent configuration policy is used to define package multicast and power management/tickle communication settings for **all** windows machines running the Altiris Agent.

Note I have found that the four configuration settings are good for a one site Notification Server infrastructure or a multiple site infrastructure where all connection speeds between sites are equal. Where connection speeds differ between sites, a custom collection can be defined for each type of site. Copies or clones of the default Agent configuration policies can then be configured to target the custom collections.

Configuring the Altiris Agent

To configure an Altiris Agent configuration policy, open the Web Console and select the Configuration Tab, then navigate to the folder **Altiris Agent > Altiris Agent Configuration**.

Select an Altiris Agent Policy to configure, for example *All Windows Mobile.*

The Details pane will show the Agent settings, consisting of the four tabs, General, Interaction, Package Multicast and Advanced Settings.

Available options within the policy are discussed in the following pages.

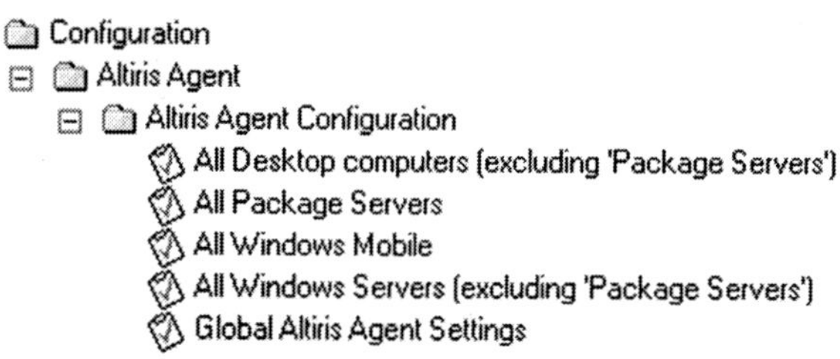

The General Tab

The General tab displays configuration options that allow the Administrator to configure communication settings for a targeted collection of Agents.

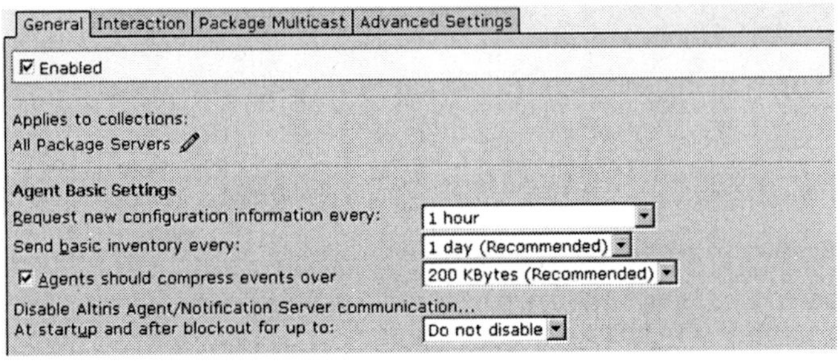

Enable Check Box – Used to enable or disable the policy.

Applies to collections – Use this to configure which machines this policy applies too. Multiple collections can be associated with a policy.

Agent Basic Settings

Request new configuration information every – How often the Agent requests configuration information. **(5-7 hours is recommended for desktops, 1-2 hours for Package Servers and 2-3 hours for servers.)**

Send Basic Inventory every – How often the Agent sends Domain Name, TCP/IP, Computer Name, Primary User, OS version and Agent Version. The default policy is send Basic Inventory every day and should be modified if you have a large number of clients. **(Recommend 5-7 days)**.

Agents should compress events over X kb – The Agent will compress event data before sending it to the Notification Server. Events are normally used to tell the Notification Server of the success or failure of a package download or task execution. Data such as Inventory data is not considered an Event.

Disable Altiris Agent/Notification Server communication – A standoff period between 0 and X minutes can be configured. Using a standoff period will ensure that all machines don't immediately contact the Notification Server when they start-up or after there has been a blockout period. **(Recommend approx 45 minutes)**

Download & Execute Options

Run from the server if bandwidth is above X – If the available bandwidth is above X, the client will execute the software package from the server instead of downloading it locally and then executing it. This is disabled by default.

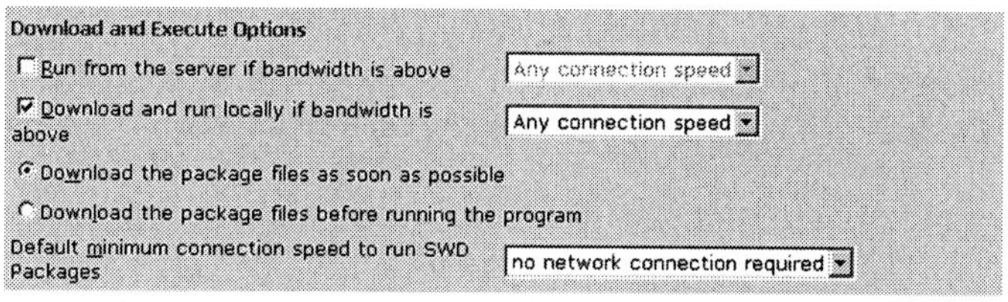

Download and run locally if bandwidth is above X – This is normally enabled with a threshold set to 'Any connection speed' and configures the client to download the package locally before execution. If both the 'Run from Server' and the 'Download and run locally' are enabled and the available bandwidth is above both set thresholds, the client will first try to execute from the server and then try to download and execute locally.

Download the package files ASAP – Clients will download the package as soon as they can, even if the package is not scheduled for execution until some time in the future. This is the default.

Download the package files before running the program – Will wait until the package is scheduled for execution before downloading it.

Note Options in the 'Advanced' tab of a Software task allow you to override the Altiris Agent download and execute behaviour. Software Tasks are discussed in the chapter 'Software Delivery Solution for Windows'.

Default minimum connection speed to run SWD packages – This is the minimum connection speed that must be available between client and the Notification Server before a software package will be executed on a client. This option does not affect package download and is useful if you are executing the package task from a server instead of downloading it first.

Bandwidth/Throttling & Blockout Settings

Never Throttle – Configures the client to never throttle bandwidth. **(Recommend throttling for all machines even in a LAN environment.)**

Enable Throttling when the connection speed is below X – Configures a client to only throttle if the threshold is below X. If this option is configured a throttle setting must be configured in the dialog.

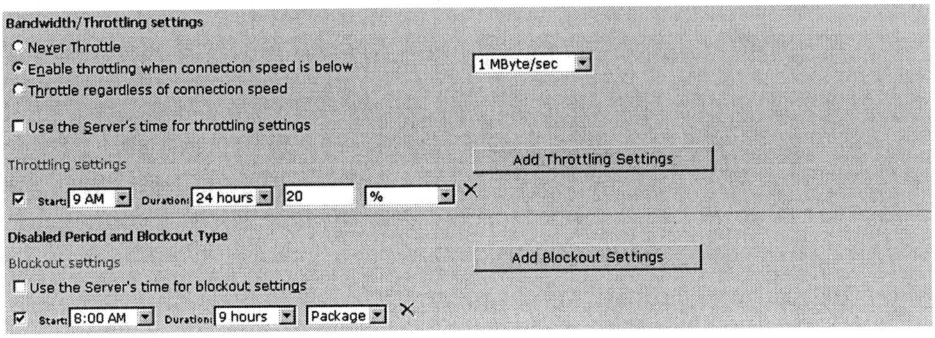

Throttle regardless of connection speed – Configures the client to always throttle regardless of the connection speed. This option, even though it is not selected by default is recommended for all desktop machines even if they are on a LAN. If desktops always throttle then it's less likely that the clients in the Altiris infrastructure will have an impact on the corporate network infrastructure.

Use the Servers time for throttling settings – This is not enabled by default and has various implications in an environment where clients from different time zones communicate with the same Notification Server.

The Add Throttling Settings Button – Allows you to add one or more throttling settings. A start time, duration and whether to use a percentage of bandwidth or a specific amount of Kbytes/sec.

The Add Blockout Settings Button – Allows you to add one or more blockout settings. A start time, duration and whether to use a 'Total' or a 'Package' blockout is available. Using 'Total' blockout stops all communications between the client and the Notification Server. Using 'Package' blockout prevents clients downloading packages but allows any other communication with the Notification Server.

Use the Servers time for blockout settings – This is not enabled by default and has various implications in an environment where clients from different time zones communicate with the same Notification Server.

The Interaction Tab

The Interaction tab displays configuration options that allow an Administrator to configure how the Agent interacts with the client.

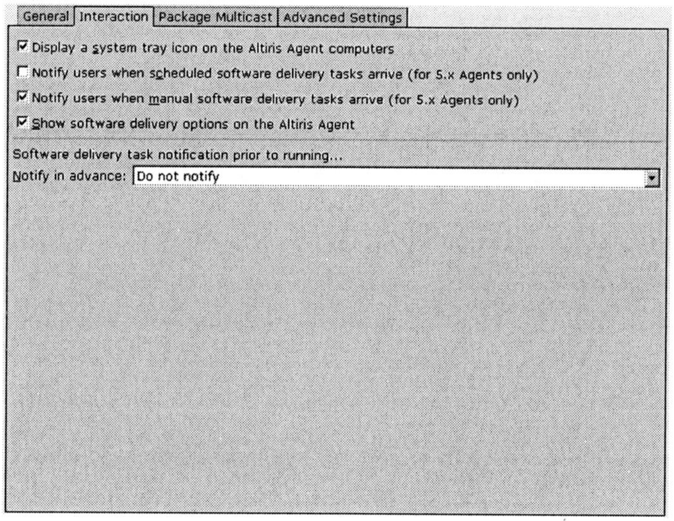

Display a system tray icon on the Altiris Agent computers – An Agent icon will be displayed on the users system tray if this option is checked.

Notify users when scheduled software delivery tasks arrive (for 5.x Agents only) – For clients running 5.x Agents, users will be notified when a scheduled software delivery task arrives.

Notify users when manual software delivery tasks arrive (for 5.x Agents only) – For clients running 5.x Agents, users will be notified when a manual software delivery task arrives. The user will then have to open the Agent interface and manually select the package to install.

Show software delivery options on the Altiris Agent – Used to configure whether or not to display the software delivery options section within the Altiris Agent interface. (**I recommend you turn this option off**.) Allowing users access to this section will allow them to disable bandwidth throttling and block network activity.

Software delivery task notification prior to running – This option is used to notify users 1 to 5 minutes prior to running a scheduled mandatory software delivery task.

The Package Multicast Tab

This tab displays options for configuring whether clients will use Package Multicast when downloading software packages and patches.

Traditionally clients download packages from a Package Server. Notification Server with SP2 adds Package Multicasting abilities to clients, which allows an individual client to temporarily act as a Package Server.

Using Package Multicast will decrease the load on dedicated Package Servers and is useful for large environments as well as small remote offices without a dedicated Package Server.

Multicast Configuration Settings

Allow Altiris Agents to use multicast for downloading packages –

Select this check box to enable Multicast for Package Downloading for clients targeted by this policy. This is disabled by default.

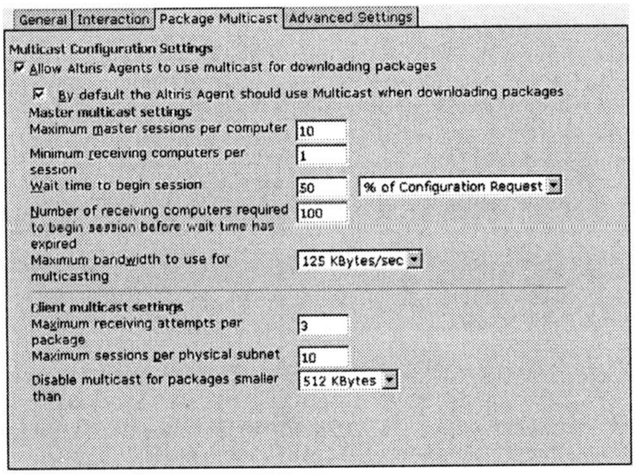

Multicast Master Settings

Maximum master sessions per computer – The maximum number of concurrent sessions for which an Altiris Agent can be the master.

Minimum receiving computers per session – The minimum number of Altiris Agents (excluding the master) that have to join the multicast session before package multicast will start.

Wait time to begin session – The maximum time to wait for the minimum number of Altiris Agents (excluding the master) to join the session, before the session times out. If the configured value is large, then more Agents will join the session but it will take longer for the package to arrive at the Agents. For example if the wait time is set to 50% of configuration update and the configuration update is set to 6 hours then the wait time will be 3 hours.

Number of receiving computers required to begin session before wait time has expired – The number of Altiris Agents (excluding the master) that will force a multicast session to begin.

Receiving Computer Settings

Maximum receiving attempts per package – The maximum number of times that an Agent will attempt to receive the same package via multicast, before defaulting to the normal package download procedure using Package Servers.
Maximum sessions per physical subnet – The maximum number of multicast sessions that can occur concurrently on a physical subnet.
Disable multicast for packages smaller than – The minimum package size that can be downloaded using multicast. Packages smaller than the configured size will use a dedicated Package Server.
By default the Altiris Agent should use Multicast when downloading packages – Use this check box to configure Multicast as the default download mechanism. (Individual packages can be configured to override this setting.)

The Advanced Settings Tab

The Advanced Settings tab displays configuration options that allow the Administrator to configure what port, multicast address, URL, Server Name and whether Power Management is enabled or not.

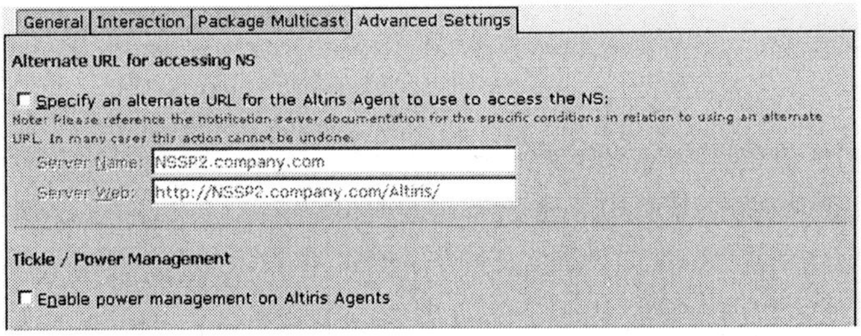

Alternate URL for accessing NS

Specify an alternate URL for the Altiris Agent to use to access the NS:
Server Name – The name of the Notification Server. Use DNS or non DNS name depending on the type of name resolution used in the infrastructure.
Server Web – The web address of the Notification Server. This setting can also be used to configure SSL and to change the default port used by the Altiris Agent when communication with the Notification Server.

Tickle / Power Management

Enabling power management on Altiris Agents allows you to wake up a managed client if it has been powered down. This is useful when deploying patches and software packages. Power Management must also be enabled if you want to force a managed client to request a configuration update or immediately send Basic Inventory.

When all options have been configured in the Altiris Agent configuration policy, return to the General tab and **enable** the policy.
When all settings for a policy are configured click **Apply** to save the configuration.

The next time machines targeted by this policy request an updated configuration they will receive and apply their new agent settings.

Global Altiris Agent Policy Settings

The Global Altiris Agent Policy applies to all clients and must be configured if Tickle and or Multicast has been enabled using any of the agent configuration policies.
If neither of these options have been enabled in any of the agent policies then the Global policy does not apply.

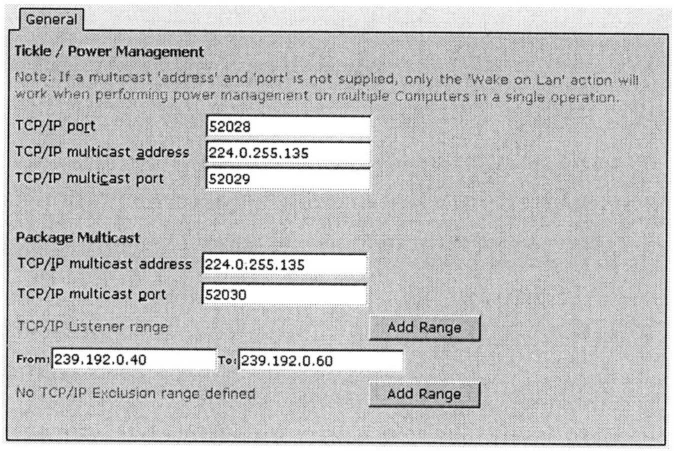

Tickle / Power Management

TCP/IP port - The Port number used by clients to listen for Power Management messages on the network.

TCP/IP multicast address - The IP Address used by clients to listen for multicast Power Management commands on the network.

TCP/IP multicast port - The multicast Port number used by clients to listen for Power Management messages on the network.

Package Multicast

TCP/IP multicast address - The IP Address used by clients to listen to multicast negotiation messages on the network.

TCP/IP multicast port - The port number used by clients to listen to multicast messages on the network.

TCP/IP Listner Range - The range of IP Address from which a the multicast session chooses from to use during the multicasting of the package by the master.

Use the first Range button to add multicast listner ranges and use the second Range button to add exclusions to a multicast range.

*When all settings have been configured, click **Apply** to save the changes. All machines with Tickle and or Multicasting enabled will recieve the new settings the next time they request a configuration update.*

Useful Altiris Agent Reports

To view the following reports open the Web Console, select the Reports Tab then navigate to **NS Infrastructure > Agent.**

Clients with no configuration in last N days

Clients that have not updated configuration in 'N' days. This could be because several issues such as a communications problem or the machine is turned off while the user is on holidays.

Configuration requests that result in error

Shows what clients had errors when requesting a configuration update from the Notification Server. Too many of these may mean that the Notification Server can not cope with the number of simultaneous configuration requests or it may simply have been that the server was down at the time.

Altiris Agent program execution (failure)

Any execution failure including an Agent rollout execution failure.

Altiris Agent basic inventory (no update 7 days)

Clients that haven't sent a basic inventory in 7 days.

Computers where the Altiris Agent installation failed

Self explanatory.

Altiris Agent installation status

Self explanatory.

Push (Altiris Agent) install failed

Self explanatory.

Discovered computers with no registered Altiris Agent

What machines have been discovered but do not yet have the Agent.

Summary

The Altiris Agent provides an interface between the client and the Notification Server. The Agent can be installed manually or using push, pull or Group Policy. Configuration setting for the Altiris Agent are controlled using an Altiris Agent configuration policy. Once the Agent is installed and configured on a client it can be managed using the Notification Server Web Console.

The next chapter, 'Administration Part II' introduces some of the common Administrative tasks you should be familiar with when administering a Notification Server.

8

Administration (Part II)

Collections

Updating Collection membership

Collection membership is automatically updated by the 'Automatic Collection Updating' setting discussed in the chapter 'Configuring Notification Server'.

To manually update collection membership, navigate to the required collection in the Resources tab.

Once the membership of the selected collection is displayed in the details pane, click the update membership button for the collection. 

Creating a new Collection

For this example we will create a collection of all machines in a specific TCP/IP range.

From the Resources tab in the Web Console select the folder in which you wish to create the new collection or create a new folder.

Right click the folder and choose **New > Collection**.

Enter a Name and description.

Set the Membership update to **Automatic**.

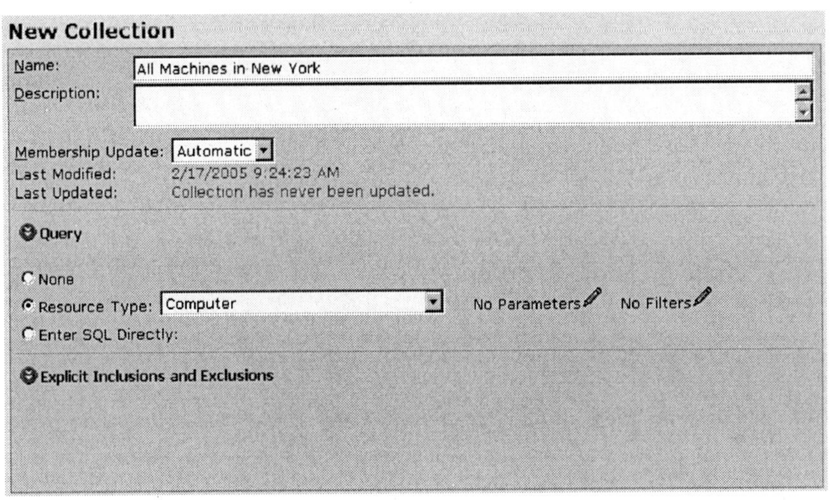

Expand the Query section and choose the option button for Resource Type. (Computer is default)

Click the Filter(s) link to display the Manage Filters dialog.

Click the New Filter button, to create a new filter.

In the New Filter dialog select *INV_AEX_AC_TCPIP* from the Table drop down.
In the field drop down choose *IP Address*.
Choose *'like'* as the operator, then enter the IP value. For example 192.168.0.% where % is a wildcard.

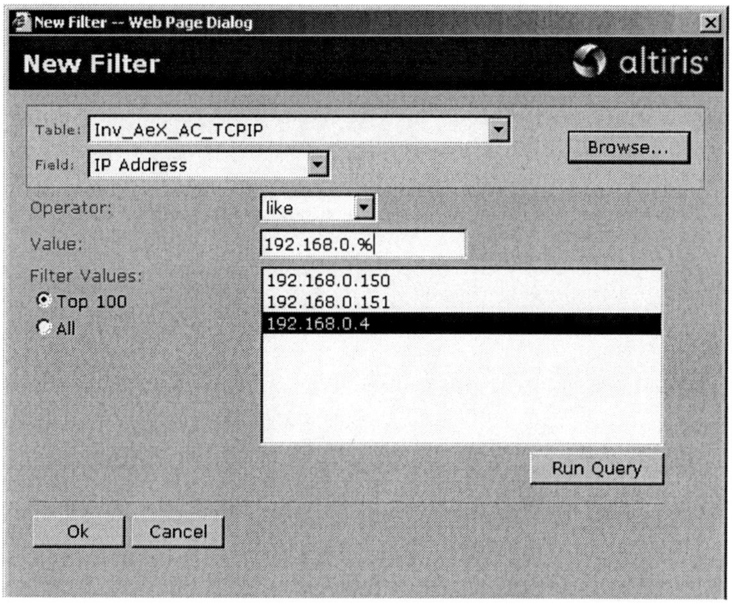

Click **OK**.

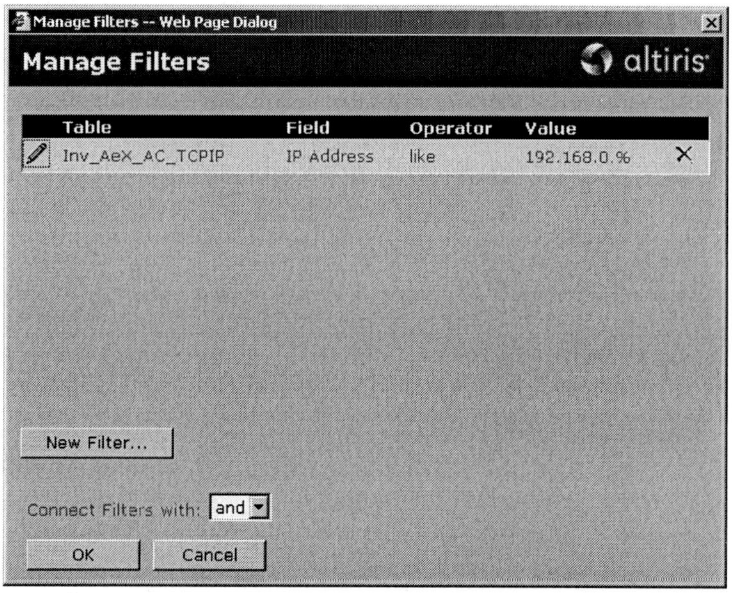

Click **OK** again to return to the collection definition.

Click **Apply** to view the collection membership.

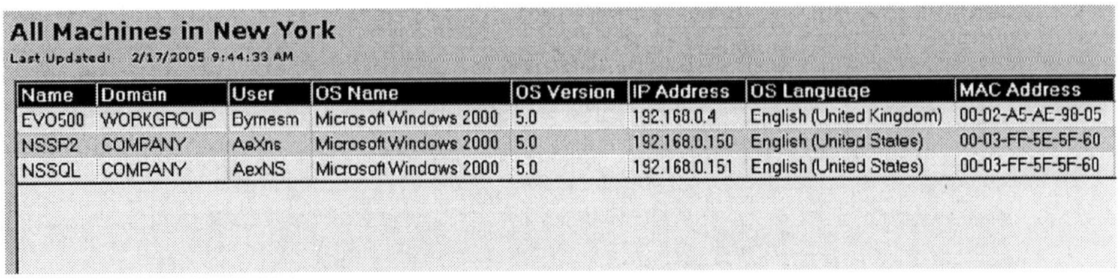

All Machines in New York

Last Updated: 2/17/2005 9:44:33 AM

Name	Domain	User	OS Name	OS Version	IP Address	OS Language	MAC Address
EVO500	WORKGROUP	Byrnesm	Microsoft Windows 2000	5.0	192.168.0.4	English (United Kingdom)	00-02-A5-AE-98-05
NSSP2	COMPANY	AeXns	Microsoft Windows 2000	5.0	192.168.0.150	English (United States)	00-03-FF-5E-5F-60
NSSQL	COMPANY	AexNS	Microsoft Windows 2000	5.0	192.168.0.151	English (United States)	00-03-FF-5F-5F-60

This collection can now be used for tasks such as software delivery or agent installation and configuration.

Using Resource Manager

Resource Manager is used to view information about a specific resource. What details appear in the Manager will be determined by the type of resource you are viewing, the Solutions installed on the Notification Server and in the case of a computer resource, what data has been reported by the computer.

To access Resource Manager, go to the Resources tab in the Web Console and navigate to a collection containing the computer you wish to explore.

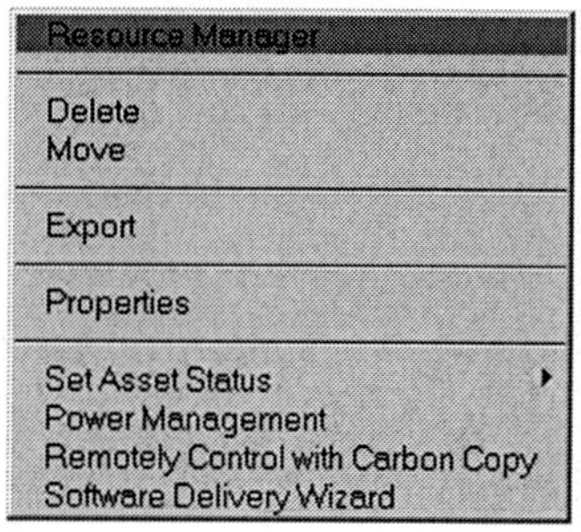

In the details pane right click a computer and choose Resource Manager from the shortcut menu. A new window is launched containing five tabs. The first of these tabs is the Summaries tab:-

Summaries Tab

The summaries tab displays a summary of the basic details and statistics for the selected computer. Extra categories may be added as solutions are installed on the Notification Server.

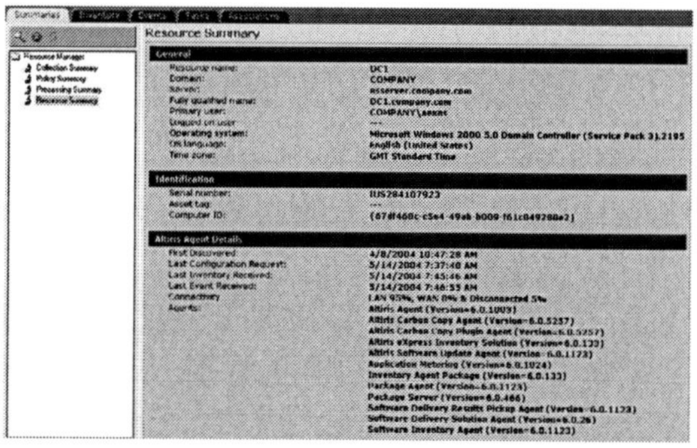

Collection Summary – Shows what collections the machine is a member of.

Policies Summary – Shows the Policies that apply to the selected machine.

Processing Summary – Details the Event History and Client Configuration Events information.

Resource Summary – Basic details for the machine including when the machine last sent a configuration request.

Inventory Tab

The Inventory Tab details Basic Inventory and Inventory Solution data, if Inventory Solution is installed. What details appear in this window will depend on the data that has been gathered from the selected machine. For example if Inventory Solution is used clients will report information such as Hardware and Software Inventory.

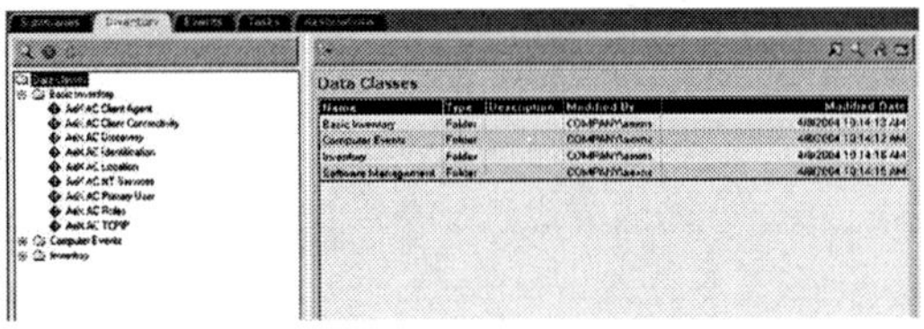

Events Tab

Contains a list of the Events a client agent has sent to the Notification Server as well as Events that have been generated by the Notification Server for that client.

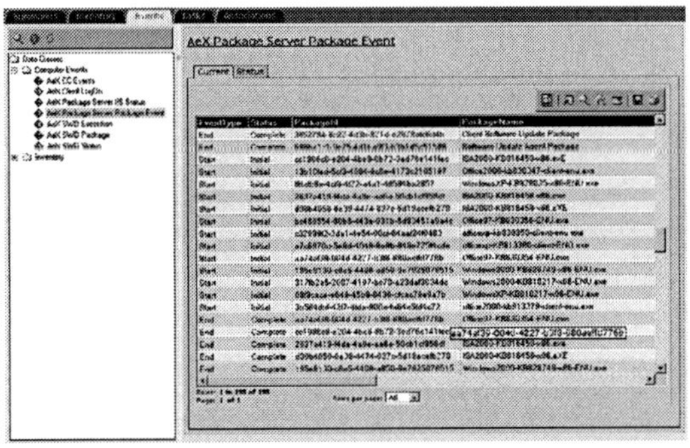

The event data that appears will always be dependent upon the agents installed on that client and the role of the client. For example in the above picture, Package Server events and statistics are reported because the selected PC is a Package Server.

Tasks Tab

Displays a list of tasks that can be executed on the client. The tasks listed depend on the Altiris solutions installed on the client.

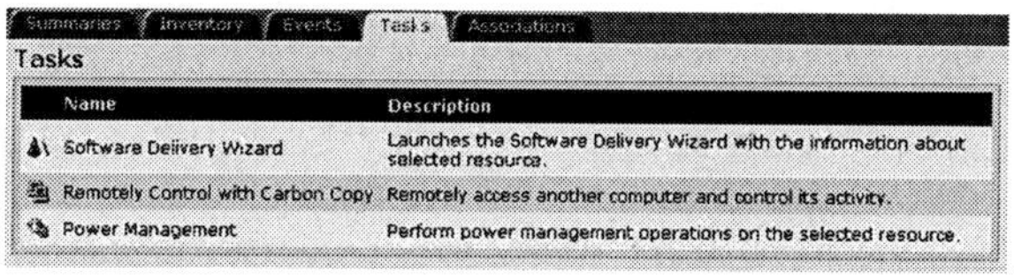

Associations Tab

Associations are links from one resource to another. This tab displays the list of resources associated with the selected recourse.

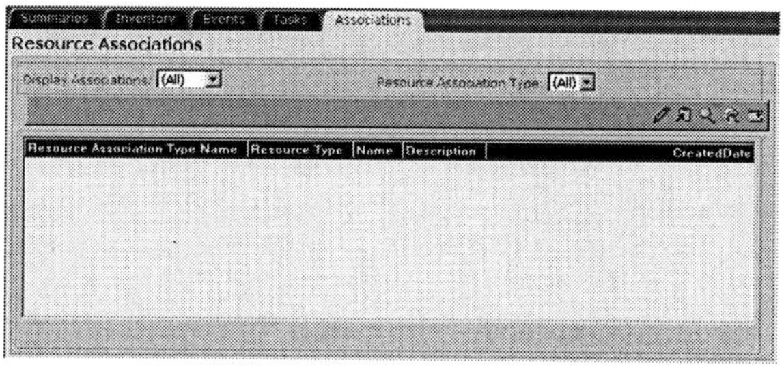

For example a computer and incident association will link the computer name and incident resource together so that the incidents associated with a computer can be viewed while exploring.

Associations are created during the installation of Notification Server and are added during Solution installation. Associations can also be manually created.

Creating an Association

In the Web Console select the Configuration tab and navigate to **Resource Settings > Resource Associations**.

Clone an existing association and give it a unique name.

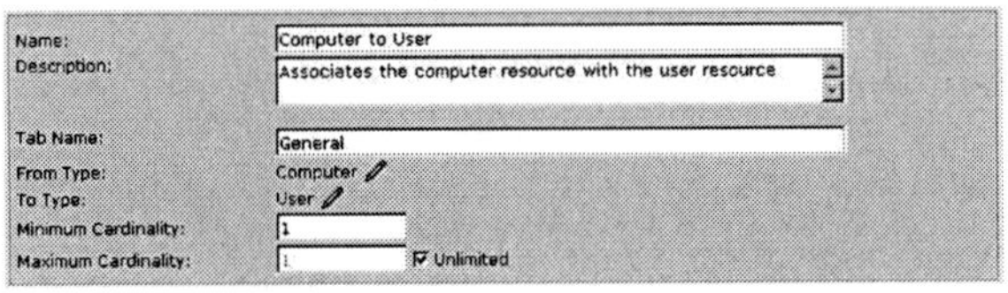

In the Edit Resource dialog enter a name and description.

Use the **'From Type'** and **'To Type'** links to select the resources.

Click **Apply** when finished.

Note Cardinality refers to the number of rows the association can return.

Deleting & Retiring computers

Machines can be retired or deleted from the database. Deleting a machine will remove all data for that machine and free up the associated license. Retiring a machine will free up the associated license and remove it from all collections and reports. However unlike deleting a machine, retiring will keep all of the associated inventory data for asset management purposes.

Deleting a computer

From the Web Console select the Resources tab and navigate to a collection containing the machine you want to delete.

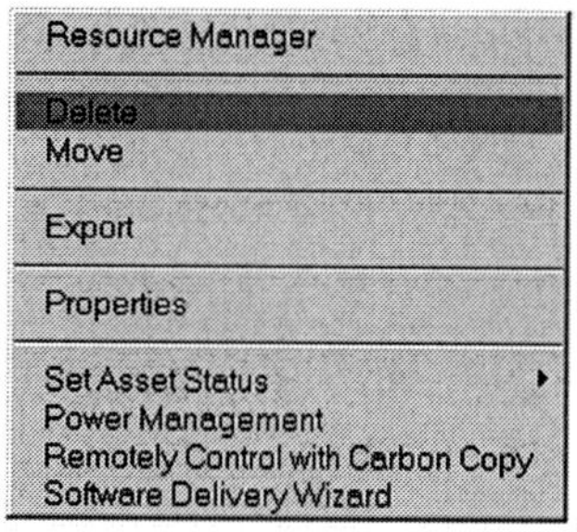

Once found, right click the machine name in the details pane and choose **Delete**. Confirm and click **OK**.

Deleting a machine from the Notification Server will not remove or disable the Agent on the client machine. If a machine is removed from Notification Server but is still a live machine, the next time the Agent on that machine requests an updated configuration it will be seen as a new machine and given a new GUID.

Retiring a computer

From the Web Console select the Resources tab and navigate to a collection containing the machine you want to retire.

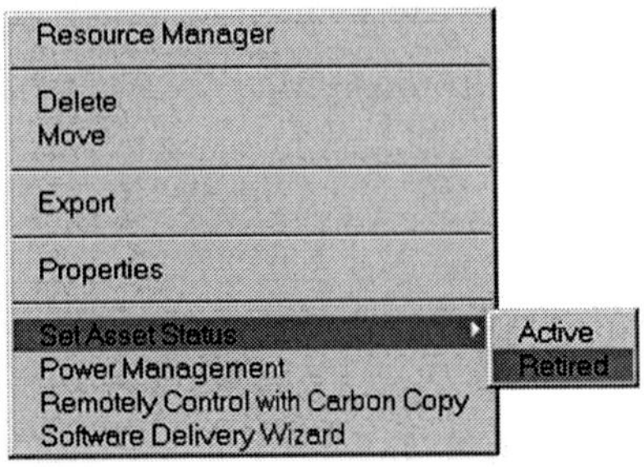

Once found, right click the machine name in the details pane and choose **Set Asset Status > Retire**.

Confirm and click **OK**.

Note A resource such as a machine should only be retired from Notification Server when it has been physically taken off the network. If a resource is retired in Notification Server but still exists on the network, Notification Server will not return client polices or process NSE files for that resource.

Power management

If Power Management has been enabled for a client through an Altiris Agent configuration Policy then you will be able to perform the following:

Forcing a machine to request a configuration update

Navigate to the Resources tab in the Web Console.
Find the collection containing the computer you want to manage.
In the details pane right click the computer and choose **Power Management**.

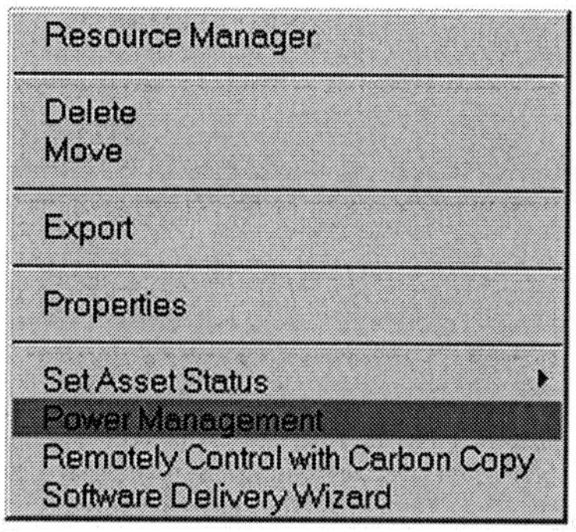

In the Power Management dialog check 'Get Client Configuration'. And click **OK**

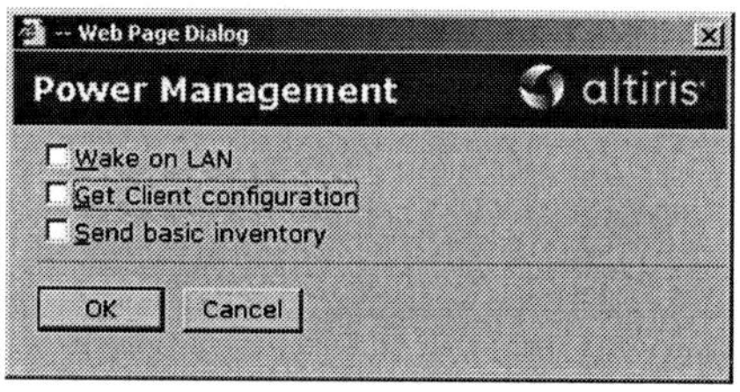

The client will receive a request from the Notification Server instructing it to request an update configuration.

Waking up a machine

Find the collection containing the computer you want to manage.
In the details pane right click the computer and choose **Power Management**.
In the Power Management dialog check 'Wake on LAN'. And click **OK**
Providing the clients network card and your network supports WOL a Wake on LAN packet will be sent to the clients MAC address instructing it to wake up.

Forcing a machine to send Basic Inventory

Find the collection containing the computer you want to manage.

In the details pane right click the computer and choose **Power Management**.

In the Power Management dialog check **'Send Basic Inventory'**. And click **OK**

The client will receive a request from the Notification Server instructing it send a Basic Inventory.

Notification Policies

A Policy consists of a set of instructions designed to automate an administrative function. For example, a policy can instruct the Notification Server to e-mail a monthly hardware inventory report or a policy can be used to configure communication settings for a Solution Agent or even deliver a software package to a targeted collection of computers. Notification Server comes with built-in Policies and Solutions come with their own specific Notification Policies. New Policies can be created and existing Policies can be edited and cloned.

Specific functions that can be automated by a policy include:

- An E-mail can be sent to a predetermined address.
- A command line can be run.
- A new incident can be created in Alert Manager (Incidents).
- An existing incident can be edited in Alert Manager.
- A new saved report can be generated.

An example of a Notification Policy can be seen below. This particular policy is configured to send an e-mail and create a report when the Altiris Agent is installed on a computer.

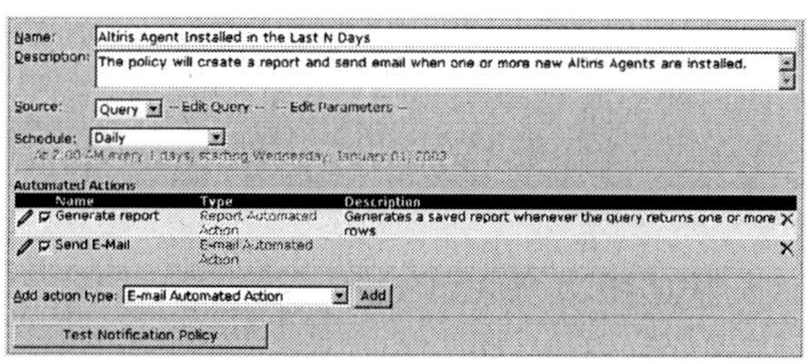

To view this Notification Policy, select the Configuration tab and navigate to **Server Settings > Notification Policies**.

To Clone a Policy

Right click the policy to clone
From the shortcut menu choose the **Clone** command
Enter the name of the new copy in the Clone Item dialog and click **OK**

Summary

In this chapter we looked some more of the common administrative tasks required when administering a Notification Server.

Notification Server comes with built-in collections that are useful for 50% of tasks. As you use CMS more you will find that custom collections are required to perform configuration and package delivery to a more granular level.

The Resource Manager is used to view information about a specific resource such as the inventory of a machine or the security of an object.

Deleting a machine will remove all data for that machine and free up the associated license. Retiring a machine will free up the associated license and remove it from all collections and reports but not delete the data for the machine from the database.

When Power Management is enabled, machines can be woken up from a powered off state, forced to send Basic Inventory and forced to request a configuration update.

A Notification Policy consists of a set of instructions designed to automate an administrative function. Notification Server comes with built-in Notification Policies mainly found in the Configuration and Tasks tab. As solutions are added to the NS infrastructure NS policies specific to that Solution may also be added.

The next chapter 'Installing & Configuring Package Servers' looks closely at all aspects of Package Servers, including installing, configuring and administration.

9

Package Servers

Introduction

Package Servers (PS) scale the Altiris infrastructure by providing more than one package source for managed clients. Clients download advertised software packages such as applications and patches from the Notification Server or from a Package Server. If no Package Servers exist in an Altiris Infrastructure then clients can only download packages from one source, the Notification Server.

Site maintenance is used to map Package Servers to TCP/IP subnets. These mapping are then used by the client to help maximize the effectiveness of Package Servers.

The addition of Package Multicast with NS SP2 now allows a client to act effectively as a Package Server. Using clients as temporary Packager Servers will take some of the load off dedicated Package Servers but can only be used in a network infrastructure that supports multicasting.

For details on the optimum number and placement of Package Servers in your Altiris infrastructure please see the chapter 'Designing an Altiris Infrastructure'.

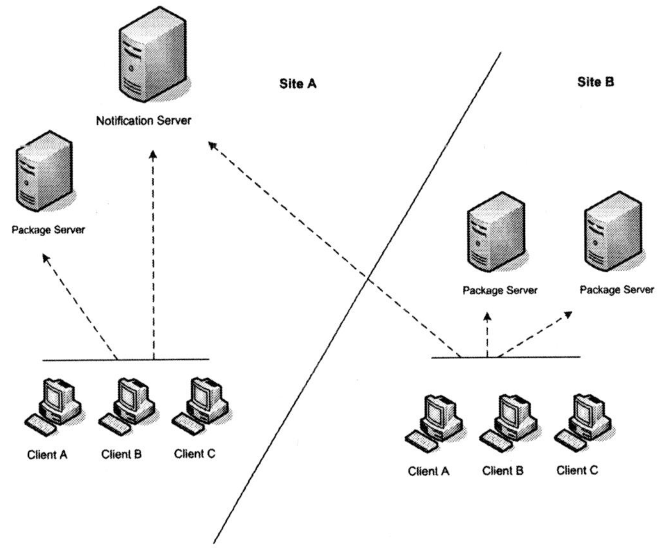

Minimum PS Software Requirements

Microsoft Windows NT/2000/XP/2003

The Altiris Agent 6.x

IIS (Optional)

For suggested hardware requirements see the chapter 'Designing an Altiris infrastructure'.

Adding a Package Server

Select the Configuration tab in the Altiris Web console and navigate to **Server Settings > Notification Server Infrastructure > Package Servers**.

Click the add Package Server button **+** and search for the machine that will be the Package Server.

In the **'Find Resource'** dialog, search for the machine that will be a Package Server. Once the machine has been found, select it and click **OK**.

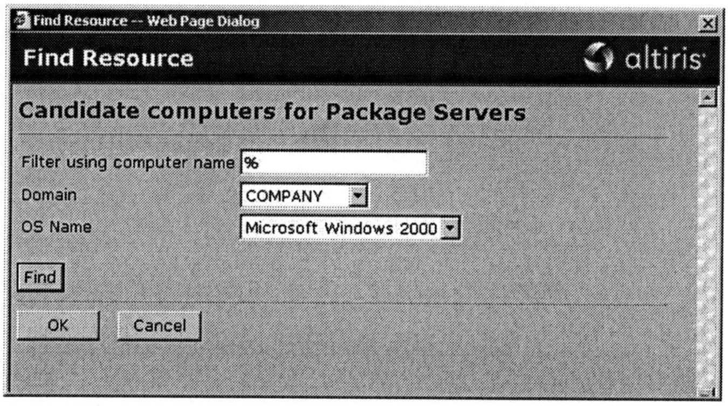

The machine will appear in the list with an asterisk to the left of the computer name. Click **Apply** to designate the machine as a Package Server.

The next time the targeted computer requests a configuration update, it will download and install the Package Server Agent.

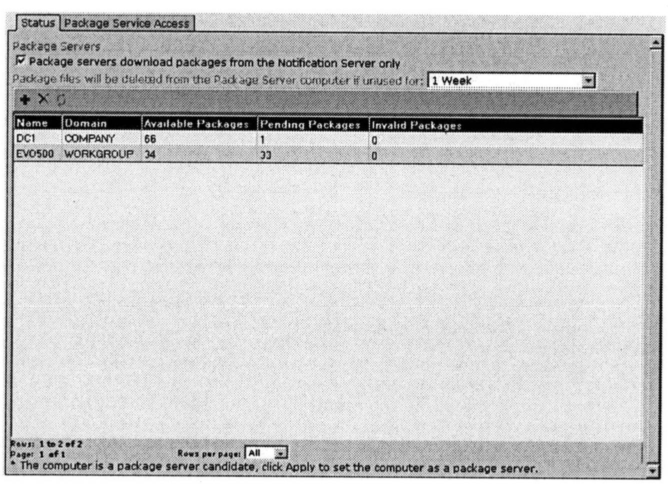

Any packages that are configured to replicate to all Package Servers will be downloaded by the new Package Server. (All patches/updates and solution agent packages are by default configured to replicate to all package servers).

Package Server Folder Structure

When the Package Server agent is installed it creates two folders, 'Package Delivery' and 'Package Server Agent' beneath the Altiris Agent folder by default. The Package Delivery folder is used to store downloaded packages. The 'Package Server Agent' folder contains files used by the Package Server agent. Both folders can be found in the root of the local Altiris Agent folder. If Internet Information Services is installed when the Package Server agent is installed a virtual web is created and mapped to the 'Package Delivery' folder.

The Package Delivery folder

Contains downloaded software packages. This folder is shared with the share name PkgSvrHostX$. (Where 'X', is the local drive letter where the Package Server Agent has been installed.)
The security permissions on the folder are, share permissions Everyone Full Control, NTFS permissions are Everyone, Read & Execute and Administrators and System Full Control.

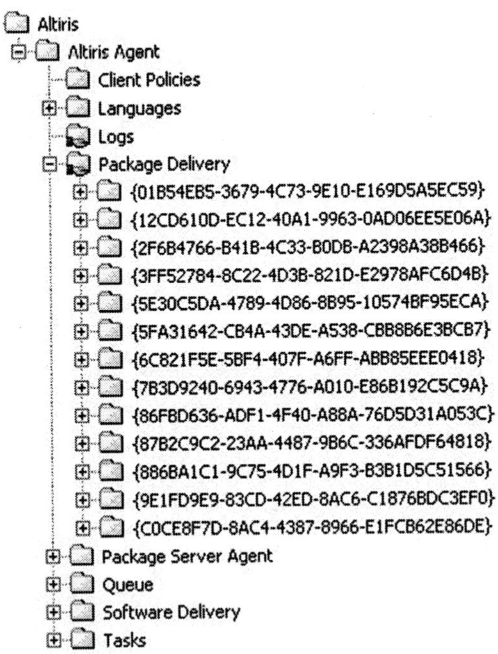

Every Package that is downloaded has a similar structure. On the root of each GUID folder are three files, log.xml, package.xml and snapshop.xml. Each GUID directory may also contain a 'Cache' folder, which contains the actual package files, but only if the package contains files and is not a command-line only package.

The Package Server Agent folder

This folder contains the files GetPackageSnapshot.asp and PackageServerStatus.xml, which are used by the Package Server Agent.

GetPackageSnapshot.asp – This file is used by the Package Server agent to get a snapshot of an existing package to see if it has changed.
PackageServerStatus.xml – This file resides in the root of the PS virtual directory and details the download status for all packages. The file can be accessed remotely using the URL http://PackageServerName/Altiris/PS/PAckageServerStatus.xml (where PackageServerName is the actual name of the Package Server).

The Package Server Web Structure

When the Package Server agent is installed, if IIS is also installed, the installation will create a virtual directory named http://localhost/Altiris/. Every time the Package Server downloads a new package it creates a GUID folder in the Package Delivery folder then creates a new virtual directory for that package. Each virtual directory is mapped to a folder of the same name under the local 'Package Delivery' folder. Clients can then download packages using a UNC or HTTP path.

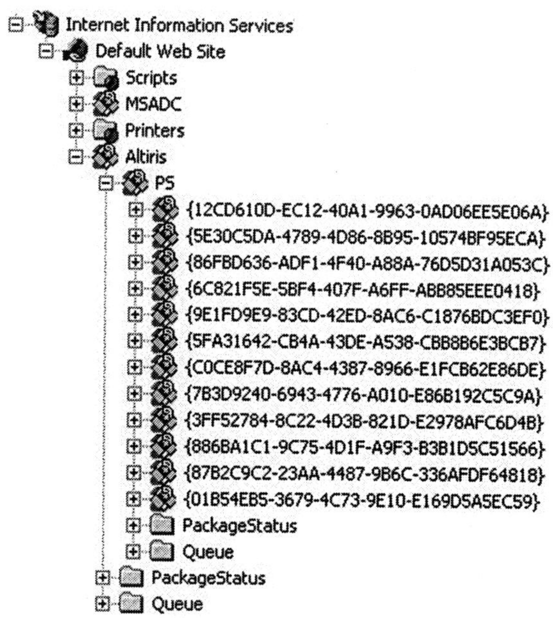

Other Files used by Package Servers

log.xml – This file contains a record of the package downloads.

package.xml – This file contains information including the list of available Package Servers to download a package from.

snapshot.xml – This file contains a snapshot of the package (file names, size and last modified time). This snapshot information is used by the Package Server agent to determine if the package is up-to-date. Only files that have changed will be downloaded if there is a change to the source package.

AeXNSPkgSvrAgent.log – Located in the Winnt\System32 folder on the Package Server. This file details the installation of the Packager Server Agent component.

Replicating a package to a selected Package Server

Use the properties of a package to configure which Package Servers will receive a specific package. Solution packages such as Agents are by default configured to replicate to all Package Servers.

From the Resources tab in the Web Console navigate to **Resources > Software Management > Software Delivery Packages > Windows**.
Right click the selected software package and choose **Resource Manager** from the shortcut menu.
In the Resource Manager window select the **Advanced** tab and choose **'Selected Package Servers'**. Check the required Package Servers then click **Apply**.
Close the Resource Manager Window.

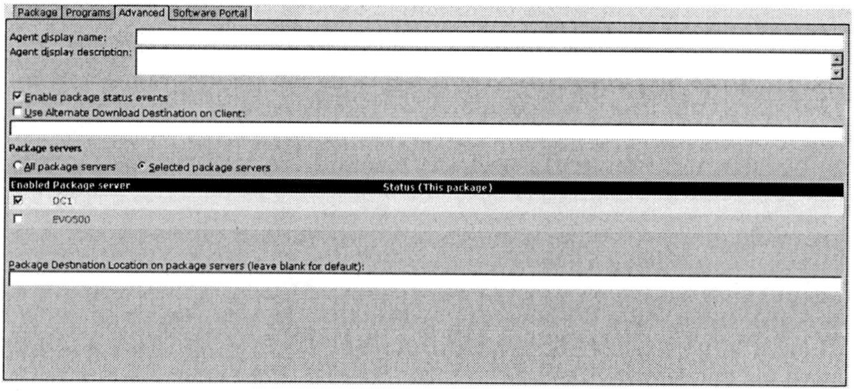

Use alternate download destination on client – When clients download packages from a Package Server or Notification Server, the client will store the package in InstallPath\Altiris\Altiris Agent\Software Delivery\GUID Folder. This option can be used to override that path. (Not recommended)
All Package Servers or Selected Package Servers – This option defines which Package Servers will receive the new package, the default is 'All Package Servers'.
Package Destination Location on Package Servers – Package Servers store packages in 'Installpath\Altiris\Altiris Agent\Package Download\Package GUID\'. Use this option to specify a different location. (The option is useful if Package Servers are low on disk space on the drive where the Altiris Agent is installed. This option is also used when replicating packages to machines that are Package Servers and also Altiris Deployment Servers. \\%PackageServer%\Express\Packages)

Replicating a software package to all Package Servers

From the Resources tab in the Web Console navigate to **Resources > Software Management > Software Delivery Packages > Windows**.

Right click the selected software package and choose Resource Manager from the shortcut menu.

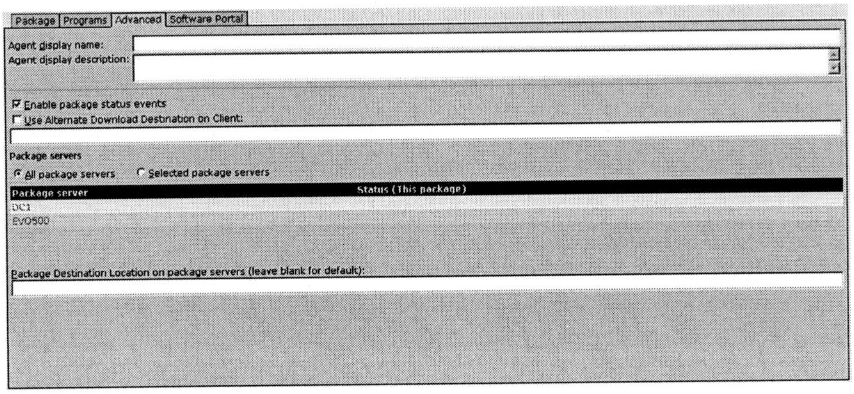

In the Resource Manager window select the **'Advanced'** tab and choose **'All Package Servers'**.

Click **Apply**.

Close the Resource Manager Window.

Updating Distribution Points

A Package Refresh schedule runs periodically on the Notification Server. Each time the schedule runs, any newly created or modified packages are updated and made available to requesting Package Servers.

The 'Update Distribution Points' button on the Advanced tab of a package allows you to force the Notification Server to refresh the selected package and not wait for the Refresh Schedule.

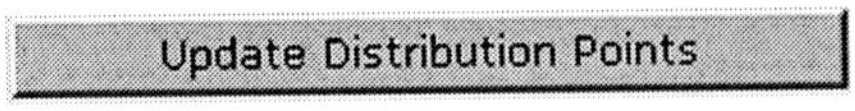

This option does **not** force targeted Package Servers to request the package but simply ensures that it is available to Package Servers before the Refresh Schedule has been run.

Package Server FAQ

When does the Package Server download new packages?

Package Servers download new packages every time the Package Server requests an updated configuration from the Notification Server.

When does a Package refresh existing Packages?

The Package Server refreshes existing packages every 24 hours by default. The Refresh will check that all packages that have already been downloaded by the Package Server have the valid files for that package. If any files are found to be corrupt or missing, the Package Server will download the missing/corrupt file(s). The refresh will not download new packages or changes to existing packages. This interval is configured through the registry and is detailed at the end of the chapter.

How does the Notification Server know which Package Servers have successfully downloaded a package?

The Package Server Agent sends back events to the Notification Server saying it has the latest Packages.

How do clients know which Package Servers have the package they want to download?

Each Package Server uses events to tell the Notification Server it has successfully downloaded a particular package. When a client next requests that package from the Notification Server it is given a list of the Package Servers that have successfully downloaded the package.

When a new Package Server is rolled out, what packages will it receive?

It will download all packages, where 'All Package Servers' has been selected on the Package Properties of a package.

Where will a Package Server get its packages?

Package Servers download packages from the Notification Server or from any Package Server that has the required package. Package Servers can be configured to only download packages from the Notification Server and not try to get packages from another Package Server. To configure this, go to the Web Console, select the Configuration tab and navigate to **Server Settings > Notification Server Infrastructure > Package Servers**. Check or uncheck the option 'Package Servers download package for the Notification Server only'.

Where will clients download software packages from?

When clients request an 'Update Configuration' they check the Notification Server to see if any packages need to be downloaded. Each package will have a list of the Package Servers that can supply that package. Clients will download packages from the nearest package source.

Package Server Registry Settings

Package Server registry settings can be found on the Package Server at **HKEY_LOCAL_MACHINE > Software > Altiris > Altiris Agent > Package Server**

AgentExecInterval (sec)	How often the Package Server refreshes existing packages. (24 Hours default)
LastPackageRefreshTime	The date and time the last package refresh occurred.
IISLogLastSentTime	The date and time the IIS logs were last sent to the Notification Server. This is only used if the Package Server is running IIS.
IISLogSendInterval (min)	This setting indicates how frequently the IIS logs are sent to the Notification Server. (24 Hours default) This is only used if the Package Server is running IIS.
PackageServerBaseDir	Where the Package Delivery folder is located.
PkgCleanupInterval (min)	How often the Package Server cleans up redundant packages.

Note Use the registry editor to edit any of the above values. Most of the values are displayed in hexadecimal, ensure that you switch to decimal values when modifying or viewing the values. The usual cautionary note applies to editing registry values.

Site Maintenance

Site Maintenance is used to assign Package Servers to sites. Package Servers will only be used by clients for downloading packages if the Package Server is in a subnet that has been assigned to a site.

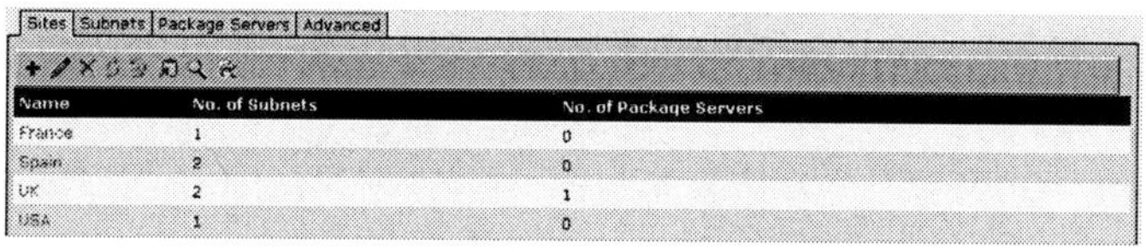

To View Site Maintenance Settings

From the Altiris Web Console select the Configuration Tab and navigate to **Server Settings > Notification Server Settings**.

Select **Site Maintenance**.

Configuring Site Maintenance

The Active Directory connector, discussed in chapter 6, can be use to populate the list of Sites and Subnets and automatically assign Package Servers to subnets. In a non Active Directory or a mixed environment, Sites and Subnets must be manually added to Site Maintenance settings. Once the sites/subnets have been added, Packages Servers can then be assigned to their respective subnets.

Manually adding a new Site and Subnet

From the Altiris Web Console select the Configuration Tab and navigate to **Server Settings > Notification Server Settings**.

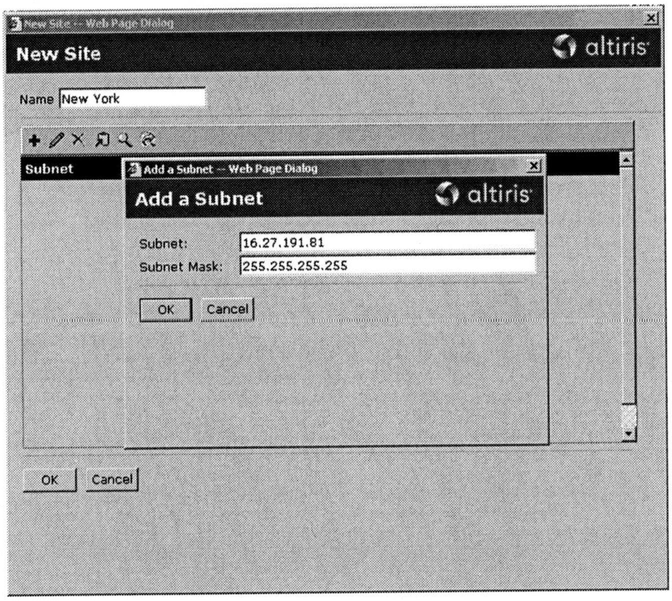

Select **Site Maintenance** and click the **Sites tab**.

Click the **plus** button to add a Site.

Enter the name for the site then click the **plus** button to add a subnet.

Enter the IP and subnet mask for the new subnet, then click **OK**.

In the New Site dialog click **OK** to return to the Site Maintenance configuration.

Manually assigning a Package Server to a Subnet

In the Site Maintenance dialog select the Package Servers tab.

Select a Package Server then click the 'Assign to Site (via Subnet)' button.

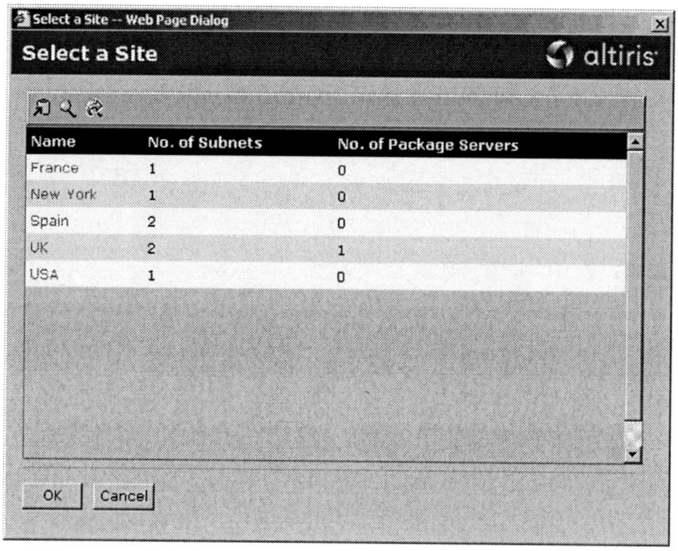

In the select a site dialog select a site then click **OK**.

The Site Maintenance update schedule

Clients request Site Maintenance information from the Notification Server. When a change is made to subnets, sites or PS mappings, either manually or through the AD connector, those changes will not be made available to a client until the site update schedule has run.

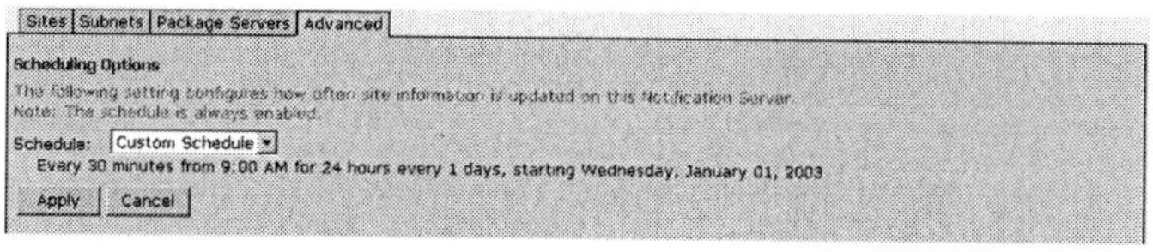

This schedule runs every 30 minutes by default and is configured through the Advanced tab of Site Maintenance. Consider changing the schedule to every 12-24 hours in large environments.

How clients use site maintenance

When a client requests package information from the Notification Server, the package location information that is returned will be determined by the Site Maintenance configuration.

- If Site Maintenance has not been configured then the client will download the package from the Notification Server or from any Package Server.
- If the client making the request is not in an assigned site then the client will only download packages from the Notification Server.
- If the client is in a site but there are no Package Servers in that site, then the client will only download the package from the Notification Server.
- If the client is assigned to a site with one or more Package Servers but the package begin rolled out is the 'Package Server Agent Package' and is not ready on any of them, the client will download the package from the Notification Server. (**Note** this only applies specifically to the 'Package Server Agent Package'.)
- If the client is assigned to a site with one or more Package Servers but the package begin rolled out is not ready on any of them, the client will retry until the package is available on one of the Package Servers.
- If the client is assigned to a site with one or more Package Servers and the package is ready, then the client will download from one of the Package Servers in the assigned site.

Removing a Package Server

In the Altiris Web console select the Configuration tab and navigate to **Server Settings > Notification Server Infrastructure > Package Servers**.

Select the Package Server from the list of servers and click the remove button 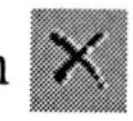 on the toolbar.

Once removed from the list, click **Apply**.

The next time the Package Server requests a configuration update, it will download the Package Server agent package if required and uninstall it. All previously downloaded packages will be removed from the Package Server folder structure.

Useful Package Server Reports

To view the following reports open the Web Console, select the Reports Tab then navigate to **Notification Server Infrastructure > Server > Package Server Status**.

Package Summary

Excellent report that allows you to see the packages, size, version and how many servers they reside on.

Recovered Packages

Lists recovered packages that failed to download and are being retried on Package Servers.

Server Load Summary

This report is used to see the load on a Package Server. The report lists the Package Servers reported total transfer rate and package downloads.

Server Summary

Summary of each individual package server, the packages hosted, and the status and disk space used.

Package Distribution Event

This report lists the status, transfer rate, and event time for each package and server.

Servers with Recovered Events

Reports on the servers with previous package download failures and are being retried.

Summary

In this chapter we looked at Package Servers. Package Servers are used to create a more scaleable solution when delivering software packages and patches to clients. Package Servers are rolled out and configured using the Web Console. When a Package Server is rolled out, an agent called the Package Server Agent is installed and a folder structure is created by the installation. A web structure is also created if the Package Server is running IIS. Once the Agent is installed it downloads packages that have been made available to it. New packages are downloaded every time the Altiris Agent on the Package Server requests an updated configuration and existing packages are refreshed every 24 hours.

The next chapter 'Inventory Solution for Windows' will look at how hardware and software inventory can be gathered from managed clients.

10

Inventory Solution for Windows

Introduction

Inventory Solution for Windows is used to gather software and hardware inventory information from managed Windows clients. Inventory can be gathered either by using the Inventory Agent installed locally on a client or by using a zero footprint inventory scan (No Agent installed). On clients were the Inventory Agent is installed, policies can be centrally configured to schedule specific types of scans on a recurring schedule.

Features

- Provides comprehensive Hardware & Software Inventory for Win32 clients.
- Can gather Inventory using WMI, Registry query or ini file query.
- Supports custom Inventory Scans.
- Supports machines that are connected, sometimes connected or never connected to the network.
- Supports zero-footprint mode. i.e. No Agent required locally to gather Inventory data.
- Inventory scans can be configured to run once and/or on a recuring schedule.
- Optimized to have as little impact as possible on clients.

Installing Inventory Solution

From the Configuration Tab in the Web Console navigate to **Upgrade/Install Additional Solutions**.

Click the **Available Solutions** tab, then click the **Solutions** button.

Select the link **'Inventory Solution for Windows'**.

A new dialog is displayed. Click **Start** to begin the installation.

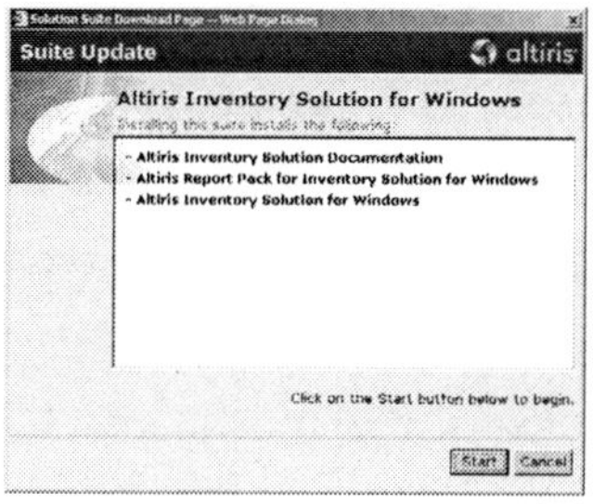

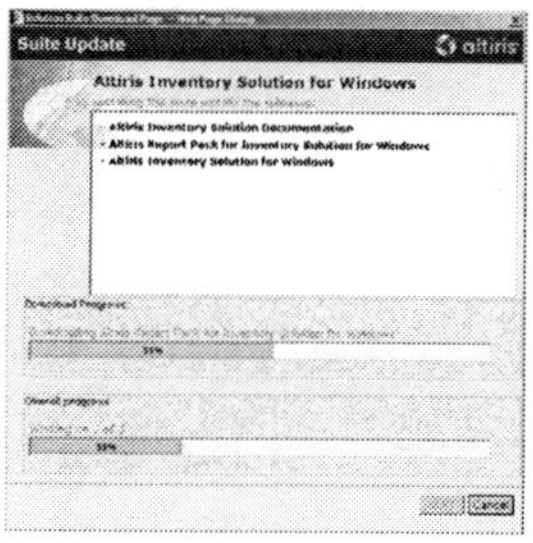

The installation will install three components, Documentation, Reporting module and the Inventory Solution itself. Reporting and documentation are now separate components from the Solution. This will allow Altiris to update individual components insted of the entire solution.

When the Solution installation is finished, apply your full license. If this solution installation is an upgrade from a previous version then there is no need to reapply the license. Solutions come with a built-in 7 day license. 30 day evaluation licenses can be downloaded from the Altiris web site.

Components added to the Web Console

Getting Started Tab – Nothing is added to this tab at this time.

Tasks Tab – The Inventory Agent configuration policies are added to **Assets and Inventory > Inventory > Windows > Inventory Tasks**. Some useful Notification Policies are also added to this tab.

Resources Tab – Nothing is added to this tab.

Reports Tab – Over 100 Inventory web reports are added.

Configuration Tab – A **Solutions Settings > Assets and Inventory > Inventory** folder, containing options to configure Normalization and Standalone Inventory. New Data classes are also added under the Resource Settings folder.

Shortcuts Tab – Nothing is added to this tab at this time.

The Inventory Agent

The inventory agent comprises of several programs, which collectively scan and gather the inventory data. The programs that make up the agent include a hardware scanner, software scanner, custom scanner, serial number scanner, Exchange User data scanner and the Collector. Collectively the Windows Inventory Agent is approximately 5MB and includes:

Software Scan *(aeXAuditpls.exe)* – Runs a detailed scan of the software installed on the computer. This agent uses a file named AuditPls.ini to determine what and how applications are reported to the Notification Server. By default, when a software scan is run, the entire hard disk is scanned for .exe files. See the section 'customising software inventory' later in this chapter for more details on AuditPls.ini.

Hardware Scan *(aeXMachInv.exe)* – This is the Hardware Agent for Inventory Solution. It reports data such as the operating system, the logged on user, local and network disks, the amount of physical memory, the TCP/IP configuration, Monitor, CPU, and PCMCIA devices.

Custom Scan *(aeXCustInv.exe)* – This Agent is used to gather inventory data from the registry, WMI, or an INI file.

Exchange User Data Scan *(aeXExchPls.exe)* – Reports data about the logged on user as found in the Microsoft Exchange Directory Service.

Serial Number Scan *(aeXSNPls.exe)* – Gathers serial number, machine make and model, BIOS, and memory module information.

Inventory Collector *(aeXNSInvcollector.exe)* – The Inventory Collector is not a scan agent. It collects and consolidates the data that each scan agent found during the scan and sends it to the Notification Server.

The Inventory Agent programs are located on the Notification Server at *InstallPath\Altiris\Notification Server\Nscap\Bin\Win32\x86\Inventory Solution\.*

Take the time to familiarize yourself with each agent file.

Configuring Inventory Scans

There are five default inventory policies that are used to configure when and what scans are executed on managed clients. The five polices are located in the Tasks Tab of the Web Console at **Tasks > Assets and Inventory > Inventory > Windows > Inventory Tasks**. Enabling any of the five policies will rollout the Inventory Agent to *All Windows computers*. I recommended that all five policies are first configured before being enabled.

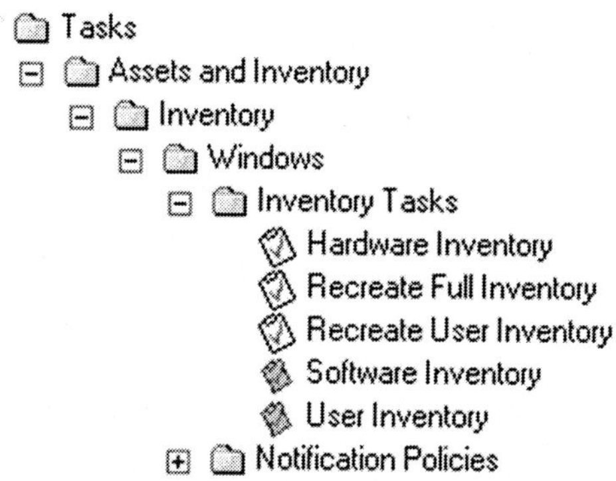

The picture above shows the five default Inventory Policies located in the Tasks Tab of the Web Console.

Note Inventory policies can be cloned and then configured to target specific machine collections. This is useful, if you do not want all windows machines to run the same inventory scans on the same schedule.

Recreate Full Inventory

This policy runs a software audit, serial number, and machine inventory and sends all inventory data to the Notification Server regardless of whether the inventory has changed since the last run. The program that is executed in a system context on the client has the command line:

AeXInvSoln.exe /cleanbeforerun /hidden /s AeXInvSolnAdm2.ini

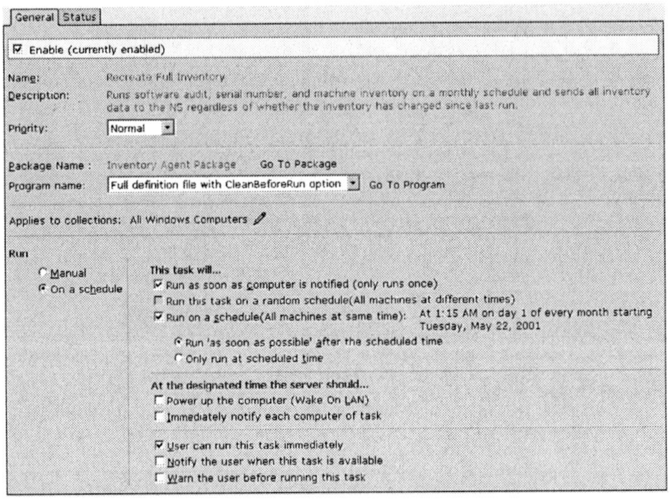

Name — The name of the Inventory Policy.

Description — The description of the Inventory Policy.

Priority — Low, Normal, High and Very High priority options are available. Tasks with a higher priority get preference over lower priority tasks.

Package Name — Name of the Inventory Package and a link to navigate to it.

Program Name — The Program that will be run by the selected schedule and a link to the Programs tab for the inventory package.

Applies to Collection — Configures which collection(s) of machines will run this scan.

Schedule — This policy runs on all Windows Machines at 1:15 am or as soon as possible after that, on the first day of every month.

Manual If Manual is selected then the user must manually start the Inventory scan. (Not normally recommended.)

Scheduled Provides options to configure when the scan starts, whether the scan only runs at the predetermined time or whether it can run ASAP after that time, if a user can start the scan through the Altiris Agent interface, and whether to let the user know when the scan is running.

Recreate User Inventory

This policy runs an end-user and exchange inventory and sends all inventory data to the NS regardless of whether the inventory has changed since the last User Inventory scan. The program that is executed in a user context on the client has the following command line: AeXInvSoln.exe /cleanbeforerun /hidden /s AeXInvSolnUsr1.ini

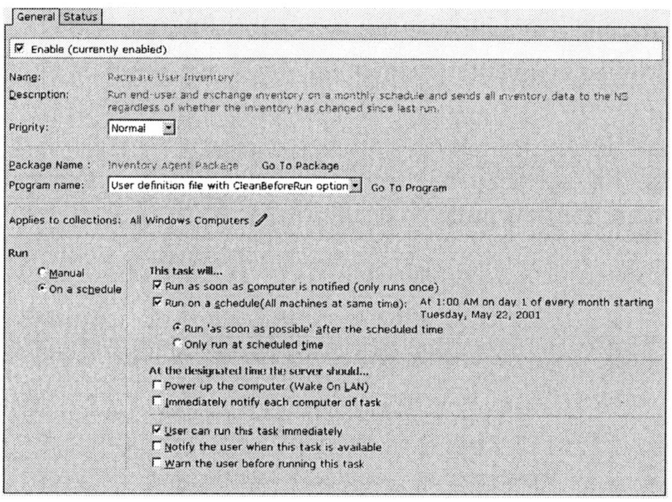

Schedule This policy runs on all Windows Machines on the first day of every month at 1:00 am or as soon as possible after that time.

Hardware Inventory

This policy runs a hardware and serial number inventory and posts the differences between the new and the last scan. The program that is executed in a system context on the client has the command line: AeXInvSoln.exe /hidden /s AeXInvSolnAdm1.ini

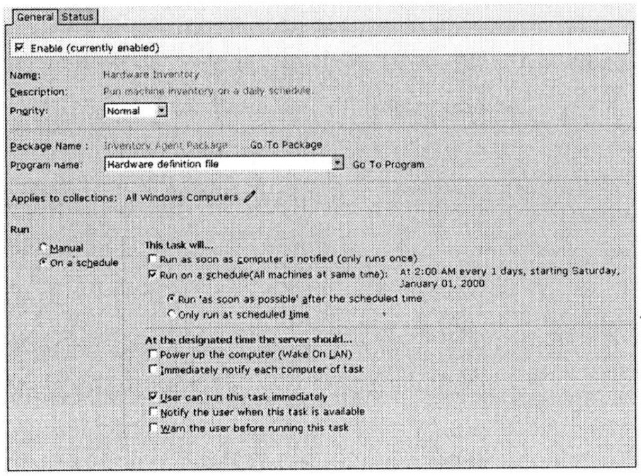

Schedule This policy runs on all Windows Machines every day at 2:00 am or as soon as possible after that time.

Software Inventory

This policy runs software audit, serial number, and machine inventory and posts the differences between the new and the last Software scan.

The program that is executed in a system context on the client has the command line: AeXInvSoln.exe /hidden /s AeXInvSolnAdm2.ini

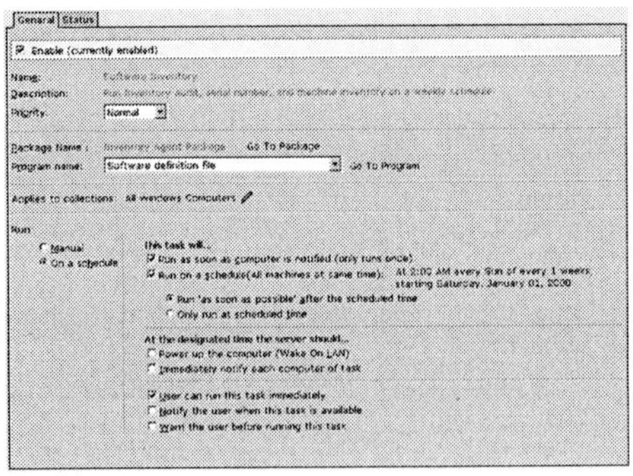

Schedule This policy runs on all Windows Machines every Sunday at 2:00 am or as soon as possible after that time.

User Inventory

This policy runs an end-user and MS Exchange inventory and posts the differences between the new and the last User Inventory scan. The program that is executed in a user context on the client has the command line:

AeXInvSoln.exe /hidden /s AeXInvSolnUsr1.ini

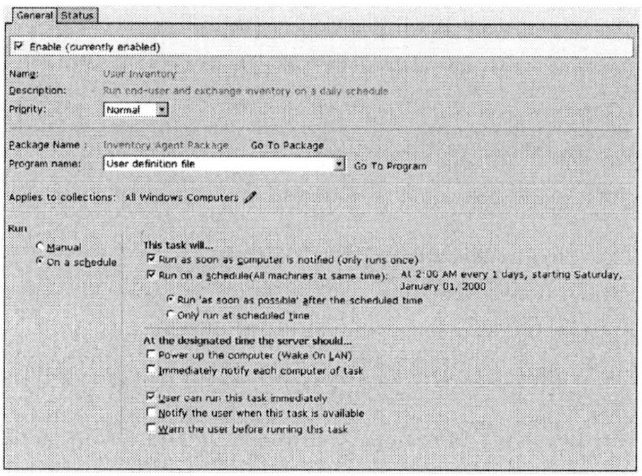

Schedule This policy runs on all Windows Machines every day at 2:00 am or as soon as possible after that time.

Rolling out the Inventory Agent

Before rolling out the Inventory Agent to clients, allow enough time for the Inventory Agent package to replicate to your Package Servers.

To rollout the agent, open the Web Console and navigate to the Tasks Tab and then **Tasks > Assets and Inventory > Inventory > Windows > Inventory Tasks**.

Select any one of the Inventory Policies.

If the selected policy has not yet been configured, do so.

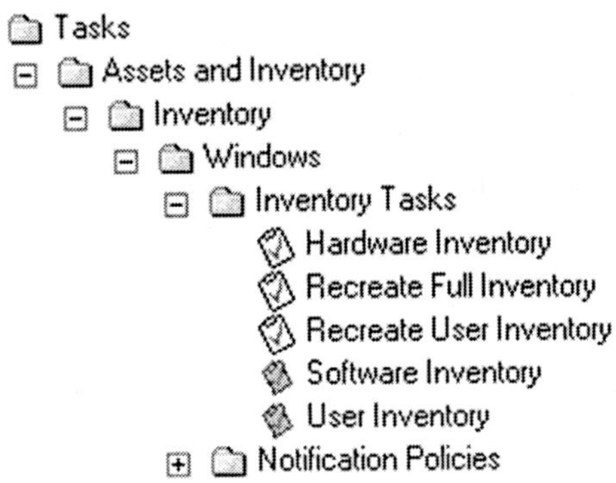

Enable the policy and click **Apply**.

The next time machines in the targeted collection update their configuration, they will download and install the Inventory Agent. An Inventory scan will then run on the client based on the configured Inventory policy schedule.

Once the Agent is installed on managed clients, configure and enable all other desired Inventory Policies. Adjust the schedule of each policy for your environment.

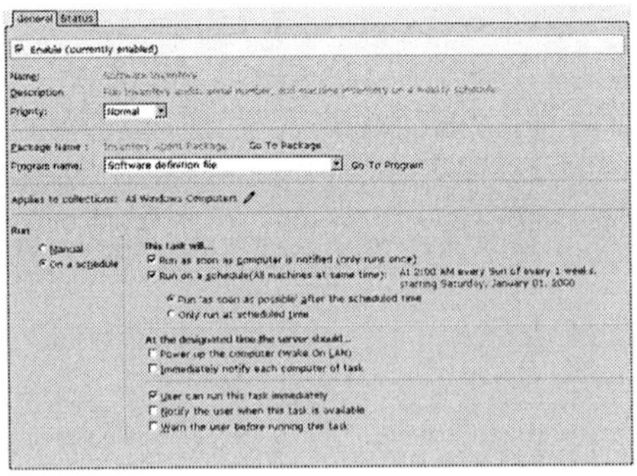

The dialog above shows the Hardware Inventory policy configured to run immediately after installation (Run once ASAP) and then again at 2:00 am on the first Monday of every month thereafter.

Inventory Agent Folder Structure

During the Inventory Agent installation a local inventory folder structure is created.

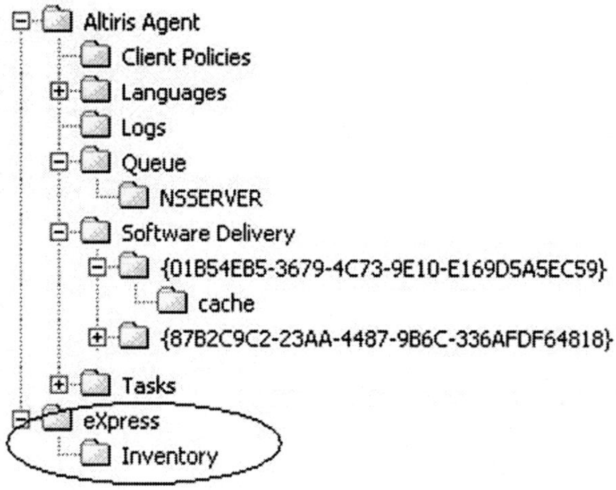

The Inventory folder is used to store the NSI files that are created by each Inventory scan agent. Once the scan is complete, the NSI files are compressed in to one NSE file and stored temporarily in the local Queue\Nsserver folder before being transported to the Notification Server.

The NSI files remain in the Inventory folder and are used by Inventory Agents to create Delta scans. (Old and new NSI files are compared and the differences sent to the Notification Server.)

The two Inventory scan policies stating with the name Recreate use the CleanBeforeRun switch to remove all NSI files from the local client Inventory folder before running an Inventory scan. This causes the Inventory scan to send a full and not delta Inventory to the Notification Server because there are no old NSI files to compare against.

Controlling the rollout of the Inventory Agent

In a small Altiris Infrastructure with good availability of network bandwidth it may not be such a hit on the network if all managed clients download the Inventory Agent around the same time, however in a large infrastructure, the network guys may come banging on your door wanting to know what's happening to 'their' network. The best way of controlling the rollout of the Inventory Agent in a large or multi site infrastructure is to target the Agent rollout site by site.

This can be achieved by creating a collection for each physical site in your infrastructure and then configuring one of the Inventory Policies to target one specific collection (site). Once the Agent has been rolled out that site, the Inventory Policies can be reconfigured to target the next site (collection) etc.

When the Inventory Agent has been rolled out successfully to all of the target machines, the scan policies can be used to control how often the inventory scans run on the targeted clients.

Inventory Data Flow

A schedule on the client starts an inventory scan.

Each scan agent creates one or more NSI files containing the scanned data and is placed in the local Inventory folder on the client.

The Collector application that forms part of the Inventory Agent collects and consolidates the data in to a single NSE file which it then sends it to the Notification Server.

The data is routed to one of the Queue folders (listed below) on the Notification Server.

When data appears in the EvtQueue, the Dispatcher Service (thread) moves the data into the Process directory. The Dispatcher Service passes the data in the Process directory to Microsoft Transaction Server.

MTS creates a process to insert the inventory data into the NS database. If the data is corrupt or cannot be processed, it is placed in the Bad folder.

Policy	Size KB
Recreate Full Inventory	400
Recreate User Inventory	80
Hardware Inventory	140
Software Inventory	400
User Inventory	80

The table above shows the approximate amount of inventory data typically generated by each of the five default policies when they are first run on a client. Subsequent executions of the last three policies will result in delta inventory of approximately 13K - 20K being sent to the Notification Server.

Notification Server folder structure

EvtQFast - This folder holds NSE files under 15 KB.

EvtQueue - This folder holds NSE files which sizes are greater than 15 KB but less than 1 MB.

EvtQSlow - This folder holds NSE files which sizes are between 1 and 20 MB.

EvtQLarge - This folder holds NSE files greater than 20MB that the Notification Server cannot process. This queue protects the Notification Server from being overloaded.

Viewing Inventory Data

Inventory can be viewed for a single or multiple machines. Use built-in and custom Inventory reports to view inventory for multiple machines.

To view the inventory of an individual machine, go to the Web Console and select the Resources Tab, then navigate to the collection containing the client you wish to view.

Once you have selected the collection right click the client in the details pane and choose **Resource Manager**.

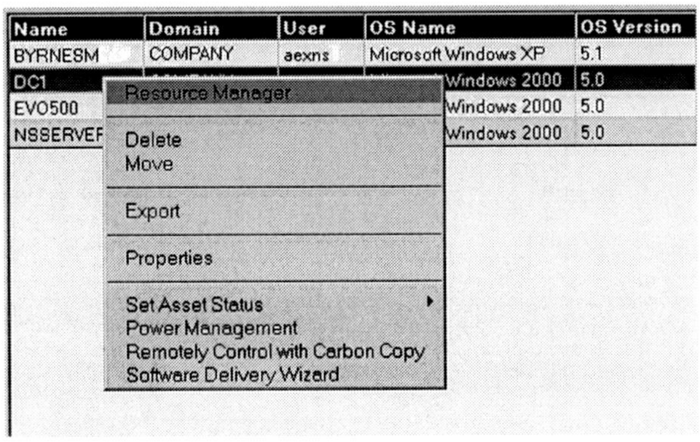

A new Window is displayed.

Select the Inventory Tab to view the clients Inventory. Expand Inventory folders as required.

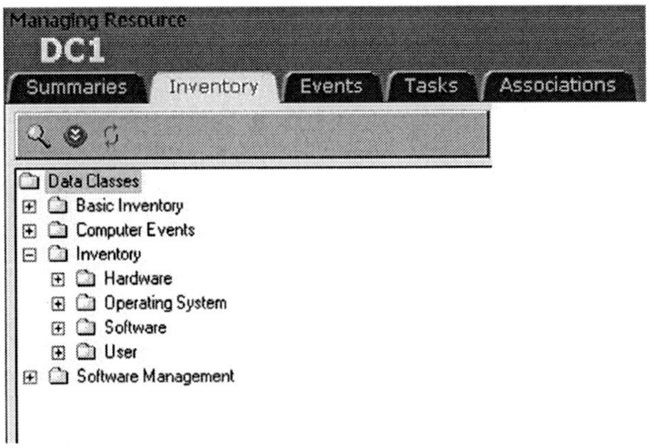

Tip To remotely connect to the Resource Manager for a specific client use the link: *http://NSName/Altiris/resource/resourcemanagerconsole.aspx?name= TargetComputerName*

Where *NSName* is the name of your Notification Server and TargetComputerName is the name of the client machine you want to view.

The Inventory Agents in detail

This section will discuss, in detail, each of the Inventory Agents, how they work, what files they use and how they can be customized. The Agents discussed include:

- The Software Inventory Agent.
- The Hardware Inventory Agent.
- The Exchange Inventory Agent.
- The Serial Number Inventory Agent.
- The Custom Inventory Agent.

The Software Inventory Agent

The software scanner is a program named AeXAuditPls.exe. This program uses an .ini file named Auditpls.ini to determine what software to scan for, which folders to scan and how to group applications together as well as much more.

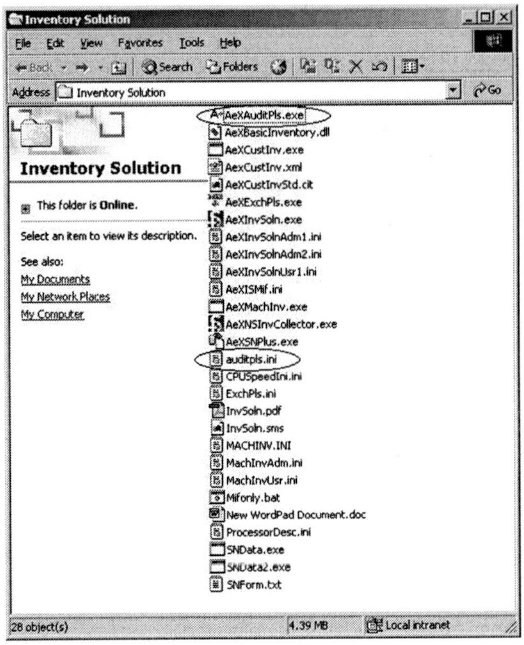

In this section we will look at how the Software Inventory scan can be customized.

Customizing Software Inventory

To customize the software scan you must edit the AuditPls.ini file in the Inventory Solution folder on the Notification Server. The application AeXAPedit is used to edit AudirPls.ini.

Note One of the common mistakes made when editing the AuditPls.ini is to edit the wrong file. Two AuditPls.ini files exist on the Notification Server, one in the Inventory Solution folder and one just one level above, in the x86 folder. The AuditPls.ini in the Inventory Folder is the file that should be edited when customising Software Inventory. The AuditPls.ini file in the x86 folder is used when using 'Standalone Inventory' discussed later.

Open the folder *InstallPath\Notification Server\Nscap\Bin\Win32\x86\Inventory Solution* on the Notification Server and make a **backup** of the file **AuditPls.ini**. Once the file has been backed up, **run** the application **AeXAPedit** application from the x86 folder on the Notification Server *InstallPath\Notification Server\NScap\Bin\Win32\x86*.

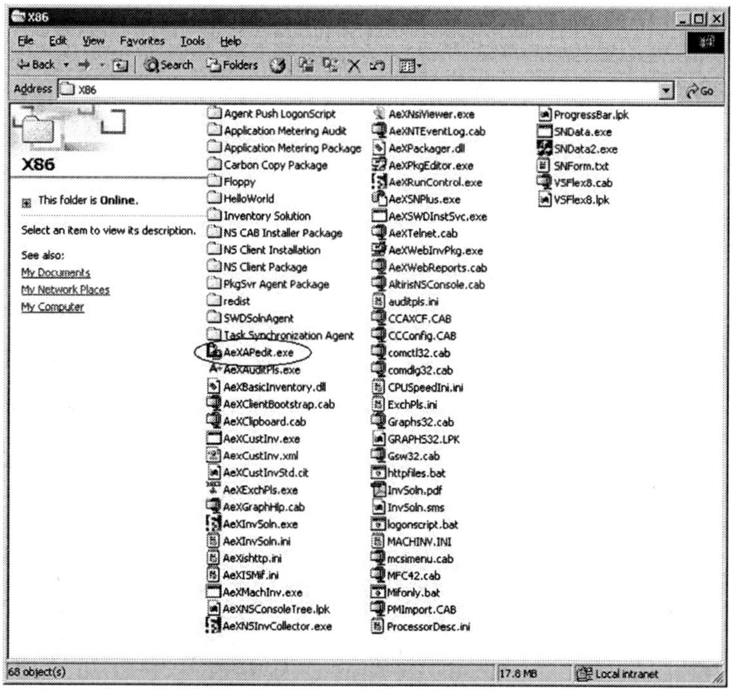

When the application opens, go to the **File** menu and choose **Open** command. Browse to the Inventory Solution Folder on the Notification Server and choose the AuditPls.ini file.

The file will take a few seconds to open.

File Masks

This dialog is used to define which extensions to scan for. The default is that .exe files will be checked for header information. From the header information the scanner will retrieve Manufacturer, Product Name Version etc.

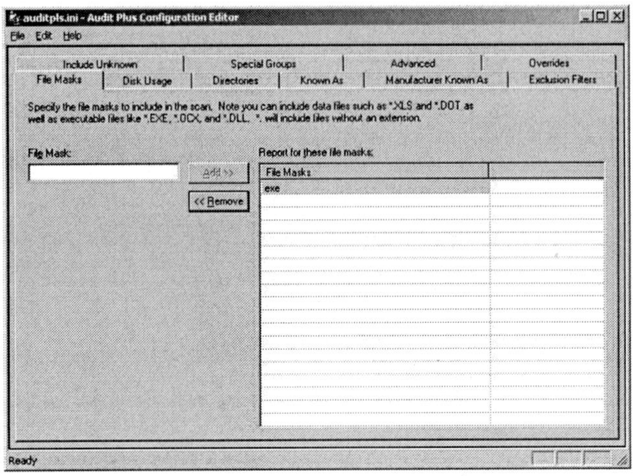

Use this dialog to add extra extensions to the Software scan.

Disk Usage

During the software scan, the extensions listed in this dialog will be scanned and the cumulative size of the files found reported to Notification Server.

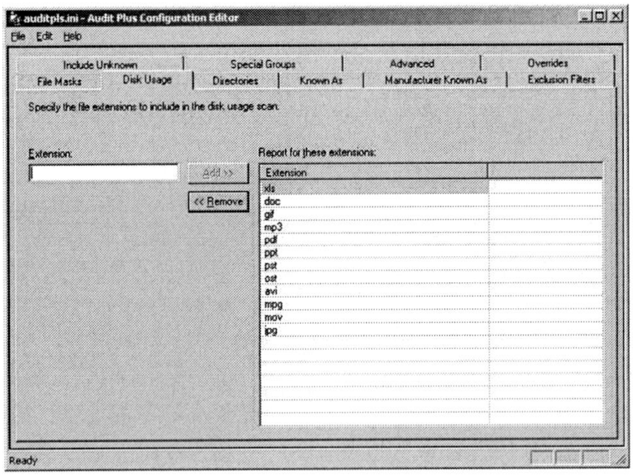

This dialog is useful if you want to see how much space is being used on a user's machine by files of a specific extension.

Directories

What folders to include and exclude in the scan. Leaving the include section blank will cause all folders to be scanned except the folders listed under exclude.

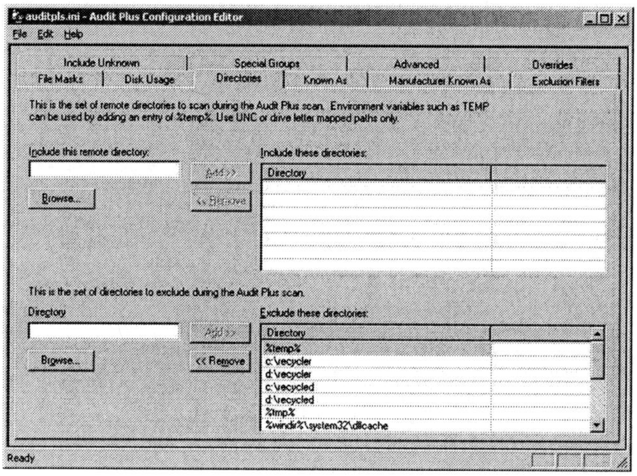

Known As

Allows you to change how the internal name of a file is reported. For example the file Mspaint.exe has the internal name MSPAINT but could appear in the Inventory as 'Microsoft Paint' if you wish.

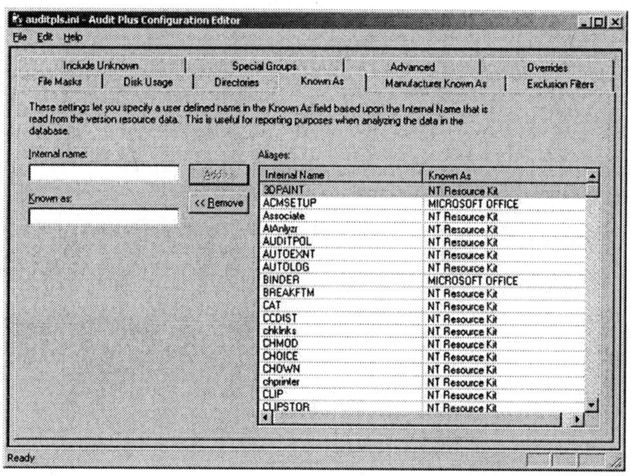

This is a purely cosmetic feature but helps to clean up how data is presented in reports.

Manufacturer Known As

Manufacturers insist on displaying their names differently for example Microsoft, Microsoft Corp, Microsoft Corporation etc. Using the Manufacturer Known As section in the AeXAPedit allows you to report applications with a consistent manufacturer name.

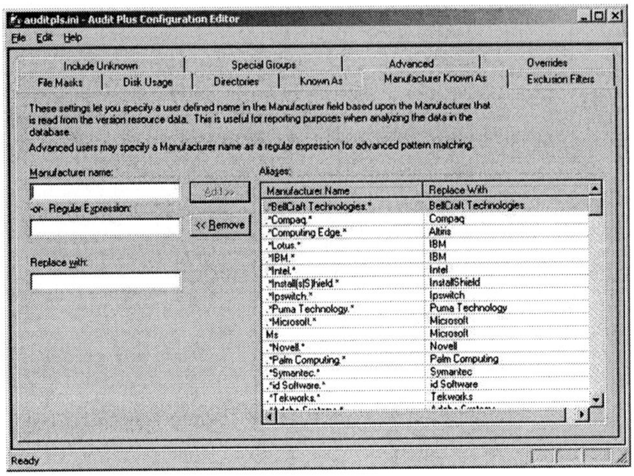

This is useful when you want to query the inventory by manufacturer at a later date.

Exclusion Filters

Allows you to exclude a specific file with specific properties from the scan.

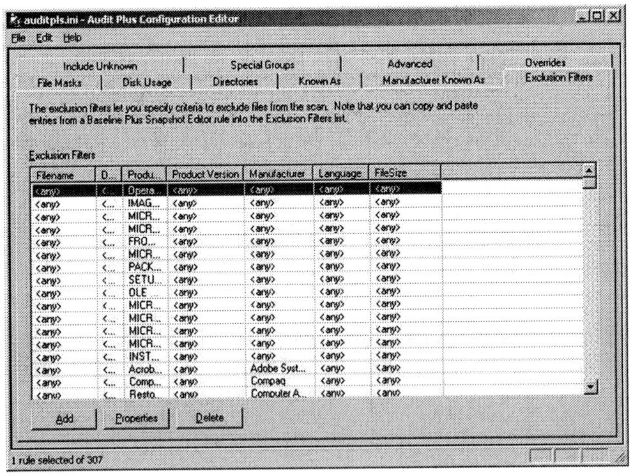

Include Unknown

Allows you to report on files with no header information in the file scanned, a DOS file is a good example.

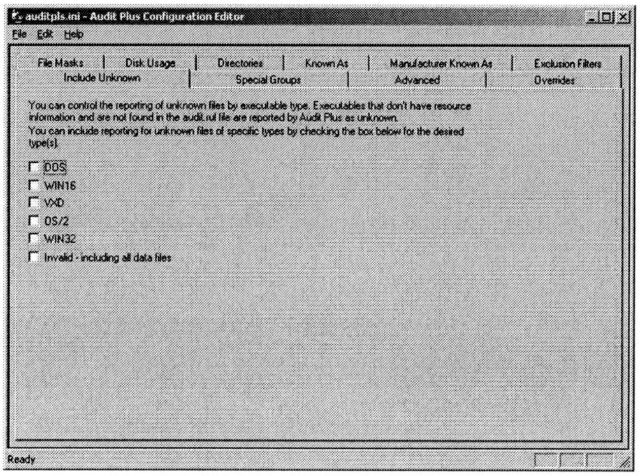

An Audit.rul file can be used to populate properties for files with no header information but using the Overrides tab section is better.

Special Groups

The Special Groups dialog allows you to collectively identify and track a group of files. For example you may want to create a special group to collectively track the components of Microsoft Office. When a special group such as Microsoft Office has been defined and the software scan runs, it will find Excel.exe, Winword.exe etc. and report it as Microsoft Office.

(When you define a special group and the group class, a new table is created in the Notification Server database.)

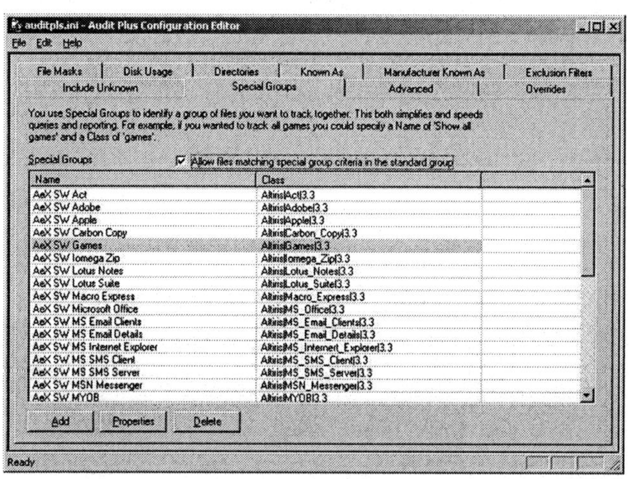

Advanced

Contains settings to override XML and MIF data generation.

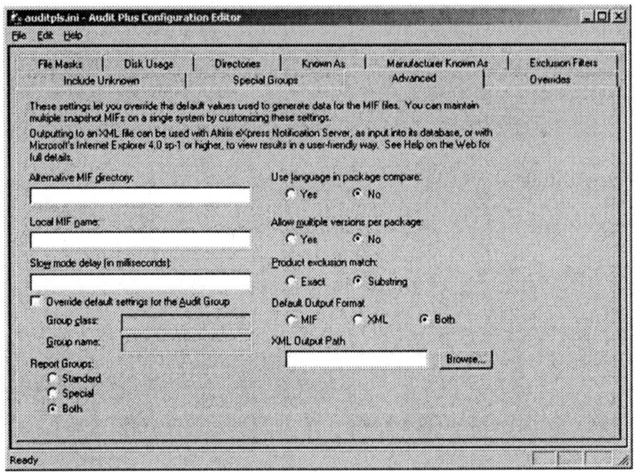

The most useful option in here is 'Slow Mode Delay' where you can specify the number of milliseconds between each file scanned. (5 to 20 is plenty) The delay will result in longer time taken to complete the software scan but will result in less impact on the client when the scan is run. The Group option lets you decide whether to report on the standard group (AeX SW Software Audit) or Special Groups defined in the Special Groups tab, or both. Default is both but the only Special Groups option could be used if you want to only report on one or two application suites.

Overrides

Allows you to override the properties of a file when reporting to the Notification Server.

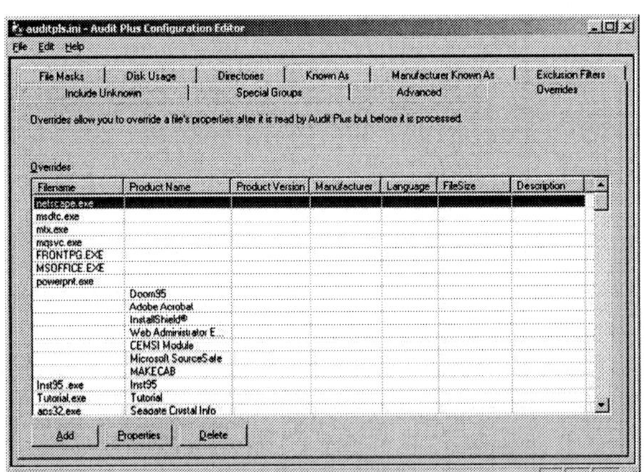

Properties of the actual file are unchanged but the properties are reported differently.

Saving the amended AuditPls.ini

The hardware Inventory scanner, AEXMachInv.exe, not only scans for hardware devices such as CPU, Monitor and Physical Memory but it also scans for the currently logged on user, Operating System version and TCP/IP information.

Updating the Inventory Agent Package

In order that clients using the Inventory Agent know that there is an updated AuditPls.ini, the Inventory Agent Package on the Notification Server must be refreshed. This can be achieved by either waiting for the Notification Server to refresh packages automatically (every 24 hours by default) or by manually initiating a package refresh through the Web Console.

To force the package update, open the Web Console and select the Tasks Tab then navigate to **Assets and Inventory > Inventory > Windows > Inventory Tasks**.

Select any of the Inventory policies. When the policy is displayed, click the *Go to Package* link to the right of the package name.

When the package properties details are displayed in the new window, click the button 'Update Distribution Points' on the package properties page.

Close the package properties window.

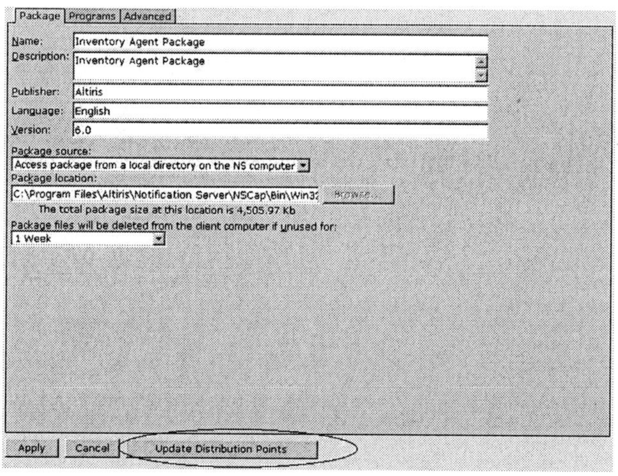

The next time a client requests a configuration update from the Notification Server, it will download the new AuditPls.ini file locally from an available package source and use it the next time a software scan is run.

The Hardware Inventory Agent

When the hardware Inventory scanner, AEXMachInv.exe runs, it scans for hardware such as PCMCIA Devices, CPU, Monitor, Physical Memory and Local Disk information and also for Logged on User, Operating System and TCP/IP information.

Three configuration files can be used to customize the hardware scanner. The files are MachInv.ini, MachInvAdm.ini and MachInvUsr.ini.

MachInvAdm.ini contains the data groups:

AeX EU Logon Users	AeX OS Internet Explorer
AeX EU Results	AeX OS Desktop
AeX OS Results	AeX OS User Profiles

When the hardware scanner is run with the command line 'aexmachinv.exe /ini MachInvAdm.ini', the scanner will only scan for the six data groups listed in the MachInvAdm.ini file.

MachInv.ini

This file is used to exclude certain data groups from the machine scan. When MachInv.exe is run with the command line 'aexmachinv.exe' and no 'ini' switch, it will scan all data groups listed in MachInvAdm.ini and MachInvUsr.ini.
MachInv.ini is read before scanning begins and any data groups listed in the file will be excluded from the scan. MachInv.ini is blank by default.

MachInvUsr.ini contains the data groups:

AeX HW CPU
AeX HW Logical Disk Changes
AeX HW Memory
AeX HW Memory Changes
AeX HW Memory Modules
AeX HW Modems
AeX HW Mouse
AeX HW Network Cards
AeX HW PCI Bus
AeX HW PCMCIA Devices
AeX HW Printer
AeX HW SCSI
AeX HW Video
AeX HW Video Monitor
AeX HW Monitor
AeX HW ActiveTcpUdpPorts
AeX DB MDAC
AeX DB ODBC Drivers
AeX DB SQL Server
AeX OS ACLs
AeX OS Admin Group
AeX OS Audit policy
AeX OS System Devices
AeX OS IIS
AeX OS Memory Management
AeX OS Network Provider
AeX OS Network Shares
AeX OS Operating System
AeX OS Provider Order
AeX OS RAS Server
AeX OS System
AeX OS TCPIP Changes
AeX OS Time Zone
AeX OS Win16 Subsystem
AeX OS Windows NT
AeX OS Windows 9x

When the hardware scanner is run with the command line 'aexmachinv.exe /ini MachInvUsr.ini', the scanner will only scan for the thirty four data groups listed in the MachInvUsr.ini file.

AeX HW Monitor and AeX HW ActiveTcpUdpPorts are new to Inventory Solution for Windows 6.1.

The Exchange Inventory Agent

Exchange Inventory agent gathers information about the Microsoft Exchange Profiles on the local machine. Two files are required for the Exchange Agent to run correctly, **AeXExchPls.exe** and **ExchPls.ini**.
When the Exchange Agent program is run, it reads the ExchPls.ini to determine what attributes are to be gathered from all of the exchange profiles on the client. The Exchange scan runs in the context of the logged on user.

Note The user must be on the network for the agent to get data from the Exchange directory.

The Serial Number Inventory Agent

The Serial Number agent gathers information about the Computer Model and Manufacturer, Serial Number, Memory Modules, BIOS and SMBIOS.
The program that is used is **AeXSNPlus.exe**. Two applications are used by the Serial Number Inventory Agent to gather SMBIOS data. They are; SNData.exe and SNData2.exe. SNData.exe is 16 Bit and SNData2.exe is the 32 Bit version.

The Custom Inventory Agent

The Custom Inventory agent, AeXCustInv.exe, is used to gather inventory data that is not collected by the other inventory agents. The agent can query WMI, Registry, File header information and data within an ini file.

Creating Custom Inventory Scans

The steps used to create a Custom Inventory Scan are similar whether you are creating a scan to query the registry, WMI, file header or an ini file on a client machine. The steps are:

1. Create an XML file containing the query.
2. Create a new .ini text file and include the appropriate syntax to run the Custom Inventory scan.
3. Create a new Program for the Inventory Agent Package.
4. Create a new Inventory policy to advertise the new Inventory program.

The following pages detail the steps used to create and rollout a custom inventory scan.

Note For information on troubleshooting custom inventory scans please see the *Appendix* at the back of this book. The ini, cit and xml files used in this section are available for download at *http://www.managingwithaltiris.com.*

Creating a Registry Inventory Scan

The first step of the following example shows the XML syntax required to query the local registry to determine what Wallpaper is set for the current user.

Step 1 - Create the xml inventory file

Create a text file and enter the data below (excluding line numbers). Alternatively, download the xml from the downloads section of www.managingwithaltiris.com. Save the text file in the *Installpath\Nscap\Bin\Win32\x86\Inventory Solution\ folder as Wallpaper.xml.*

```
1  <?xml version="1.0" encoding="windows-1252"?>
2  <InventoryClasses>
3  <InventoryClass name="Wallpaper Data" manufacturer='Altiris' description=
   " platform='Win32' version='1.0' mifClass='Altiris|WallPaper|1.0'>
4  <xml xmlns:s="uuid:BDC6E3F0-6DA3-11d1-A2A3-00AA00C14882"
   xmlns:dt="uuid:C2F41010-65B3-11d1-A29F-00AA00C14882"
   xmlns:rs="urn:schemas-microsoft-com:rowset" xmlns:z="#RowsetSchema">
5          <s:Schema id="RowsetSchema">
6          <s:ElementType name="row" content="eltOnly" rs:updatable="true">
7          <s:AttributeType name="c0" rs:name="Wallpaper" rs:number="1"
           rs:keycolumn="true" mifAttrId="1">
8          <s:datatypc dt:typc="string" dt:maxLength="25"/>
9          </s:AttributeType>
10         </s:ElementType>
11         </s:Schema>
12         <rs:data>
13 <%set path="HKEY_CURRENT_USER\Control Panel\Desktop"%>
14         <z:row
15                 c0="<%writexml "reg:%path%\Wallpaper"%>"
16         />
17         </rs:data>
18         </xml>
19 </InventoryClass>
20 </InventoryClasses>
```

Line 3 – Defines the table name within the Altiris database (Wallpaper Data) where the data will be stored. If the table does not exist, it will be created. **Note** Manufacturer must always be 'Altiris'.

Line 7 – Defines the name (Wallpaper) and length (25) of the first column in the new table.

Line 13 – Defines the registry path, with line 15 defining the data value within the path to be captured.

Step 2 - Create an ini which will be used by the Inventory Agent

Create a new text file named WallpaperName.ini and enter the two lines below:

```
Aexcustinv.exe /in .\Wallpaper.xml /out Wallpaper Version.nsi
Aexnsinvcollector.exe /hidden /nsctransport /v default /useguid
```

Save the ini in the Installpath\Nscap\Bin\Win32\x86\Inventory Solution\ folder on the Notification Server.

The syntax above will run the Custom Inventory scan using Wallpaper.xml. Any results of the Inventory scan will then be output to a file named 'Wallpaper Version.nsi' to the local Inventory folder on the client. The inventory Collector will then transport the Inventory data to the Notification Server.

Step 3 - Create a new Inventory Program for the Custom Inventory Scan

Now that the XML and ini files have been created, a new program must be added to the existing Inventory Package. This new program will contain the command-line to run the custom inventory scan.

Select the Tasks Tab in the Web Console and navigate to **Assets and Inventory > Inventory > Windows > Inventory Tasks.** Select any of the Inventory configuration policies.

To the right of Program name click the *Go to Programs* link.

The package properties are displayed in a new window.

In the Programs tab click the **New** button at the top right corner of the dialog

Name the Program 'Desktop Settings'.

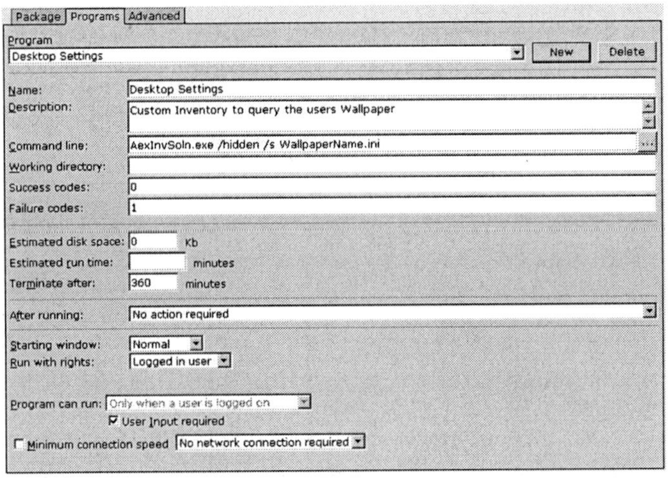

Enter the command line AexInvSoln.exe /hidden /s WallpaperName.ini

Verify the privileges that the inventory policy will run under. i.e. System, or User account. For this example we will use the logged on user.

Click **Apply**, then click the **'Update Distribution Points'** button.

Step 4 - Create a new Inventory policy

From the Tasks Tab in the Web Console navigate to **Tasks > Asset and Inventory > Inventory > Windows > Inventory Tasks**.

Clone an Inventory policy by right clicking an existing policy and choosing **Clone**.

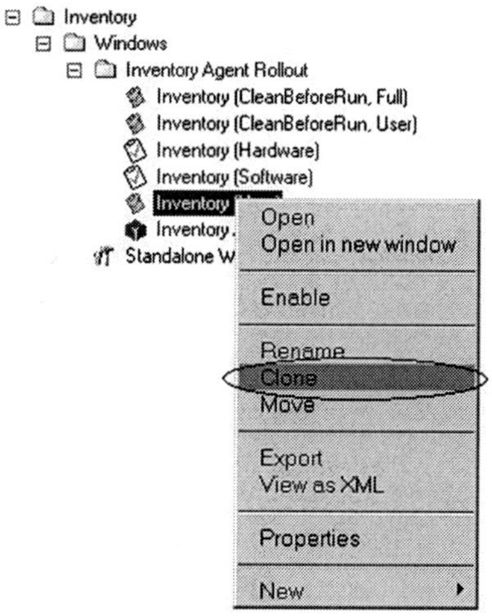

Name the cloned policy 'Wallpaper Inventory'.

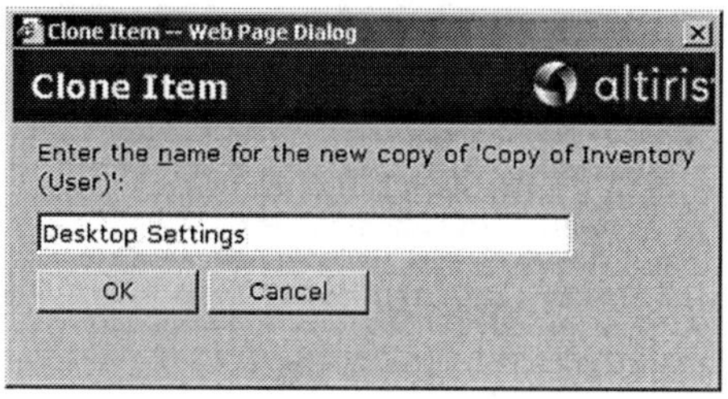

Change the description for the policy.

Select your new Program 'Desktop Settings' from the Program Name drop down list.

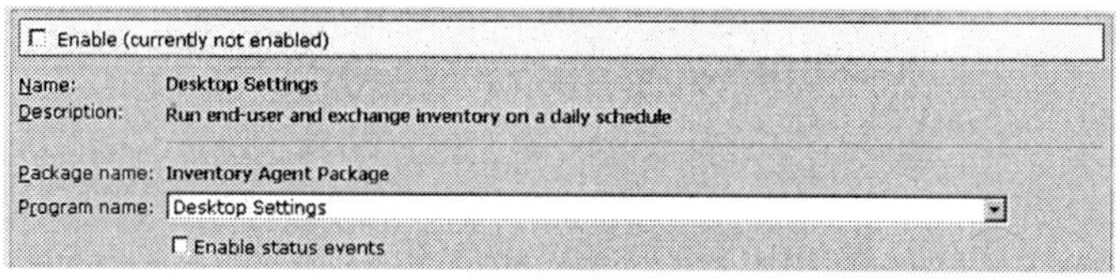

Configure the collection that should run this custom inventory policy.

Configure the scheduling options. For example you may wish to run the policy ASAP.

Enable the policy using the checkbox.

Click **Apply**.

The next time machines in the targeted collection request a configuration update, they will see the new Inventory policy and start the custom scan based on the schedule.

Viewing Custom Inventory

When a custom inventory scan is run for the first time on a client machine, the inventory that is gathered, is uploaded to the NS database and a new database table is created for that custom data. This process creates a new Data class which is added to the Default Folder of Data classes, as shown below. I recommend that you move any new data classes created by custom inventory scans to a more appropriate folder, such as a custom inventory folder.

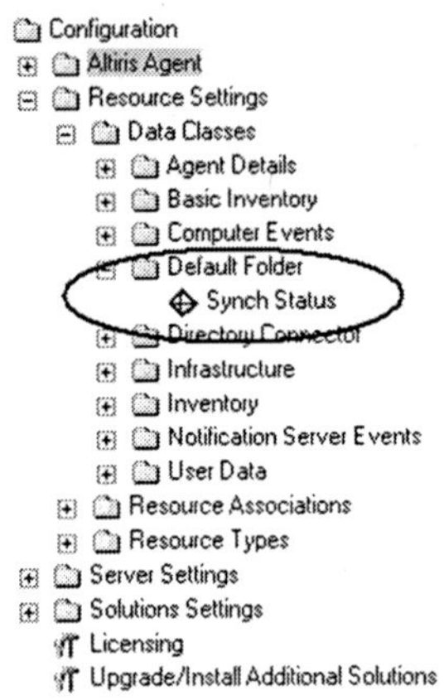

To create a custom data class inventory folder

Open the Web Console and select the Configuration Tab, then navigate to **Resource Settings > Data Classes > Inventory.**

Right click the Inventory folder and choose **New > Folder**.

Give the folder the name Custom Inventory and click **Apply**.

To move a custom data class

Right click the new data class in **Configuration Tab > Resource Settings > Data Classes > Default Folder** and choose move.

In the move item dialog, select the newly created 'Custom Inventory' folder as the destination for the new data class.

Now when the Inventory of a client is viewed in Resource Manager, the Custom Inventory folder will appear within the Inventory folder structure if that client has run the custom Inventory scan.

Example: WMI Inventory Scan

The following example can be used to query WMI for the name and status of all services running on a client machine.

```
<?xml version="1.0" encoding="windows-1252"?>
<InventoryClasses>
<InventoryClass name="AeX OS Service Status" manufacturer='Altiris' description=''
platform='Win32' version='1.0' mifClass='Altiris|ServStat|1.0'>
        <xml xmlns:s="uuid:BDC6E3F0-6DA3-11d1-A2A3-00AA00C14882"
        xmlns:dt="uuid:C2F41010-65B3-11d1-A29F-00AA00C14882"
        xmlns:rs="urn:schemas-microsoft-com:rowset" xmlns:z="#RowsetSchema">
        <s:Schema id="RowsetSchema">
        <s:ElementType name="row" content="eltOnly" rs:updatable="true">
        <s:AttributeType name="c0" rs:name="Service Name" rs:number="1"
        rs:nullable="true" mifAttrId="1">
        <s:datatype dt:type="string" dt:maxLength="200"/>
        </s:AttributeType>
        <s:AttributeType name="c1" rs:name="Running" rs:number="2"
        rs:nullable="true" mifAttrId="2">
        <s:datatype dt:type="string" dt:maxLength="200"/>
        </s:AttributeType>
        </s:ElementType>
        </s:Schema>
        <rs:data>
        <%foreach wmiobject="o" namespace="root\CIMV2" wql="select * from
        Win32_Service"%>
        <z:row
                c0="<%writexml "wmi:o.Name"%>"
                c1="<%write "wmi:o.State"%>"
        />
        <%next%>
        </rs:data>
        </xml>
</InventoryClass>
</InventoryClasses>
```

Follow the instructions from the previous section to create a custom inventory using the above xml syntax. Download the above xml from the downloads section of the http://www.managingwithaltiris.com web site.

Tip Download the WMI Object Browser from the Microsoft web site and get familiar with WMI objects and properties.

Example: ini file Inventory Scan

The following example can be used to query an ini file and retrieve a line of text within the file. The file that will be queried is the oeminfo.ini file. The contents of the oeminfo.ini file and the Inventory XML are displayed below. The line that this custom inventory will retrieve is the 'model' line.

Oeminfo.ini:

```
[General]
Manufacturer=Company
Model=Desktop Build Version 1.2a
[Support Information]
Line1=For support please call your local IT HelpDesk
Line2=Information you may be asked for will include:
```

Sample XML:

```
<?xml version="1.0" encoding="windows-1252"?>
<InventoryClasses>
<InventoryClass name="AeX SW Image Version" manufacturer='Altiris' description=''
platform='Win32' version='1.0' mifClass='Altiris|ImageVer|1.0'>
    <xml xmlns:s="uuid:BDC6E3F0-6DA3-11d1-A2A3-00AA00C14882"
    xmlns:dt="uuid:C2F41010-65B3-11d1-A29F-00AA00C14882"
    xmlns:rs="urn:schemas-microsoft-com:rowset" xmlns:z="#RowsetSchema">
    <s:Schema id="RowsetSchema">
    <s:ElementType name="row" content="eltOnly" rs:updatable="true">
    <s:AttributeType name="c0" rs:name="Model" rs:number="1"
    rs:keycolumn="true" mifAttrId="1">
    <s:datatype dt:type="string" dt:maxLength="200"/>
    </s:AttributeType>
    </s:ElementType>
    </s:Schema>
    <rs:data>
        <%set filepath="c:\winnt\system32\oeminfo.ini"%>
        <z:row
        c0="<%write "ini:%filepath%\[General]\Model"%>"
        />
    </rs:data>
</xml>
</InventoryClass>
</InventoryClasses>
```

Gathering Inventory Data from a machine not connected to the network

Some machines in your Enterprise may not be connected to the corporate network but you may want to get a one-off Inventory from them anyway.
Altiris provide the Floppy Disk Inventory method to gather inventory from such machines.

Note Using the floppy disk method does not require the machine to have the Altiris Agent.

There are two packaged Inventory files used when running Inventory from a floppy disk. Both files are in:

InstallPath\Altiris\Notification Server\Nscap\Bin\Win32\x86\Floppy\.

- **Win32invfloppy1.exe** contains the programs to execute a Software, Custom, Machine and Exchange Inventory scan.
- **Win32invfloppy2.exe** contains the programs to execute a Serial number inventory scan only.

Creating Inventory Disks

You will need three blank floppy disks for this procedure.
Label the first disk Inventory Program 1, the second disk Inventory Program 2, and the third disk Inventory Data.

Copy the file Win32invfloppy1.exe from InstallPath:\Altiris\Notification Server\Nscap\Bin\Win32\x86\Floppy\ to the first Inventory Program floppy disk.

Copy the file Win32invfloppy2.exe from InstallPath:\Altiris\Notification Server\Nscap\Bin\Win32\x86\Floppy\ to the second Inventory Program floppy disk.

Gathering the Inventory

From the client machine that you want to capture inventory data, insert the first program disk and run the command A:\Win32Invfloppy1.exe from the **Start > Run** command.
The Inventory scan will take a few minutes to run.
Insert the data disk when prompted.
When the scan is complete, there will be an NSE Inventory data file and a DOS batch file named PostInv.bat on the data disk.
If you also need a Serial Number scan repeat the previous steps using Program Disk 2 but use the command A:\Win32Invfloppy2.exe.

Posting the Inventory

When all required Inventory scans have been run, go to any machine connected to the network and insert the Data Disk. From the **Start > Run** command run the command

A:\PostInv.Bat Nsserver (Where Nsserver is the name of your Notification Server)

Gathering Inventory from a machine without the Altiris Agent

There are two ways to run the Inventory Agents without having the Altiris Agent installed locally. They are:

- Run **AexInvSoln.exe** from the Notification Server using a UNC path.
- Run the Inventory web package, **AeXWebInvPkg.exe** from the Notification Server using a HTTP or UNC path.

The primary difference between the two methods above is that the first method will run the Agents across the network while the second method will extract the Agents locally to the machine before running.

Using AexInvSoln.exe

The **first** way is to run **AexInvSoln.exe** from the Notification Server using a UNC path. When AexInvSoln.exe is run from the x86 folder on the Notification Server, the program looks for the file named AexInvSoln.ini in same folder to determine what agents to run. Edit AexInvSoln.ini if you want to modify what agents will run during the scan.

If you want to run the Inventory scan using a logon script it is suggested that you copy the contents of the root of the x86 folder to your logon share point.

Using AeXWebInvPkg.exe

The **second** way to run the Inventory scan without the Altiris Agent installed, is to use the Web Inventory Package (**AeXWebInvPkg.exe**). This package contains all of the Inventory scan agents and their respective configuration files.

When the package is run, all files are extracted to the local Temp folder on the client and then the scan is run.

This Web Inventory Package can be run using a UNC path or URL.

> http://NSName/Aexns/Nscap/Bin/Win32\x86/AeXWebInvPkg.exe ***or***
> \\NSName\Nscap\Bin\Win32\x86\AexwebInvPkg.exe.

Note The AeXWebInvPkg.exe package is complied during Inventory Solution installation and is configured to point to the local Notification Server name upon which Inventory Solution was installed. The AeXWebInvPkg package can be edited using the Web Package Editor which is located in the InstallPath\Altiris\Notification Server\Nscap\Bin\Win32\x86\ and has the file name **AeXPkgEditor.exe**. Editing can be used to change the Notification Server name and alter the command lines for each Inventory Agent included in the package.

An administrator could also e-mail the package file to a user and ask them to run it. (The AeXWebInvPkg.exe can also be copied to a share on a different server which clients can access)

Using Inventory Solution with a Port Other Than 80

Configure your IIS server to support the monitoring of additional ports.

From Windows 2000, click **Start** > **Programs** > **Administrative Tools** > **Internet Services Manager.**

Double-click on the server name in the left pane.

Right-click Default Web Site and select Properties.

Select the Web Site tab.

Click **Advanced**.

Click **Add**.

In the TCP Port field, enter your desired port number.

Click **OK**.

Click **OK**.

Click **OK**.

Alter the Inventory Solution INI files (AeXInvSolnX.ini).

Alter the AeXNSInvCollector.exe line so you are using the following URL format:

http:// server : port /Altiris/NS/postevent.asp

For example:

AeXNSInvCollector /url "http://myserver:8082/Altiris/NS/postevent.asp"

Normalization

Normalization reduces data redundancy/duplication and makes the NS database more efficient by dividing very large tables into smaller tables and by dividing tables that contain repeated information into separate tables, eliminating duplication.

Data normalization only needs to be done once per table and only needs to be done if you have upgraded from a previous version of Inventory Solution, to version 6.1.

To use Data Normalization

In the Altiris Console, select the Configuration tab then navigate to **Solutions Settings > Assets and Inventory > Inventory > Windows > Normalize.**

A data class requiring normalization will have the notation *Requires Normalization* in square brackets after the class name.
Select the Data Classes to normalize.
Use the *Run Now* button to start normalization immediatly or use the schedule to run it later.

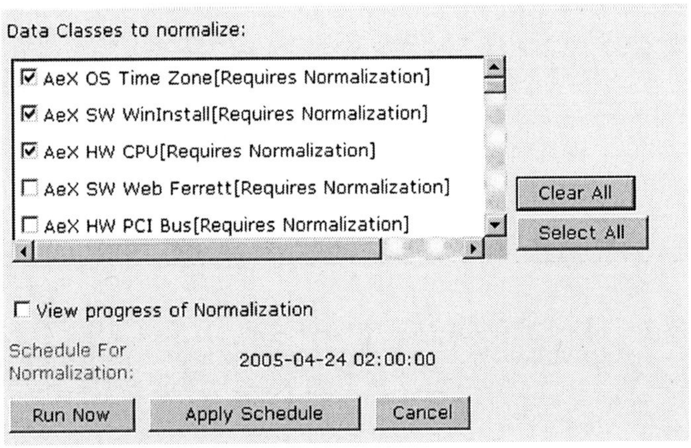

Once a Data Class has been normalized, the Class will have the notation *Normalized* in square brackets after the class name.

Normalization of a large number of data classes can take a long time and should be performed out of hours. During the process the Notification Server is paused.

Removing Inventory Solution

If you do not intend to use Inventory Solution anymore, disable all Inventory scan policies in the Tasks Tab of the Web Console (see below). Allow all clients to request an update configuration so that they have a chance to disable all Inventory policies. Use **Add/Remove** Programs in Control Panel on the Notification Server to remove Inventory Solution for Windows.

Note Removing Inventory Solution will disable the Inventory Agent on client machines. Once Inventory Solution has been removed it will not be possible to view client inventory data through the web console or reports, however the data will remain in the Notification Server database.

Disabling the Inventory Agent

Go to the Tasks Tab in the Web Console and navigate to **Tasks** > **Assets and Inventory** > **Inventory** > **Windows** > **Inventory Tasks**.
Disable all of the Inventory scan policies.

The Inventory Agent will be disabled the next time clients request a configuration update.

Useful Inventory Reports

To view the following reports open the Web Console, select the Reports Tab then navigate to **Assets and Inventory > Inventory > Win32.**

'N' Most Recent Inventory Captures

This report displays the 'N' most recent Inventory captures from clients. (Inventory Agent > Inventory Capture folder of reports)

Computers Requiring Resources

Useful pre-migration report that allows you to report on which computers do not meet a minimum hardware requirement. (Upgrade Analysis > Windows 2000/XP upgrade folder of reports)

Internet Explorer Components by Version

Reports versions of IE funnily enough!. (Software Applications > Web Browsers folder of reports)

Count of Computers by Computer Model

Self explanatory.(Hardware > Manufacturer and Model folder of reports)

Count of Computers by Form Factor

Self explanatory. (Hardware > Form Factor folder of reports)

Count of Operating System, Version and Service Pack

Self explanatory. (Software/Applications > Operating Systems folder of reports)

Summary

In this chapter we saw that the Inventory Agent compromises of several programs which collectively scan and report inventory data to the Notification Server. Configuration policies are used to schedule when Inventory scans run on a client machine and each type of scan agent can be customised. Custom Inventory scans can be used to scan and report Inventory data that is not normally reported by the default scan agents.

The next chapter, 'Software Delivery Solution for Windows' looks at how you can define, deliver and install/execute software packages on managed Windows clients.

11

Software Delivery Solution for Windows

Introduction

Altiris Software Delivery Solution for Windows provides the ability to define, deliver and install/execute software packages on machines running Windows 9.x or higher.

Features

- Software Packages can be targeted to machines based on Inventory.
- Domain, Non-Domain and 'Locked Down' machines can be targeted for Software Delivery.
- Lots of fantastic web based Reports to view the state of software delivery.
- Packages can be deployed as mandatory or optional.
- Multicasting, a feature of NS SP2, allows clients to temporarily act as package servers for a package.
- If your network supports WOL and your clients are correctly configured then a software package can be sent immediately to a managed client without having to wait for the configuration cycle.
- WOL can be used when delivering a package to a client.
- A simple and an advanced Wizard to guide you through deploying software.
- A software package can be targeted at multiple collections.
- A client can be configured to start the package command line from the package source, if the bandwidth is above a certain threshold.
- Sequential software delivery tasks allow you to chain the delivery and execution of multiple software delivery packages together.

Terms Used in this module

Software Package

The file(s) or command that will be downloaded by the client. A package could be a UNC or HTTP path to a setup or batch file on a server or it could be a folder containing the files necessary to install an application.

Software Delivery Task

Defines what collection of machines the software package is for and whether it will run on a schedule or must be run manually. A Software Delivery Task is sometimes called a software advertisement because it advertises a package to clients.

Files used by Software Delivery Solution

AeXSWDSolnAgent.exe

This is the Software Delivery Solution agent install package. Any machine that you want to target with software packages must have this agent installed.

AeXSWDSolnAgentUninst.exe

This is the Software Delivery Solution agent uninstall package. When the policy to uninstall the Software Delivery Solution Agent is enabled in the Web Console, clients targeted by the policy use this file to uninstall the Agent.

Installing Software Delivery Solution for Windows

From the Configuration Tab select **Upgrade/Install Additional Solutions**.
Click the **Solutions** button if it is not already selected.
Select the Software Delivery Solution for Windows link.
Click **Start** and follow the on screen prompts.
Installing Software Delivery Solution will install three solutions, Task Synchronization Solution, Software Delivery Solution and Software Portal Solution.

Once installed, apply your full license. Solutions come with a built-in trial license. 30 day licenses can be downloaded from the Altiris web site. If the solution installation is an upgrade from a previous version then there is no need to reapply the license.

Components added to the web console

Getting Started Tab – Nothing is added at this time.
Tasks Tab – The Software Delivery Wizard and Software Delivery Notification Policies are added.
Resources Tab – A Software packages folder lists all created software packages.
Reporting Tab – A Software Delivery Dashboard summarizes the status of software delivery tasks. Over thirty web based software delivery reports are also added to the Software Management/Software Delivery folder.
Configuration Tab – Configuration and rollout options for installing and uninstalling the Software Delivery and Task Synchronization Agent as well as a Software Portal configuration policy.
Shortcuts Tab – No shortcuts are added automatically by the Solution installation.

Installing the Software Delivery Agent

Allow enough time after the Solution installation for the Software Delivery Agent to replicate to Package Servers.

Software Packages can only be delivered to managed clients running the Software Delivery Agent. To install the Agent go to the configuration Tab in the Web Console and navigate to **Solution Settings > Software Management > Software Delivery > Windows > Software Delivery Solution Agent Rollout > Software Delivery Agent Install**. The Policy is disabled by default.

Select the Collection(s) that the Agent will be installed too.

The installation schedule can be configured to run on a predetermined schedule (recommended) or require manual intervention by the user.

Agent installation will not inhibit a user while they are working and the installation does not require a reboot.

Once you are happy with the installation choices, enable the Agent Installation Policy and click **Apply**.

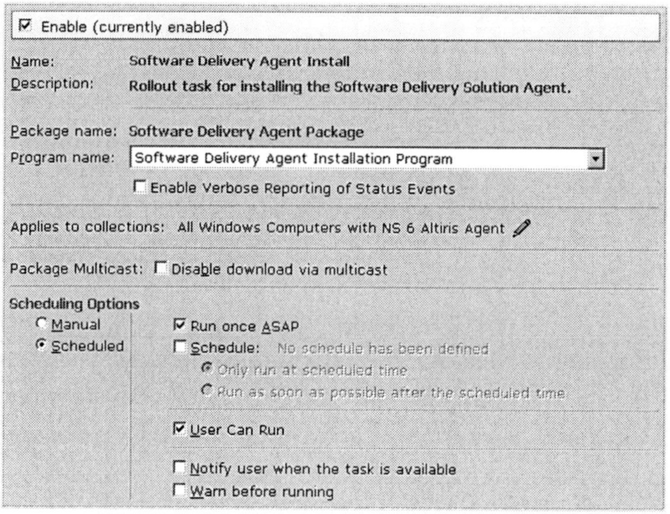

The next time clients in the target collection(s) request a configuration update, they will download the Software Delivery Agent (approx 850 KB) and start the installation based on the schedule or wait for manual intervention, depending how the rollout policy was configured. Once the Software Delivery Agent is installed clients can be targeted with Software Delivery packages.

Note Clients will download the Software Delivery Agent install files from the Notification Server or from a Package Server, if configured.

Software Delivery Agent folder structure

When the Software Delivery Agent is installed on a managed client, a software delivery structure is created beneath the local Altiris Agent folder. This folder structure is used to store downloaded software packages. Each software package created on the Notification Server is given a unique GUID. Every time a client downloads a package, a folder is created under the software delivery folder on the client for that package. The new folder created on the client is given the same name as the package GUID.

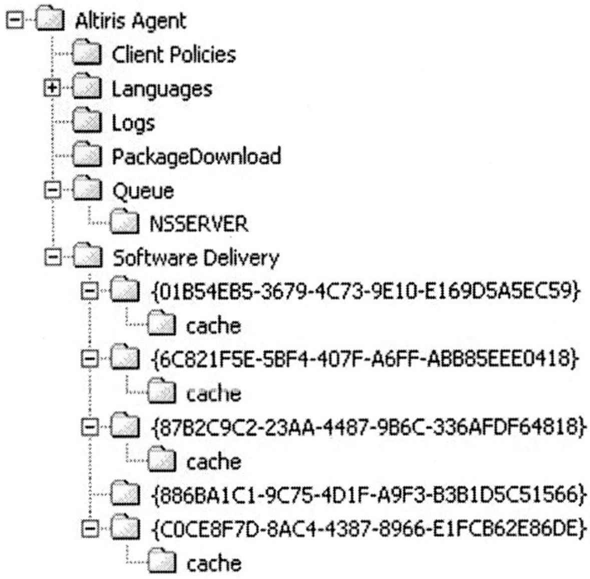

If the package downloaded by the client contains files, then a cache subfolder is created beneath the GUID folder and the package files are stored there. If the package contains no files and is perhaps a command line to a network installation then no cache folder is created.

Installing the Task Synchronisation Agent

The Task Synchronization Agent is used by Software Delivery Solution and other Altiris solutions that synchronize the execution of tasks on an Altiris Agent. The Agent should be rolled out to any clients that have the Software Delivery Agent installed.

In the web console select the configuration tab and navigate to **Solution Settings > Task Synchronization > Synchronization Agent Rollout**.
Select the policy '**Task Synchronization Agent Install**'.

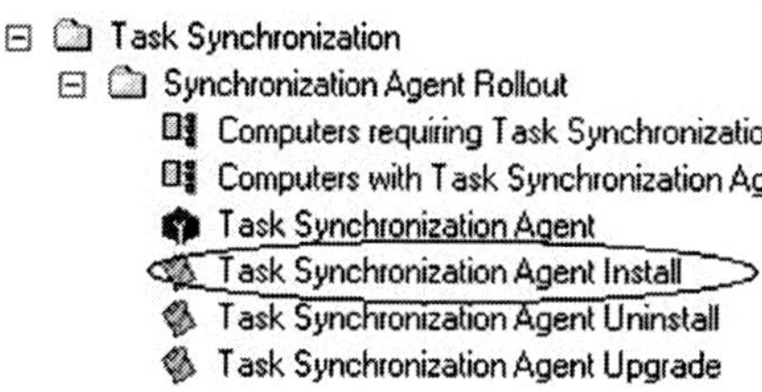

Use the 'Applies to collection' link to select the target collection(s) or leave the default 'All windows computers with the NS 6 agent installed'.

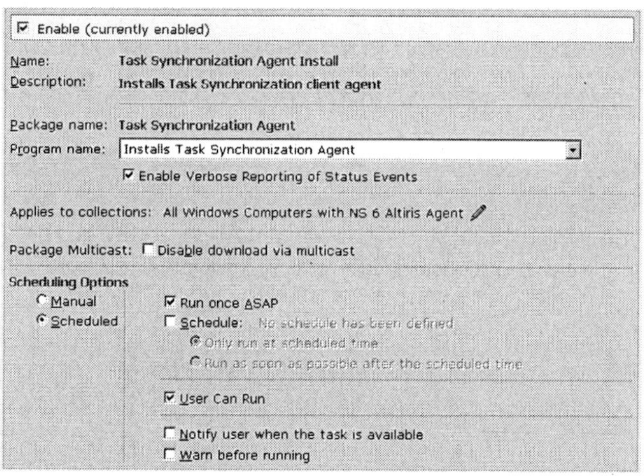

Configure the scheduling options to determine when you want to rollout and install the agent, then enable the policy and click **Apply**.

The next time that clients in the targeted collection update their configuration, they will download and install the Task Synchronization Agent based on the configured schedule.

Deploying Software to Clients

To deploy a software package to Windows clients you will need to; create a Software Package and then create a Software Delivery Task to deliver that package.
There are several ways to create software delivery packages and tasks including:

- Using the Software Delivery Wizard in simple mode.
- Using the Software Delivery Wizard in advanced mode.
- Manually create the Software Package and Software Delivery Task

Using the Software Delivery Wizard in simple mode combines the two tasks of Package and Task creation and is easy to use but doesn't offer all of the available configuration options.
Using the Software Delivery Wizard in advanced mode offers more of the available configuration options than simple mode.
Manually creating Packages and Tasks provides access to all configuration options.

My preferred method is to use the Wizard in Advanced mode to create the basic Package and Task and then if required, perform manual configuration of the Package and Task. The following pages will walk you through using the Wizard as well as creating and modifying packages and tasks manually.

Creating a Software Package Source

A software package typically consists of a file or group of files which are downloaded by the client machine and is either run manually by the user or runs on a preconfigured schedule. Software Packages can also contain no files. A package without files may contain a command line that points to a UNC or HTTP path and is typically used for network installations.

Creating a Package Source

A Software Package Source can be a folder on the local Notification Server, a folder under a share on another server or a folder under a web server folder structure. To create a local package source on the Notification Server, create a local folder anywhere on the local hard disk of the Notification Server and copy the required files that will make up the package to the folder. For example, to create an Office 2003 package source, copy the Office 2003 CD contents to a folder on the local Notification Server. There is no need to share the folder as Notification Server will create a virtual directory through IIS to allow Package Servers to download the package. (If no Package Servers are in your infrastructure clients can download the package directly from the Notification Server.)

My preferred structure as shown above is to create a folder named Packages and then create sub folders for each package under this structure.

Using the Software Delivery Wizard (Advanced)

Using the Software Delivery Wizard in advanced mode will guide you through the task of deploying software and at the same time provide access to most of the available task and package options.

Step 1 - Launch the Wizard

Select the Tasks Tab in the Web Console then navigate to **Software Management > Software Delivery > Windows > Software Delivery Tasks**.

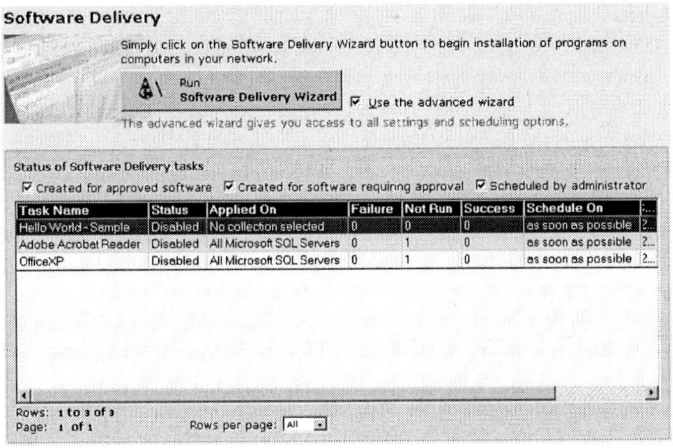

Choose Wizard and Status.

Check the **Use the Advanced Wizard** check box then click the **Software Delivery Wizard** button.

Step 2 - Choose a New or Existing Package

The first Wizard Dialog offers the option to, Deliver an Existing Package of Software or Create and Deliver a new package of Software. **If you already have a packge source, select the package, click Next and go to step 4.** If you are creating a new package, read on.

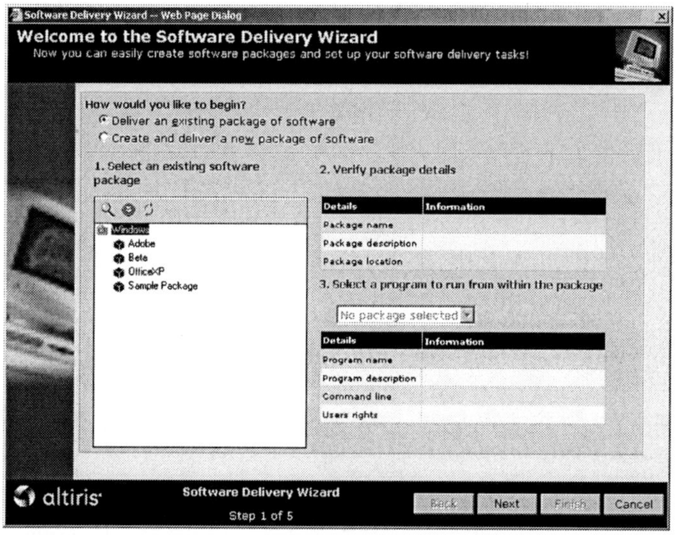

Choose the option to **Create and Deliver a new package of Software**.

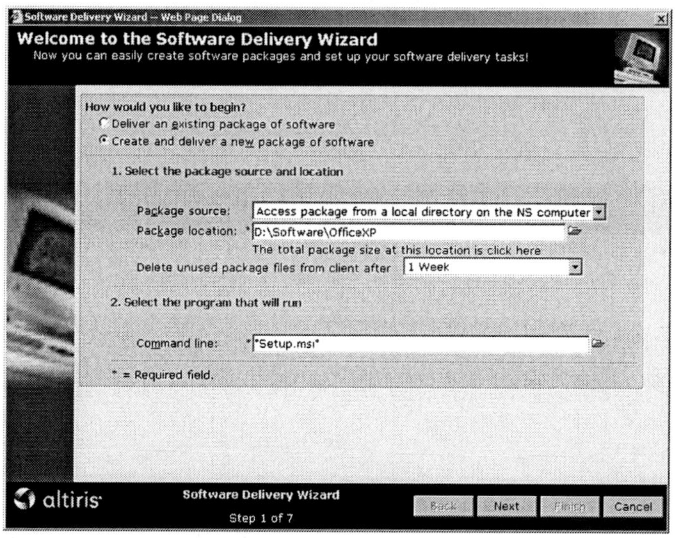

Choose the Package Source and use the Browse buttons to enter a Folder Path and Command-line. Include any required switches in the command line. e.g. "Install.exe" /Q. The option *Delete unused package files from the client* will remove the packge files from the client (Not the Package Servers) after one week by default. The four choices for Package Source and an explanation of each follow;

Package does not contain source files -

This option can be used when you want to run a command locally on the client. A good example of using a package without source files would be if you wanted to run notepad remotely on a client. Because the file Notepad.exe will not be part of the package, the file must already exist on the client. A path to the executable may be required if current user environment path statement on the client does not include the folder containing the command to execute.

Access the Package from a local directory on the Notification Server -

This is probably the most commonly used package option. Files are stored locally in a folder on the NS. All files and sub folders become part of the package. When the targeted client machine requests the package, it will download the entire package locally before executing the command line for the package.

Access the Package from an existing UNC -

This option is similar to the previous option but in this case the package files exist on a machine other than the Notification Server. When the targeted client machine requests the package, it will download the entire package locally before executing the associated package command line.

Access the Package from a URL -

This option is similar to the previous option but in this case the package files exist on a web server. When the targeted client machine requests the package, it will download the entire package locally using HTTP before executing the associated package command line.

Configure the package source options as appropriate.
Click **Next**.

Step 3 - Configure the Program Options

This dialog lets you select how to run the program, which rights to use and what to do when the program is finished. Options included are:

Select the User rights for the Program to run

Run with rights – Lets you choose which rights the program will run under, options are; Logged on User, System Account or Specific Account.

Program Can Run – Mandatory field used to limit when the Program can run. Options include, Only when a User is logged on, Only when no User is logged on and Whether or not a User is logged on. This option is not available if the System account was specified previously.

User Input Required – This option is optional and is only required when a User is logged on. The option allows Users to interact with the executed installer/application which is useful if input is required during installation. I would recommend including answer files and silent install switch with the command line to ensure that users don't need to interact with an installation program.

Run once for each logged on user – Self explanatory.

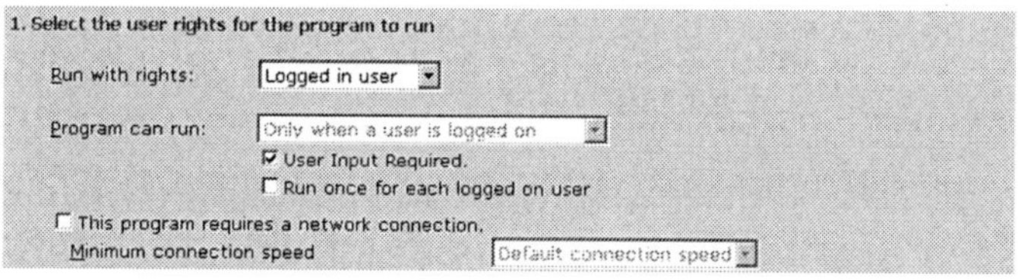

This program requires a network connection – If a Program requires a network connection to run successfully this option should be checked. The option should be used when, running an application or installation across the network or when installing an application that requires connection to a server or web site to download installation or configuration files to complete the installation. Using this option and the next option 'Minimum connection speed' you can configure the Program to only execute if the minimum connection speed configured is available.

Minimum connection speed – The minimum connection speed that must exist for the Program to run. (This option is used in conjunction with the previous option.)

Select the windows style in which the window will run

Select the Window style – Normal, Hidden, Minimized or Maximized. (This option only seems to apply to DOS type windows.)

Select the action to take after the program is finished running

When the program is finished – Do nothing, Restart the computer or Logoff the current user.

Select the program execution properties

Working directory – Optional field used to specify the working directory required by the application installer.

Success codes – Applications normally return 0 as a success code. If the application being deployed doesn't return 0 as a success code use this optional field to specify additional success codes. To enter multiple codes separate each code with a comma. For example 7,8.

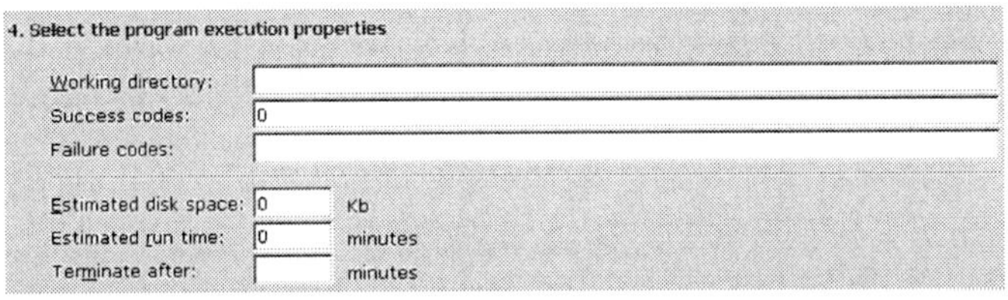

Failure codes – Applications normally return 1 as a failure code. If the application being deployed doesn't return 1 as a failure code use this optional field to specify additional failure codes. To enter multiple codes separate each code with a comma. For example 9,10.

Estimated disk space – The amount of space required for the installation. This will not limit the disk space available for the installation.

Estimated run time – The estimated time it will take to complete the installation. Users can view this estimate if they view the properties of this program through the Altiris Agent interface.

Terminate after X minutes – If the installation takes more than X minutes the program will abort.

Configure the program options as appropriate and click **Next**.

Step 4 - Configure the Collection and Schedule

Step four is used to configure what collection of computers you want the package delivered to and when you want the Package Program to run. Other options in this step also allow you to configure when the package is available for clients to download and if a package expires.

Select the collection to which the package will be delivered

Applies to collection - Select a collection(s)

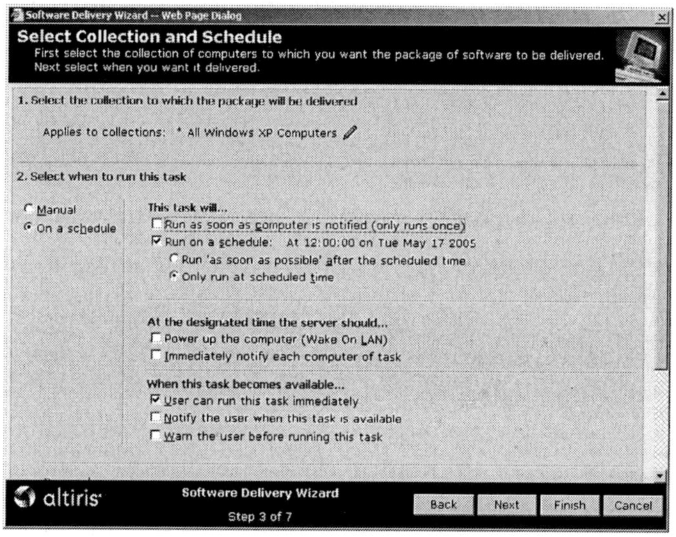

Select when to run this task

Run – Manual or On a Schedule.

Configuring a Task to run on a schedule effectively makes it a mandatory installation. Choosing Manual means that the Administrator is relying on the User to start the installation manually.

Manual

Notify the user when this task is available On/Off – Displays a Notification to the user that a Software Task is available.

Warn the user before running this task On/Off – Select this to warn the user before a Software Delivery task is run.

On a schedule

Schedule – Run as soon as computer is notified (only runs once). This option makes a Task mandatory. The next time a machine in the targeted collection(s) requests an update configuration it will download and install the package ASAP.

Run on a schedule – Used to configure when the command-line is executed.

Power up the computer (Wake On LAN) – The Agent must be configured for 'Tickle/Power Management' through an Altiris Agent configuration Policy.

Immediately notify each computer of task – Doesn't wait for clients in the targeted collection to request an update to their configuration. Using this option will cause all targeted machines to run the task. Ensure that you allow time for the associated software package to replicate to all designated Package Servers before using this option.

User can run this task immediately – Used to allow users through the Altiris Agent interface to manually start the Task.

Notify the user when this task is available – Displays a Notification to the user that a Software Task is available.

Warn the user before running this task – The user is warned before the Task runs.

Remove this task after successful install – The Task is not available through the Altiris Agent interface after it has been run once.

Availability – Allows you to control during what period the Task is available.

Use the Servers Time – On/Off. This option is useful in an environment with multiple time zones.

Configure the collection and schedule options as appropriate and click **Next**.

Step 5 - Configure the Package Options

This step allows you enable and disable package delivery event logging as well as configure which package servers will receive this package.

Package Servers

All Package Servers - Choose this to replicate the package to all Package Servers.

Selected Package Servers - Choose this to replicate the package to selected Package Servers.

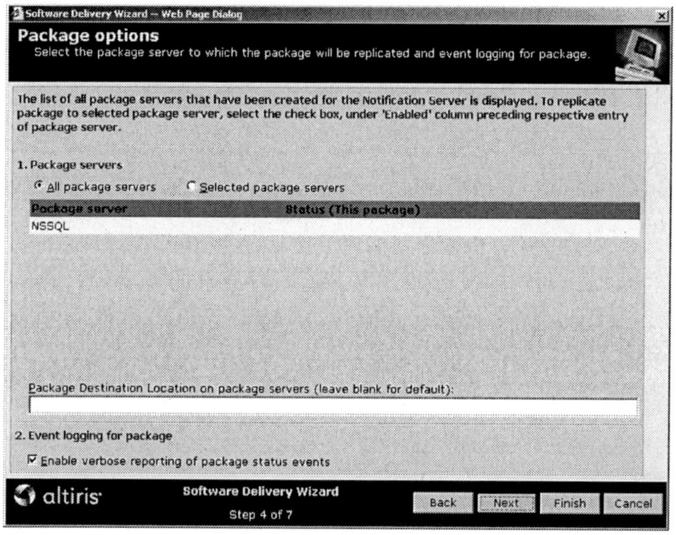

Package Destination location on Package Servers - Use this option to change the destination on the Package Servers to a path other than the default.

Event Logging for Package

On/Off Enable verbose reporting of package status events - Use this to enable or disable reporting of the package download status. If this is disabled you will not be able to report on the success or failure of clients downloading this package.

When all options have been configured, click **Next** to continue.

Step 6 - Configure the Advanced Options

This step is used to configure the name and description of the task as displayed in the Altiris Agent user interface on the client as well as download and execute options.

Specify the name and description of the SWD task that is displayed on the Agent UI

Name – This is the name that will appear for this Software Task in the clients Altiris Agent interface.

Description – This is the description that will appear for this Software Task in the clients Altiris Agent interface.

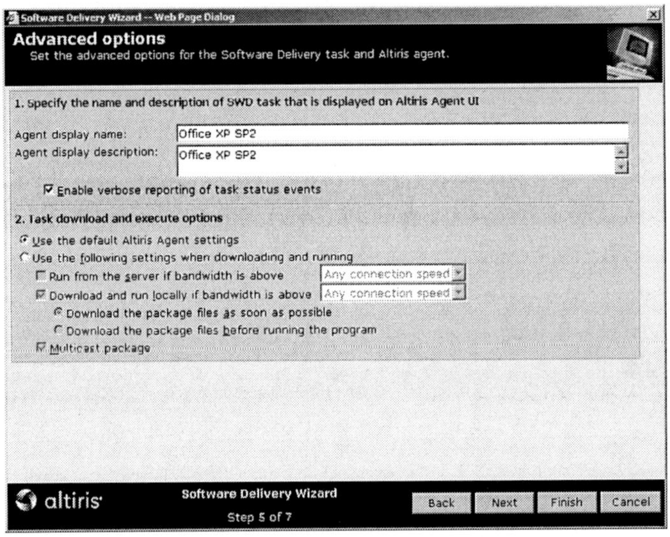

Enable verbose reporting of task status events – On/Off. Enabling this task will allow reporting on the success or failure when it runs on a targeted client.

Task download and execute options

Use the default Altiris Agent settings – Uses the settings for download and execute as configured in the Altiris Agent configuration. **Or**

Use the following settings when downloading and running – Overrides the download and execute options as configured in the Altiris Agent configuration.

Run from the server if bandwidth is above X – Instead of downloading the package locally and then running it, the command line for the package is executed from the Package Server. (Like a network install)

Download and run locally if bandwidth is above X – Downloads the package locally before executing if the bandwidth is above the set threshold.

Download the package files as soon as possible – Download the package as soon as the client is aware of the Package even if the package command line is not due to be immediately executed. **Or**

Download the package files before running the program – Download the package just before it is due to be executed.

Package Multicast – Overrides the multicasting settings for this package on the targeted Altiris Agents.

Click **Next** once the options have been configured.

Step 7 - Configure Software Portal Settings

If a new package is being deployed this step appears. This step is used to configure if the package is available to users of the software portal. For more information on the software Portal see the next chapter.

If this package will not be made available through the portal click **Next** to continue, otherwise, configure which roles will have, Install Software and Install on Approval permissions.

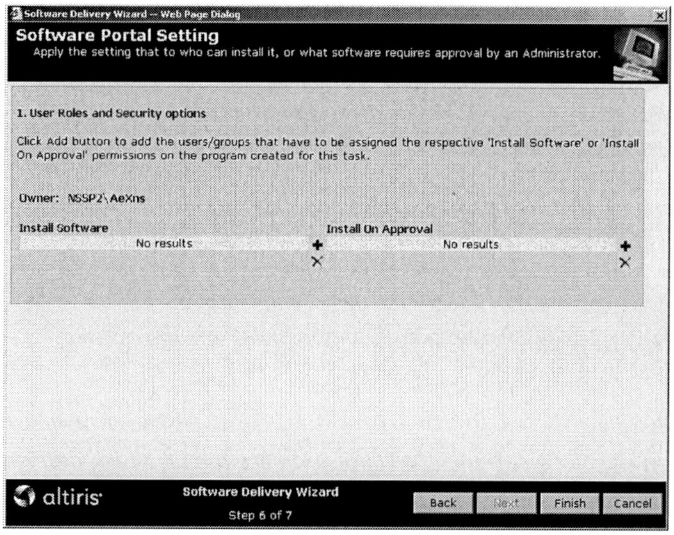

Step 8 - View the Summary

The final step allows you to Enable or Disable the Software Delivery Task, configure the download priority and change the package, task and program name.

Enable/Disable the Task – Enable or Disable.

Set Priority of the task

Priority – Low, Medium, High or Very High. Determines the order in which packages will be downloaded. (Not executed. This setting is only for download order.)

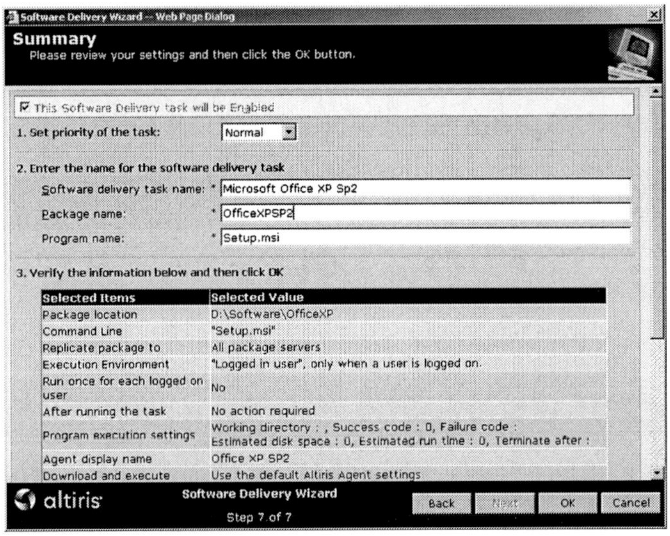

Enter the name of the Software Delivery task

Software delivery task name –

The Delivery Task is enabled by default. Click **OK** to finish.

The next time clients that are targeted by this software delivery task request an update configuration from the Notification Server, they will see the new task and run it based on the configured schedule.

When and whether clients download the software package will depend on the Package Software Task and Altiris Agent configuration. By default package download and execute options are defined by the Altiris Agent configuration. Individual packages can be configured to override the Agent setting. See the configuration section of the chapter 'The Altiris Agent' for more detail.

Manually creating a Software Package and Software Delivery Task

Step 1 - Create a Package Source

See creating a Package Source earlier in this chapter.

Step 2 - Create and Configure the Software Package

From the Web Console go to the Resources Tab and navigate to **Resource Management > Resources > Software Management > Software Delivery > Windows**

Right Click the Windows folder and choose **New > Software Delivery Package**

A new explorer Window displays the properties of the New Package

Four tabs are included: Package, Programs, Advanced and Software Portal. A description of the options contained within each tab follows.

The Package Tab

The Package tab primarily contains options used to configure the package source location.

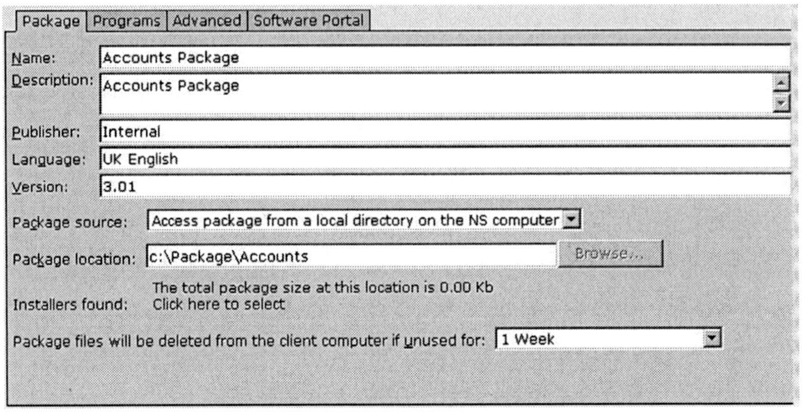

Name – Enter the name of the package. This field is mandatory.

Description – An optional field allowing you to enter a description. Even though the field is optional, I would suggest entering a short description as this will help later when you have lots of packages.

Publisher – Optional field where you can enter the publisher of the application or package. Useful if you later want to query packages by publisher.

Language – Optional Language information.

Version – Optional version information.

Package Source – Mandatory information indicating where the package files are i.e. Local folder, UNC, URL or no files.

Package Location – Mandatory information indicating where in the 'Package Source' the package files are located i.e. The actual path for example c:\Test. If there are no source files in the package, this option will not appear.

Package Directory – This option will only appear if the Package Source selected is a URL source. Use this option to specify a folder beneath the URL specified.

Installers Found – If there are no source files in the package, this option will not appear. If there are source files this link will allow you to display the MSI and Wise application installers found within the package.

Package Type – Is it an SMS, Win32 or Unix package. If there are no source files in the package, this option will not appear.

Package files will be deleted from the client computer if unused for X – This is used to remove software packages from clients that have not accessed the package for X. If there are no source files in the package, this option will not appear.

The Programs Tab

The Programs tab primarily contains options used to configure what account and command line is used to run/install the software package.

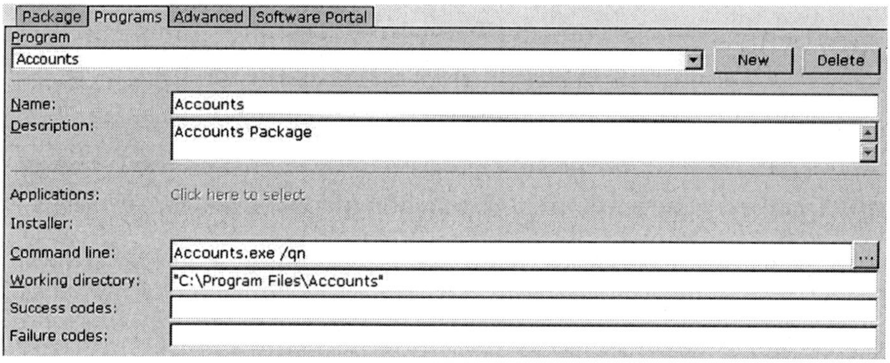

The first time you visit the Programs Tab for a new package, no Program will be defined, click the **'New'** button to create a new program. This will expand the dialog to reveal the following options some of which are optional.

Name – A mandatory field that indicates the Program name.
Description – Optional field used to provide a description. Useful if you have multiple programs associated with one package.
Applications – If installers were configured in the Programs tab within the package, this link will be active and allow you to choose a specific application. Using this option allows you to tie a program to a defined application.
Installer – If applications was previously configured, the installer for the application will be displayed.
Command line – A mandatory field used to provide the command line used to run the program. Include any optional switches and parameters in this field.
Working directory – Optional field used to specify the working directory required by the application installer.

Success codes – Applications normally return 0 as a success code. If the application being deployed doesn't return 0 as a success code use this optional field to specify additional success codes. To enter multiple codes separate each code with a comma. For example 7,8.

Failure codes – Applications normally return 1 as a failure code. If the application being deployed doesn't return 1 as a failure code use this optional field to specify additional failure codes. To enter multiple codes separate each code with a comma. For example 9,10.

Estimated disk space – The amount of space required for the installation. This will not limit the disk space available for the installation.

Estimated run time – The estimated time it will take to complete the installation. Users can view this estimate if they view the properties of this program through the Altiris Agent interface.

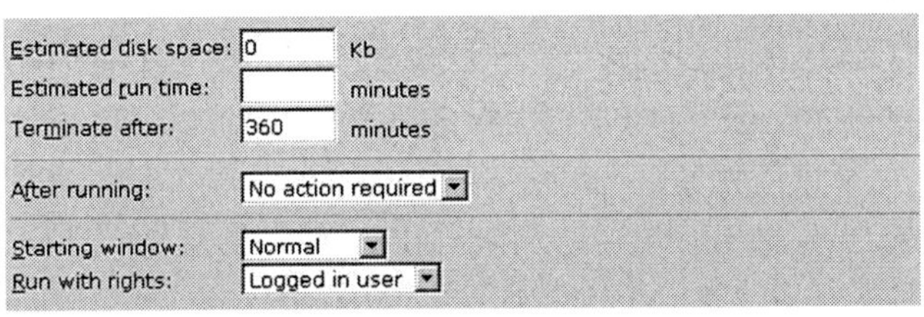

Terminate after X minutes – If the installation takes more than X minutes the program will abort.

After running – Mandatory field used to specify what happens when the installation has completed. The choices are, Reboot, No Action Required or Logoff the user.

Start window – Normal, Hidden, Minimized, Maximized.

Run with Rights – Mandatory field used to specify what right to use when running the Program. The choices are, the Logged on User, System Account and a Specified User Account. This is particularly useful when users are not local administrators on their machines. Keep in mind that the System Account is good for installing any application but does not have any access rights outside of the local machine. Generally the best option is to use a specific account with administrative rights on the target machine(s).

Program Can Run – Mandatory field used to limit when the Program can run. Options include, Only when a User is logged on, Only when no User is logged on and Whether or not a User is logged on. This option is not available if the System account was specified previously.
User Input Required – This option is optional and is only required when a User is logged on. The option allows Users to interact with the executed installer/application which is useful if input is required during installation. I would recommend including answer files and silent install switch with the command line to ensure that users don't need to interact with an installation program.

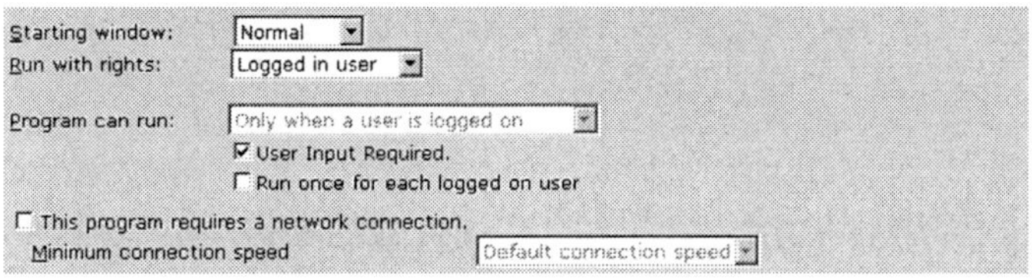

Run once for each user logged on user – Self explanatory.
This program requires a network connection – If a Program requires a network connection to run successfully this option should be checked. The option should be used when, running an application or installation across the network or when installing an application that requires connection to a server or web site to download installation or configuration files to complete the installation. Using this option and the next option 'Minimum connection speed' you can configure the Program to only execute if the minimum connection speed configured is available.
Minimum connection speed – The minimum connection speed that must exist for the Program to run. (This option is used in conjunction with the previous option.)

The Advanced Tab

This tab lets you configure which Package Server(s) will receive the package as well as options to configure another download path.

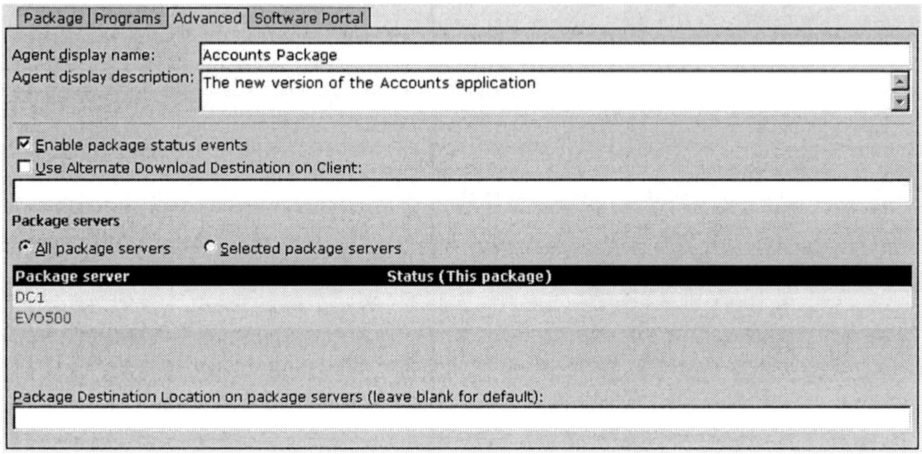

Agent Display Name – The name that will appear in the Altiris Agent interface.
Agent Description – The description that will appear in the Altiris Agent interface.
Enable Package Status Events – Can be set to on or off. With this option 'on', the agent will send package download events to the Notification Server. (Approximately 16k)
Use alternate download destination on client – The default on the client is to download packages to InstallPath\Altiris\Altiris Agent\Software Delivery\GUID Folder. (Where GUID is a unique name given to the folder. e.g. A654FRD5643). This option can be used to override the download path. The option is normally used if replicating packages to Altiris Deployment Servers.
All Package Servers or Selected Package Servers – This option defines which Package Servers will receive the new Package, the default is 'All Package Servers'.
Package Destination Location on Package Servers – The default package location is Installpath\Altiris\Altiris Agent\Package Download\Package GUID\Cache. Use this option to specify a different location.

The Software Portal Tab

This tab is used to configure whether users can access and request this package through the Software Portal interface.

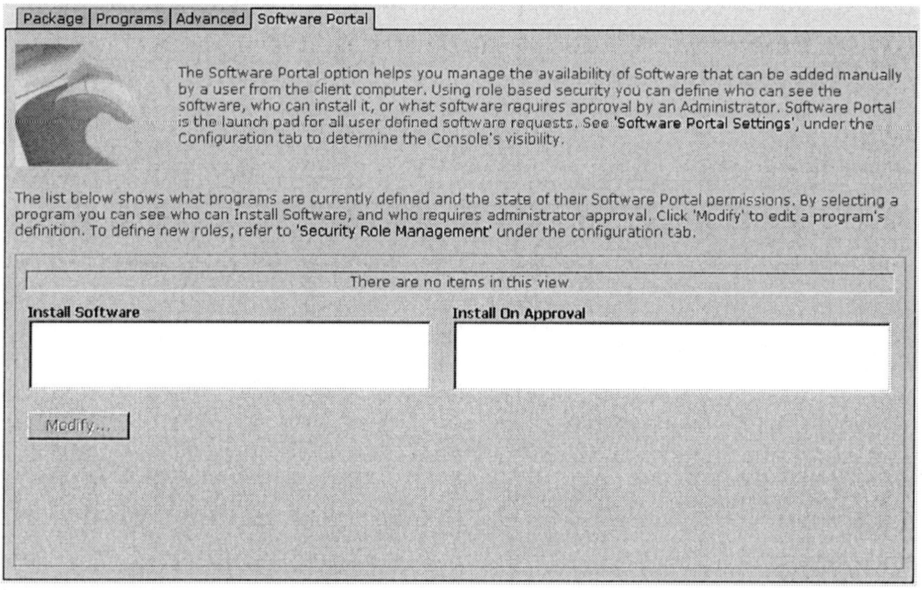

The Software Portal is discussed in the next chapter.

Once all options have been configured, click **Apply**.

Step 3 – Creating a Software Delivery Task

Now that the Software Package has been created, you must advertise the package to clients by creating a Software Delivery Task.

From the Web Console go to the Tasks Tab and navigate to **Software Management > Software Delivery > Windows > Software Delivery Tasks**.

Right click Software Delivery Tasks and choose the **New > Software Delivery Task** command.

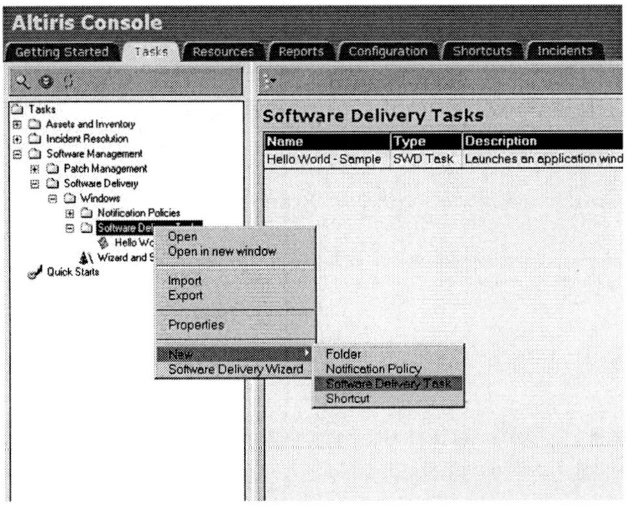

The Software Delivery Task dialog is displayed below and described in the following pages.

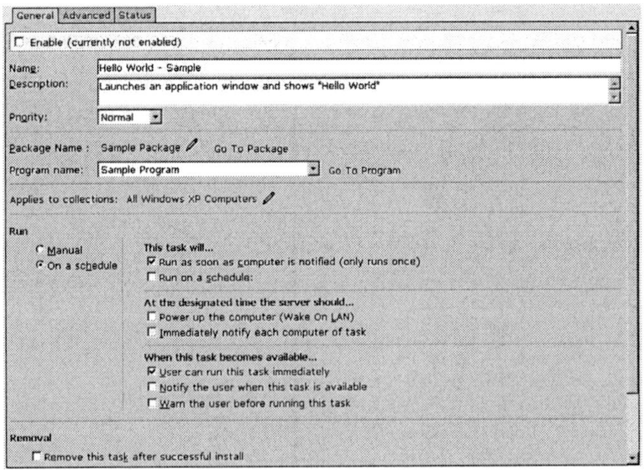

Software Delivery Task Options

The General Tab

The General Tab provides options to allow the Administrator to configure which collection(s) of machines will receive the Software task and whether the Program for the package will be automatically run on a schedule or rely on the User manually starting the install.

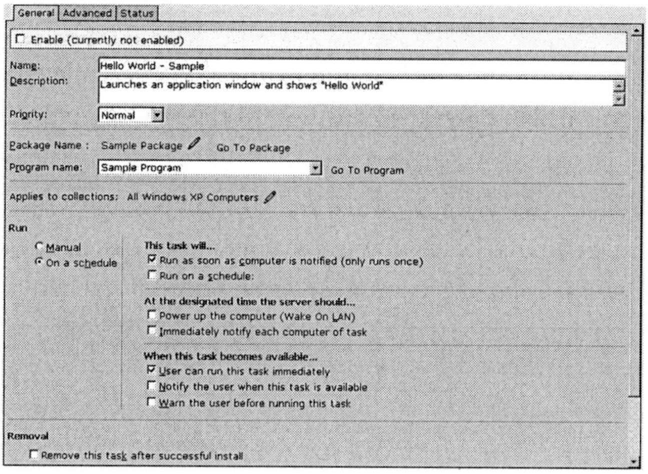

Enable/Disable the Task – Enable or Disable.

Name – The Task name as viewed in the Web Console.

Description – The Task description as viewed in the Web Console.

Priority – Low, Medium, High or Very High. Determines the order in which packages will be downloaded. (Not executed. This setting is only for download order.)

Package Name – Select what Software Package is associated with this task.

Program Name – Once the Package has been selected, select the Program Name (Command Line).

Applies to collection(s) – Configures which collection(s) of machines will be targeted.

Run – Manual or On a Schedule.

Configuring a Task to run on a schedule effectively makes it a mandatory installation. Choosing Manual means that the Administrator is relying on the User to start the installation manually.

Manual

Notify the user when this task is available On/Off – Displays a Notification to the user that a Software Task is available.
Warn the user before running this task On/Off – Select this to warn the user before a Software Delivery task is run.

On a schedule

Schedule – Run as soon as computer is notified (only runs once). This option makes a Task mandatory. The next time a machine in the targeted collection(s) requests an update configuration it will download and install the package ASAP.
Run on a schedule – Used to configure when the command-line is executed.
Power up the computer (Wake On LAN) – The Agent must be configured for 'Tickle/Power Management' through an Altiris Agent configuration Policy.
Immediately notify each computer of task – Doesn't wait for clients in the targeted collection to request an update to their configuration. Using this option will cause all targeted machines to run the task. Ensure that you allow time for the associated software package to replicate to all designated Package Servers before using this option.
User can run this task immediately – Used to allow users through the Altiris Agent interface to manually start the Task.
Notify the user when this task is available – Displays a Notification to the user that a Software Task is available.
Warn the user before running this task – The user is warned before the Task runs.
Remove this task after successful install – The Task is not available through the Altiris Agent interface after it has been run once.
Availability – Allows you to control during what period the Task is available.
Use the Servers Time – On/Off. This option is useful in an environment with multiple time zones.

Once you have configured the available options in the General Tab move to the Advanced Tab. The Advanced Tab provides options to configure what name and description appears in the clients Agent interface as well as whether to override download and execute options configured on the Altiris Agent.

The Advanced Tab

Agent Display Name – This is the name that will appear for this Software Task in the clients Altiris Agent interface.

Agent Display Description – This is the description that will appear for this Software Task in the clients Altiris Agent interface.

Track the status events for this task – On/Off. Use this to track status events for the Task.

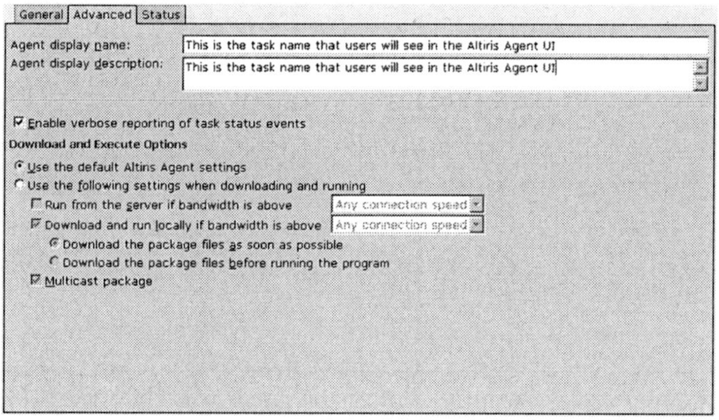

Use the default Altiris Agent settings – Uses the settings for download and execute as configured in the Altiris Agent configuration. **Or**

Use the following settings when downloading and running – Overrides the download and execute options as configured in the Altiris Agent configuration.

Run from the server if bandwidth is above X – Instead of downloading the package locally and then running it, the command line for the package is executed from the Package Server. (Like a network install)

Download and run locally if bandwidth is above X – Downloads the package locally before executing if the bandwidth is above the set threshold.

Download the package files as soon as possible – Download the package as soon as the client is aware of the Package even if the package command line is not due to be immediately executed. **Or**

Download the package files before running the program – Download the package just before it is due to be executed.

Multicast Package - Multicasting must be enabled through the Altiris Agent policies for this to work. Select this option to multicast the package to other clients receiving the package. (A client temporarily becomes a PS for this package.)

The Status Tab

This dialog displays the list of computers this Task last ran on and the status i.e. success or failure. If this is a new Task or if the **'Track the status for this task'** option in the Advanced tab was not enabled for the task then no status information will be displayed in this page.

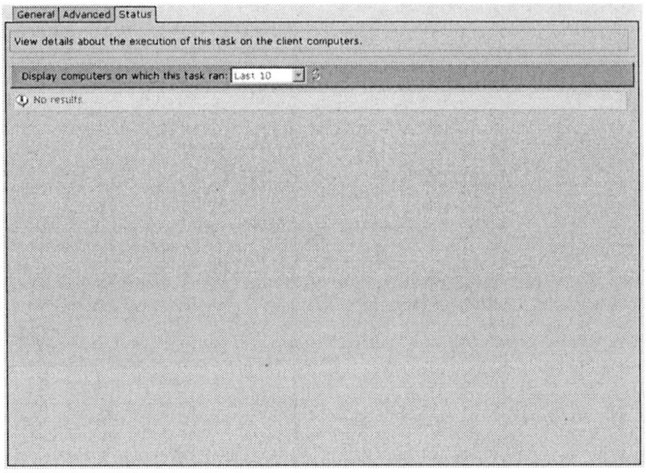

Final Step –

Once you have configured the available options, **enable** the Task in the General Tab and then click **Apply**.

The next time clients in the targeted collection(s) request an update configuration from the Notification Server, they will see the new Software Delivery task. Clients will run the software task based on the configured schedule. Use the built-in reports to determine the success and failure of the software deployment.

Sequential Software Delivery Tasks

Sequential software delivery tasks allow you to chain the delivery and execution of multiple software delivery packages together. A sequential task also provides the ability to configure the execution order of the tasks and any task dependencies.

For example, you can have two tasks, Task 1 and Task 2 in one sequential task. After setting the execution order, you can configure a dependency for Task 2 to only execute if Task 1 executed successfully.

Creating a sequential Software Delivery Task

Open the web console and select the Tasks tab then navigate to **Software Management > Software Delivery > Windows > Sequential Software Delivery Task**.

Right click the Sequential Software Delivery Task folder and from the shortcut menu choose **New > Sequential Software Delivery Task**.

Configuring a sequential Software Delivery Task

When the properties of the new task are displayed, enter a name and description.

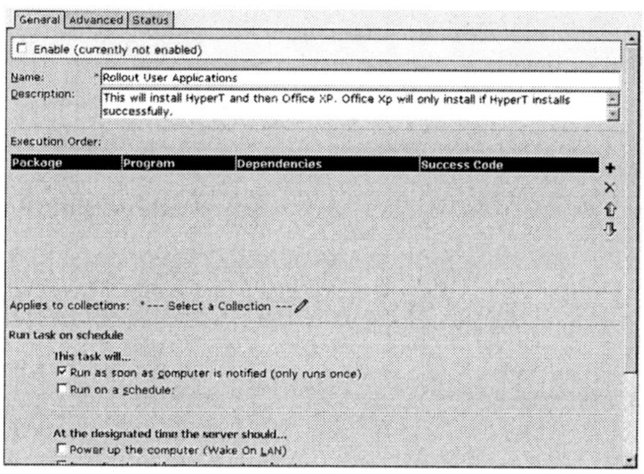

Use the **Add** button to display the Software Delivery Program Selector dialog.

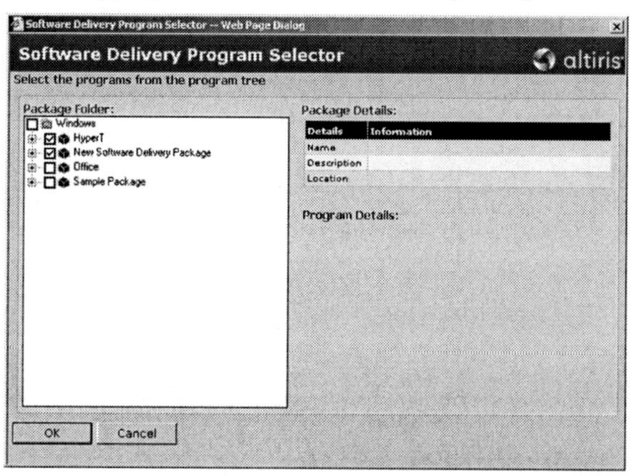

Check the programs required then click **OK**.

The selected programs are displayed in the sequential software delivery tasks dialog.

Execution Order:

Package	Program	Dependencies	Success Code
HyperT	HyperT	-- No dependency --	0
Office	Install Office XP	-- No dependency --	0

Configuring the Task execution order

The program at the top of the list is the first program that will run on the targeted machines. Use the up and down arrows to alter the sequence.

Configuring Dependencies

The dependencies link for each program is used to configure dependencies. In the above example, we want to configure the second program (Office) to only run if the first program (HyperT) runs successfully, in other words returns a success code of 0. (The return code is defined in the package tab of the package properties.)

Click the dependencies link for the second package and select the first task as a dependency.

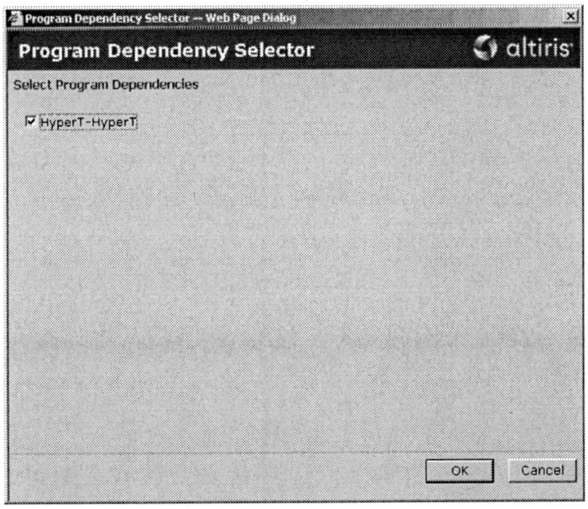

Click **OK**.

Execution Order:

Package	Program	Dependencies	Success Code
HyperT	HyperT	-- No dependency --	0
Office	Install Office XP	HyperT-HyperT	0

The first package is now configured as a dependency for the second package. The second task will only run if the first task returns a success code of 0.

Completing the configuration

To complete the configuration of the sequential software delivery task, you will need to configure the target collection(s) for the task, the scheduling options, the download and execution options in the advanced tab and then enable the policy.

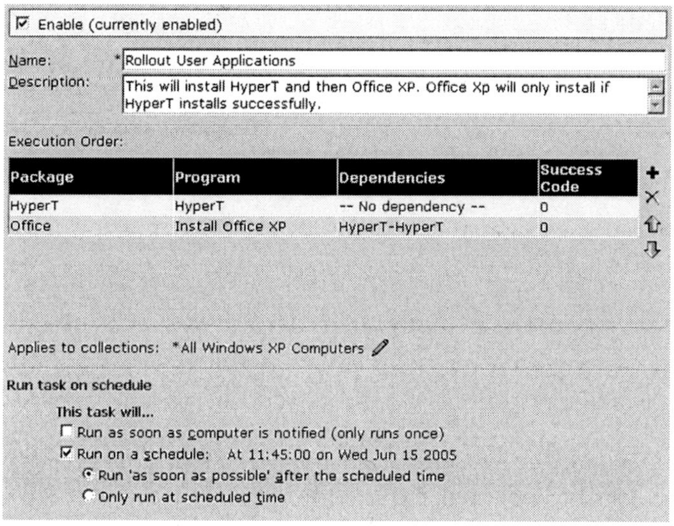

The next time clients in the targeted collection(s) request an update configuration they will see, download and execute the sequential task based on the how that task has been configured.

Removing Software Delivery Solution

If you do not intend to use Software Delivery Solution anymore, use the Software Delivery Agent Uninstall Policy to remove the Agent from all machines (See below). Allow all clients to request an update configuration so that they have a chance to uninstall the Agent.

Use **Add/Remove** Programs in Control Panel on the Notification Server to remove the Solution.

Un-Installing the Software Delivery Agent

Go to the Configuration Tab in the Web Console and navigate to S**olution Settings > Software Management > Software Delivery > Windows > Software Delivery Solution Agent Uninstall > Software Delivery Agent Uninstall**.

This Policy is disabled by default.

Select the Collection(s) that the Software Delivery Agent will be uninstalled from.

Schedule the uninstall to begin as required.

Enable the Agent Uninstall Policy.

Click **Apply**.

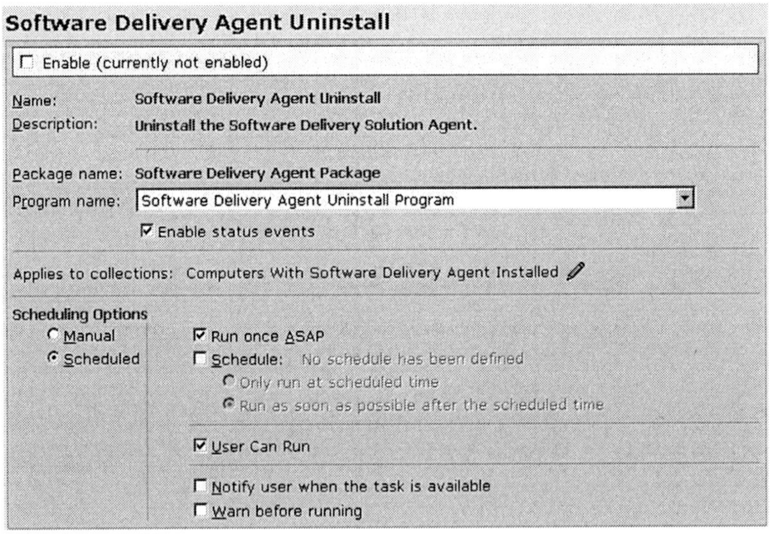

The Software Delivery Agent will be uninstalled the next time clients in the target collection(s) request a configuration update. The software delivery folder structure is also removed.

Useful Software Delivery Reports

To view the following reports open the Web Console, select the Reports Tab then navigate to **Software Management > Software Delivery > Windows folder**.

Package Download - Summary

This report displays a summary of the packages downloaded by clients. The report also shows the transfer rates and duration of the download. Only data for the Packages with Verbose reporting enabled will be displayed.

Program Execution - All

This report will list all program execution regardless of status. Only data for the Tasks with Verbose reporting enabled will be displayed.

Program Execution - Failed

This report will list all failed program execution. Only data for the Tasks with Verbose reporting enabled will be displayed.

Program Execution - Success

This report will list all successful program execution. Only data for the Tasks with Verbose reporting enabled will be displayed.

Software Delivery Task Summary - All Activity

This report displays a summary of all software delivery task activity. Only data for the Tasks with Verbose reporting enabled will be displayed.

Summary

This chapter walked you through the process of installing Software Delivery Solution, rolling out the Software Delivery Agent and then guided you through creating and rolling out software packages to managed clients.

The two primary elements in software delivery are the software package and the delivery task. The package defines the files and command-line used. The Task advertises the software package to clients and defines when the client will download and execute the package and associated program.

The next chapter 'Software Portal Solution' looks at how you can use the Software Portal to allow users to manually install approved software as well as request approval to install software through a special web interface.

12

Software Portal Solution

Introduction

The Software Portal is a self-service solution that allows users to manually install and request software through a web interface. When a user opens the Portal interface, a list of 'approved software' and' software requiring approval' is displayed based on the users login. Approved Software is software that can be installed immediately by the user. Software Requiring Approval is software that the user can not immediately install, but can use the Portal interface to request installation of that package.

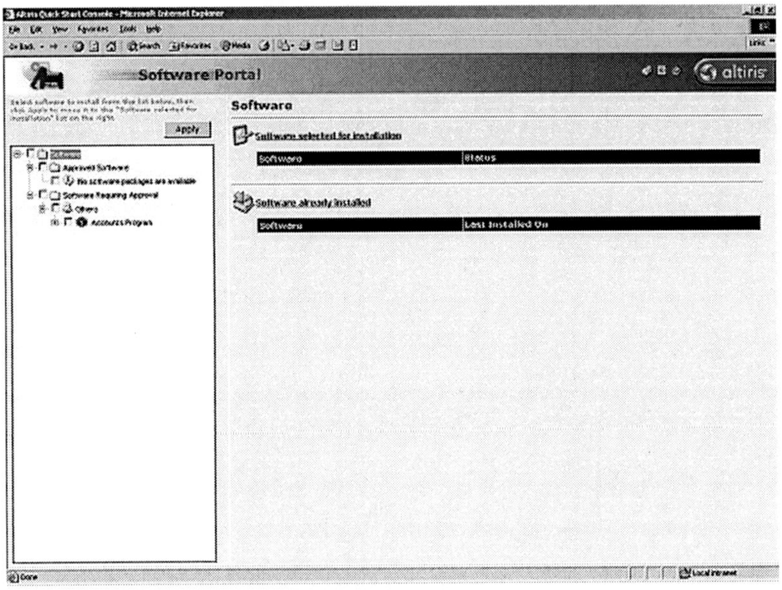

In the diagram above there are no approved software packages listed and there is one software package that requires approval by the Administrator. In this instance, the user must request approval before the package can be run/installed.

Which packages appear in the Portal interface, will be determined by the logon credentials of the currently logged on user.

Installing Software Portal Solution

Software Portal Solution is installed as part of the Software Delivery Solution for Windows installation. See the previous chapter 'Software Delivery Solution for Windows' for further details.

Components added to the web console

- A 'Software Portal' folder containing three new reports are added to the Reports Tab.
- A Software Portal configuration page is added to **Configuration Tab > Solution Settings > Software management > Software Delivery > Software Portal Configuration**.
- A Task Synchronization folder containing packages, collections and policies to rollout the 'Task Synchronization Agent' is added to **Configuration Tab > Solution Settings > Task Synchronization**.
- An extra tab 'Software Portal' is added to the properties of all existing and future software packages.

Configuring and using Software Portal

The steps required to begin using the Portal are relatively straight forward. Effectively you need to ensure that the Software Delivery Agent is installed on client machines. Then you need to configure Portal access and finally configure the necessary permissions on software packages that you want to make available through the portal.

Step 1 – Rollout out the Software Delivery Agent

If managed clients do not already have the Agent, go to the section 'Installing the Software Delivery Agent' in the previous chapter 'Software Delivery Solution for Windows' and rollout the Agent.

Step 2 - Configuring Software Portal Access

The Software Portal configuration page in **Configuration tab > Solution Settings > Software Management > Software Delivery > Software Portal Configuration** allows you to configure how users will access the Software Portal web page. There are three choices:

- Show link for Software Portal in Start Menu
- Show link for Software Portal in "Add Remove Programs" dialog box
- Show link for Software Portal in Altiris Agent's context menu

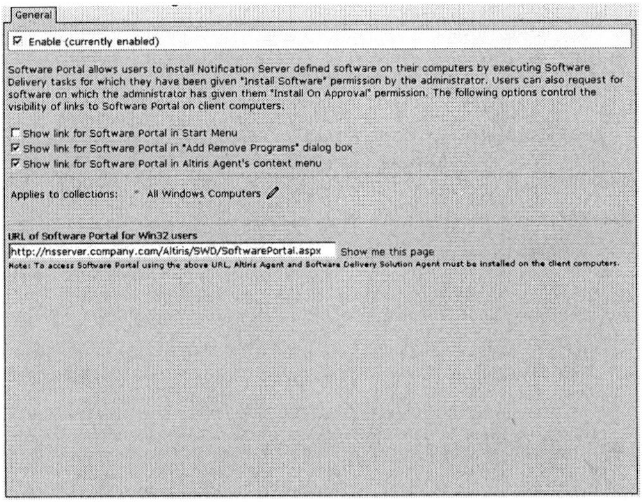

Enable one or more of the available options, then click **Apply** when finished.

The next time that clients in the targeted collection update their configuration, they will configure Software Portal access.

Step 3 – Configure a software package for Software Portal

Select the Resources tab in the Altiris Web Console and navigate to **Software Management > Software Delivery Packages > Windows**.

Right click an existing package and choose **Resource Manager** from the shortcut menu.

Select the Software Portal tab to display the dialog below.

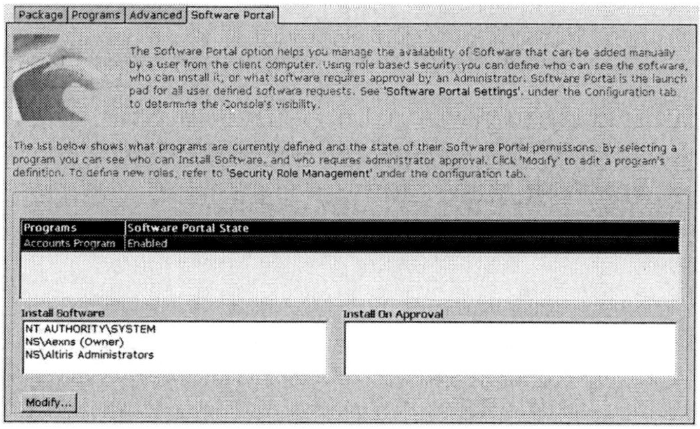

The default permissions are that Altiris Administrators, the creator/owner of the package and the System account have the 'Install Software' permission.

To change these permissions click the **Modify** button.

Click the **Add** button to add a new user group. The Role dialog is displayed.

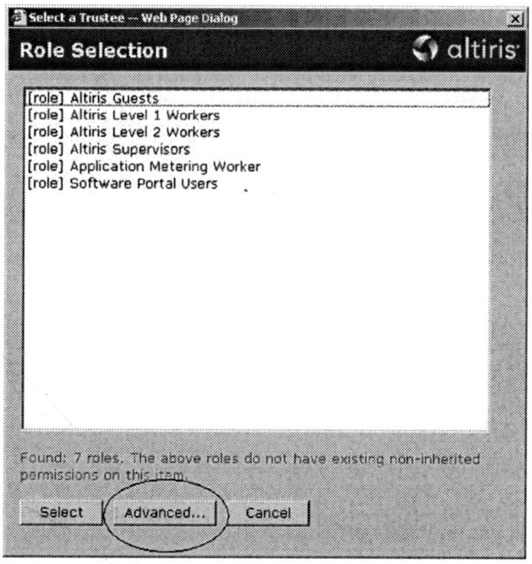

Click the **Advanced** button within the Role dialog to select users and groups.

Use the **Find** button to view the available users and groups.

Select the user or group, that you want to grant access too.

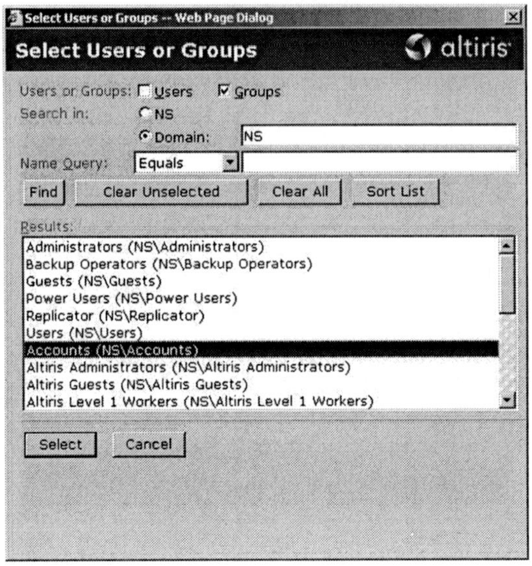

Click the **Select** button to display the **Edit Permissions** dialog. Select the permission 'Install Software' or 'Install on Approval' and click **Select**. Wait until the Security Descriptor dialog is refreshed.

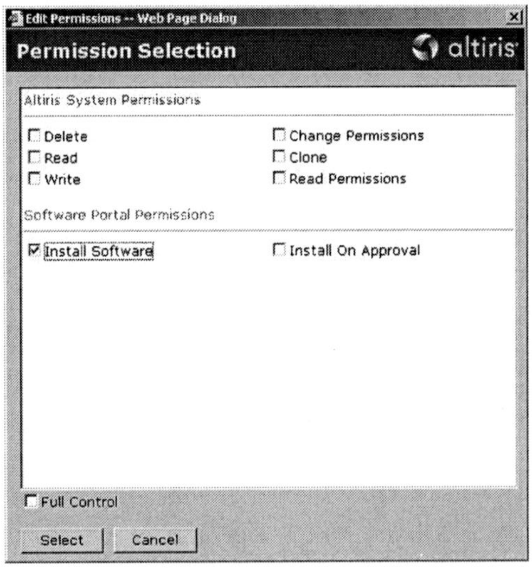

Repeat the previous actions to add more users or groups.

When all users and groups have been selected and configured, click **OK** to close the Security Descriptor dialog. The Selected package is now configured and will be available to the selected groups through the portal interface.

Installing a package using the Portal

When a user displays the Software Portal interface they will be offered packages where they have been given the 'Install Software' or the 'Install on Approval' permission.

Approved packages appear in the approved section as shown below.
For a user to install an approved package, the user simply opens the Portal interface, checks the required package to install and clicks **Request**.

Packages requiring approval appear in the Software Requiring Approved section as shown below.
For a user to request a package requiring approval, the user simply opens the Portal interface, checks the required package in the Software Requiring Approval section and clicks **Request**.
The user then has to wait for the Administrator or Helpdesk person to approval or deny the request.

Approving and denying Software Requests

When a user requests a software package through the Software Portal, an incident is created for the Notification Server Administrator. Through the incident, the Administrator can approve or reject a software request from a user. By default, all software that requires approval will be added to the Asset Management queue. Whomever is assigned to this queue will be responsible for approving or denying each software request.

Approving a Software Request

Connect to the Web Console using the Application Identity account and select the **Incidents** tab.

If this is the first time you have accessed Incidents, enter the application identity account details. (Only 'Full Name' is required.)

Select 'All Open Incidents' from the Query dropdown to display the new request as show in the figure below.

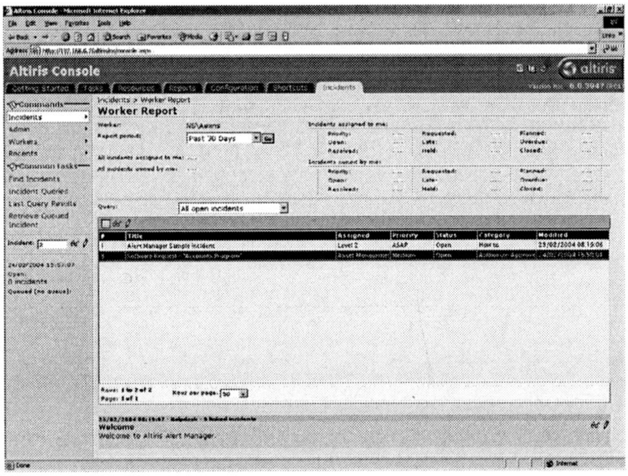

Open the new Software Request incident by double clicking it.

The incident properties page will be displayed. Two links are shown to allow approval or denial of the software request.

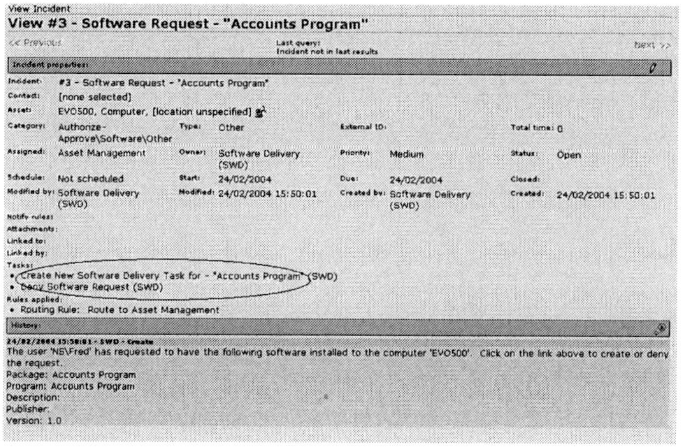

To approve a software request click the link 'Create New Software Delivery Task for ....'. A new window is launched.

A new software delivery task is created for the approved package. The task configuration will determine when the software package runs on the requesting user's machine.

Configure the task in the same way as any other software delivery task.

Once the task has been configured **enable** it and then click **Apply**.

Denying a Software Request

From the Web Console select the Incidents tab.

Open the software request incident.

The incident properties page will be displayed. Two links are shown to allow approval or denial of the software request.

Click the link 'Deny Software Request'. A new window confirms the denial.

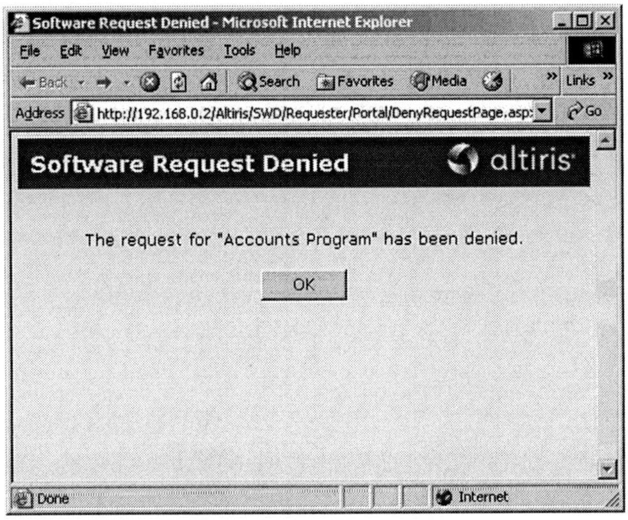

When a request has been denied, the status displayed on the requesting users Software Portal interface will change to 'Rejected by administrator'.

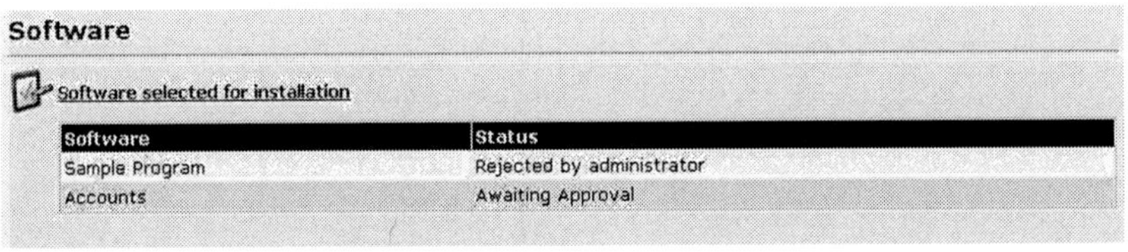
Software

Software selected for installation

Software	Status
Sample Program	Rejected by administrator
Accounts	Awaiting Approval

Useful Software Portal Reports

To view the following reports open the Web Console, select the Reports Tab then navigate to **Software Management > Software Delivery > Windows > Software Portal folder**.

Request Activity Summary

Summarizes the number of requests per package.

Software Requests by Machine

Displays the list of packages and the machines that have requested the package.

Software Requests by User

Displays the list of packages and the users that have requested the package.

Summary

In this chapter we looked at using Software Portal to allow users to manually install and request software through the Software Portal interface.
Users are given access to the portal through a policy on the Notification Server. Packages that are to be made available to users through the portal can be given the 'Install Software' and/or the 'Install on Approval' permissions. The Install Software permission allows a user to manually install the software package without intervention. The Install on Approval permission allows a user to request permission to install a software package. When a user requests to install a package, an incident for that request is generated in Incident Manager on the Notification Server. This incident is used to approve or deny a request.

In the next chapter 'Application Metering Solution' we will look at how application usage can be monitored.

13

Application Metering Solution

Introduction

Application Metering is used to monitor when and how often an application is run on a client machine. Application Metering can be used on an on-going basis to monitor application usage or occasionally to check which applications are being used and then harvest licenses based on the metering data.

Features

- Monitor the number of times an application is run.
- Prevent a user from using an application during certain periods.
- Discover what Win32 applications are run the first time on a client.
- Track when an application is started or stopped and how long an application is in use.
- The same AuditPls.ini used to customize Inventory reporting can also be used by application metering.
- License harvesting can be accomplished through the use of Inventory Solution and Application Metering Solution. Inventory Solution will report which applications are installed and Application Metering will report which applications are being used. Comparing the two sets of data will allow you to determine what applications are installed but are not being used.

What types of applications can be monitored?

Windows NT/W2K/XP	Win32 apps only
Win 9.x/ME	Win32 & Win16 apps

Installing Application Metering Solution

From the Configuration Tab in the Altiris Web Console select **Install/Upgrade Additional Solutions**.
Click the **Solutions** button and select the Application Metering link.
Click **Start** and follow the on screen prompts.

Once installed, apply your full license. If this solution installation is an upgrade from a previous version then there is no need to re-apply the license. Solutions come with a built-in 7 day license. 30 day licenses can be downloaded from the Altiris web site.

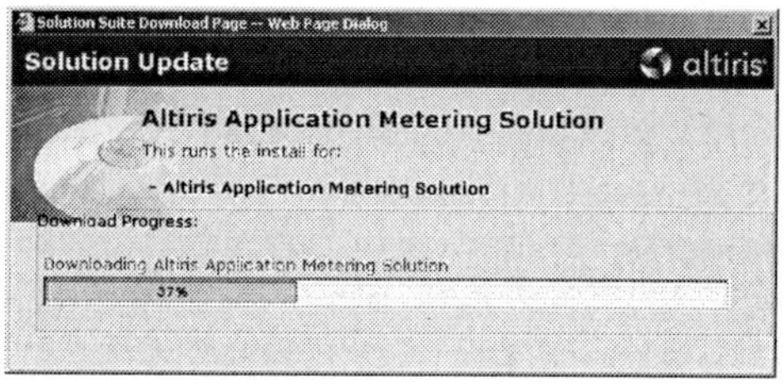

Important

Immediately after installing the solution, navigate to the **Tasks Tab** then **SoftwareManagement > Application Metering > Application Monitors**.
Disable all Monitors including:-

All Applications; Pinball 3D; All Office application monitors.

Then select the **Configuration Tab** and navigate to **Solution Settings > Application Metering > Application Metering Solution Configuration Policy**.
Disable 'Discover and report on all new Win32 applications executed on client machines'. Click **Apply**.

You can enable Discovery and the selected monitors later when you fully understand the implications.

Components added to the Web Console

Getting Started Tab – The Application Metering Solution installation does not add to the Getting Started tab at this time.
Tasks Tab – Application Metering Monitors are added to the **Software Management > Application Metering folder**.
Resources Tab – Nothing of any significance is added at this time.
Reporting Tab – Over 30 reports are added to the **Software Management > Application Metering folder**.
Configuration Tab – An Application Metering folder is added to the Solutions Settings folder. The folder contains policies to install, upgrade, uninstall and configure the Application Metering agent.
Shortcuts Tab – No shortcuts are automatically added by the Application Metering Solution installation.

Application Metering Traffic

There are two types of data sent from the client to the Notification Server, **Application Events** and **Application Metering Summary** data.

The Application events Start, Stop, Win32 Discovery and Denial are always sent **immediately** from the client to the Notification Server. Each Event is approximately 2KB.
Application Metering Summary data includes information such as when an application was run and for how long it was run. Application Summary is sent from the client to the Notification Server based on a schedule every 1, 2, 7 or 14 days. Metering Summary data is approximately 7 to 10KB based on 10 applications.

Configuration Application Metering Solution

From the Altiris Web Console select the **Configuration Tab** and navigate to **Solution Settings > Application Metering > Application Metering Solution Configuration Policy**.

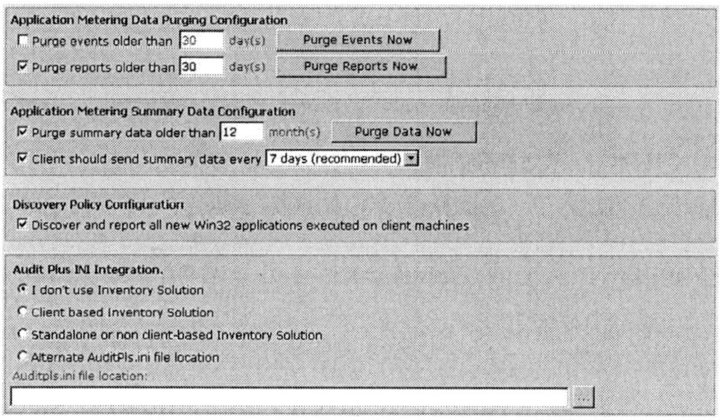

Application Metering Data Purging Configuration

Purge Events older than X Days – Deletes start, stop and denial events from the database if older than X Days.

Purge Reports older than X Days – Deletes reports older than X Days. This does not delete the default solution reports.

Both of the previous options also have a **'Purge Now'** button to allow you to purge data immediately without having to wait for the schedule.

Application Metering Summary Data Configuration

Purge Summary Data older than X months – Automatically deletes application summary data older than X months from the database.

Client should send summary data every X Days – Configures how often a client sends application metering summary data to the Notification Server. Application Metering Summary includes what application and how many times that application has been run. This option configures application metering summary data it does not affect Application Metering Events or Win32 discovery data which are sent immediately to the Notification Server.

Application Discovery – Discovery is used to find out what Win32 applications are run on a client machine. If Win32 discovery is enabled, the client will report immediately to the Notification Server (HTTP port 80) when a Win32 application is run on a client machine for the first time. Each application discovered will generate an event of approximately 2KB. The record of the discovered applications is stored locally in a text file on the root of the Altiris Agent folder named AeXAMDiscovery.txt.

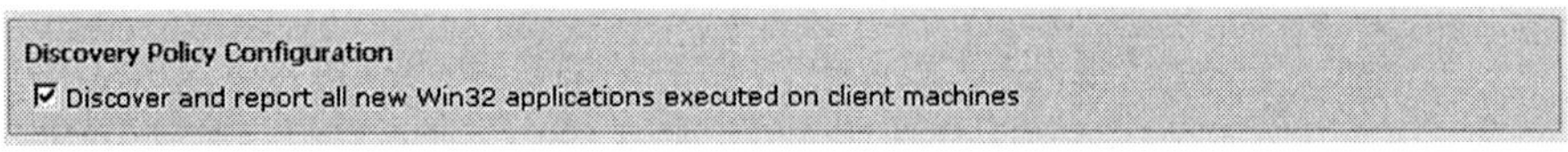

Audit Plus ini Integration

Auditpls.ini is used by Inventory Solution to customise the software inventory scan as well as streamline what is reported to the Notification Server.

The application Metering Agent can use the same Auditpls file as the Inventory Solution Agent to streamline what is reported to the Notification Server. When the metering agent is installed on a client, a new dummy Auditpls.ini is created on the client for the metering agent. If you are using Inventory Solution as well as Application Metering, it is preferable to use the same Auditpls.ini for both solutions as this incurs less administrative overhead. There are four options included in this section of the Application Metering Agent configuration:

I don't use Inventory Solution – The metering agent will use the auditpls.ini in the local Altiris Agent folder. The file is created during the Application Metering Agent installation and has the default auditpls settings.

Client based Inventory Solution – (This option is greyed out if you don't have Inventory Solution installed.) Selecting this option will configure the Application Metering Agent to use the same Auditpls.ini as Inventory Solution. This will help to report data consistently between Inventory and Application Metering Solutions.

Standalone or Non-Client based Inventory – This option can be used for clients that do not report data to the Notification Server. (Standalone Inventory is where you either manually or through a logon script execute the Inventory agent AexWebInvPkg.exe on a client. This means that the client does not have a copy of the Inventory agent installed locally and so does not have a copy of the Auditpls.ini for Inventory Solution.)
Alternate Auditpls.ini location – Allows you to specify a different location for the Auditpls.ini. This option is rarely used but allows you some flexibility if the previous options do not meet your needs.

Once you have configured the desired options in the Application Metering Solution Configuration policy, click **Apply**.
The settings configured will apply to all managed clients running the Application Metering Agent.

Deploying the Application Metering Agent

From the Altiris Web Console select the **Configuration Tab** and navigate to **Solution Settings > Application Metering > Application Metering Agent Rollout**.

Select the policy 'Win32 Application Metering Agent Install/Upgrade'.

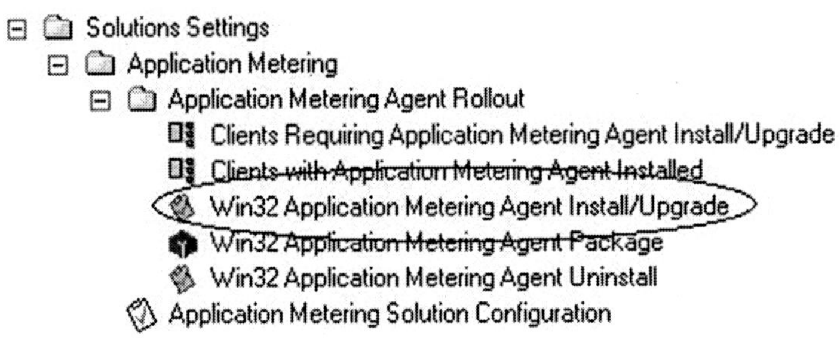

Use the **'applies to collection'** hyperlink to target which machines will install the agent. The default collection is, 'Clients requiring the Application Metering Agent install/upgrade'.

Configure the scheduling options as required.

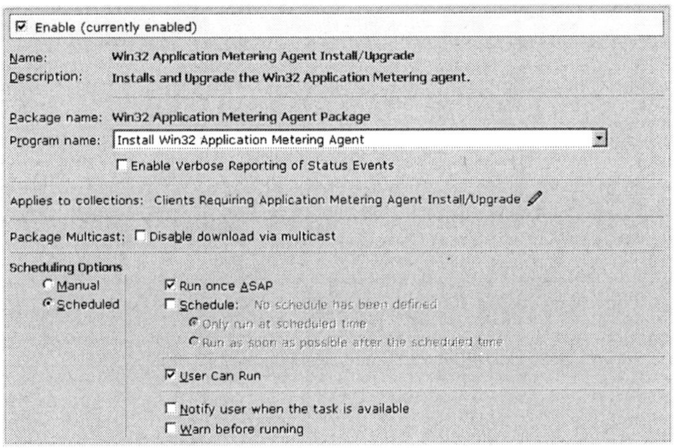

Enable the policy and click **Apply**.

The next time machines in the target collection(s) update their configuration; they will download and install the agent based on the scheduling options.

Files used by the Application Metering Agent

AMAgent.exe – The installation file. The agent is installed using the syntax 'AMAgent.exe -s -a /s' and uninstalled using the syntax 'AMAgent.exe -s -a /s /oRemove'.

AeXAMAgentInst.log – This file is used to log the installation of the agent and is stored in the root of the Altiris Agent folder on the client.

AeXAMInventory.txt – This file is used to record details of Win32 and Win16 (Only on 9.x) run on a client and is used by application monitors not by Win32 discovery. The details recorded include application .exe and manufacturer information as well as the number of times the application has been run, who ran the application and when it was first and last run.

AeXAMDiscovery.txt – Records details of Win32 applications first run on a client. The details include application .exe and manufacturer information but **not** how many times the application has been run or when it was run. Application Monitors do not use this file only Win32 discovery.

AuditPls.ini – Auditpls.ini is used by the Application Metering Agent to customize and streamline how information is reported to the Notification Server. The Application Metering Agent can be configured to use another Auditpls.ini or the same Auditpls.ini as the Inventory Solution Agent. Integrating Inventory Solution with Application Metering Solution is discussed later in this chapter.

Application Discovery

Discovery will report **immediately** to the Notification Server when a Win32 application is run for the first time on a client machine. (Note that it will only report the first time the application is run.) Discovery does not report how many times an application is run or when it is started or stopped. Application Discovery uses a local client text file named AeXAMDiscovery.txt on the root of the Altiris Agent folder, to track what Win32 applications have been run once on a client. When a Win32 application is first run and reported to the Notification Server, the application name is added to the text file and so subsequent executions of the same application do not get reported to the Notification Server. Each discovered application will generate approximately 2KB.

Enabling and Disabling Application Discovery

From the Altiris Web Console select the **Configuration Tab** and navigate to Solution **Settings > Application Metering > Application Metering Solution Configuration Policy**.

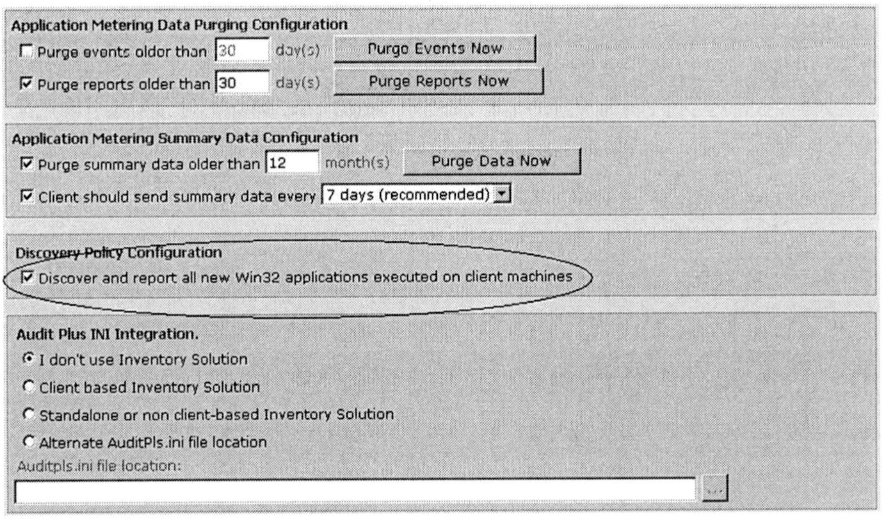

Enable/Disable Application Discovery.

Click **Apply**.

The next time machines in the target collection(s) update their configuration they will start Win32 Application Discovery.

This policy setting applies to all managed clients running the Application Metering Agent.

Application Monitoring

As the name implies, Monitoring is used to monitor not just discover what applications are in use. Application Monitors can be configured to be much more granular than Win32 Discovery as they allow you to monitor specific application usage as well as report Start, Stop and Denial Events to the Notification Server. Unlike Application Discovery, Monitoring can be targeted at specific collections of managed clients.

The Application Metering Solution installation creates predefined monitoring policies for many commonly used applications. If you want to monitor an application that has a predefined monitor, simply enable the policy. If you want to monitor an application that does not have a predefined monitor then you must create a Monitor for that application.

Viewing Application Monitors

From the Web Console select the **Tasks tab** and navigate to **Software Management > Application Metering**.

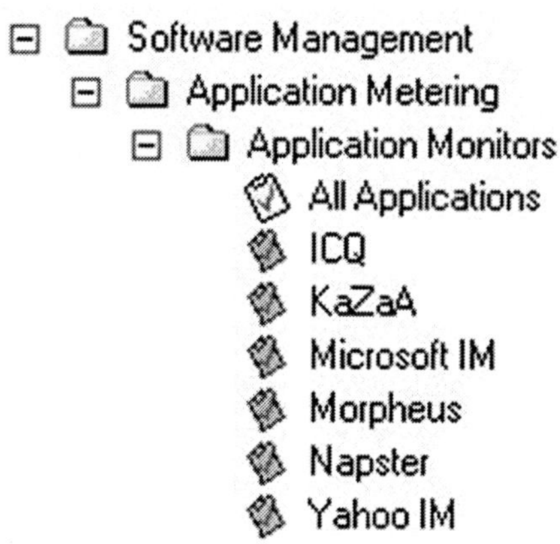

Select an application monitor such as 'Napster' in the Treeview pane. And view the details of the monitor in the details pane.

Configuring an existing Application Monitor

From the web console select the Tasks tab and navigate to **Software Management** > **Application Metering Solution** and then the folder name and the policy you want to configure.

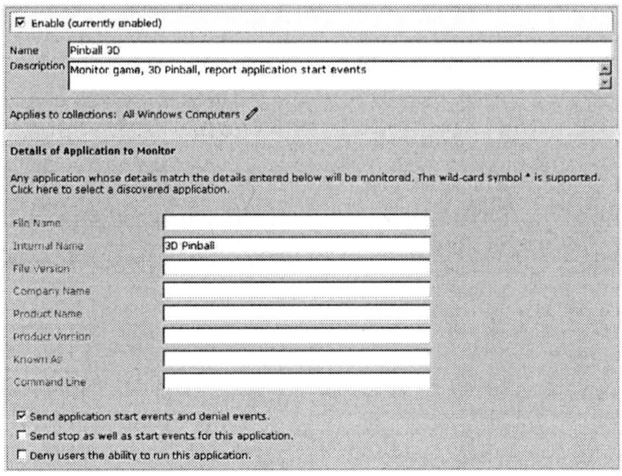

Applies to collection – Defines the collection(s) of managed clients that will monitor the defined application.

Details of Application to monitor – This section allows you to specify the details of the application(s) to monitor. You can enter the specific details for the application, such as the file name or the internal name. Wildcards (% and *) can also be used.

Send application Start and Denial events – If enabled, this option **immediately** sends a Start event to the Notification Server when the application is started. Enabling this option will also send a Denial event immediately to the Notification Server if the monitor has been configured for Denial.

Send Stop as well as Start events for this application – This option is only selectable if the previous (Start/Denial) option is checked. This option will send Stop events **immediately** to the Notification Server when an application is closed. Using Start and Stop events will allow you to see how long an application was run for.

Deny users the ability to run this application – Enabling this option will expand the dialog to show 'Denial Message Options' and 'Denial Time Options'. Enabling the 'Deny' option will prevent users from running that application on the target machine at the specified time. Denial is on a per application basis, it does not matter what user is logged or what privileges they have.

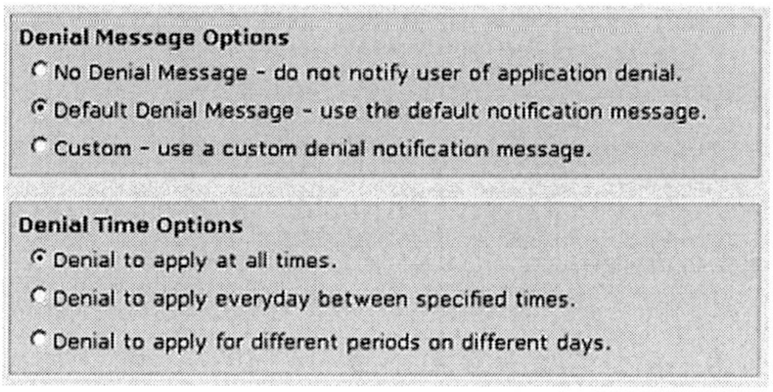

The Denial Message Options section allows you to configure what message, if any, appears when a user tries to run a denied application.
The Denial Time Options section allows you to configure when an application can not be run on a machine.

Once all desired options have been configured, **enable** the policy and click **Apply**. The next time machines in the targeted collection request a configuration update, an updated client policy, detailing the application to monitor, will be downloaded and applied to the client. The client will then monitor the application based on the configured policy.

Creating a new Application Monitor

From the Web Console select the Tasks tab and navigate to **Software Management > Application Metering Solution** and then a folder of your choice.

Right click the folder name and choose **New > Application Monitor Policy**.

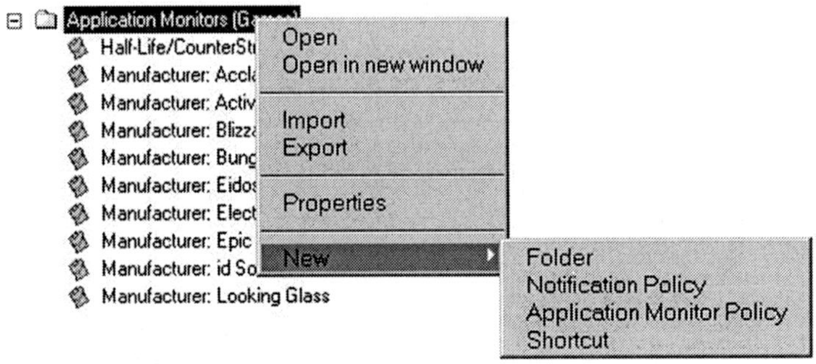

Enter a name and description for the new monitor.

Use the Applies to Collection link to select the target collection(s).

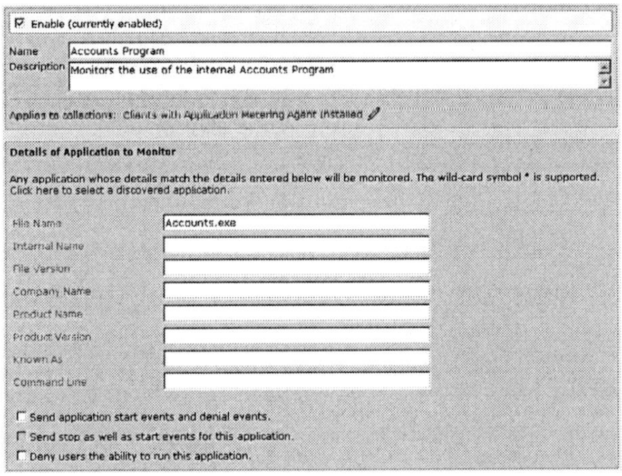

Enter the criteria for the application such as file name and or internal name. The more specific you are, the less likely it will be that you will monitor applications other than the application you want to monitor. See the previous page for detail on the available configuration options.

Configure Start, Stop and Denial Events.

Enable the Policy and click **Apply**.

The next time machines in the targeted collection request a configuration update, a new client policy, detailing the application to monitor, will be downloaded and applied to the client. The client will then begin to monitor the application specified.

Viewing Application Monitoring Data

Application monitoring data can be viewed using the built-in reports provided with Application Metering Solution.

In the Web Console select the Reports tab and navigate to **Software Management > Application Metering**.

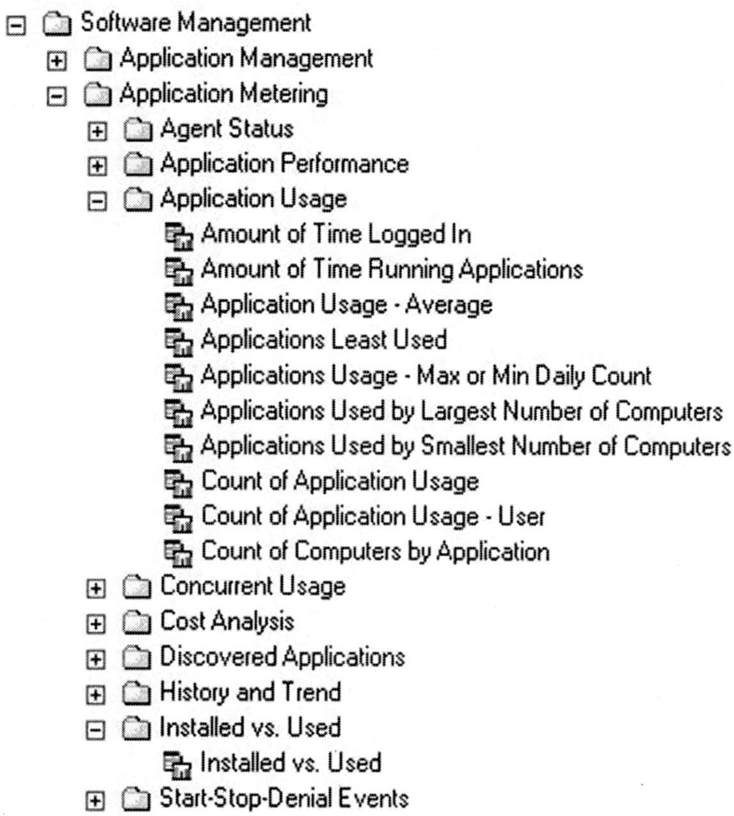

Navigate to the **Application Usage** folder and select an appropriate report.

Removing Application Metering Solution

If you do not intend using Application Metering Solution anymore, use the 'Win32 Application Metering Agent Uninstall' Policy to remove the agent from all managed clients (See below).
Wait until the clients have uninstalled the Application Metering agent, then use **Add/Remove Programs** in Control Panel on the Notification Server to remove the Solution.

Uninstalling the Agent

From the Altiris Web Console select the Configuration Tab and navigate to **Solution Settings > Application Metering > Application Metering Agent Rollout**. Select the policy 'Win32 Application Metering Agent Uninstall'.

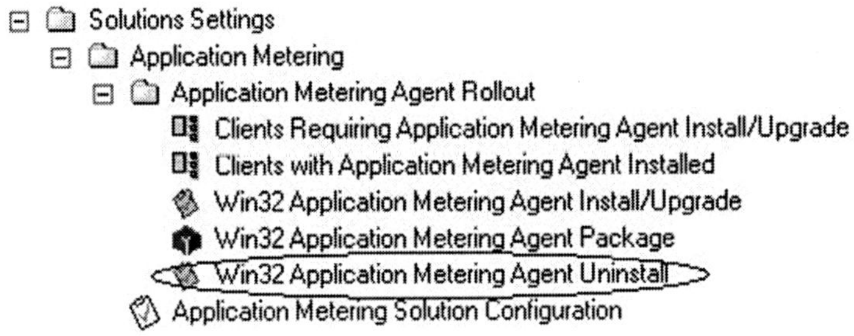

Use the **'applies to collection'** hyperlink to configure the collection(s) that will uninstall the agent. The default collection is, 'Clients with the Application Metering Agent installed'.
Configure the scheduling options as required.
Enable the policy and click **Apply**.

The next time machines in the target collection(s) update their configuration they will uninstall the agent based on the policy schedule.

Useful Application Metering Reports

To view the following reports open the Web Console, select the Reports Tab then navigate to **Software Management > Application Metering folder**.

Application Metering Agent Not Reporting Data

This report details any machine not sending data to the Notification Server. This is useful when identifying machines with metering agent or communication issues.

Application Metering Agent Rollout Status

This report details the Application Metering Agent installation status. Enable status events on the install policy to receive status data.

Count of Computers by Application

This report details a list of monitored applications that have been run, along with the number of computers that run the application.

License Comparison (Used vs. Installed vs. # Licenses)

This report displays the number of machines with installed products compared to the number of machines that use the products. Inventory Solution is required to provide the number of products installed data.

Count of Computers by Discovered Applications

This report displays the number of computers upon which a discovered application was run.

Installed vs. Used

This report details all of the applications discovered in the enterprise. Filters can be applied to show how many of the discovered applications have been used.

Summary

This chapter looked at installing and configuring Application Metering Solution for Windows.

Managed clients run the Application Metering Agent and can be configured to use Application Monitors and or Win32 Discovery to report what applications are used by a user. Win32 discovery will report all Win32 applications that are first run on a managed client running the Metering Agent. Application monitoring policies report start, stop and denial events for a specific application.

The next chapter 'Carbon Copy Solution' looks at using Carbon Copy to remotely control and manage remote clients.

14

Carbon Copy Solution

Introduction

Carbon Copy is primarily a web based remote control tool but also includes the ability to transfer files, initiate a chat session, remotely print and access a remote clipboard.

Features

- Built-in security allowing you to control who can remote control clients.
- Transfer files between a local and remote computer.
- Multiple configuration policies can be created to configure different collections of machines with different Carbon Copy configurations.
- Remote chat (Voice and Text).
- Remote clipboard allows you to cut/copy and paste between a local and a remote clipboard.
- Remote printer allows you to locally print documents from a remote computer.
- Remote control allows you to fully remote control a Windows 98 or above remote client.

Ports used by Carbon Copy

Carbon Copy uses TCP port 1680 and UDP ports 1680 - 1701.
To change port assignments use the Carbon Copy configuration file CCWin32.ini.

Installing Carbon Copy Solution

From the Configuration Tab in the Web Console select **Install/Upgrade Solutions**.
Click the **Solutions** buttons.
Select the Carbon Copy Solution for Windows link.
Click **Start** and follow the on screen prompts.

Once installed, apply your full license. Solutions come with a built-in 7 day license. 30 day evaluation licenses can be downloaded from the Altiris web site.

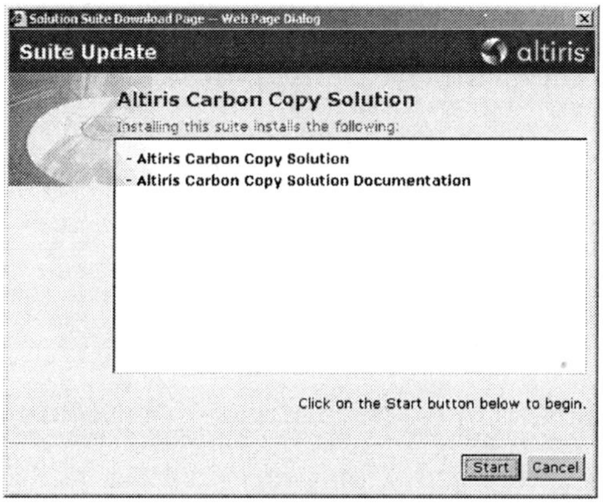

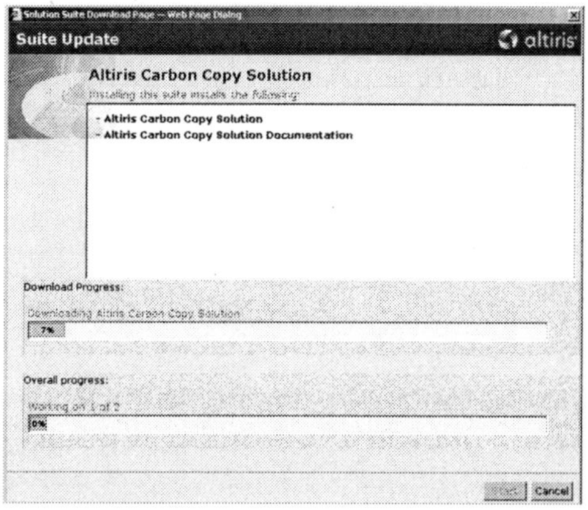

Components added to the Web Console

Getting Started Tab – The Carbon Copy Solution installation does not add to the Getting Started tab at this time.
Tasks Tab – Under the Incident Resolution folder in the Task Tab two new folders are added, Carbon Copy and Tools. The Carbon Copy folder contains two Notification policies, one policy creates a daily Carbon Copy usage report and the other creates a helpdesk work item on a weekly basis that identifies machines without login security. The Tools folder contains a link to remote control a client using Carbon Copy.
Resources Tab – The Carbon Copy Solution installation does not add to the Resources tab at this time.
Reporting Tab – Approximately 14 Carbon Copy status and summary reports are added.
Configuration Tab – A new folder in the path Solution *Settings\Incident Management\Carbon Copy* is created. This folder contains Agent rollout, upgrade and configuration policies and packages for the Carbon Copy Agent.
Shortcuts Tab – No shortcuts are added automatically by the Carbon Copy Solution installation.

Deploying Carbon Copy Agent

To remote control a client, the client must have the Carbon Copy Agent installed. There are two policies to rollout the Carbon Copy agent, they are, **Reboot** and **No Reboot**. The 'Reboot' policy will reboot the client after installation, the 'No Reboot' will not, funnily enough.

In practice it is best to rollout the agent with the 'No reboot' Policy and wait for the user to manually reboot the machine.

Select the Configuration Tab in the Web Console and navigate to **Solution Settings > Incident and Management > Carbon Copy > Carbon Copy Agent Rollout**.

Select the appropriate policy. (No Reboot should definitely be used for servers.)

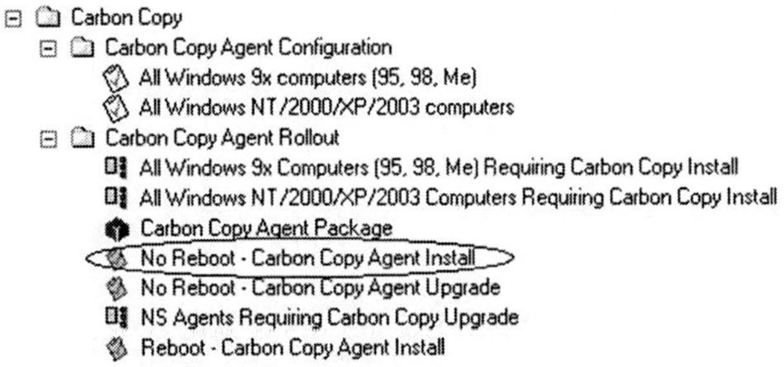

Select the target collection(s) and set the schedule for installation of the agent. Enable **Status Events** if required then enable the Policy and click **Apply**.

The next time machines in the targeted collection(s) update their configuration they will download and install the Carbon Copy Agent based on the configured rollout policy schedule.

Staggering the agent rollout

The agent installation can be staggered across an enterprise by targeting the install policy (Reboot or No Reboot) at a specific collection of machines and not 'All machines requiring the agent'. Location specific collections can be used to control this type of rollout.

Configuring the Carbon Copy Agent

There are two policies used to configure the Carbon Copy Agent. One policy is for Windows 9.x machines and the other for Windows NT/W2K/XP machines. Both policies are located in the **Configuration Tab > Solution Settings > Incident Management > Carbon Copy > Carbon Copy Agent Configuration**.

Both policies can be cloned to provide the ability to have multiple configuration policies for managed machines. Using multiple configuration policies is discussed later in this chapter.

Configuring the Carbon Copy Agent for Windows NT type machines

From the Web Console go to the Configuration Tab and navigate to **Solution Settings > Incident Management > Carbon Copy > Carbon Copy Agent Configuration**. Select the policy 'All Windows NT/W2K/XP computers'.

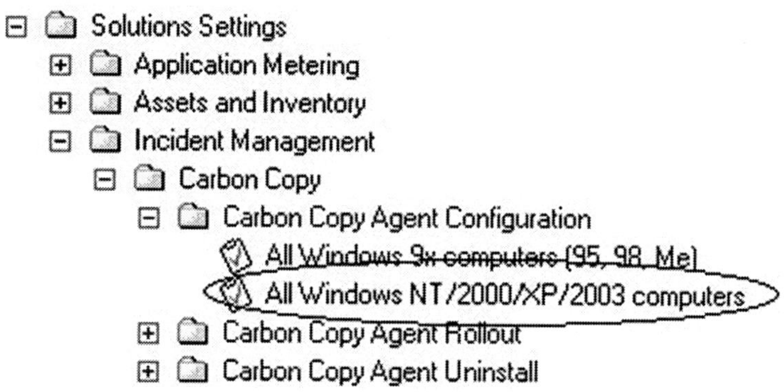

This configuration policy has the tabs, General, Authentication and Advanced Settings and is detailed in the following pages.

General Tab

Enabled check box – To enable or disable the policy. Only enable the policy when you have finished configuration in all three tabs. Leave the policy enabled even after all clients have received their Carbon Copy configuration. Leaving the policy enabled ensures that any new clients get the appropriate configuration.
Applies to collection – The group(s) of machines that will be targeted with these Carbon Copy settings.

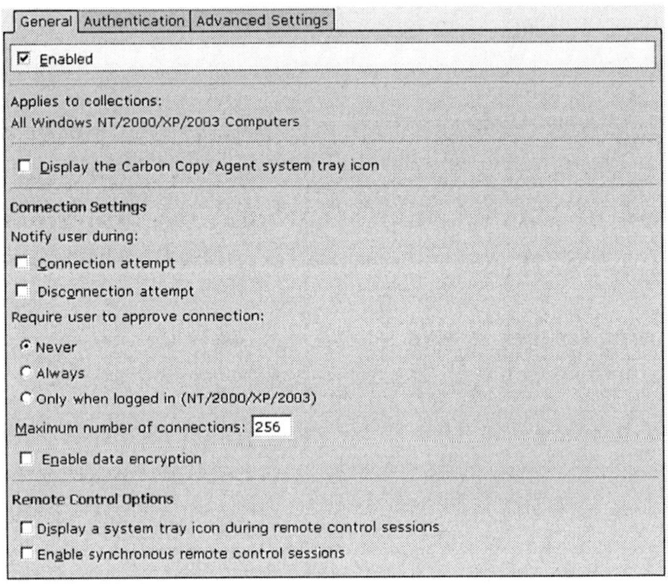

Display the CC Agent on system tray – A yes/no option which configures whether to show a Carbon Copy icon on the system tray. My advice is 'No' as users won't mess if they don't know it's there.

Connection Settings Section

Notify user during:
Connection attempt – I would advise you to set this to 'Yes' so that users are made aware that someone is trying to remote control their machine. (Good Politics too!)
Disconnection attempt - I would advise you to set this to 'Yes' so that users know when the remote control session is over.
Require user to approve connection: Never, Always, Only when logged in. – Set this to 'Only when logged in' for the most politically friendly option. Administrators can only remote control when the user is not logged on, or when the user is logged on and allows the connection.

Maximum no of connections – Handy if you want up to 256 remote connections to a single machine!
Enable data encryption – Set this to 'Yes' to ensure that data is encrypted between the console and the remote machine.

Remote Control Options Section

Display a system tray icon during remote control sessions – This displays a remote control icon on the user's system tray once the remote control connection is established and authenticated.
Enable synchronous remote control sessions – There are two modes of display, synchronous and asynchronous. Asynchronous mode is now the default in Carbon Copy 6.x. Asynchronous is not real time, meaning that what the administrator is seeing in the remote control window is not exactly what's on the users local screen (But close enough for troubleshooting). With Synchronous mode set to 'on', the remote and local user screen show exactly the same in real time but the overall operation is slower, particularly on the user's machine.

Authentication Tab

The Authentication Tab includes configuration settings that determine whether a login name and password are required to remote control a machine. For NT type machines a local or AD group can be used to allow remote control. The most secure method of login is to use Active Directory Groups. With AD Groups, an Administrator or helpdesk person can simply be added to a group with the right to remote control machines.

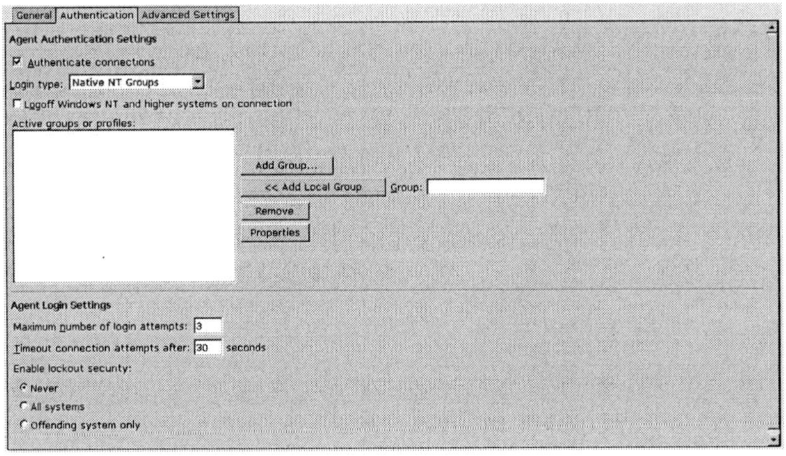

Agent Authentication Settings Section

Authenticate connections – When the Authenticate connections option is checked, a login credential is required to remote control a remote computer.

Login type choices are Native NT Groups, AD Groups or Carbon Copy Profiles – Native NT Groups are generally used configure Carbon Copy Agent settings in a non Active Directory Domain or Workgroup environment. AD Groups are used in an Active Directory environment and Carbon Copy Profiles are generally used in a Windows 9.x environment.

Logoff Windows NT and higher systems on connection – On a Windows NT/W2K/XP type machine if this option is set to 'Yes', when a remote control session is started with a client, the currently logged on user is automatically logged off. *(Users love that one!)* This option does not affect Windows 9.x clients.

Active Groups or Profiles Section

This section allows you to add the groups and profiles that will be given the right to perform actions such as remote control. The available options will change depending on the **Login Type** chosen.

In a typical environment, a group for remote control is created in Active Directory. Users that are permitted to perform remote control are added to the group. The group is then given permission to remote control by adding it as an authorized group within the authentication tab of the configuration policy.

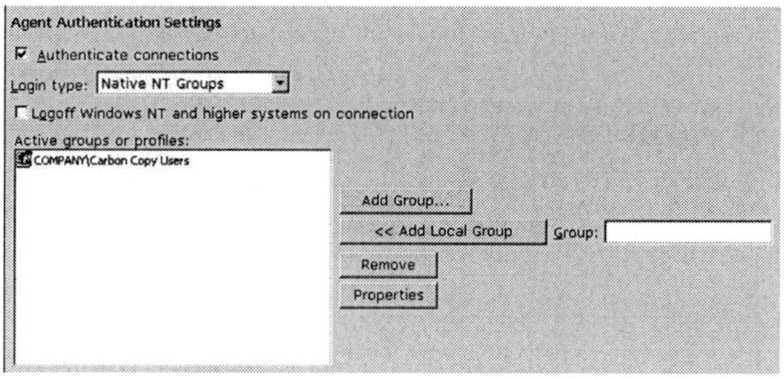

Add Group Button – Allows you to add AD groups. The user establishing the connection must be a member of the AD group.

Add Local Group Button – Type a local group name in the **Group** box then click the **Add Local Group** button. The group specified must be a local group on the machine that you are connecting too. The person establishing the connection must be a member of the local group.

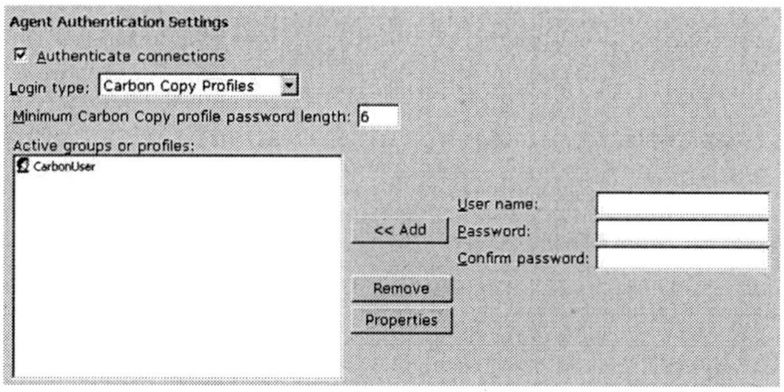

User Name and Password Buttons – Only appear if the login type is Carbon Copy Profiles. Profiles are typically used for Windows 9.x machines. The name and password supplied must be known by the user attempting to establish the remote connection.

Remove Button – Allows you to remove a group listed.

Properties Button – Select a listed group and click properties to configure which tools the members of the selected group can use. Security can be applied at a tool level.

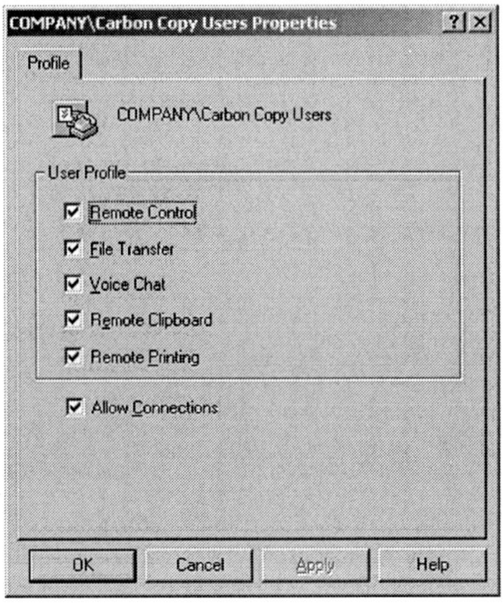

Agent Login Settings Section

Maximum number of login attempts – The maximum number of times a login can be tried to remote control a machine.

Timeout connection attempts after (30 sec) – The maximum number of seconds a login can be tried to remote control a machine.

Enable lockout security – The choices are, Never; All systems and Offending system only - If the maximum number of login attempts or the timeout connection attempts after is reached or exceeded, do you want to disable Carbon Copy logins for all systems, the offending system or Never disable Carbon Copy logins.

I generally use either Never or the Offending System only. Using the All Systems option means that if a helpdesk worker or Administrator exceeds the password or time threshold then all remote control logins are disabled.

Advanced Settings Tab

The Advanced Settings Tab includes configuration settings that allow an Administrator to protect the Carbon Copy user interface on the client, as well as add specific Carbon Copy agent settings at a granular level.

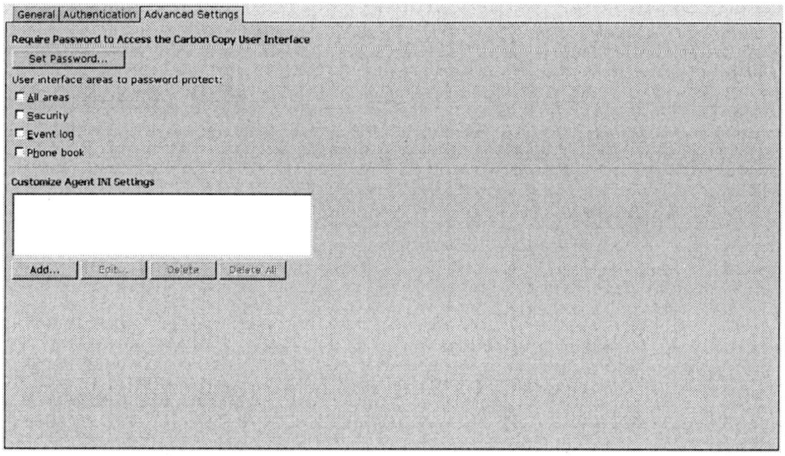

Require password to access the Carbon Copy User Interface – Allows the option to protect the Carbon Copy client interface on the client using a password. The entire interface can require a password or just certain areas of the interface.

User interface areas to password protect – Allows selected areas of the Carbon Copy user interface to be protected. Hiding the Carbon Copy icon will prevent users from accessing the interface. The following checkboxes can be used to set interface security on certain areas.

All areas –	Requires a password to access all areas of the agent interface.
Security –	Requires a password to access the Security section of the interface.
Event log –	Requires a password to access the Event Log section of the interface.
Phone book –	Requires a password to access the Phone Book section of the interface.

Customize Agent ini settings Section

This section allows an Administrator to add Carbon Copy client settings that are not available through the normal agent configuration in the Web Console.

To change the TCP port used by the Carbon Copy Agent

In the Advanced Settings tab of the Carbon Copy configuration policy click the Add button in the Customize Agent INI settings section. Enter the following:

Section	Carbon Copy
Key	TCP_PORT
Value	A value between 1024 and 65535.

Click **OK.**

Repeat the previous steps to add other values.

Check the Altiris support site for more information on the available options.

Completing the agent configuration

Once you have selected your configuration choices, return to the General Tab and **enable the policy** then click **Apply**.

The next time machines in the targeted collection(s) update their configuration they will download and apply the new Carbon Copy Agent configuration.

Using multiple configuration policies

Using multiple configuration policies is useful when you want different machine collections to have different Carbon Copy configurations. In previous versions of Carbon Copy, all machines shared the same configuration policy.
In the current release, the default configuration policies can be cloned, renamed and configured to target a specific collection of machines.

From the Web Console go to the Configuration Tab and navigate to **Solution Settings > Incident Management > Carbon Copy > Carbon Copy Agent Configuration**.
Right click the 'All Windows NT/W2K/XP machines' policy and choose **Clone** from the shortcut menu.
Give the cloned copy a new name such as 'Carbon Copy configuration for Servers'.
Configure the policy to target machines in a specific collection.
Configure all other available options and click **Apply**.

Repeat the above steps for each policy you want to configure. Ensure that machines are not targeted by more than one policy.

Using Remote Control

Remote control of a client is initiated using the Altiris Web Console.

Select the Tasks Tab in the Web Console and navigate to **Incident and Resolution > Tools > Remotely Control with Carbon Copy**.

Enter the name of the machine to remote control or use the 'Click to Select' to select the machine from the list of available machines.

Click the **Connect** button. 

Enter an authorized name and password if requested.

(Another way to start a remote session, is to right click a computer and choose 'Remotely Control with Carbon Copy' from the shortcut menu.)

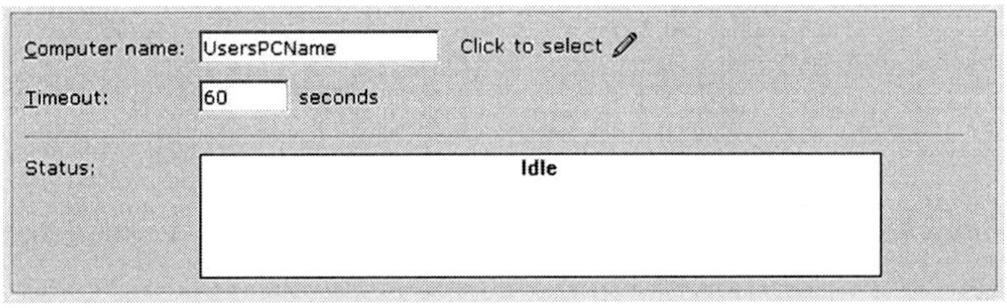

Once connected, a remote control window is opened. The window includes several buttons which allow you to manage and configure the remote control session. The buttons are detailed as follows:

 Exit the Carbon Copy session

 Full Screen view

 Windowed View

 Stretch to Window

 Send CTRL + Alt + DEL keys

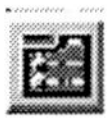 Remote Control Option Page

 Synchronous Display

 Asynchronous Display

 Reboot remote machine

Carbon Copy Utilities

Carbon Copy Solution Web-hosted Console utilities are launched from the console. When you launch the console, the Carbon Copy Solution utilities are downloaded to your computer. The utilities and any configuration changes will remain locally until the console is purged from its temporary location.

To use any of the Carbon Copy utilities, the Advanced Console must be displayed and a connection must be made to a client running the Carbon Copy Agent. Once connected, the Advanced Carbon Copy connection console activates the buttons below.

Display the Basic Console.

Display the Advanced Console.

Disconnect from a remote machine.

Connect to a remote machine.

Remote control the connected machine.

File Transfer allows you to drag and drop files between local and remote machines connected through a Carbon Copy session.

Remote Clipboard allows the local and the remote machines to share a common clipboard.

Voice Chat lets you communicate using voice or text. Multiple connections to a chat session are allowed.

Remote printing allows you to print to a printer connected to a remote machine through a Carbon Copy session.

File Transfer

The file transfer is similar to Microsoft's File Explorer. When File Transfer is launched, a split window will display the local and remote drive content. This window can be used to perform similar tasks to that performed in Explorer, such as copying, renaming and deleting files. Drag and drop or menus can be used to accomplish most file maintenance tasks.

Use the File Transfer icon  to start a file transfer session with a connected user.

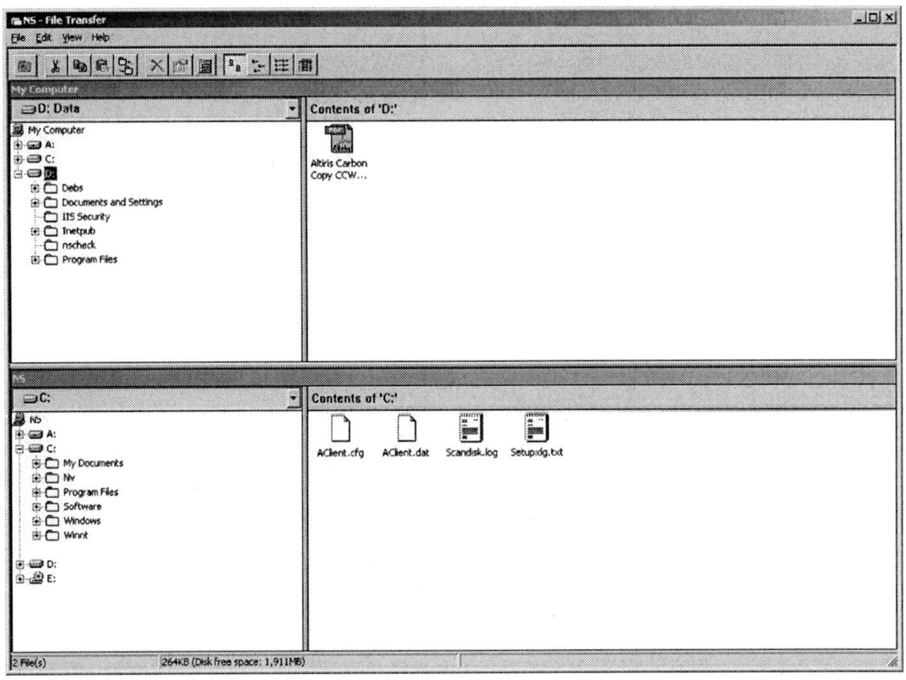

Configuring Carbon Copy File Transfer

The Options command in the View menu of the File Transfer window allows you to configure file transfer options.

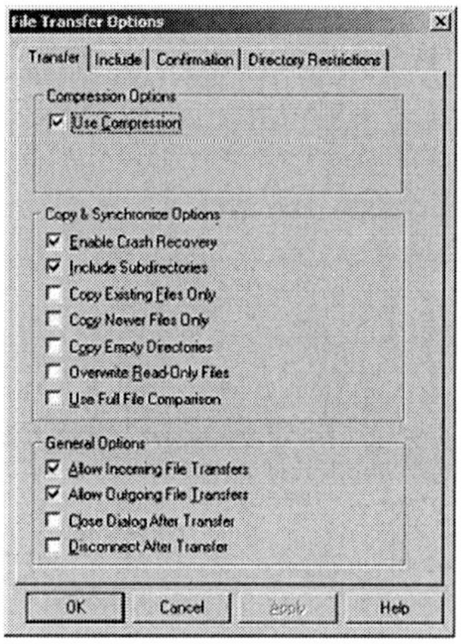

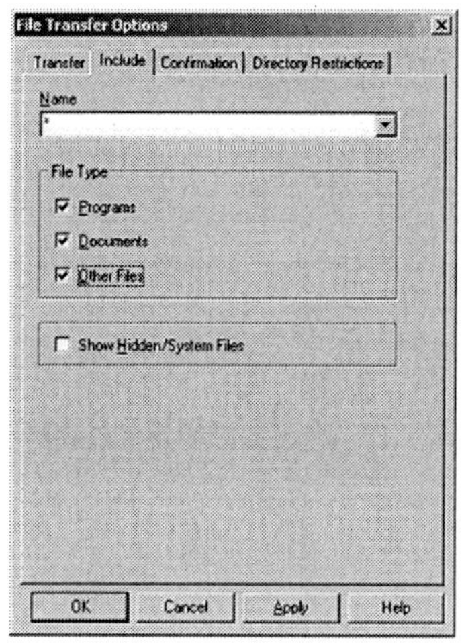

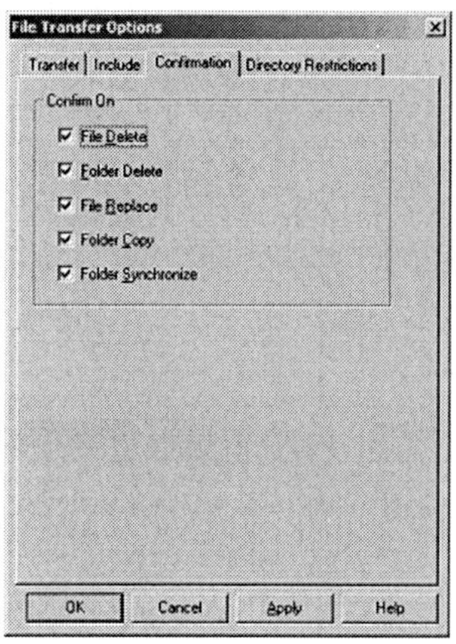

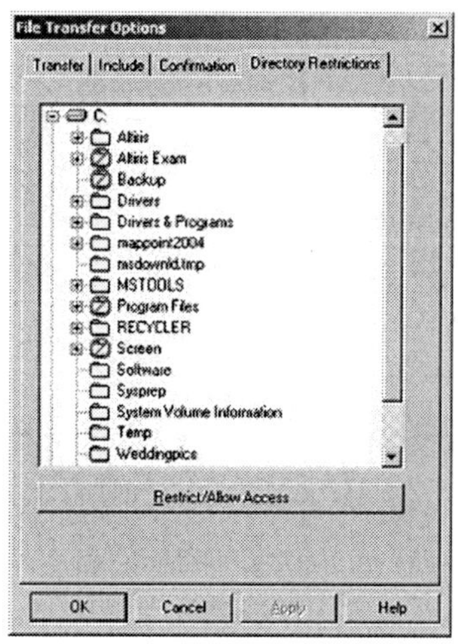

The options included are displayed above and include the ability to control what files are seen in the window and if any restrictions apply.

Voice Chat

Carbon Copy Voice Chat is used to allow people to chat over a Carbon Copy connection. A sound card, speakers and a microphone are required on each machine for successful voice chat. If a computer is not correctly equipped with the necessary hardware, Voice Chat defaults to Text Chat.

Use the Chat icon to initiate a chat session with a connected user. 

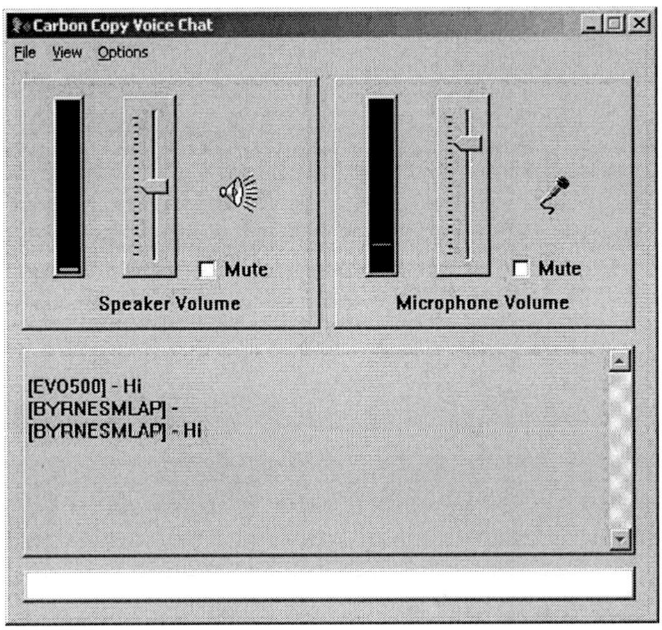

The dialog shows speaker and microphone controls as well as the text chat box.

Remote Clipboard

Remote Clipboard allows the local and the remote machines to share a common clipboard. Nothing needs to be configured for remote clipboard to work. Once remote clipboard is active on all connected machines, a clipboard is shared. If a user on a remote machine copies text or graphics, it is copied to the shared clipboard and can be pasted locally by all other connected machines.

Using Remote Clipboard

Start a Carbon Copy client connection.

Use the Remote clipboard icon  to start sharing a clipboard with the remote machine.

A minimized button for remote clipboard appears on the Taskbar of each connected machine.

From the Web Console highlight some text or graphic and use the 'CRTL + C' to copy the selected text or graphic to the shared clipboard.

Instruct the user to open a new document and press 'CTRL + V' or Edit > Paste. This will paste what you copied to a document in the remote machine.

Using Remote Printing

Remote Printing allows the Carbon Copy Console to locally print documents from a client computer.

Configuring Remote Printing

Before Remote Printing can be used, a new Carbon Copy printer must be created on the managed client, this can be done either locally or through a remote control session.

From the client machine select Printers from the **Windows Start > Settings menu**.

Click **Add Printer**.

Select Local Printer and click **'Next'**. (Uncheck the 'Automatically detect and install my plug and play printer')

Select the Carbon Copy Printer Port and click **Next**.

Select the console's printer manufacturer and model. Click **Next**. (The driver must match the default printer on the Notification Server)

Type in a printer name and click **Next**.

If you are using NT/2000 or XP, you will be prompted to share the printer. Click **Not Shared** and then click **Next**.

Do not print a test page click **Next** then **Finish**.

Using Remote Printing

Start a Carbon Copy client connection. Once connected, use the Remote Printer icon to activate remote printing. 

You can now remotely print documents from the client computer.

Removing Carbon Copy Solution

If you do not intend using Carbon Copy Solution anymore, use the 'No Reboot - Carbon Copy Agent Uninstall' policy to remove the agent from all managed clients (See below).
Wait until all clients have uninstalled the Carbon Copy agent and then use **Add/Remove Programs** in Control Panel on the Notification Server to remove Carbon Copy Solution.

Uninstalling the Carbon Copy Agent

Uninstalling the Agent is required if you want to remove the CC agent from a machine or a collection of machines.
Select the Configuration Tab in the Web Console and navigate to **Solution Settings > Incident and Management > Carbon Copy > Carbon Copy Agent Uninstall**.
Select the 'No Reboot - Carbon Copy Agent Uninstall' Policy.

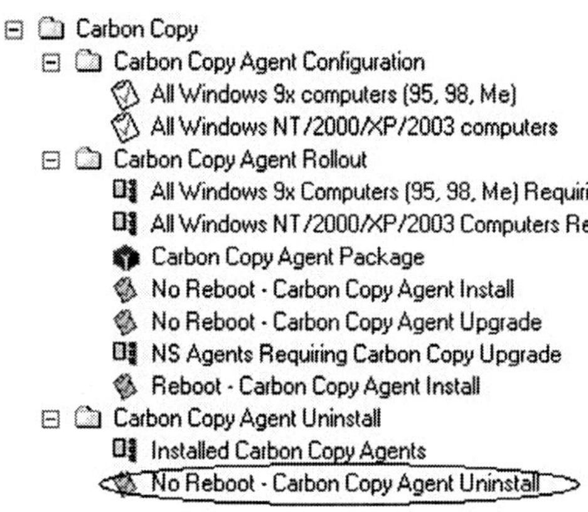

The default target collection is 'Installed Carbon Copy Agents'.
Enable status events if required. Enabling status events for this policy will allow you to report on which machines successfully or unsuccessfully executed the policy to remove the agent. Status events for this policy will generate network traffic of approximately 2-12 KB per client.
Set the scheduling options and **enable** the policy.
Click **Apply**.

The next time machines in the targeted collection update their configuration they will uninstall the Carbon Copy Agent based on the configured schedule.

Useful Carbon Copy Reports

To view the following reports open the Web Console, select the Reports Tab then navigate to **Incident Management** > **Carbon Copy folder**.

Carbon Copy Agents by Operating System

This report displays a graph of machines with the Carbon Copy agent installed by operating system.

Carbon Copy Agents by Version

This report displays a list of machines with the Carbon Copy agent installed as well as operating system information and agent version.

Carbon Copy Events by Computer

This report displays a list of events reported by the Carbon Copy agent over the last 'N' days.

Carbon Copy Session Activity in the Last 'N' Days

This report displays a list of connection and remote tool activity over the last 'N' days.

Summary

This chapter looked at installing and configuring Carbon Copy Solution.
Carbon Copy Solution provides the ability to remote control as well as transfer files, remotely print and remotely chat with a remote machine. All machines that will be remote controlled must have the Carbon Copy Agent which is installed and configured using policies on the Notification Server.

In the next chapter 'Patch Management' we will look at managing Microsoft operating system and application patch deployment.

15

Patch Management Solution

Introduction

Altiris Patch Management Solution provides the ability to scan computers for security vulnerabilities, report on the findings and distribute Microsoft security patches. This chapter will guide you through the installation, configuration and use of this solution.

Features

- Patch Management no longer relies on MBSA for patch management. An Agent reports patch, applications, OS and service pack levels to the Notification Server.
- Once a bulletin is enabled, the patches for that bulletin are automatically downloaded.
- Reporting has been improved.
- Patch Management Solution provides support for English, French, German, Japanese, and Spanish software updates.
- Overall manageability and ease of use have been improved.

An Overview of Patching

The process of evaluating and deploying patches using Altiris PM is relatively straight forward. The basic steps are:

1. Client reports patch inventory

Clients run the Software Update Agent and the Inventory Rule Agent. The Inventory Agent is an agent specific to Patch Management and is not related to the Inventory Agent for Windows agent. The Inventory agent scans the client periodically for patch specific information and sends it to the Notification Server. This information is used by Patch Management Solution to create specific Patch Management collections when a related software bulletin is enabled.

2. Software bulletin information is downloaded from Altiris

Software bulletin information is downloaded from the Altiris Web site at the time of installation and thereafter on a recurring schedule. The bulletin information includes patch details, severity rating, rules for collection creation and the download location for the patch on the Microsoft website.

3. The Patch Management Administrator enables a bulletin

Using the Web Console, an administrator enables one or more bulletins. Patches associated with each bulletin are downloaded from the Microsoft website and placed in the configured Downloads folder on the Notification Server.

5. The Patch Management Administrator deploys the patch

When all of the patches for an enabled bulletin have been downloaded, the Administrator can then create a Software Update task for each software bulletin to deploy. Patch Management Solution then creates a Software Update package for each software update and associates one or more programs with the package.

6. Client checks and installs updates

When the client receives the Software Update task, the Software Update Agent first checks that the software update is required, then if required, downloads the Software Update package and launches the required program to install the software update. Periodically the Software Update task is re-evaluated to ensure that the patch is still installed and if needed, the software updates are reinstalled.

Installing Patch Management Solution

In the Web Console select the Configuration tab and navigate to **Install/Upgrade Additional Solutions**.

Click the **Solutions** button in the Available Solutions tab and select the Patch Management Solution link. Click **Start** and follow the on screen prompts.

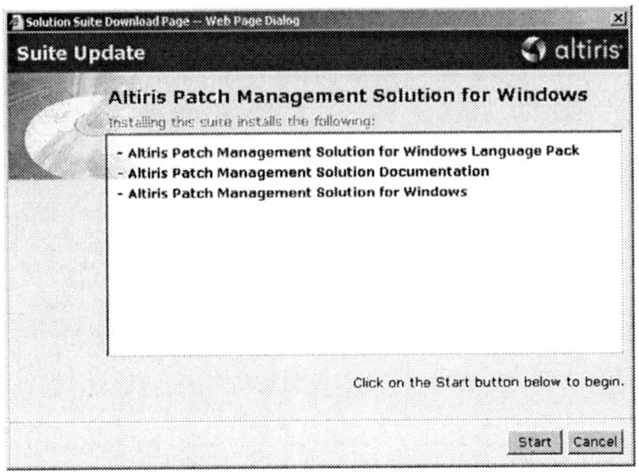

Once installed, apply your full license. Solutions come with a built-in trial license. 30 day licenses can be downloaded from the Altiris web site.

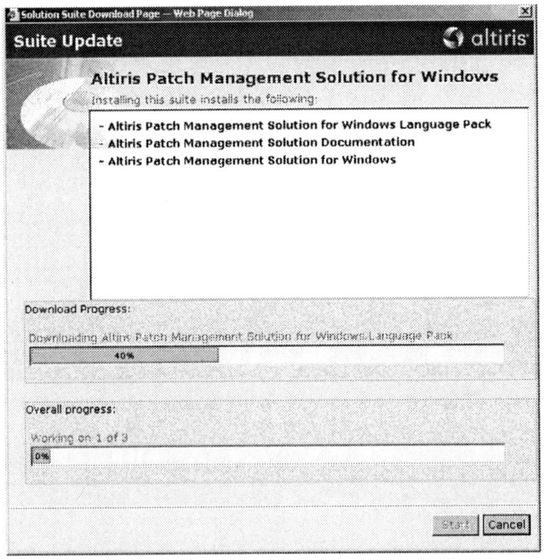

Note PM should not be installed through a Terminal Server or remote session.

Components added to the web console

The following components are added to the Notification Server Web Console by the Patch Management Solution installation.

Tasks Tab – Tasks to allow you to display, enable and disable software bulletins as well as view and create software deployment Tasks.

Resources Tab – Numerous collections are created by the Patch Management installation.

Reports Tab – A Patch Management Dashboard and over 30 Patch Management reports.

Configuration Tab – A Patch Management folder under *Solution Settings > Software Management* containing options to configure core Patch Management settings, Inventory schedules as well as Software Update Agent install/uninstall and configuration policies. Under the Solution Settings folder an Inventory Rule Management folder is also added.

Using Patch Management with a Proxy Server

Background tasks are used by Patch Management Solution to perform actions such as downloading patches. If a Proxy Server sits between the Notification Server and the Internet then the Notification Server must be configured with credentials to access the Proxy.
In Notification Server SP2 (6.0.5287) a proxy configuration page is provided to configure proxy settings. See the chapter 'Configuring Notification Server' for more details.

Patch Management Folder Structure

When Patch Management Solution is installed, a Patch Management folder structure is created under the Altiris Notification Server install path. The structure includes:

Downloads folder

Contains the Microsoft bulletin definition file, PMImport.cab, downloaded from the Altiris website. Any updated versions of PMImport.cab will be downloaded to this folder.

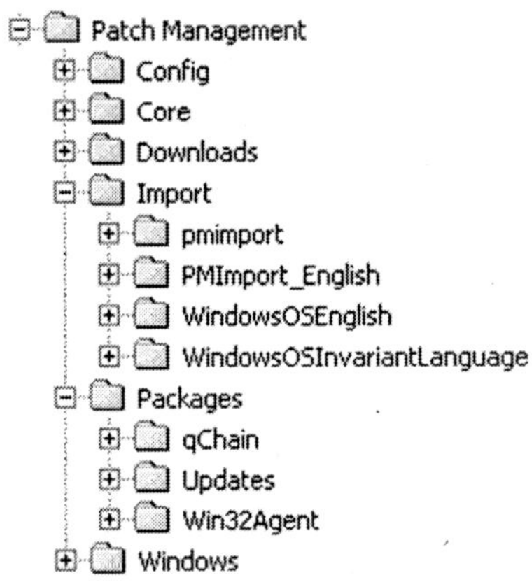

If Patch Management is configured to use multiple languages, one PMImport_Language.cab will be downloaded for each language selected.

Import folder

After the PMImport file is downloaded to the Downloads folder, the xml bulletins within the file are extracted to the Imports folder. The import process then takes these files and imports them in to the NS database.

Qchain & Win32 Agent folders

The Qchain folder contains the application QChain.exe, used to install multiple patches and suppress reboots. The Win32 Agent folder contains the Patch Management Agent.

Updates folder

When a bulletin is enabled through the console, the patches for the bulletin are downloaded from the Microsoft web site and placed in the updates folder. A separate folder is created for each bulletin and patch.

Configuring Patch Management Solution

Configuration is divided into two sections, Server configuration and Client configuration. In this section we will look at configuring the server components.

Configuring the Server components

Step 1 – Configure Patch Management Core Solution Settings

These settings are Global and apply to all machines regardless of platform. Patch Management Solution supports English, French, German, Japanese, and Spanish software updates. The settings in this dialog allow you to select the languages that Patch Management can manage.

From the web console select the **Configuration Tab** and navigate to **Solution Settings > Software Management > Patch Management > Server Settings > Global Settings > Patch Management Core Configuration**.

The default is that Patch Management will download only English patches and not exclude patches for any applications.

The *Locale Selection Option* section lets you configure which languages will be managed by Patch Management. If *Manage all software management resources* is selected or additional languages are added, then the patches for that language will be downloaded when the Download Software Update Packages Policy runs.

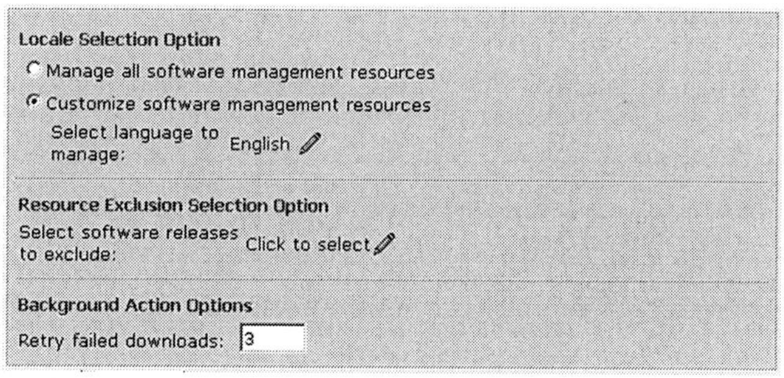

The Resource Exclusion Selection Option allows you to exclude software updates by excluding software releases that are not relevant to your organization. For example if you don't use Microsoft FrontPage then don't include patches for that product.

The last option, Background Action Options lets you configure how many times the software update download process will retry when attempting to download.

When all options have been configured, click **Apply**.

Step 2 – Configure Download Software Update Packages

This step is used to configure where patches will be stored on the Notification Server. The settings are Global and apply to all machines regardless of platform.

From the Web console select the **Configuration Tab** and navigate to **Solution Settings > Software Management > Patch Management > Server Settings > Global Settings > Download Software Update Packages**.

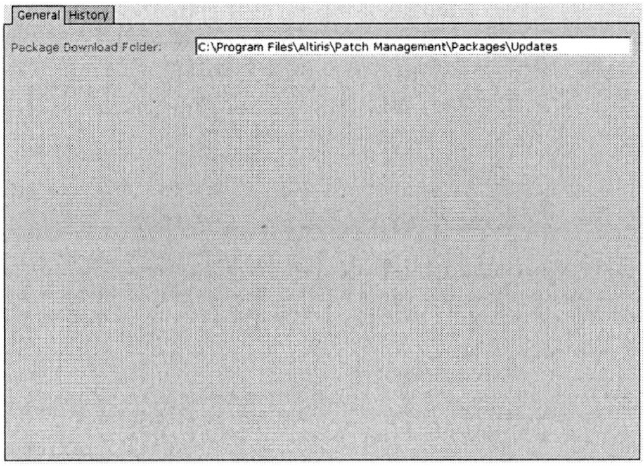

Enter the name of the folder where downloaded patches will be saved on the Notification Server or leave the default path. Ensure that you have enough space for current and future packages.

For troubleshooting purposes use the History tab to view the download history.

Step 3 – Configure Download Qchain

Qchain is used when installing multiple patches.

From the Web console select the **Configuration Tab** and navigate to **Solution Settings > Software Management > Patch Management > Server Settings > Microsoft Settings > Download Qchain**.
Enable the schedule and click **Apply**.

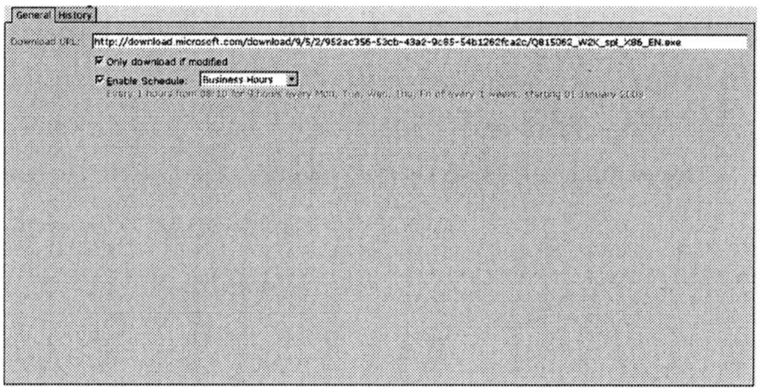

The policy will download the Qchain.exe file to a folder named Qchain in the Patch Management > Packages folder structure on the Notification Server. The policy will also download a patch named Q815062_W2K_spl_X86_EN.exe to the 'Downloads' folder. This patch fixes some Qchain issues when rolling out older patches.

Step 4 – Configure Import Microsoft Software Management Resources

This policy performs three tasks:-

- Downloads updated versions of the PMImport.cab file from an Altiris website.
- Extracts the bulletins from downloaded PMImport.cab file and populates the Import folder under the Patch Management folder structure on the Notification Server.
- Imports the extracted bulletins in the Import folder to the Notification Server database.

From the web console select the **Configuration Tab** and navigate to **Solution Settings > Software Management > Patch Management > Server Settings > Microsoft Settings > Import Microsoft Software Management Resources**.

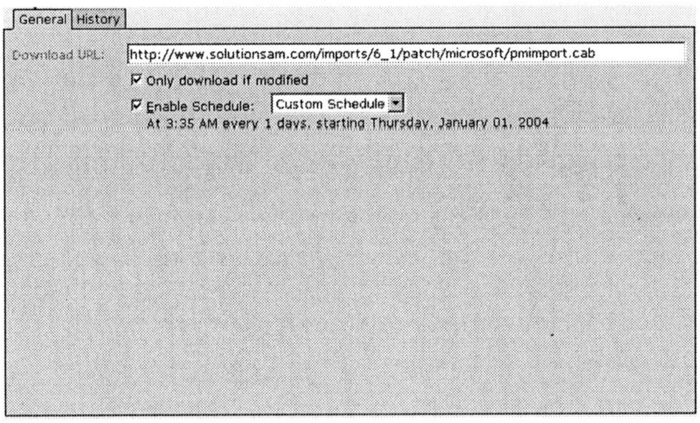

When Patch Management is first installed the Import policy is automatically launched and begins the process of downloading the PMImport.cab file.
The default schedule will check for updates to the cab file(s) at 2:20 am every day. Configure the schedule if required.

Starting the Import immediately

To configure the policy to begin the download immediately, **right click** the **Import Microsoft Software Management Resources** policy in the treeview pane and from the shortcut menu choose the command **Start Task**.

Once the schedule has run, an updated PMImport.cab (if available) is downloaded to the 'Downloads' folder under the Patch Management folder structure. The xml bulletins are then extracted from the cab file and copied to the 'Import' folder under the Patch Management folder structure.
Once the Import folder has been populated, the bulletins are imported in to the Notification Server database. The import can take up to 30 minutes to complete.

When the import has finished, the bulletins can be viewed in the Tasks tab of the Web Console.

Viewing imported bulletins

From the **Web Console** navigate to the **Tasks Tab** then **Software Management > Patch Management > Manage Software Updates**.

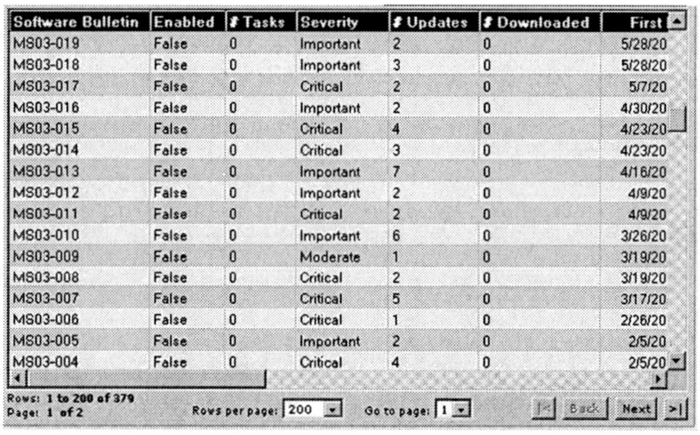

Software Bulletin	Enabled	# Tasks	Severity	# Updates	# Downloaded	First
MS03-019	False	0	Important	2	0	5/28/20
MS03-018	False	0	Important	3	0	5/28/20
MS03-017	False	0	Critical	2	0	5/7/20
MS03-016	False	0	Important	2	0	4/30/20
MS03-015	False	0	Critical	4	0	4/23/20
MS03-014	False	0	Critical	3	0	4/23/20
MS03-013	False	0	Important	7	0	4/16/20
MS03-012	False	0	Important	2	0	4/9/20
MS03-011	False	0	Critical	2	0	4/9/20
MS03-010	False	0	Important	6	0	3/26/20
MS03-009	False	0	Moderate	1	0	3/19/20
MS03-008	False	0	Critical	2	0	3/19/20
MS03-007	False	0	Critical	5	0	3/17/20
MS03-006	False	0	Critical	1	0	2/26/20
MS03-005	False	0	Important	2	0	2/5/20
MS03-004	False	0	Critical	4	0	2/5/20

Rows: 1 to 200 of 379
Page: 1 of 2
Rows per page: 200
Go to page: 1
Back Next

Note If no bulletins appear in this list, use the history tab on the 'Configure Import Microsoft Software Management Resources' policy and the NS event logs to troubleshoot.

Step 5 – Configure the Microsoft Settings Policy

This policy is used to configure some of the default settings in the 'Distribute Software Update Wizard'. The policy is also used to configure Microsoft Update distribution.

From the Web console select the **Configuration Tab** and navigate to **Solution Settings > Software Management > Patch Management > Server Settings > Microsoft Settings > Microsoft**.

There are three tabs; General, Package Server and Advanced.

The *General* tab provides an option to configure the default target collection displayed in the first step of the Distribute software Update Wizard.

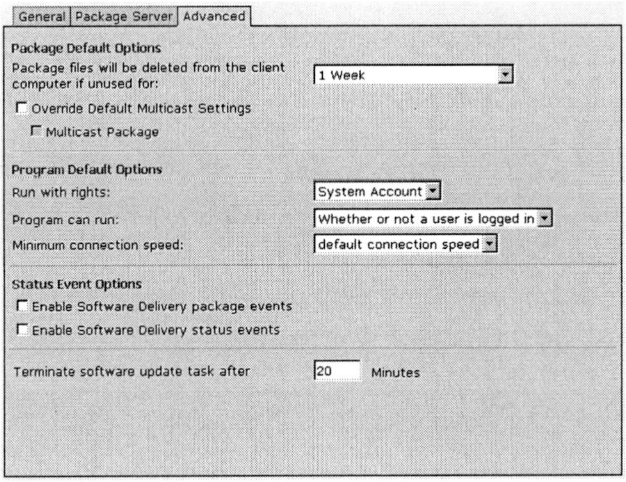

The *Package* Server tab provides options to override the default package server replication settings. These options are the same as normal package server replication options, which you should already be familiar with.

The *Advanced* tab provides options to configure Package Defaults, Program Defaults and Status Events.

When all available options have been configured, click **Apply**. Then right click the Policy name in the tree view pane and click **Enable** from the shortcut menu.

Final Server Configuration Check

The content of the folder structure should now be populated with the files necessary to use Patch Management.

Downloads Folder

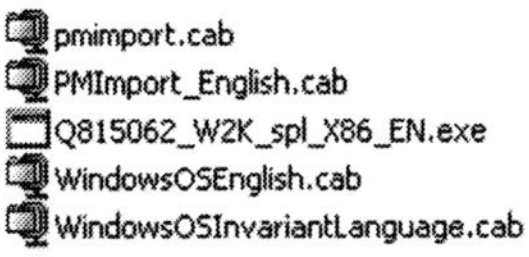

PMimport Folder

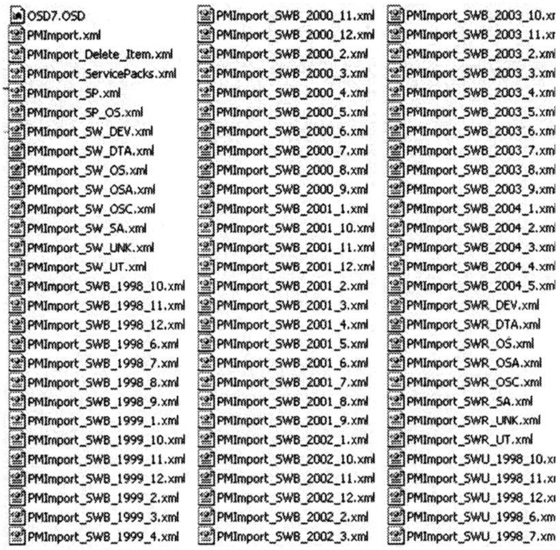

Import Folder

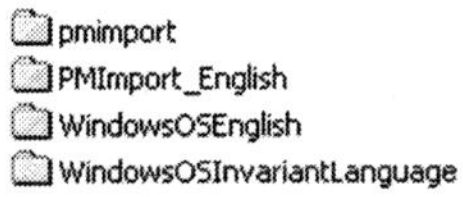

Qchain Folder

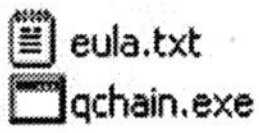

Now that the Server Background actions have been configured, the client configuration can begin.

Configuring the Client components

Configuring the client components of Patch Management Solution includes:

- Configuring the Patch Management Software Inventory scan policies.
- Configuring the Software Update Agent configuration policies.

Step 1 – Configuring the Patch Management Software Inventory scan policies

For a client to be successfully managed by Patch Management it must have the Software Update Agent and the Inventory Rule Agent. The Inventory Agent, which is not related to the Inventory Agent for Windows Agent, is used to report Operating System, MSI application, Installed applications and Software Update installation data to the Notification Server. This data is then used by Notification Server to determine which clients need specific updates and patches. There are four Inventory scan policies used to configure the Inventory Rule Agent.

To configure the Inventory Rule Agent, open the Web Console select the Configuration tab and navigate to **Solution Settings > Software Management > Patch Management > Windows > Software Inventory**.

Default Windows OS Inventory Policy

This first policy is a Global policy (Not platform specific) used to configure the Inventory Rule Agent to gather Inventory data on the operating system version. The data is then used to determine what OS components are required to be installed before installing software updates

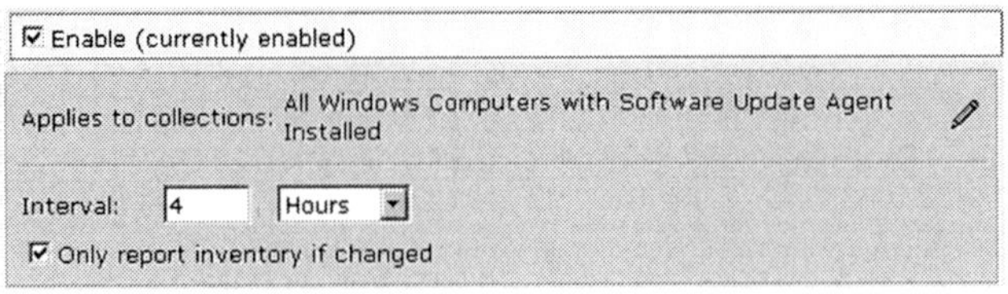

Default Windows Software Release Inventory Policy

This policy is also a Global policy and is used to configure the Inventory Rule Agent to gather Inventory data on the operating system software release and service pack level. The data is then used to determine which software updates need to be installed

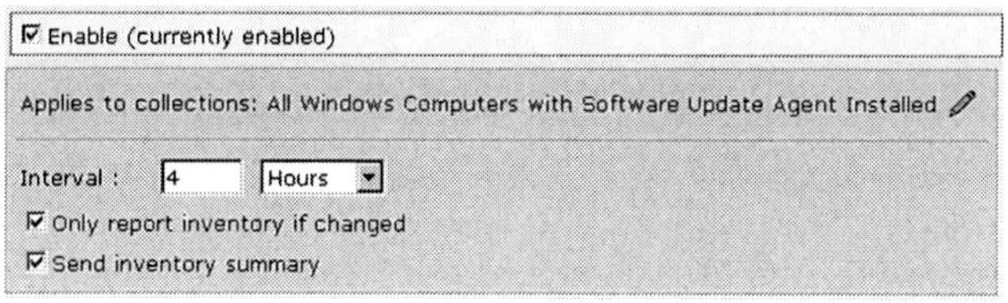

Default Microsoft Software Inventory Policy

This policy applies only to the Microsoft platform and is used to configure the Inventory Rule Agent to gather Inventory data on the installed applications found on the client machine. The data is used by the Notification Server to create application specific collections.

Microsoft Vulnerability Analysis Policy

This policy applies only to the Microsoft platform and is used to configure the Inventory Rule Agent to gather Inventory data on which software updates have already been installed on the Altiris-enabled computer. This data helps you determine which software updates need to be installed on the computer.

By default all Inventory Agent policies run every 4 hours.
Configure each of the Inventory policies as appropriate then click **Apply** to save any changes.

Step 2 – Configuring the Software Update Agent configuration policies

These policies are used to configure how the Software Update Agent runs on the client. There are three configuration policies. Each policy has the same configuration settings but targets different OS type and Service Pack levels. The policies are:

- Windows Computers (NT 4 & Pre Windows 2000 SP2) with Software Update Agent.
- All Windows Computers (Post Windows 2000 SP2) with Software Update Agent.
- All Windows Computers (Windows 95, 98 & ME) with Software Update Agent.

There is a Pre and a Post SP2 policy because Pre SP2 Windows systems may replace newer files when a patch is applied, Post SP2 Windows systems will not allow newer files to be replaced when a patch is applied.

From the Web Console select the Configuration Tab and navigate to **Solution Settings** > **Software Management** > **Patch Management** > **Windows** > **Software Update Agent Configuration** > **Microsoft**.

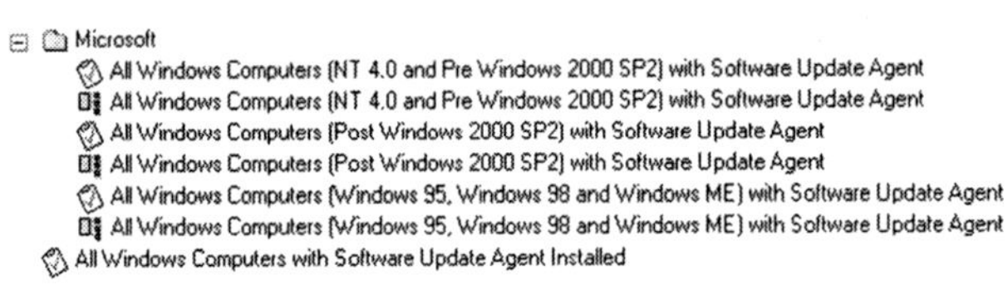

Select one of the three configuration policies.

The details of the policy are displayed in the details pane.

The policy has a **General** tab allowing you to configure the target collection and whether to reapply patches by default.

Configure as appropriate and click **Apply**.

Step 3 – Configuring the Software Update Agent Settings

The Software Update Agent Settings Policy provides options to configure how often updates are installed as well as reboot and notification configuration for all clients.

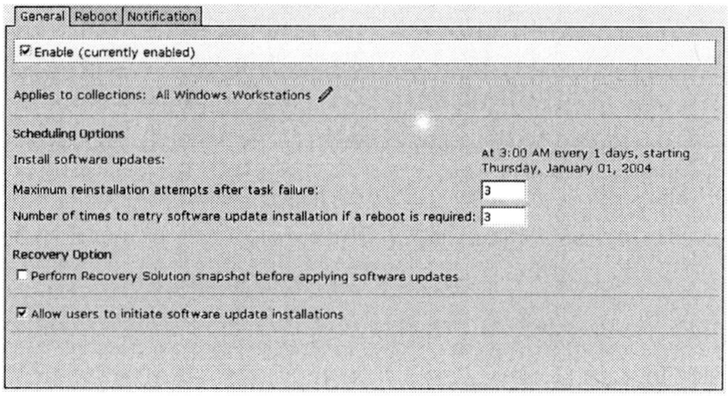

The General Tab

Options in the *General* tab provide the ability to configure:

Applies to collection - The target collection(s) for the policy
Install software updates - The patch installation schedule.
Maximum reinstallation attempts - Default is to try up to three times to install an update where the task has failed.
Number of times to retry a software update installation if a reboot is required - A patch requiring a reboot is not considered installed until a reboot has occurred. The Update Agent will install this type of patch up to three times.
Perform Recovery Solution snapshot before applying software updates - If Recovery Solution is installed and the client is running the Recovery Agent, a snapshot can be performed prior to installing patches.
Allow users to initiate software update installations - Allows users to manually start the installation of an update.

The Reboot Tab

Options in the *Reboot* tab provide the ability to configure the default reboot options and the default notification configuration.

If a patch installation requires a reboot after the patch has been installed, options in this policy allow you to configure whether the system will; Not reboot, Reboot automatically or Reboot on a predefined schedule.

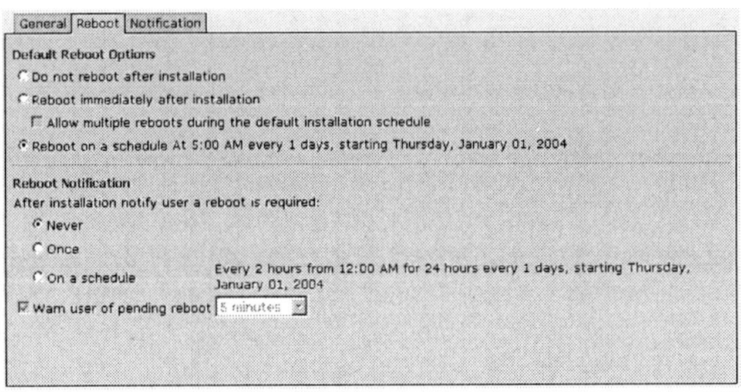

The Reboot Notification section in this tab is used to configure whether the user will be notified that their system requires a reboot; Never, Once or on a predefined schedule. The user can also be notified X minutes before the system actually reboots.

The Notification Tab

Options in the *Notification* tab provide the ability to configure the notifications, if any, users receive prior to installing a patch.

Notify in advance - Notifies the user that a patch will be installed in X minutes.
Show the Software Update Monitor progress dialog - Displays a progress dialog when the patch is installing.
User can defer reboot - Allows the user to defer a reboot for X minutes.
Custom Notification Messages - Can be used to customize reboot and update message for the user.

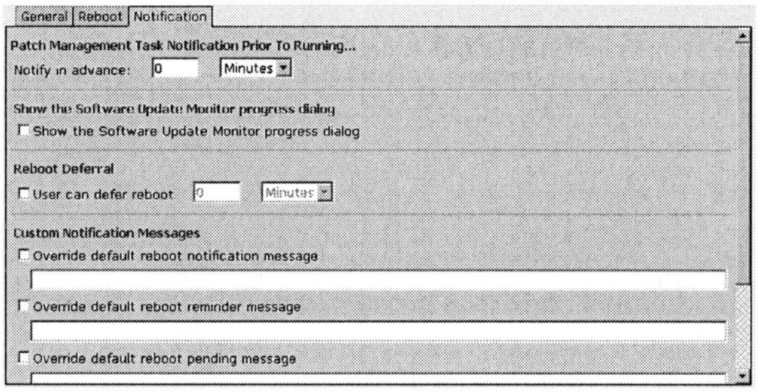

When all options have been configured, click **Apply** to save the changes to the Patch Management Agent settings Policy. The client components are now configured.

Deploying the Software Update Agent

The Agent is rolled out using the Software Update Agent Install policy. The installation will install the Software Update Agent, Package Agent and the Inventory Rule Agent.
From the Web Console select the Configuration tab and navigate to **Solution Settings > Software Management > Patch Management > Windows > Software Update Agent Rollout > Software Update Agent Install**.

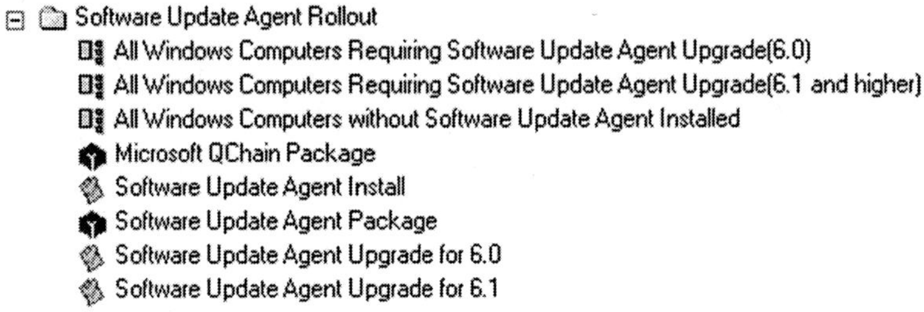

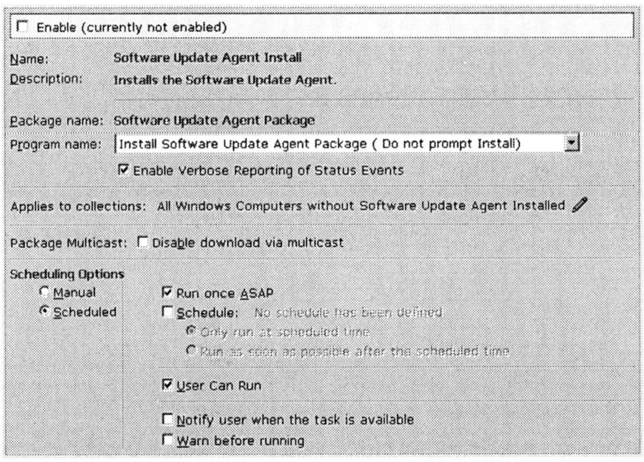

Use the policy to configure when the client should install the Software Update Agent. Once configured, **Enable** the policy and click **Apply**.

The next time clients in the targeted collection update their configuration they will see the policy and install the Update Agent and the Inventory Rule Agent based on the schedule.

Vulnerability Analysis

The Default Microsoft Vulnerability Analysis Policy is used to report missing patches on clients. Once this policy has run at least once you can view the list of missing patches for clients.

From the Web Console select the **Tasks tab** and navigate to **Software Management > Patch Management > Manage Software Updates**.

The default view will show all Bulletins imported from PMImport.cab. This is the list of all security bulletins from that have been released by Microsoft since 1998.
In the **Show** drop-down choose **Detected Microsoft Vulnerabilities by Computer**.

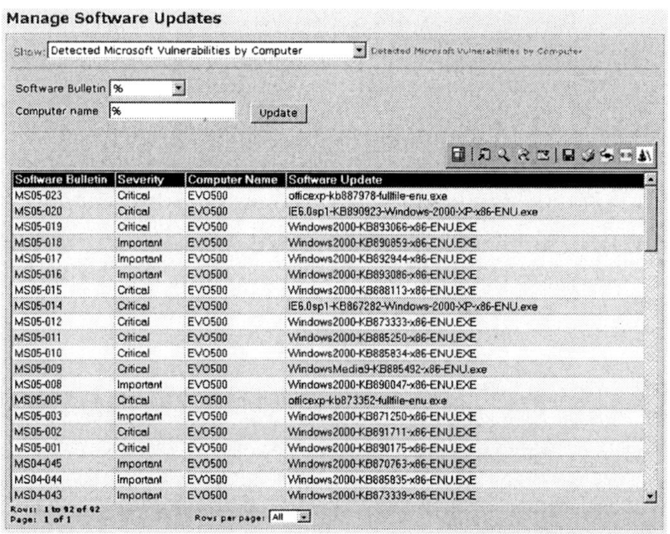

Software Bulletin	Severity	Computer Name	Software Update
MS05-023	Critical	EVO500	officexp-kb887978-fullfile-enu.exe
MS05-020	Critical	EVO500	IE6.0sp1-KB890923-Windows-2000-XP-x86-ENU.exe
MS05-019	Critical	EVO500	Windows2000-KB893066-x86-ENU.EXE
MS05-018	Important	EVO500	Windows2000-KB890859-x86-ENU.EXE
MS05-017	Important	EVO500	Windows2000-KB892944-x86-ENU.EXE
MS05-016	Important	EVO500	Windows2000-KB893086-x86-ENU.EXE
MS05-015	Critical	EVO500	Windows2000-KB888113-x86-ENU.EXE
MS05-014	Critical	EVO500	IE6.0sp1-KB867282-Windows-2000-XP-x86-ENU.exe
MS05-012	Critical	EVO500	Windows2000-KB873333-x86-ENU.EXE
MS05-011	Critical	EVO500	Windows2000-KB885250-x86-ENU.EXE
MS05-010	Critical	EVO500	Windows2000-KB885834-x86-ENU.EXE
MS05-009	Critical	EVO500	WindowsMedia9-KB885492-x86-ENU.exe
MS05-008	Important	EVO500	Windows2000-KB890047-x86-ENU.EXE
MS05-005	Critical	EVO500	officexp-kb873352-fullfile-enu.exe
MS05-003	Important	EVO500	Windows2000-KB871250-x86-ENU.EXE
MS05-002	Critical	EVO500	Windows2000-KB891711-x86-ENU.EXE
MS05-001	Critical	EVO500	Windows2000-KB890175-x86-ENU.EXE
MS04-045	Important	EVO500	Windows2000-KB870763-x86-ENU.EXE
MS04-044	Important	EVO500	Windows2000-KB885835-x86-ENU.EXE
MS04-043	Important	EVO500	Windows2000-KB873339-x86-ENU.EXE

The Default Microsoft Vulnerability Analysis Policy must have run on at least one computer for any vulnerabilities to be displayed.

Downloading Patches

Before a patch can be deployed it must be first downloaded to the Notification Server. Most bulletins include patches for a different variety and service pack level of operating system. Enabling a bulletin will automatically download all patches for the bulletin into the Updates folder on the Notification Server.

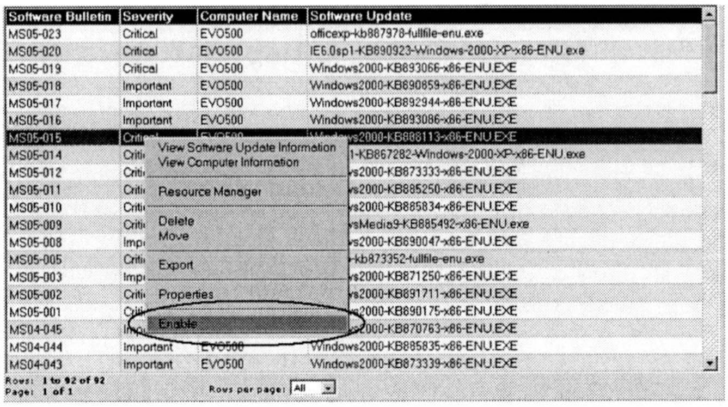

In the All Software Bulletins list enable each bulletin by right clicking one bulletin at a time and choosing **Enable** from the shortcut menu or select multiple bulletins and use the **Enable** button on the patch toolbar.

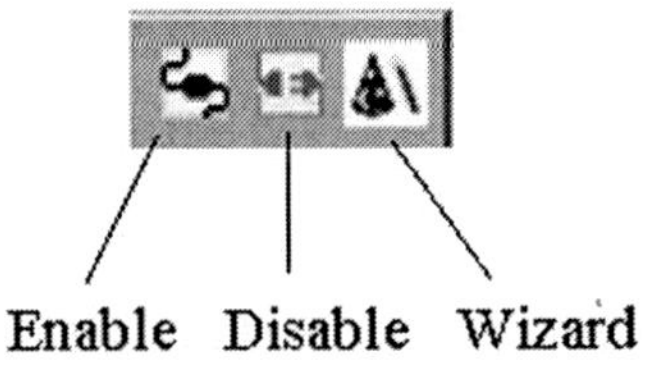

In the background, Patch Management will download the patches for each enabled bulletin to the Updates folder.

Allow some time for the patches to download and check the Updates folder on the Notification Server to see the patches arrive.

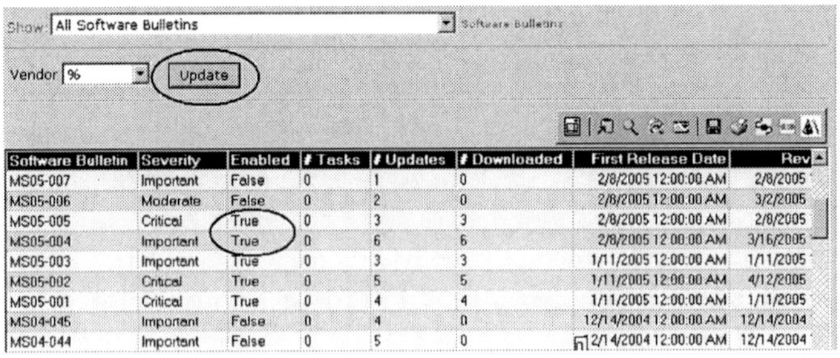

Use the **Update** button to refresh the enabled status of the bulletin.

As patches are downloaded each associated update is saved to a sub-folder of the bulletin folder.

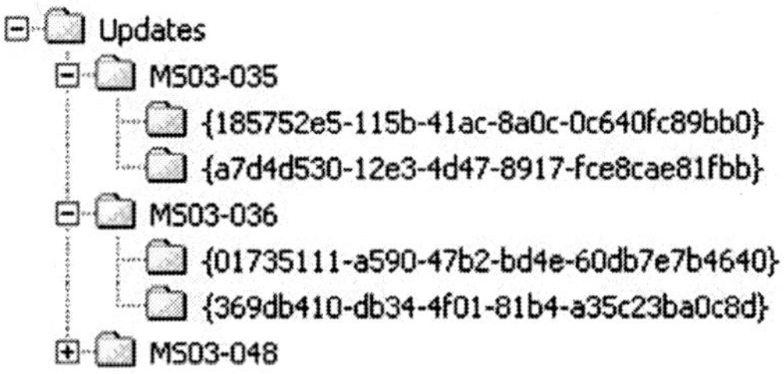

While patches are being downloaded, change the Show dropdown on the bulletin page to **All Software Bulletins**.

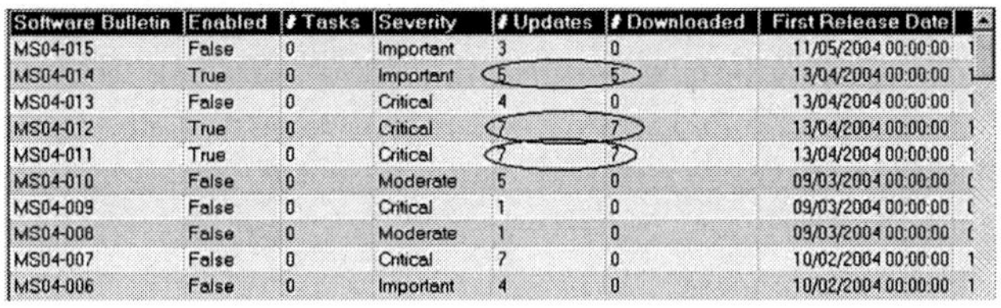

Software Bulletin	Enabled	# Tasks	Severity	# Updates	# Downloaded	First Release Date
MS04-015	False	0	Important	3	0	11/05/2004 00:00:00
MS04-014	True	0	Important	5	5	13/04/2004 00:00:00
MS04-013	False	0	Critical	4	0	13/04/2004 00:00:00
MS04-012	True	0	Critical	7	7	13/04/2004 00:00:00
MS04-011	True	0	Critical	7	7	13/04/2004 00:00:00
MS04-010	False	0	Moderate	5	0	09/03/2004 00:00:00
MS04-009	False	0	Critical	1	0	09/03/2004 00:00:00
MS04-008	False	0	Moderate	1	0	09/03/2004 00:00:00
MS04-007	False	0	Critical	7	0	10/02/2004 00:00:00
MS04-006	False	0	Important	4	0	10/02/2004 00:00:00

When the **Updates** and the **Downloaded** numbers are equal, the download is complete. Use the **Update** button to refresh the status.

The client and server portions of Patch Management configuration are now complete.

Deploying Patches

Once the chosen bulletin(s) has been enabled and the associated patches have been downloaded, the patch can be deployed.

Step 1 – Starting the Wizard

The Software Update Task is used to advertise the bulletin and associated patches to managed clients. Wait until all updates for a bulletin show as downloaded. **Right click** the enabled bulletin and choose **Distribute Software Updates**.

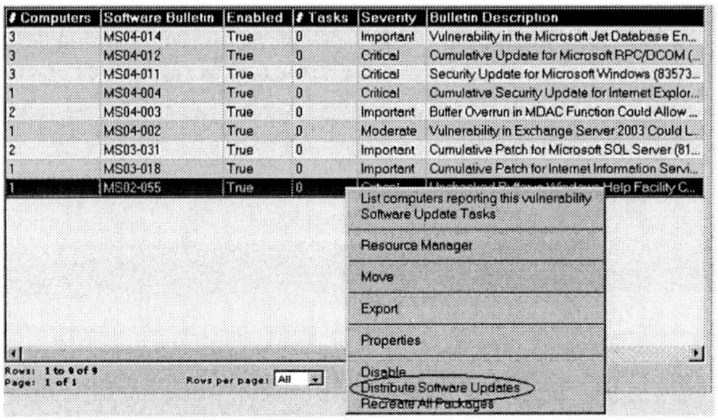

The Distribution Software Update Wizard is launched. The first step is primarily used to enable the task and configure the target collection.

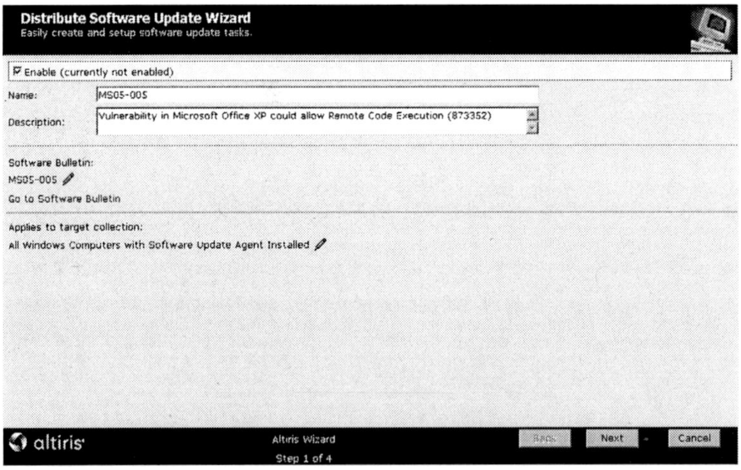

Check the Software Update Task name and description and double check that the Bulletin name is correct. Everything else in this dialog should be OK.

Click **Next** to continue.

Step 2 – Configure the Reboot and download options

The second step in the wizard allows you to configure when the patch is installed, the reboot options and multicast options. All of these settings apart from the multicast option are taken from the Patch Management Agent Settings Policy in the Configuration tab. You can use these default settings of override the settings for this patch.

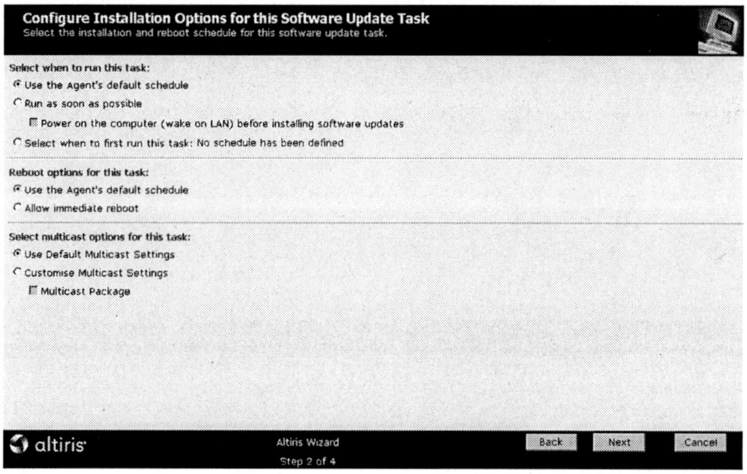

The default multicast option is taken from the Microsoft Policy in the Configuration tab. Configure all options and click **Next** to continue.

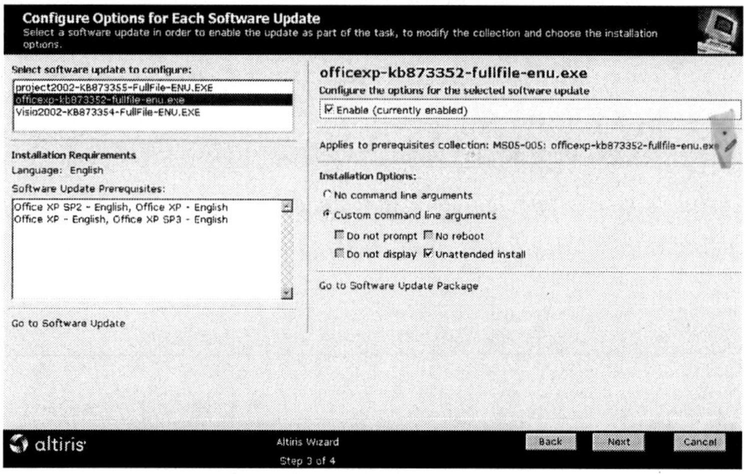

Step 3 – Configure the Patch Installation Options

The third step in the Wizard displays the patches associated with the bulletin. Each patch can be individually configured by clicking the name of the patch in the Select Software to Configure box and then configuring the Installation Options.
Configure any changes to the Installation options if required then Click **Next**.

Step 4 – Final Step

The final step in the Wizard displays a summary of the patches that will be deployed using this Software Update Task.

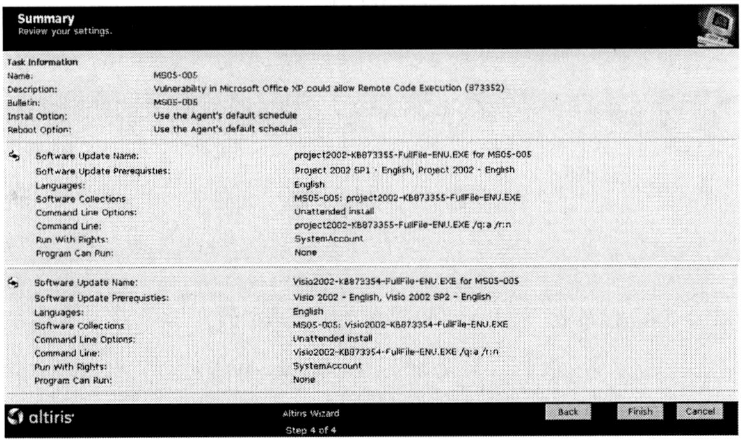

Click **Finish** to complete the Wizard.

*When Finish is clicked, a new Software Update Task is created in **Tasks Tab > Software Management > Patch Management > Software Update Task > Microsoft.** One new package for each patch in the bulletin is also created at **Resources Tab > Resources > Software Management > Software Patch Packages > Software Updates > Security Updates.***

The next time clients in the targeted collection update their configuration they will see the advertised bulletin and install it based on the configured schedule.

On the Client

The next time clients in the targeted collection update their configuration they will see the advertised bulletin and install it based on the configured schedule.

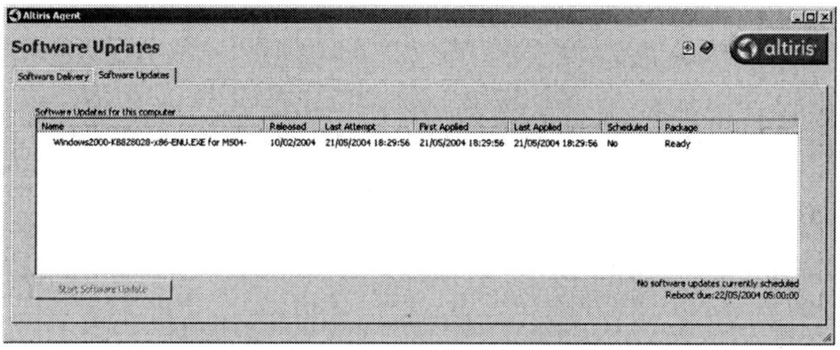

The dialog above shows that the patch has successfully executed on the client and a reboot is scheduled for 5:00 am.
To view this page, go to a client machine and display the Altiris Agent interface, then select the Software Updates tab.

Note Patches are targeted to all Windows machines but will only be download and run by clients requiring the update/patch.

Using Reports to Monitor Patch Deployment Progress

To view patch management reports open the Web Console, select the Reports Tab then navigate to **Software Management > Patch Management**.
Use the list of useful patch management reports at the end of this chapter for more information.

Removing Patch Management Solution

If you do not intend using Patch Management Solution anymore, use the 'Software Update Agent Uninstall' policy to remove the agent from all managed clients (See below).
Wait until all clients have uninstalled the agent and then use **Add/Remove Programs** in Control Panel on the Notification Server to remove Patch Management Solution.

Uninstalling the Software Update Agent

Select the Configuration Tab in the Web Console and navigate to **Solution Settings > Software Management > Patch Management > Windows > Software Update Agent Uninstall.**
Select the 'Software Update Agent Uninstall' Policy.

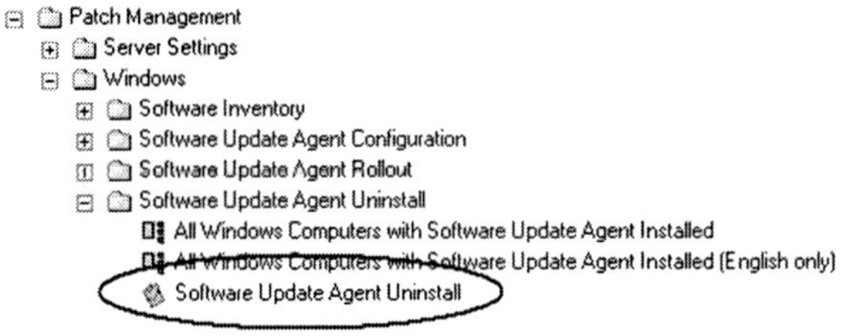

The default target collection is 'All machines with the Software Update Agent Installed'.
Enable verbose status reporting if required. Enabling status reporting for this policy will allow you to report on which machines successfully or unsuccessfully executed the policy to remove the agent. Status events for this policy will generate network traffic of approximately 2-12 KB per client.
Set the scheduling options and **enable** the policy.
Click **Apply**.

The next time machines in the targeted collection update their configuration they will uninstall the Software Update Agent based on the configured schedule.

Useful Patch Management Reports

To view the following reports open the Web Console, select the Reports Tab then navigate to **Software Management > Patch Management**

Inventory Agent Installation Summary

This report is in the Agent Information folder and lists computers with the Inventory Agent installed.

Software Update Agent Installation Summary

This report is in the Agent Information folder and lists computers with the Software Update Agent installed.

Task Execution by Computer

Summarizes the execution results for all scheduled software update tasks by software bulletin. (Agent Task Execution folder)

Microsoft Software Update Compliance by Bulletin

Lists the overall compliance percentage based on the number of software update tasks and the number of installed software updates. (Compliance folder)

Software Update Packages - Errors

Lists any software update package that reported errors during download. The report can be used to identify computers with communication errors.

Detected Microsoft Vulnerabilities by Computer

Summarizes the vulnerabilities found on all computers. (Vulnerability Analysis folder)

Summary

In this chapter we looked at using Altiris Patch Management to deploy Microsoft patches to managed clients.

To deploy patches to clients, the client must have the Software Update Agent installed. Once clients have the Agent, the Inventory Rule agent which is rolled out with the Update Agent, reports the MSI, Installed applications and OS Service pack level to the Notification Server. This inventory is used to target clients with a patch. When a bulletin is released from Microsoft, Altiris update the PMImport.cab file on the Altiris website. A policy on the Notification Server downloads this file, extracts it and imports it in to the Notification Server database.

The import populates the list of patch bulletins. These can be viewed in the Tasks tab. When a bulletin is enabled, the Notification Server automatically downloads the patches for that bulletin from the Microsoft website. Once all patches for a bulletin have been downloaded, the bulletin can be deployed using the Distribution Software Update Wizard.

The next chapter 'Reporting' guides you through viewing and creating reports.

16

Reporting

Introduction

Altiris Solutions come with an excellent range of built-in reports. Each solution installed will add its own set of reports. Reports are located in the Reports tab of the Web Console.

Main Reports Toolbar

 Run this report in the same Window.

 Run this report in a new Window.

 View saved reports.

 Schedule this report to run.

 Edit the parameters of this report. (Most built-in reports cannot be edited.)

 Used to display the details of a report in a new Window.

Report Sub Toolbar

 Create a collection based on this reports SQL.

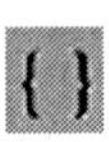 Create a collection based on this reports result.

 Turn off the parameters for this report.

Viewing a Solution Report

From the web console select the **Reports** tab and navigate to the category of report you wish to view. Drill down through the folders until you find the report you want.

Once a report is selected, the details pane displays the options to run the report in the same window or in a new window.

Select the link to 'Run the report in a new Window'. 

Some reports will run and display the results immediately while others will offer options to further specify what is to be returned in the selected report. If you are prompted for parameters, configure them, then click the **run** button. 

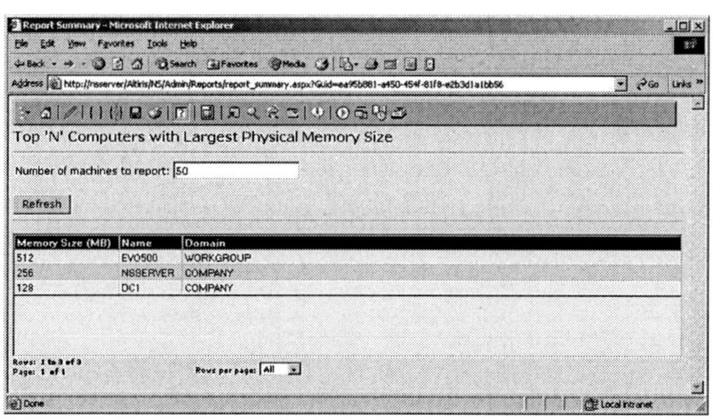

Saving a Report

When you run a report in the Web Console, the results are from the data contained in the database at that moment in time. Saving a report allows you capture a data snapshot so that the data can be viewed at a later date.

To save a report

Open the Web **Console** and select the **Reports** tab then navigate to a report.
Run the report in the same window or in a new window.
When the results are displayed click the Save button and enter a name for the saved report and click **OK**.

To view a saved report

Open the Web Console and select the Reports tab then navigate to the required report.
In the details pane click View Saved Reports.
A list of saved reports are displayed.
Click on the magnifying glass to the left of the report name to display it.

Scheduling a Report

Scheduling a report to run is useful if you want to automatically run and save a report at a specific date and time. For example you may want to automatically run and save a patch vulnerability report before and after patches have been applied.

To schedule a report run

Open the Web Console and select the Reports tab then navigate to the required report.
In the details pane click *Schedule this report to run.*
Enable the schedule and use one of the shared schedules or a custom schedule.
Click **Apply**.
When the scheduled report runs, it will create and save a report based on the data in the database at that time. To reports results can be view from within Saved Reports.

Cloning a Report

Right click the selected report in the left hand pane and choose **Clone**.
The Clone Item dialog appears asking for a name for the copied report. Enter the name and click **OK**.

Editing a Report

Only new or cloned copies of the built-in reports can be edited.
Select a new or cloned report to edit and click the **Edit** button. 
The queries and parameters for the report are displayed.

Exporting and Importing a Report

Export – Select the report in the Treeview pane. Right click the report name and choose **Export**. Select where to store the exported xml.
Import – Select the target folder in the Treeview pane. Right click the folder name and choose **Import**. Navigate to the exported xml report and click **Open**. The report is added to the selected folder.

Viewing the SQL of a Built-in Report

To view the SQL of a built-in report, the report must first be cloned.
Select the Reports tab in the Web Console and navigate to a built-in report.
Right click the report name and choose **Clone** from the shortcut menu.
Enter a new name in the Clone Item dialog and click **OK.**
The *Edit this Report* button will now be visible and can be used to view the SQL, parameters, views and drilldowns for the report.

Creating Custom Reports

A report can be created by creating the new report from scratch or by cloning an existing report and then modifying it's queries and parameters.
To guide you through the creation of reports we will start by creating a simple report that will list all machine names and their TCP/IP address that exist in the Altiris database.

Creating a Simple Custom Report

In this example we want to create a report that will list all machines and their TCP/IP address.
From the web console select the Reports tab and navigate to the folder in which you want to create the new report.
Right click the folder and from the shortcut menu choose **New > Report**.

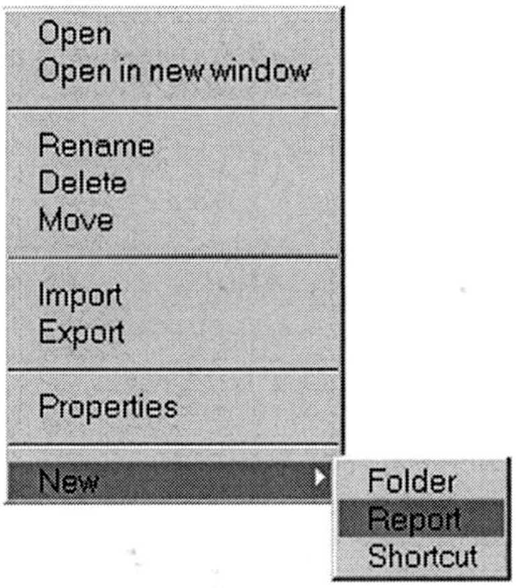

The Query Builder is launched and offers a choice of four different reports.

Enter a report name and description. Select **Simple Report** in the report type section.

Each of the **Content** choices needs to be configured.

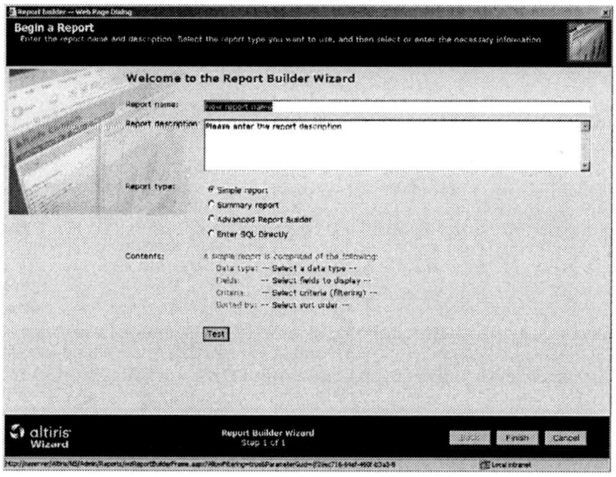

Click the **Data type** link to choose the resource type to be included in the report.

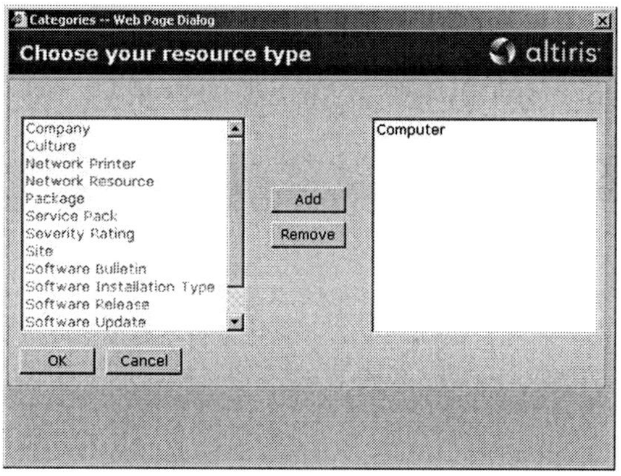

Only one resource can be chosen. Use the **Add** button to add the Computer resource, then click **OK**.

The next link, 'Fields' determines what columns of data are displayed in the report. Click the Fields link and navigate to the *Data Classes > Basic Inventory folder*. Choose the two fields;

Basic Inventory > AeX AC Identification > Name

Basic Inventory > AeX AC TCPIP > IP Address.

Use the **Add** button to add the selected fields to the Selected Fields pane.

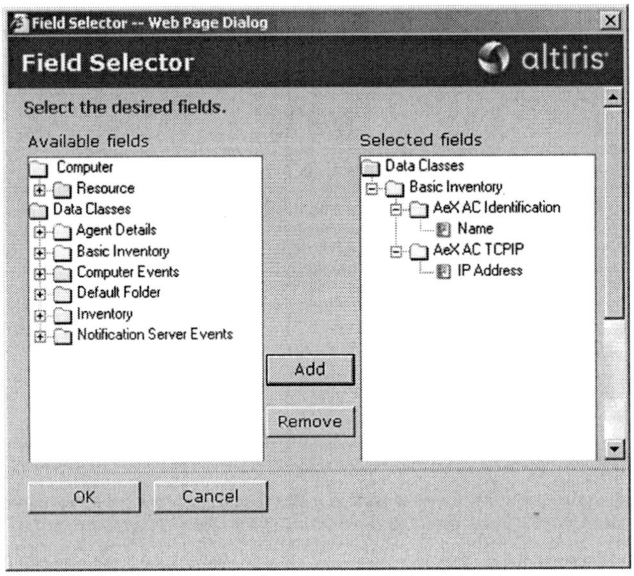

Click **OK** to return to the wizard.

Click the Criteria link and in the Condition dialog click the **New Condition** button. Choose **[Inv_AeX_AC_Identification].[Name] Like %** as the criteria. The percentage symbol is a wildcard meaning all.

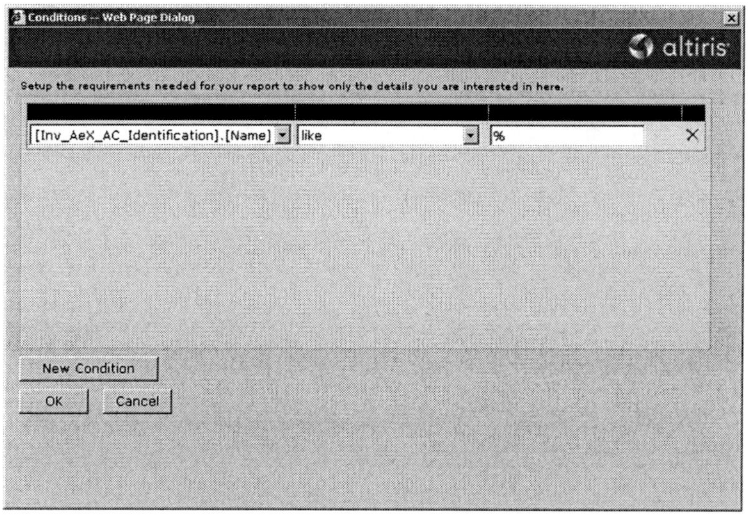

Click **OK**.

When you have returned to the Report Wizard, click the Sorted by link to launch the sort dialog. Choose the column to sort by and select either Ascending or Descending.

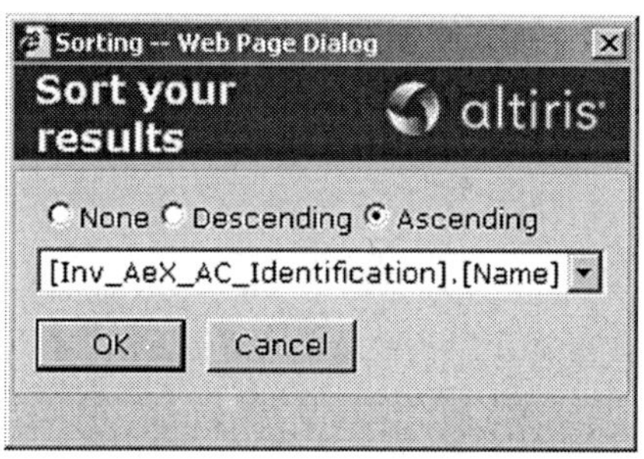

Click **OK** to return to the Wizard.

The report builder wizard dialog should look like the picture below. Use the **Test** button to test your report. If the message 'no records returned' is displayed, either your criteria has returned no data i.e. there are no machines in the database (Unlikely) or there is something wrong with the criteria or fields.

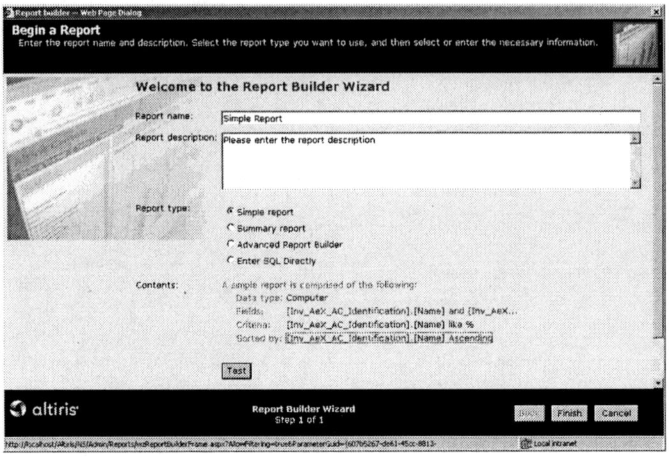

Click **Finish** to complete the wizard.

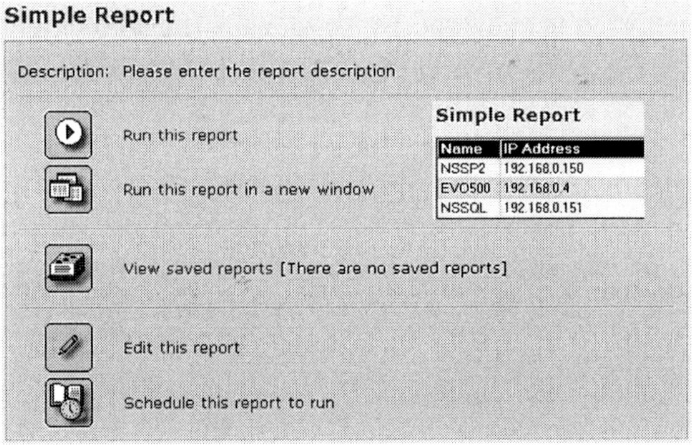

Run the report to display the results. In this instance all machine names and their associated IP Addresses are returned.

Adding Parameters to a Report

The basic report that was created previously, displays all machine names with their associated IP Addresses. A percentage symbol was used as the parameter for this report to specify that all machine names should be returned. If we want to be able to specify the machine name or part of the name when the report is run then we can use a new parameter to achieve this.

Select the previously created report and click the *Edit this report* button in the details pane.
This will display the report properties.

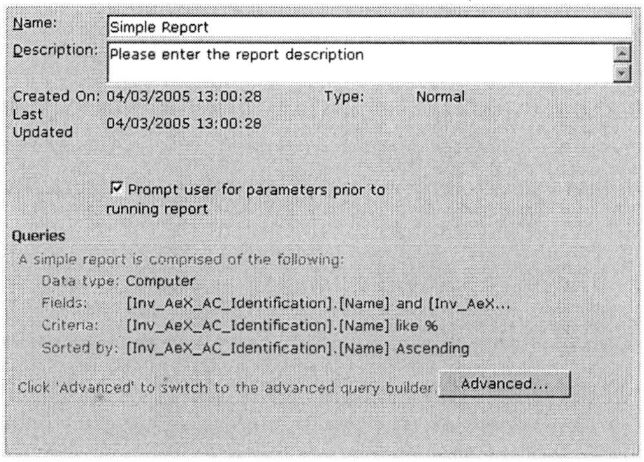

Click the **Advanced** button to re-launch the wizard.

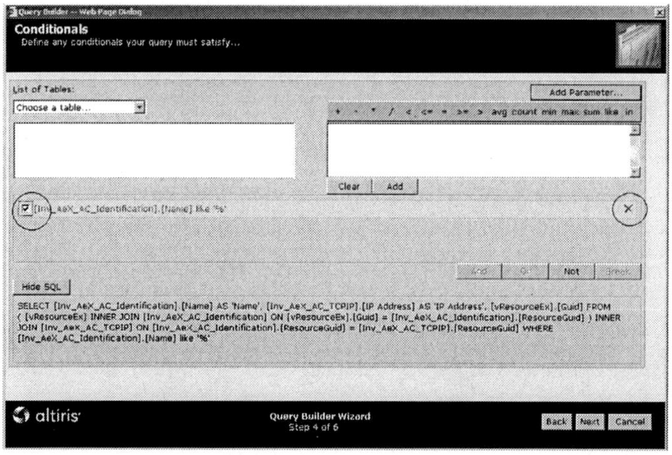

Use the **Next** button to move through the Wizard until you get to the Conditionals dialog. **Delete** the previous Parameter by checking the box for that parameter and clicking Delete.

In the List of Tables Dropdown choose the *Inv_AeX_AC_Identification* table. Then choose the *Name* field from the list of fields.

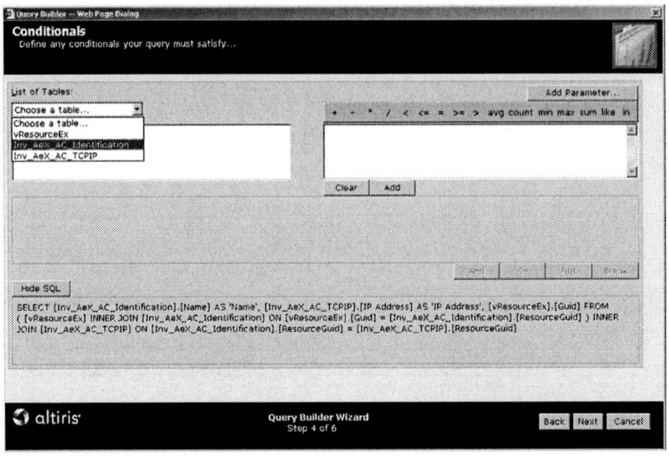

When the *Name* field is selected, it will populate the conditionals to the right. Select the word **LIKE** to add it after the table and column name.

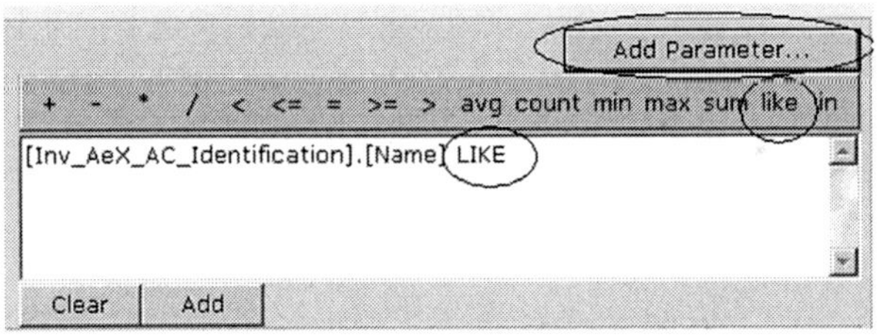

Click the **Add Parameters** button to launch the Add Parameters dialog..

In the Add Parameters dialog, click the **New Local parameter** button.

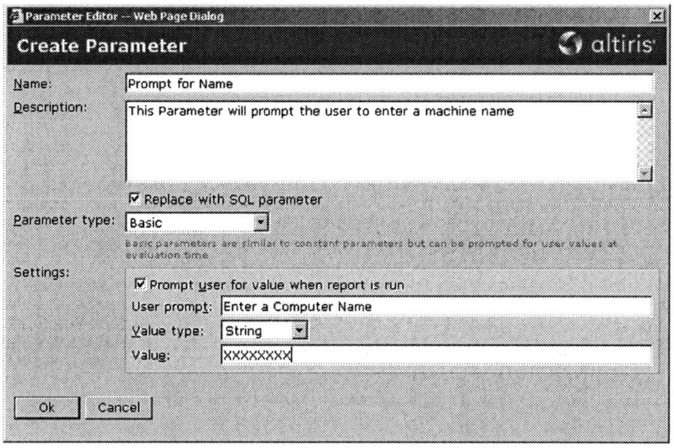

Enter the parameters as shown above then click **OK**.

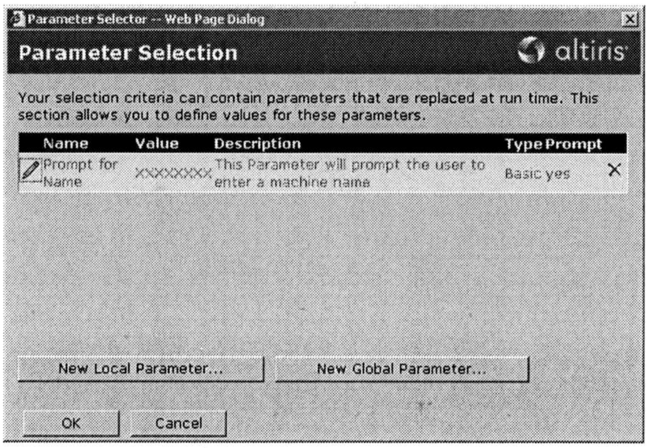

Once the Parameter is displayed in the Parameter Selection dialog, click **OK**.

In the Conditionals dialog, the new local parameter will be displayed as show below.

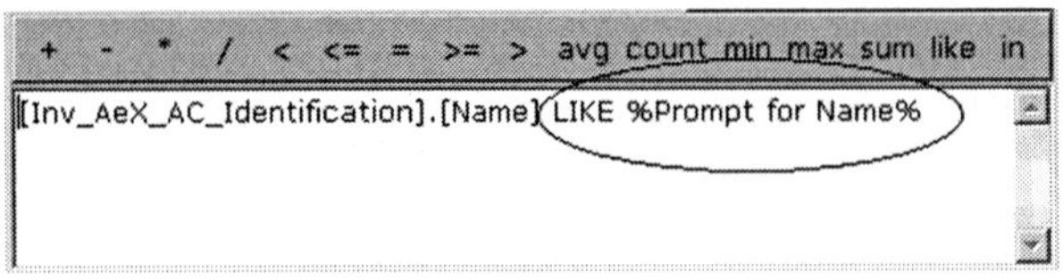

Click the **Add** button to add the new parameter.

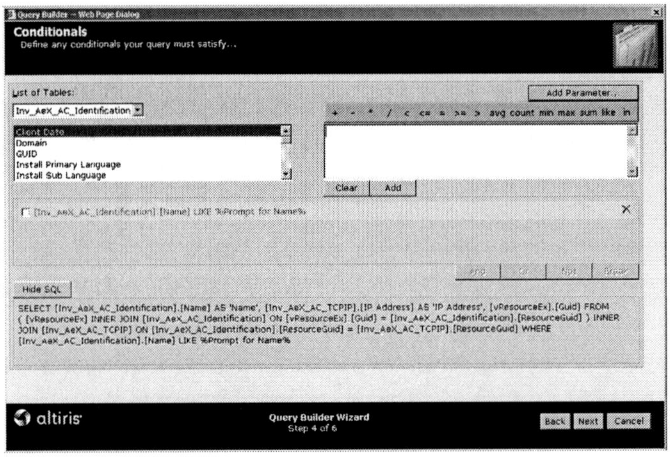

The new local parameter has now been added.

Use the **Next** button to continue to the end of the Wizard.

Click **Finish** to exit the Wizard.

Immediately upon exiting the Wizard, click **Apply** to save your changes.

With the modified parameter, when the report is now run, it will not just automatically display all computers, but will first prompt the user to enter the computer name or part of a name as the criteria for the report. What is entered will then be passed to the reports query as a condition.

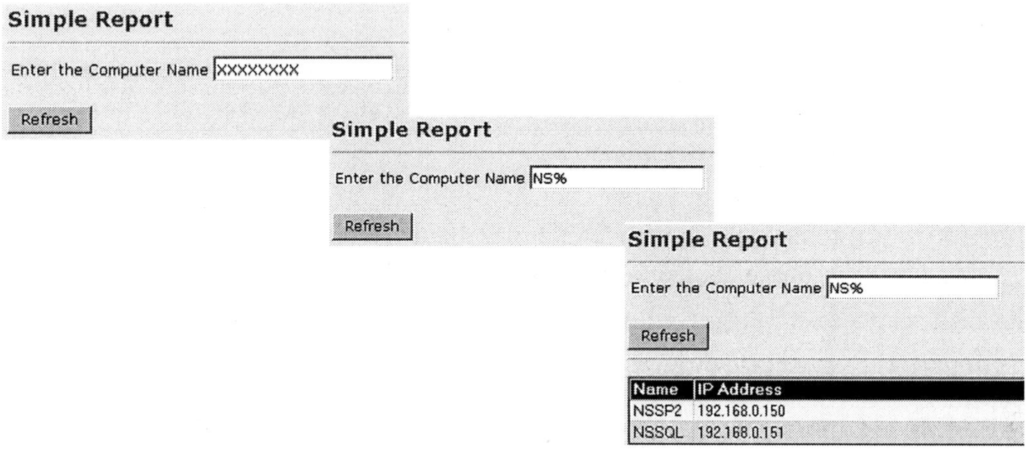

The pictures above show the user entering NS% as the criteria for the report which then displays all machines starting with the characters NS.

Modifying Report Views

Editing a Report View allows you to determine whether a reports result appear in a Table, Chart or Pivot format.

To modify a Report View

Navigate to the report in the reports tab and select it.
In the details pane click the **Edit this Report** button. Edit this report

When the details of the report are shown, click the **Views** button for the query level you want to change. Three views are available, Table, Graph and HTML.
In the Configure Report Views dialog check the type of view you want for the selected query level. For example a Graph. (Uncheck any checked options.)
Configure the options for the selected view. For example 3D Pie chart with X and Y axis titles.

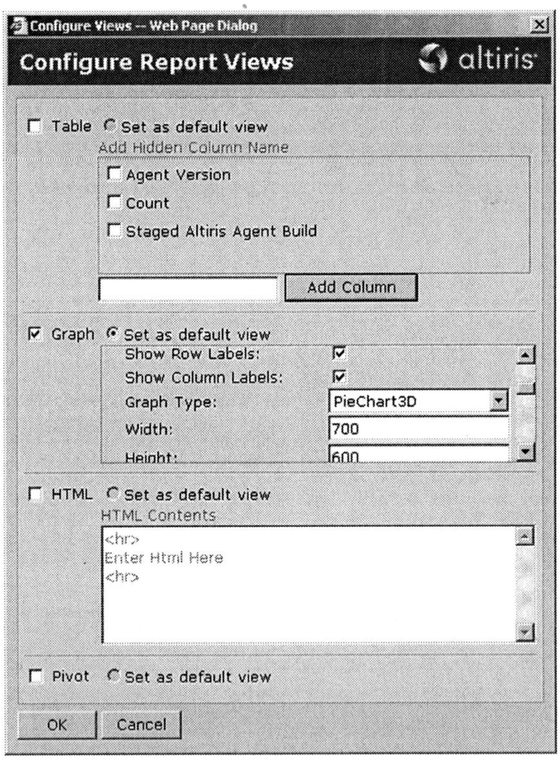

Click **OK** when finished.

Click **Apply** to save the changes in the report details.

When the report is now run, the new view will be displayed.

Creating a collection from a reports results

Display the results of a report.

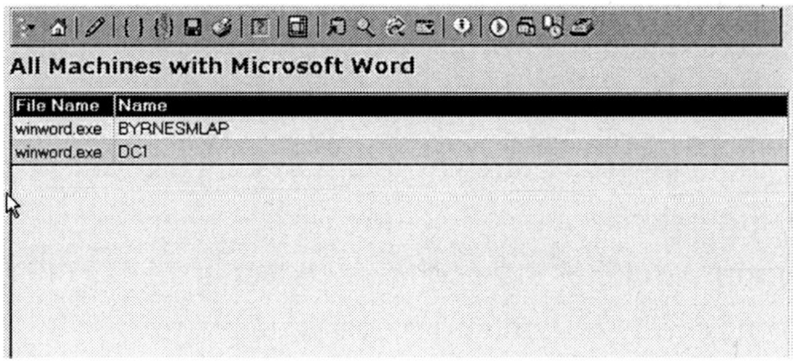

Click the 'Create collection from this reports results' button.

A new collection is created and saved in **Resource tab > Collections > Computer Collections > My Collections**.

The collection is given the name **Collection from report:** Report name.

Once the collection is created you will be returned to the reports window.

The new collection can be edited and the parameters, criteria and fields modified.

Creating a collection based on the SQL of a report

Display the results of a report.

Click the 'Create collection based on this reports SQL', button.

A new collection is created and saved in **Resource tab > Collections > Computer Collections > My Collections**.

The collection is given the name **Collection from report:** Report name.

The collection properties are displayed.

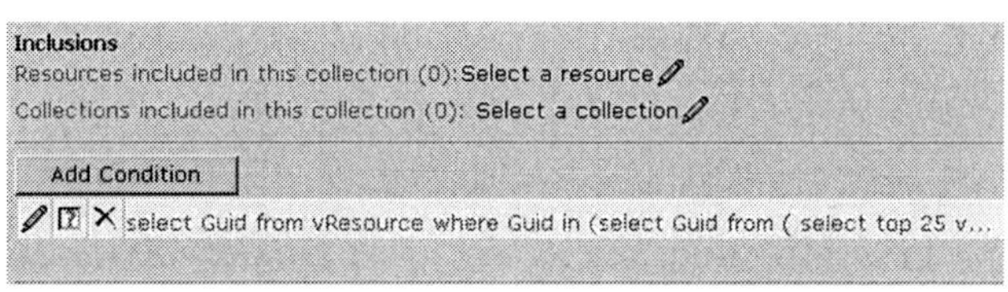

From here you can modify the parameters and also view and edit the SQL for the report.

Summary

Reports are used to view data in the Notification Server database. Each Solution installed comes with built-in reports which allow you to view data for that Solution. Reports are viewed in the Reports tab of the Web Console and are arranged into folders.

Built-in reports can be viewed, cloned and exported. Custom or cloned reports can be edited, cloned and deleted.

The results of a report can be used to create a collection. The collection can be used when targeting agent configuration and package delivery.

The next chapter 'Inventory forwarding' examines how Inventory data can be forwarded from one Notification Server to another.

17

Inventory Forwarding

Introduction

Inventory Forwarding is used to forward Inventory data from one Notification Server to another. Forwarding is used in an environment with multiple Notification Servers. One or more Notification Servers can be configured to forward Inventory data to a central Notification Server, creating a central repository for Inventory.

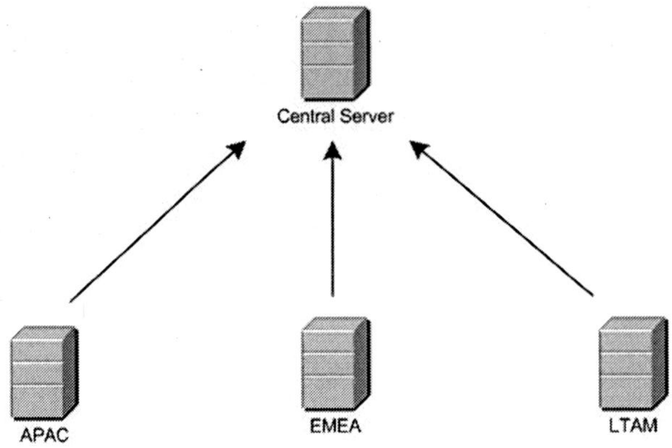

In a multiple Notification Server infrastructure, such as the one shown above, clients send Inventory data to their regional Notification Server. Forwarding rules are used on each regional server to forward Inventory data to a central Notification Server. The central Notification Server contains inventory data from all regions and can be used for reporting and support.

Important

Ensure that the receiving Notification Server is running the same solutions and versions as the sending Notification Servers.

Configuring Inventory Forwarding

From the Configuration Tab in the Web Console navigate to **Server Settings > Notification Server Infrastructure > Inventory Forwarding**.

When Inventory Forwarding is opened for the first time there are no forwarding rules to display.

Click the **Add Rule** button to add a rule. 

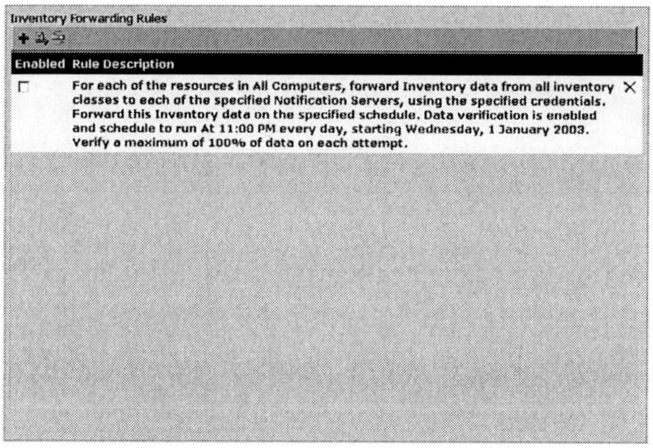

To configure the new rule **click each hyperlink** within the rule and configure each associated option in turn. Most options are self-explanatory. Two of the configuration options that you may not understand are **Data Verification** and **Verify a maximum percentage of data**.

Data verification simply checks the data forwarded. The target Notification Server will compare what it has received against what is in the source database.

Verify a maximum percentage of data allows you to configure a percentage of the data that will be verified during the forwarding process.

Once the rule has been configured, enable it and then click **Apply**. Data will be forwarded based on the rule schedule.

Note

The Forward button  can be used to start a rule immediately. Using the forwarding button will forward any inventory data changes since the last forward.

The Resynchronize  button can also be used to start a rule immediately. Using the Resynchronize button will forward all inventory data **regardless of whether there have been any changes since the last forward**.

Tasks performed from a central Notification Server

In a scenario where there are three regional servers (APAC, EMEA and LTAM) forwarding data to a central Notification Server, the following could be done at the central server:

- View all machines from all regions.
- Create reports using the Inventory data from all regions.
- Launch a Carbon Copy session from the central Notification Server, providing the client is running the Carbon Copy agent and the central Notification Server has Carbon Solution installed.

The following could not be done from the central Notification Server:

- Target regional machines with patches using Patch Management Solution. This would have to be done from the regional Notification Server.
- Target regional machines with software packages using Software Delivery Solution. This would have to be done from the regional Notification Server.
- Configure Solution agent settings for regional computers.
- Configure Altiris agent settings for regional computers.

Note In an Altiris infrastructure **data flows up, it does not flow down**. This is why the functionality of a central Notification Server (repository) is currently limited. It is hoped that future releases of Notification Server will allow policies, tasks, patches and packages to be created at a central level and will automatically roll down to the Notification Server clients at a regional level.

Registry Recommendations

The following registry settings are recommended on a machine that will receive forwarded inventory.

Key	Default Value	Recommended
FastQueueThreshold	15 KB	1500 bytes (15 KB)
SlowQueueThreshold	2097 KB	8000 KB (8 MB)
LargeQueueThreshold	2097 KB	8000 KB (8 MB)

The above settings are in the root of *HKLM\Software\Altiris\Express\Notification Server*.

Extra Logging

To enable more comprehensive logging during the Inventory forwarding process configure the following:

Key	Type	Value
InvForwardFullLoggingEnabled	REG_DWORD	1 for on, 0 for off

The above logging setting is not created during the NS installation. You must manually create the key in the root of *HKLM\Software\Altiris\Express\Notification Server* if required.

Useful Inventory Forwarding Reports

To view the following reports open the Web Console, select the Reports Tab then navigate to **Notification Server Infrastructure > Server > Inventory Forwarding folder**.

Computers never forwarded

This report lists the machines that have never forwarded inventory.

Inventory forwarding status

This report lists the destination server which is receiving forwarded inventory and the last time inventory was sent.

Summary

This chapter looked at forwarding inventory data from one Notification Server to another. The basic procedure is to ensure that the target and source Notification Servers are running the same Solutions and versions. Rules are then created on the source Notification Server to determine what inventory data is forwarded, what server(s) it is forwarded too and when it is forwarded.

In the next chapter 'Upgrading Notification Server' we will look at the procedures used to upgrade an Altiris 5.5 SP3 Notification Server to Notification Server 6.x.

18

Upgrading NS from 5.5 to 6.x

Introduction

The process of upgrading from Notification Server 5.5 SP3 to 6.x is straight forward, there are however certain steps that need to be completed in order that the upgrade be successful.

Server Upgrade Requirements

- Notification Server 5.5 SP3. (Older versions are not supported.)
- Meets the minimum hardware and software requirements as detailed in the chapter 'Installing Notification Server Framework'.

Step 1 - Upgrade the Altiris Agent

Use Notification Server 5.5x to upgrade all managed clients to Altiris Agent 6.x. Download the AexAgentRollout.exe from www.solutionsam.com/solutions/5_5/ and install it on your Notification Server. Reboot the server if prompted.

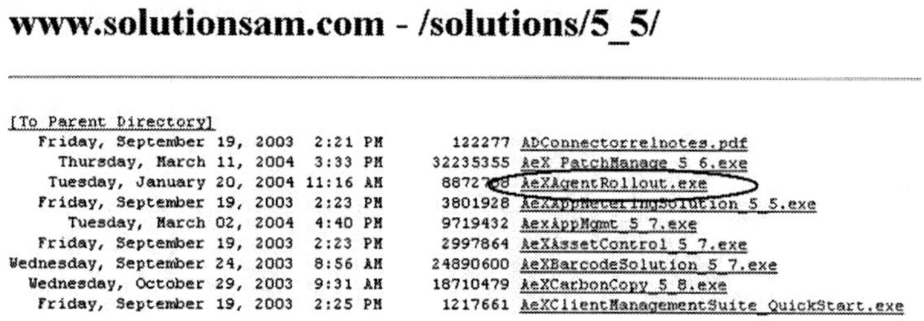

Once installed, open the web console and navigate to **Altiris eXpress Configuration > Policies > Notification Server Client Agent Rollout Jobs**.

Configure and **enable** either or both of the Upgrade policies. If you wish, turn on Status Events for the policy and use reporting to check on the upgrade status. The **NS Client Version** report in the **Reports > Client Deployment** folder is useful for this.

The next time managed clients request a configuration update they will see that there is a new version of the Altiris agent. The client will download and install the upgrade based on the policy schedule.

Step 2 - Upgrade the Package Server Agent

Once all clients have upgraded to Altiris Agent 6.x, upgrade the Package Server Agent on Package Servers. In the Web Console navigate to **Altiris eXpress Configuration > Policies > Package Server Agent Rollout Jobs**.

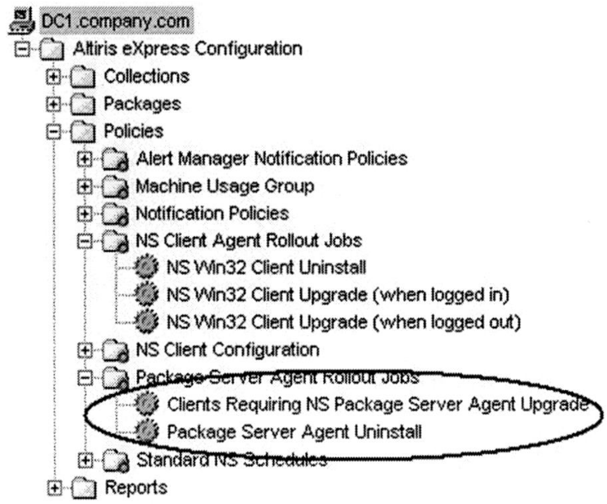

Configure and **Enable** the policy, Clients Requiring NS Package Server Agent Upgrade. If you wish, turn on Status Events for the policy and use reporting to check on the upgrade status.

The next time a Package Server request a configuration update it will see that there is a new version of the Package Server agent. The server will download and install the upgrade based on the policy schedule.

Step 3 - Blockout Clients

Configure the Altiris Agents to Blockout all communications during the time you are upgrading the Server.

Clients will be unable to communicate during the upgrade process anyway but this stops the few clients that may try to send inventory data prior to starting the upgrade. This step is recommended but not essential.

Step 4 - Backup the Notification Server

Backup the folder structure and the Altiris database, using whatever means you have available. Ensure that you backup any custom inventory ini or xml files as well as AuditPls.ini and any other custom files you may have.

Step 5 - Remove all Altiris Solutions

Remove all Solutions using Add/Remove Programs in Control Panel.

Step 6 - Remove Notification Server software

Remove Notification Server using Add/Remove Programs in Control Panel. Once the Notification Server software has been removed, **reboot the server**.

Step 7 - Remove redundant files

Remove any Temporary Internet files and any Aex*.* files from the root of your NT folder.

Step 8 - Double the size of your database if required

If your NS 5.5 database has a fixed size, double it using SQL Enterprise Manager before installing NS 6.x.

Step 9 - Install Notification Server 6.x

Use the chapters 'Installing the Notification Server Framework' and 'Configuring Notification Server' to guide you through the process of installing Notification Server 6.x. **In the last step of the installation choose to use an existing database rather than create a new database**. Choose the name of the Notification Server 5.5 database which is AeXNS by default.

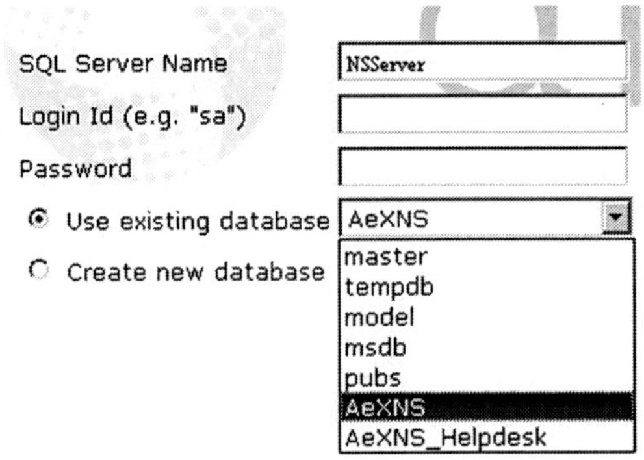

Step 10 - Verify

Verify the version as displayed in the console banner and examine the log files to ensure everything is working OK. (http://NSServer/aexns/celogview.asp)

Step 11 - Install Solutions

Use Upgrade/Install Additional Solutions in the Configuration Tab of the Web Console to install the required solutions. Apply your production licenses once installed.

Step 12 - Upgrade the Altiris Agent, Package Server Agent and Solution Agents

Use the Altiris Agent upgrade policy to upgrade all managed clients. When all clients including the Package Servers have been upgraded, use the Package Server agent upgrade policy to upgrade the Package Servers. When the Package Servers have been upgraded to the latest version of the agent use the upgrade agent policies in each Solution to upgrade all clients with the latest version of the respective Solution agent. Enable one Solution Agent upgrade at a time to avoid flooding the network.

This completes the upgrade process.

Summary

In this chapter we looked at the process of upgrading an existing Altiris 5.5 infrastructure to version 6.x. The upgrade involved upgrading clients and package Servers prior to upgrade, then removing all Solutions and the Notification Server software from the Notification Server. Once the software was removed the new version could be installed along with version 6.x of the Solutions. Solution Upgrade Policies are then used to upgrade solution agents on clients.

The next chapter 'An Introduction to Deployment Solution' provides a guide to designing, installing, configuring and using Deployment Solution.

19

An Introduction to Deployment Solution

Introduction

Altiris Deployment Solution is a collection of tools and components that offers operating system deployment, remote control, imaging, configuration, computer "personality" migration and software deployment across hardware platforms and operating systems.
This chapter will discuss these tools and provide an overview of a typical design, installation, basic configuration and usage.

Deployment Solution Features

- Create and Deploy images
- Migrate personal information from one computer to another
- Backup and restore a client registry
- LAN optimized Remote control and chat sessions
- LAN optimized software delivery
- Create application packages
- Execute commands remotely
- Execute DOS and Windows scripts
- Manage the Deployment Server using Win32 and or Web type consoles
- Support for PXE
- Supports BIS (Certificate for DOS communications)
- Supports Wake on LAN (Wake a machine from a powered off state)

There are some duplication of features between Deployment Solution and other CMS Solutions, for example, Deployment Solution offers software delivery as does Software Delivery Solution. The difference between the two, is that Software Delivery Solution can deliver software to clients in a multi-site enterprise, but because Deployment Solution can not utilize the scalability of Package Servers, it can only be used to delivery software to clients within a single well connected site.

Typically, I use Deployment Solution to build and migrate machines and then use CMS Solutions such as Patch, Software Delivery and Inventory Solutions to manage the machine after they have been built/migrated.

Things to be aware of

Package Servers do not natively integrate with a Deployment Solution infrastructure. Clients run a standalone agent specifically to communicate with a Deployment Server. The client does not support Package Servers, checkpoint recovery or bandwidth throttling.

Features such as Software Delivery are LAN based, in that when a software package is deployed from the Deployment Server, the client pulls the package directly from the source server and does not use Package Servers.

Unlike Carbon Copy Solution, the remote control feature of Deployment Server is not optimized for WAN connectivity and incurs more overhead on the client being remote controlled.

The Deployment Server has its own database separate to the Notification Server database.

The Deployment Server PC Transplant component does not support PCT Web Stores making it less scalable than its Solution equivalent.

There are no built-in reporting facilities.

Ports used by Deployment Solution

UDP 67 & 68 for DHCP and PXE requests

UDP 4011 for PXE requests when PXE is installed on the same machine as the DHCP server

TCP 402 used for client communication with the Altiris Server Service

UDP 402 for Wake on LAN

TCP 401 used by client for multicast image deployment and tickle

UDP 1758 & 1759, for TFPT and MTFTP transfer of PXE images

TCP 1010 for PXEConfig to communicate with the PXE Configuration service

For a real-time migration (Peer to peer) ports 4949, 3829, 4950, 4951, and 4952 are used.

TCP 8081 is used when connecting directly to a Deployment Server Web Console

TCP/HTTP port 8080 is used when connecting from the Notification Server Deployment Console to a Deployment Server

Dynamic ports are used for file transfer but can be configured through the console

Deployment System Component Overview

An Altiris Deployment System, typically compromises of the following components:

The Deployment Consoles

A Deployment Console is used to manage a Deployment Server and the clients that have registered with that Deployment Server. There are three consoles:

- The Deployment Console is a Win32 application that is used to connect to an Altiris Deployment server. Typically the Win32 console is installed on the Deployment Server and also on an administrator's workstation.
- The Deployment Web Console is a http/web based console and provides access to one Deployment Server at a time. This console does not provide 100% of the functionality provided by the Win32 console.
- The Notification Server Deployment View is a plug-in solution for Notification Server that provides access to multiple Deployment Servers but does not provide 100% of the functionality provided by the Win32 console.

Deployment Server Access Point (Datastore)

This is a shared folder containing the files and programs used to manage Deployment Server clients. This folder is created during the installation of Deployment Server and is shared with the share name 'Express'.

Database

The database stores and maintains all of the information about the clients that connect to the associated Deployment Server. Typical information includes the client hardware configuration, basic application installation information, services and network configuration.

According to Altiris, Deployment Solution 6.1 supports MSDE 2000 (2,500 max clients) or SQL 2000 (5,000 max clients).

The Deployment Server

The Deployment Server is the primary connection point between client computers and the Deployment System.

Deployment Server Windows Agent

Managed Devices are the clients that are managed by Deployment Server. Typically, clients are desktops, servers or handhelds. Any client that will be managed requires a Deployment Server client called the Deployment Agent. There are three client agents:

- Deployment Agent for Windows - AClient
- Deployment Agent for UNIX - ADLagent
- Deployment Agent for DOS - BootWorks (Non PXE)

Note Bootworks will be considered out of scope for this chapter.

The Deployment Server Agent

Not to be confused with the Aclient above, this is an Agent that plugs in to the Notification Server Altiris Agent and provides the ability to replicate the Deployment Server database to the Notification Server. One of the reasons that you may want to do this, is to provide Deployment Server reporting through the Notification Server console.

RapidDeploy

RapidDeploy (Rdeploy.exe) is the imaging engine for Deployment Solution and is used for cloning and deploying Windows, Linux, and other operating systems using unicast and multicast technology.

PC Transplant (PCT)

PCT provides the ability to capture Desktop Settings, Application Settings, Printers and Files/folders. There are three versions of PCT. They are:

- Deployment Server PCT - Comes as part of Deployment Solution.
- PCT Solution - Comes with CMS L1 and integrates with Notification Server.
- Standalone PCT - Purchased as a separate Win32 product and requires no other Altiris components.

RapidInstall

This application comes with Deployment Server and provides the ability to create application packages using snapshot technology.

PXE Server

A Pre-boot Execution Environment (PXE) Server provides management in a DOS environment. This functionality is required if you want to perform management functions such as image capture and deployment without the need for manual intervention.

Bootworks

Provides management in a DOS environment for machines whose network card does not support PXE. Instead of the client downloading a network boot floppy through PXE, the network boot disk image is stored locally on the client hard disk.

DHCP

DHCP is used to service clients with a TCP/IP address and related configuration. To use PXE, you must have a Dynamic Host Configuration Protocol (DHCP) server on your network so that when a client performs a network/PXE boot, it can obtain TCP/IP addressing information.

Client Access Point

The Client Access Point is where Altiris program files, image files, registry files, application packages, Personality Packages, script files etc are stored. When a computer is being deployed or managed, Deployment Server will store and retrieve the required components from the Client Access Point.
(The default path to the CAP is Program Files\ Altiris\eXpress\Deployment Server.)

DS Infrastructure Design Examples

The following section, provides design examples to help clarify where the various components sit within a Deployment System. The examples will provide a basic understanding of a design but do not attempt to cover all scenarios.

Single Site - Example A

In the following design, Deployment components have been installed on separate servers.

Components such as the CAP and Deployment Server have been installed on Server 1 while the Deployment Server database is hosted on Server 3 and PXE is on Server 2.

All of the clients are Windows machines and use the Altiris Deployment Agent (Aclient) to communicate with the Deployment Server.

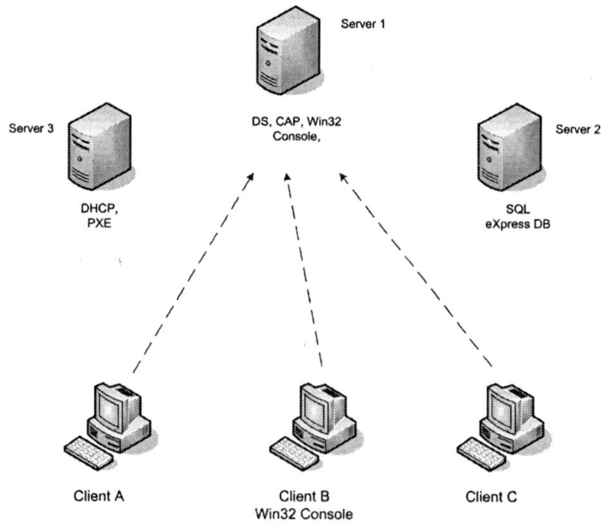

DS - Deployment Server
CAP - Client Access Point
SQL - Database

Administration of the Deployment Server can be performed from 'Client B' or physically at the Deployment Server (Server 1) or through Terminal Services using the Win32 console.

Clients use the DHCP and PXE server when performing actions at a DOS level, for example downloading an image.

Single Site - Example B

In the following design, all of the Deployment components including the Database, CAP and Deployment Server have been installed on the same server, Server 1.

All of the clients are Windows machines and use the Altiris Deployment Agent (Aclient) to communicate with the Deployment Server.

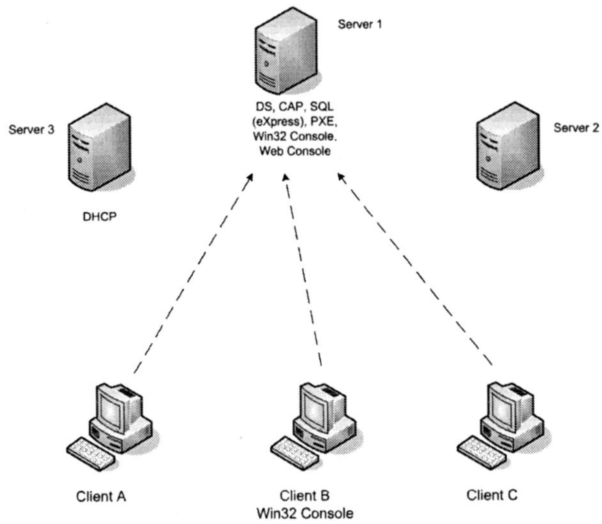

DS - Deployment Server

CAP - Client Access Point

SQL - Database

Administration of the Deployment Server can be performed using the Win32 console from 'Client B' or physically at the Deployment Server (Server 1).

Administration can also be performed by connecting to the Web Console on the Deployment Server from any compliant server or client.

Multiple Sites - Example C

In the following two site design, each site has its own Deployment Server.

All of the clients are Windows machines and run the Altiris Deployment Agent (Aclient). Each client is configured to communicate with its respective site Deployment Server.

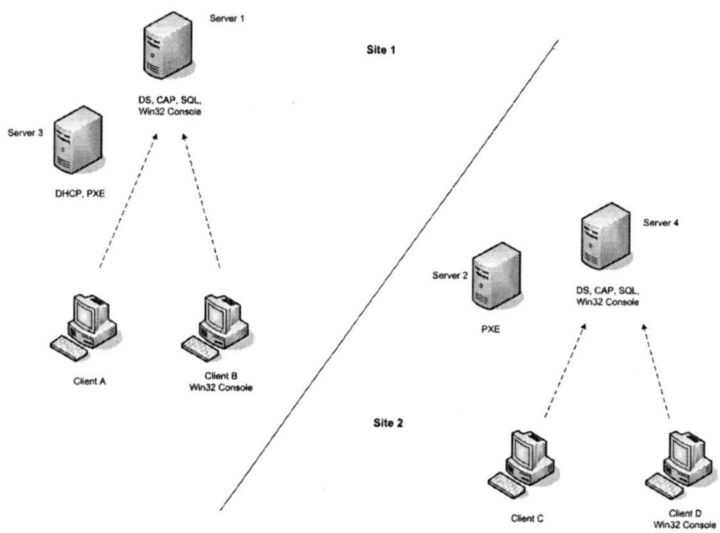

DS - Deployment Server
CAP - Client Access Point
SQL - Database

Administration of the Deployment Server in Site 1 can be performed using the Win32 console on the Site 1 Deployment Server (Server 1) or from 'Client B or D'. Administration of the Deployment Server in Site 2 can be performed using the Win32 console on the Site 2 Deployment Server (Server 4) or from 'Client B or D'.

Note An IP Helper on the connecting site switches will be required by clients in Site 2 to enable communication with the DHCP server.

Multiple Sites - Example D

In the following design, each site has its own Deployment Server. Site 1 also has a Notification Server with Deployment Solution installed. The addition of this solution to the Notification Server, provides the ability to manage multiple Deployment Servers.

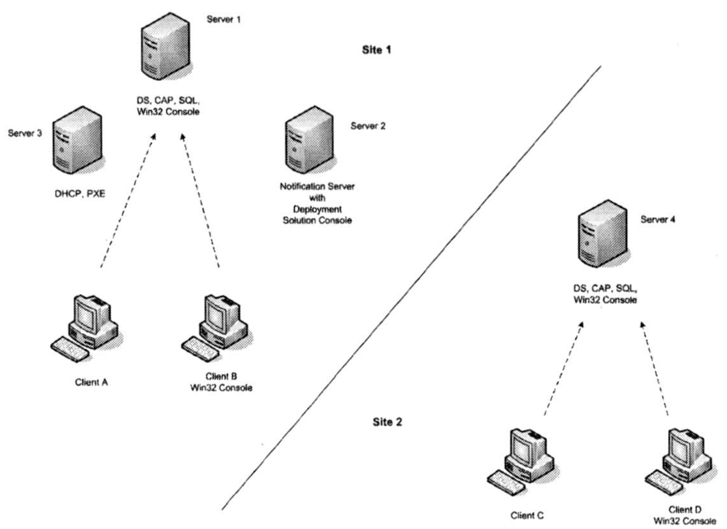

DS - Deployment Server
CAP - Client Access Point
SQL - Database
NS - Notification Server

To administer a site Deployment Server, an administrator can run the Win32 console from 'Client B', 'Client D' or directly from either Deployment Server.
Deployment Server management can also be performed centrally from the Notification Server in site 1. Using the Notification Server console removes the need for multiple installations of the Win32 console.

Note The Win32 console is still installed on each DS to provide some form of redundancy in the event of a Notification Server failure.

The next section in this chapter looks at installing Deployment components.

Installing Deployment Components

Installing Deployment Solution in to Notification Server

Installing Deployment Solution on the Notification Server will add a Deployment tab to the Notification Console (Altiris Console) and provide the ability to manage multiple Deployment Servers. The installation also extracts the files required to install Deployment Server and related components.

Step 1 - Installing Deployment Solution on the Notification Server

Open the Altiris Console and select the Configuration Tab then navigate to Upgrade/Install Additional Solutions.

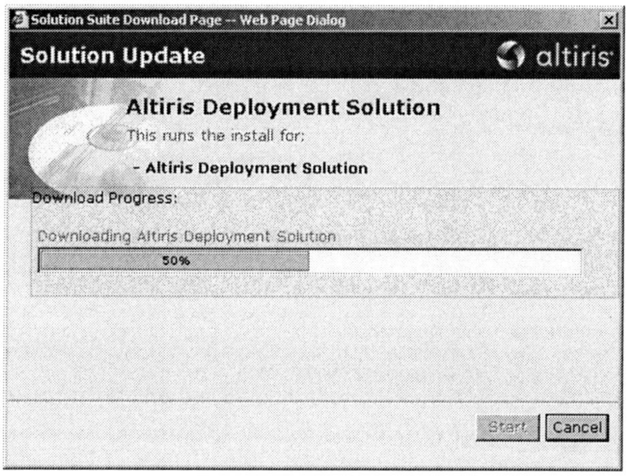

Select the Solutions button and scroll down to Deployment Solution.
Click the **Deployment Solution link** and follow the on-screen instructions.

When the installation has completed, use F5 key to refresh the Notification Server Web Console. A Deployment tab will now be visible within the console.

Apply Deployment Solution Hotfixes

It sometimes happens that even though you install a Solution through the console, the installation may not include all up to-date Hotfixes.

In the Web Console select the Configuration tab and then navigate to **Upgrade/Install Additional Solutions**. Click the **Segments** button.
Scroll down to the **Solution Hotfixes section** and see if there is a Hotfix for Altiris Deployment Solution. If there is, click the link to begin the installation and follow any on-screen instructions.

Changes to the Web Console

The installation of Deployment Solution modifies and adds the following:

The Altiris Console

A new tab labelled Deployment is added to the Web Console. This tab is used to add, connect too and manage Deployment Servers.

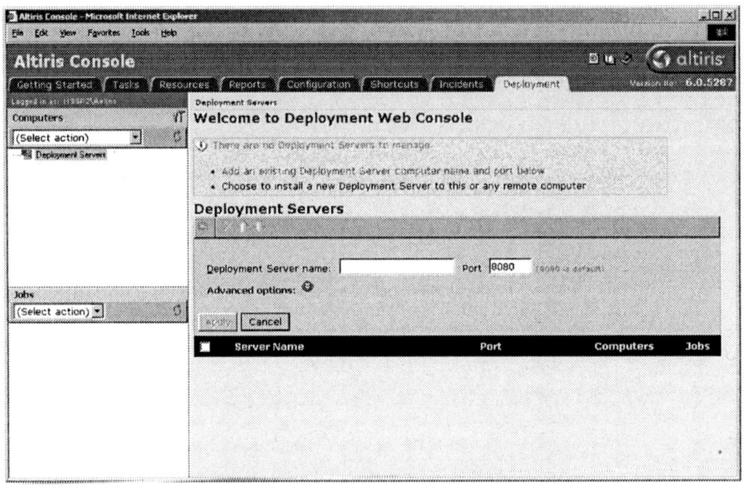

The Configuration tab

This tab contains a Deploy and Migrate folder under the Solution Settings folder. The folders contain policies to perform a push installation of Deployment Server as well as rollout and configure the Windows Agent and the Deployment Server Agent.

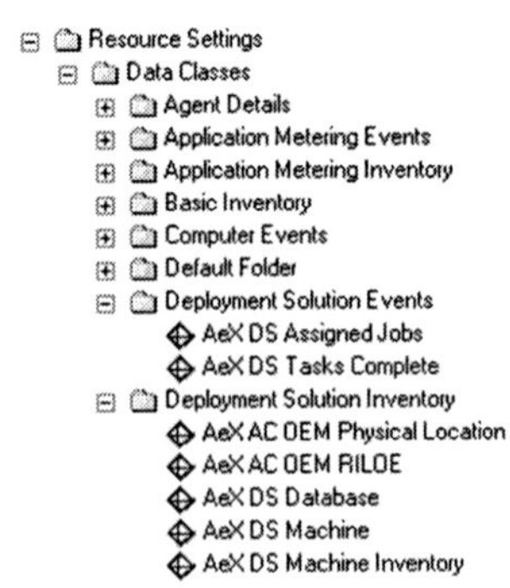

In the Data Classes folder extra data classes are added during the installation.

The Tasks tab

A new Deployment folder is added containing options to, replicate application packages, images and Jobs between Deployment Servers.

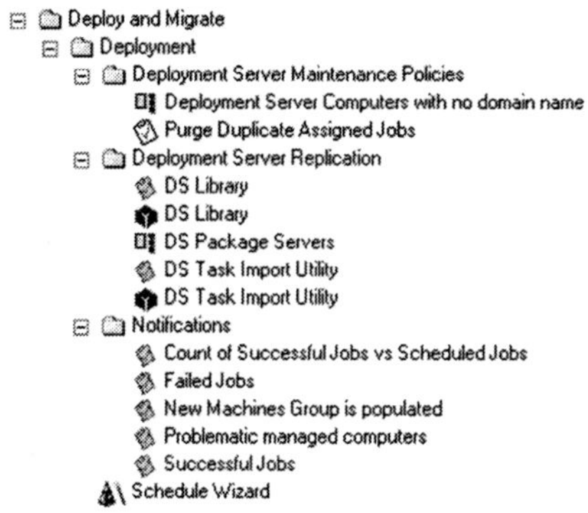

A wizard is also added to guide you through the process of deploying a job to clients managed by a Deployment Server.

Folder additions

The installation of Deployment Solution on the Notification Server adds the following folders.

The NSCap folder now has four new folders:-

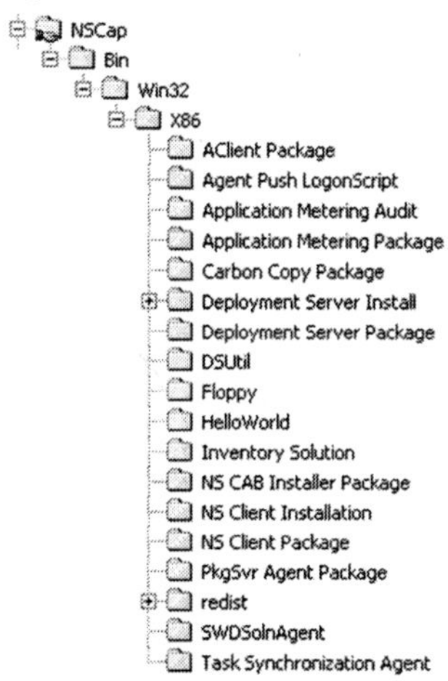

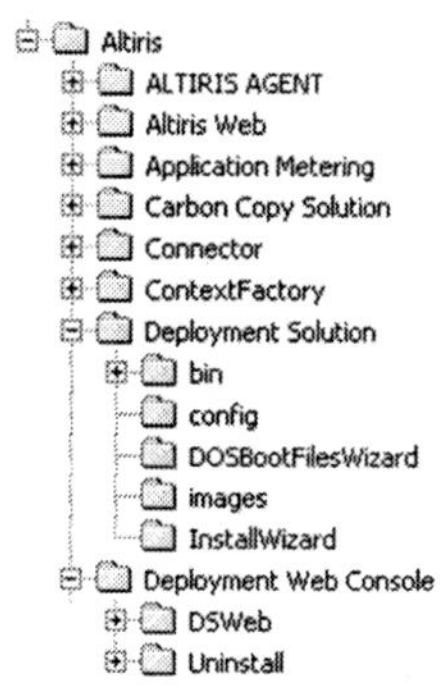

The **Aclient** folder contains the agent that runs on clients managed by the Deployment Server.

Deployment Server Install folder contains the files necessary to perform a full installation of Deployment Server and components.

Deployment Server Package folder contains the Deployment Server Agent which is used to replicate data from a Deployment Server to the Notification Server.

The **DSUtil** folder is used when replicating Deployment Server Jobs between Deployment Servers.

Installing Deployment Server

Now that Deployment Solution has been installed, we can proceed with the installation of Deployment Server. For the purpose of this exercise we will install Deployment Server and components on a server other than the Notification Server. It should also be noted that Deployment Solution is not a requirement for Deployment Server but it is useful if you want to centrally manage several Deployment Servers. *This section steps you through the installation but does not detail every option in every dialog. See the Altiris DS documentation for full details.*

To obtain just the files necessary to install Deployment Server without the need to first install Deployment Solution, go to http://www.altiris.com/eval. Choose Deployment Solution for Clients and then download the zipped file, Deployment Solution 6.x for Clients (Windows). Once downloaded, unzip the file to a local folder. The file will be named Altiris_DeploymentSolutionWin_6_1.exe, double click it and choose Extract Only button.

Step 1 - Install SQL 2000 with SP3a or higher

During the installation of Deployment Server a database named eXpress is created. As with Notification Server, Deployment Server uses an SQL type database to store data. The database can be SQL or MSDE (Testing only) and be installed locally or remotely. Install MSDE or SQL 2000 with SP3a or higher either on the machine that will be the Deployment Server or on another machine. The same SQL server used by Notification Server can also be used.
(For full instructions on installing SQL or MSDE see the Microsoft documentation.)

Step 2 - Install the Altiris Agent

Install the Altiris Agent on the machine that will be the Deployment Server.
For information on installing see the chapter 'The Altiris Agent' earlier in this book.

Step 3 - Configure the server as a Package Server (Optional but recommended)

Once the Altiris Agent has been installed on the machine that will be the Deployment Server, add it as a Package Server, using the NS Web console. Configuring a Deployment Server as a Package Server will allow jobs, images and application packages stored on a central location to be replicated to this new Deployment Server. See the 'Package Server' chapter earlier in this book for instructions on adding a Package Server.

Step 4 -Install Deployment Server

Once Deployment Solution has been installed, the installation files used to install Deployment Server will reside under the NSCAP share on the Notification Server. If the new server has also been configured as a Package Server then the installation files will be replicated to the default package location under the local Altiris Agent folder structure on that server (InstallPath\Altiris\Altiris Agent\Package Delivery).

Before you begin the installation, ensure that you have the following:

- A Deployment Server Service Account with administrative rights on the SQL server and the machine that will be the Deployment Server.
- A Windows 95 or 98 SE CD/DOS boot disk for the PXE installation.
- An SQL/MSDE server to host the Deployment Server Express database.
- A Deployment Server license file (.lic file).
- The machine that will be the Deployment Server has been assigned a static IP address.
- IIS is required if you intend to install the Web Console. (Suggest that you do)

Begin the installation by connecting to the install files source, for example *\\NSServer\NSCAP\Bin\Win32\x86\Deployment Server Install* folder on your Notification Server.

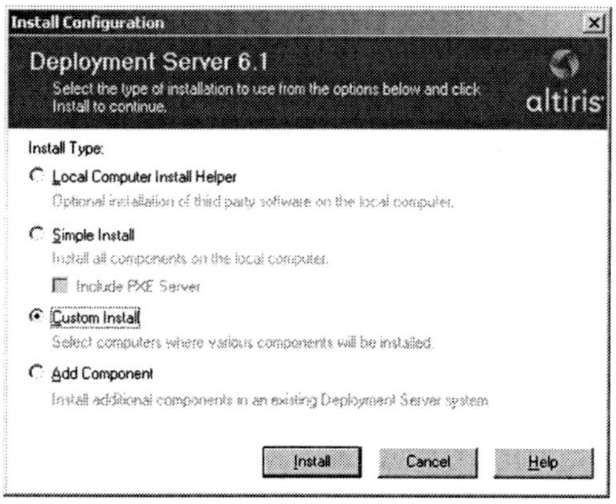

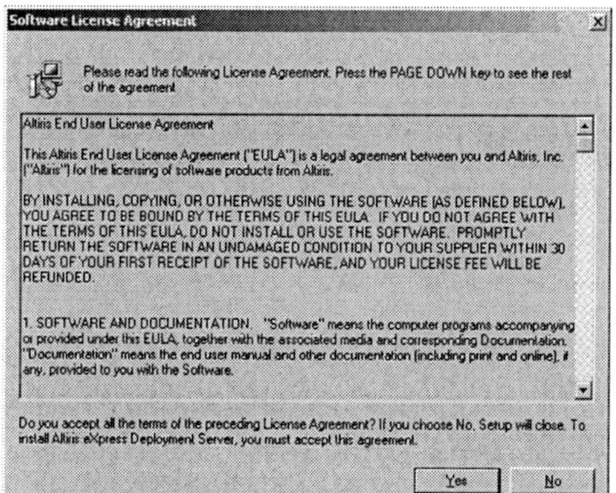

Double click the **axInstall.exe** file. *(If you have not installed Deployment Solution but manually downloaded and extracted the Deployment Server files, then go to your extracted file source and double click axInstall.exe.)*

Choose **Custom** Install and click the **Install** button. Read the licensing agreement and click '*Yes*' if you agree.

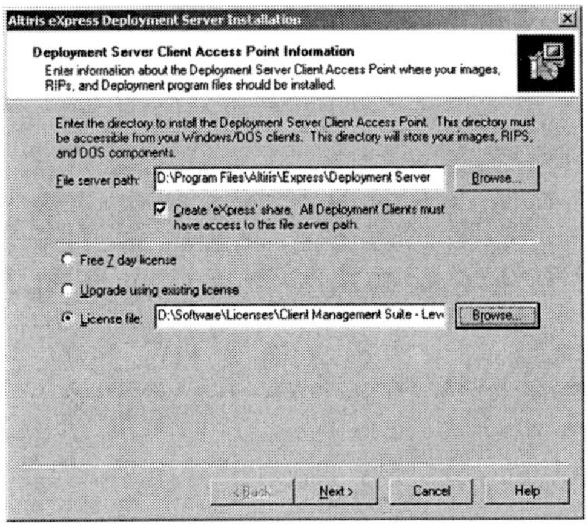

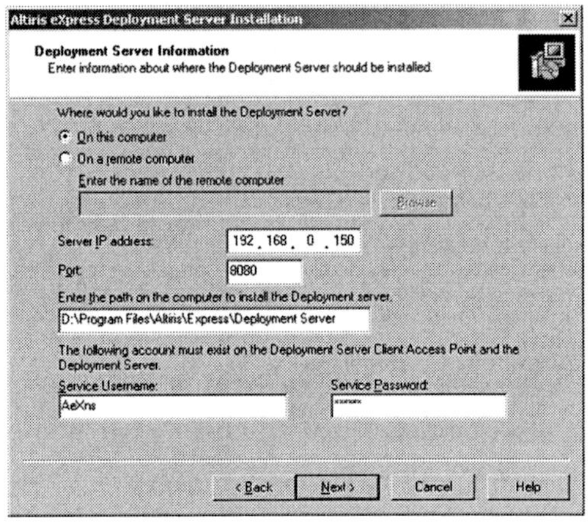

Enter the path were the Client Access Point (CAP) will be installed. The CAP is shared with the name Express by default, and is used by Windows and DOS clients.

In the licensing section **enter the path to your Deployment Server license file** or use the evaluation license for now. Click **Next** to continue.

When asked where Deployment Server (Deployment Server Services etc.) will be installed, choose 'On this Computer'. Check the TCP/IP address and Port. Enter the path which in this case will be the same as the CAP path, then enter the service account name and password. Click **Next** to continue.

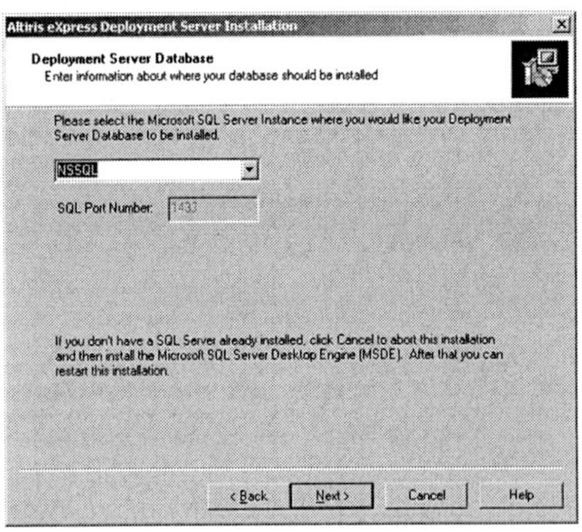

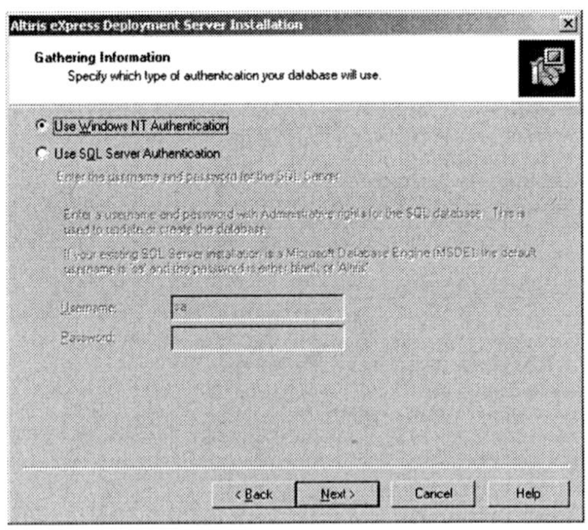

In the next step enter or **choose the name of the SQL server** that will host the Express database for Deployment Server. The SQL/MSDE server can be local or remote, in fact it can even use the same SQL server hosting the Notification Server database.

Choose the type of SQL authentication, Windows is preferred. Click **Next** to continue.

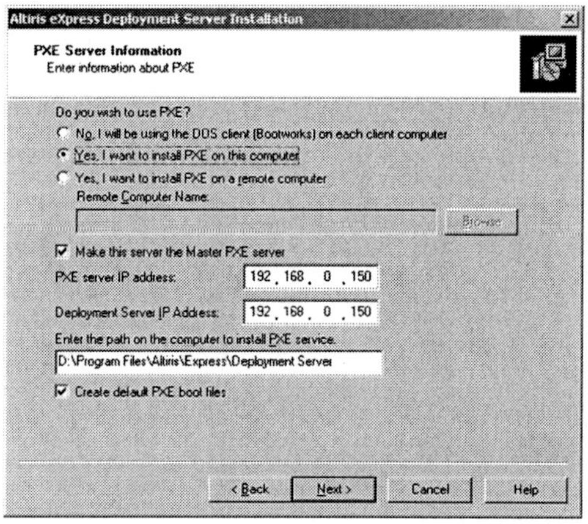

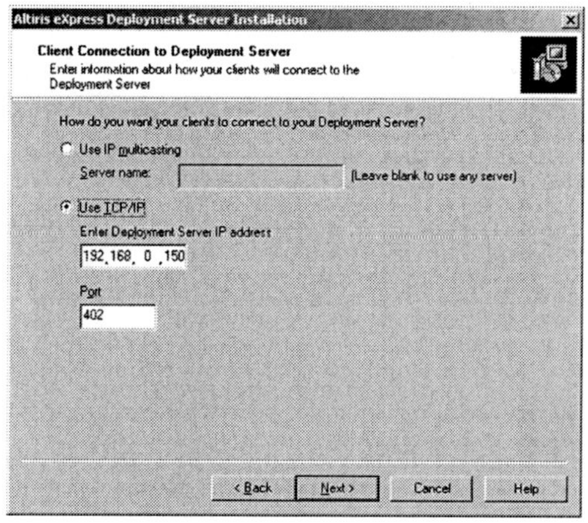

If PXE will be installed on this machine, choose 'Yes, I want to install PXE on this computer'. Check the IP addresses and the path are correct, leave everything else as default and click **Next**.

The next step lets you decide how clients will connect to this Deployment Server. IP multicasting means that clients will pickup the first Deployment Server available, I would suggest use TCP/IP and the specific address of the Deployment Server. 402 is the default port used by the clients to connect to Deployment Server. Click **Next**.

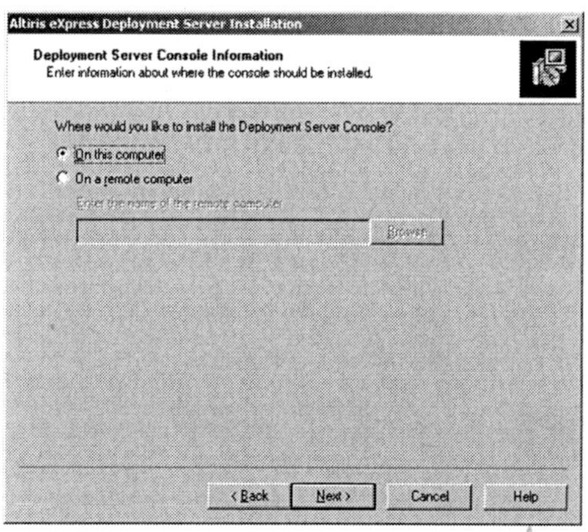

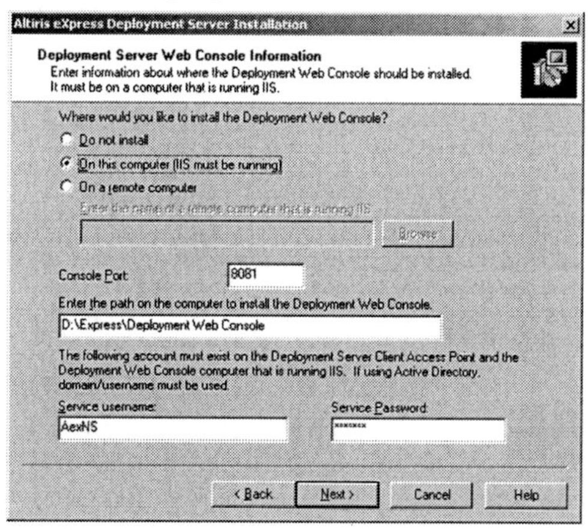

Install the Win32 console on the same machine as Deployment Server. Additional Win32 consoles can be installed later if required. Click **Next**. Install the Deployment Server Web Console on this machine to the default path. Use the default port unless it conflicts with another application on the Deployment Server and a service account that can access the CAP.

Installing the DS Web Console provides the ability to manage any Deployment Server through a web browser and can be installed on any machine running IIS. Click **Next**.

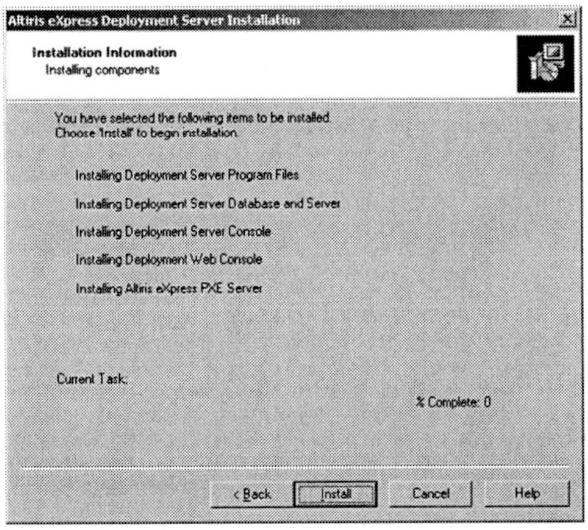

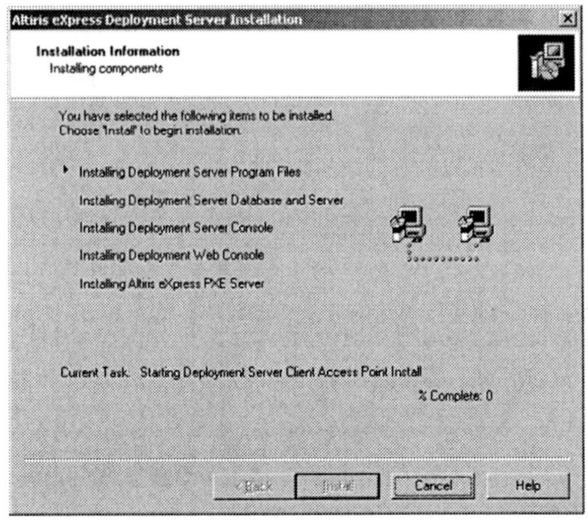

Click **Next** then click the **Install** button to being the installation.

If you chose to install PXE during the installation, the Configure Boot Disk Creator dialog will be displayed during the installation. Choose one of the three available options were the installation can find the DOS files, then click **Next**.

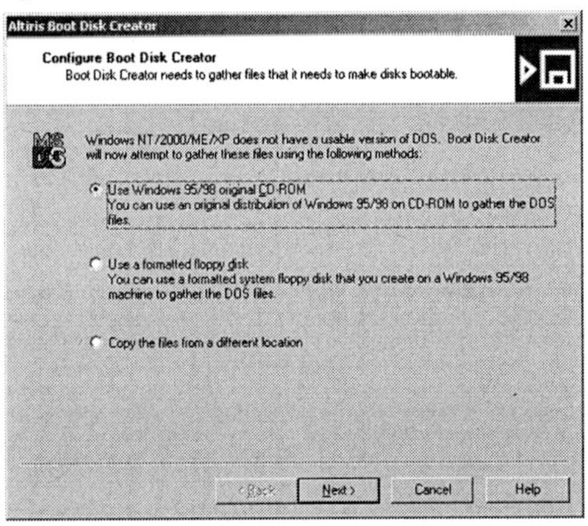

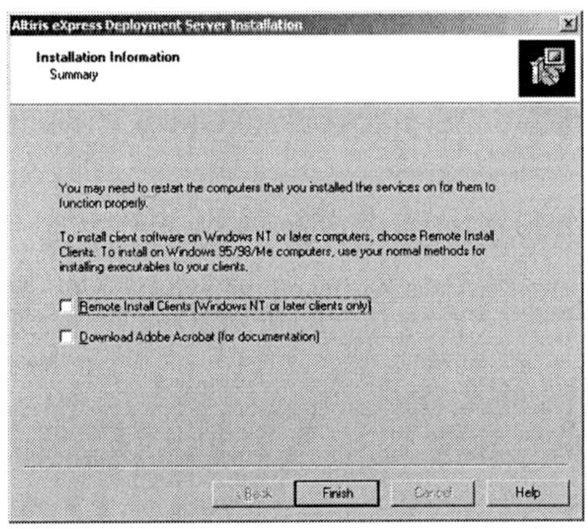

These files will be used later when configuring PXE boot files. (A Windows 98 SE CD or source is preferred.)

The installation will take about 10 minutes depending on the specification of the machine. The last dialog offers the opportunity to remotely install the Deployment Server agent and download Adobe Acrobat reader. It is worth having Acrobat Reader so that you can read the Deployment Server User Guide but I wouldn't bother rolling out the Deployment Server client at this time. At this stage the Deployment Server installation is complete.

Step 5 -Install Deployment Server Hotfixes

To determine if there are available service packs or Hotfixes for Deployment Server, connect to the Internet and navigate to http://www.altiris.com/support/updates. Choose Altiris Deployment Solution from the updates list.

An update or hotfix can be either; *Windows* or *Console*.

Windows updates and fixes are applied to the actual Deployment Server for Windows server.

Console updates and fixes are for Deployment Solution for Notification Server and are applied to the Notification Server.

When you have determined the level of service pack or hotfix available, return to your Deployment Server and open the Win32 console. Use the Help menu and the **About** command to determine the current hotfix/service pack level.

If the service pack or fix level displayed is lower than that available from the updates web site, return to the updates site and download then install the appropriate fix.

Deployment Server Consoles

The Web Console

The Web console is used to interface with and mange clients that are connected to a Deployment Server. To access the console, open a browser and go to *http://servername/DSweb* (where *servername* is the name of the Deployment Server).

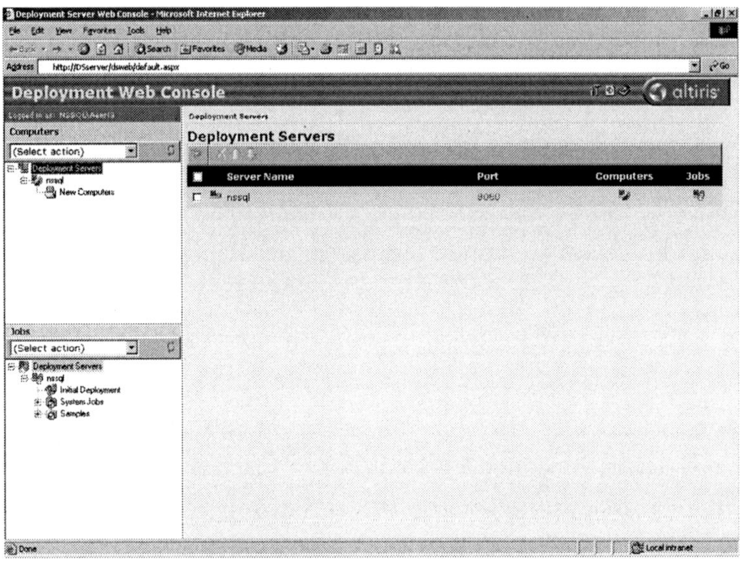

The web console offers most of the functionality offered by the Win32 console and has the advantage of being accessible through a browser without the need to install additional components.

The Deployment Server Win32 Console

The Win32 console is used to interface with and manage clients that are connected to a Deployment Server. This interface provides access to all Deployment Server functionality.

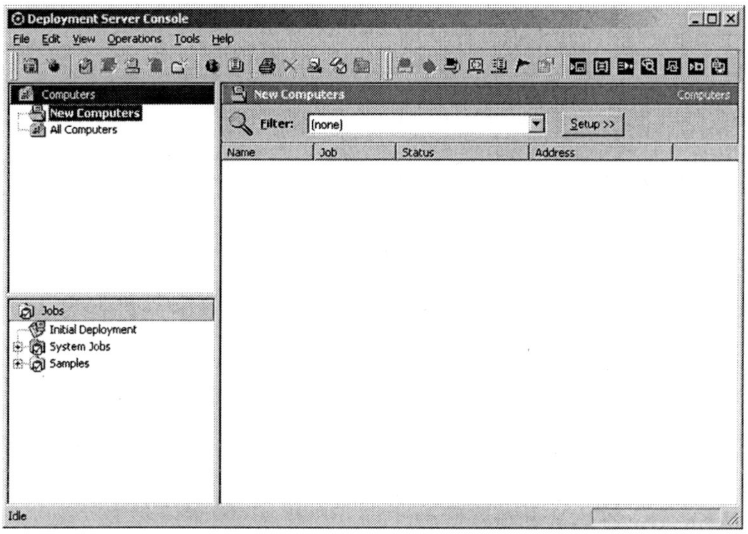

Apart from the obvious menu and task bar, the console has a Computers pane, Jobs pane and details pane.

To install an additional Deployment Server Win32 console

Connect to the *NSCAP\Bin\Win32\x86\Deployment Server Install* folder on your Notification Server or wherever you have your Deployment Server installation files.

Double click the axInstall.exe file.

In the installation Configuration dialog choose 'Add Component'. Click the **Install** button to continue.

Read and agree any licensing to continue.

Enter the path to the Deployment Server Client Access Point (CAP). This is normally *\\DSserver\Express* where DServer is the name of your Deployment Server. Click **Next**.

Choose the option 'Install an Additional Deployment Server Console'. Click **Next**.

Choose either on the local machine or a remote machine. Click **Next**.

Click **Install** to begin the installation.

When the installation has completed, click the **Finish** button.

The installation adds a Deployment Server Win32 Console shortcut to the local desktop and the **Start > Programs** section of the Start menu.

The Notification Server Deployment Web Console

Using the Notification Server Web Console offers the advantage of providing the ability to manage more than one Deployment Server through one web interface.

The first time you view the Deployment tab through the Notification Server Web Console you are prompted to add a Deployment Server that will be manged through the Notification Server interface.

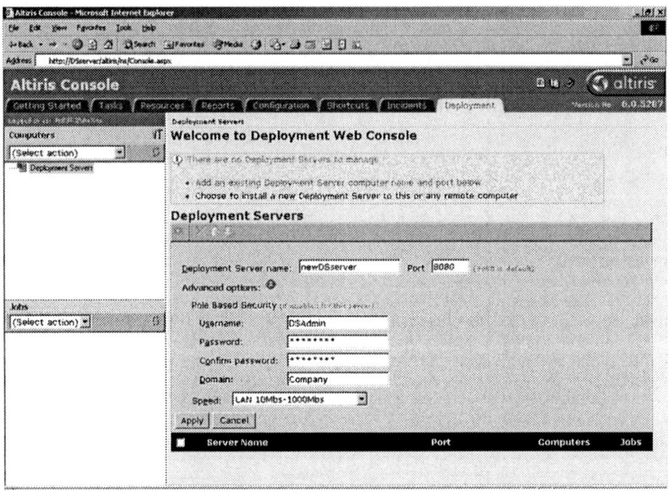

Open the Web Console and select the **Deployment** tab then enter the name of the new Deployment Server.

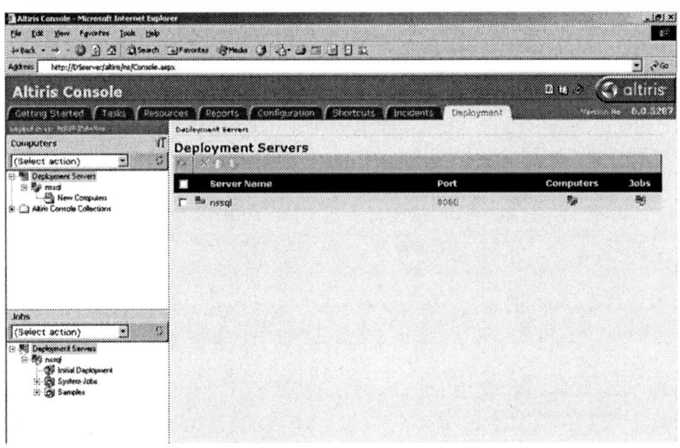

If role based console security (discussed later), has been configured for the selected DS, expand the *Advanced options* and enter the configured credentials. Click **Apply** to add the Deployment Server.

Once added, this new DS can be managed from within the Notification Server Web console. *The NS Deployment Web console offers the same functionality as the DS Web Console with the addition of being able to manage multiple Deployment Servers.*

Post Installation Configuration Tasks

The following section provides an overview of some of the important configuration options available in Deployment Server.

There are two areas where configuration of Deployment Server is performed; The first set of configuration options are available from the **Options** command in the **Tools** menu of the Win32 console and the second area is using the Altiris Express Server icon in Control Panel.

Configuring Options

Open the Win32 Console and from the Tools menu choose the Options command.

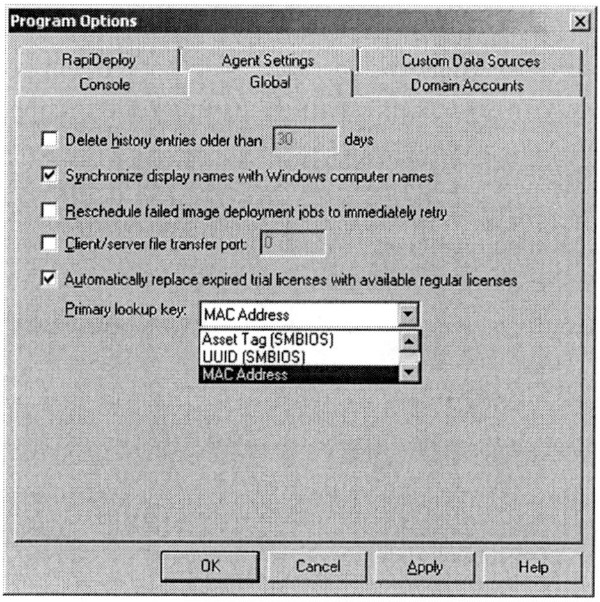

Global Options

Select the **Global tab** to display the available options.

Delete history entries older than X days - The number of days an entry is kept in the history until it's deleted.

Synchronize display names with Windows computer names - Automatically update the name displayed in the console when the client computer name changes.

Reschedule failed image deployment jobs to immediately retry - Immediately retry a failed image deployment job and continue to retry until the job succeeds or is cancelled.

Client/server file transfer port - Specifies a static TCP port for file transfers to the clients. The default value is 0 and will cause the server to use a dynamic port. This is a useful setting if you have a firewall and need to use a specific port instead of a dynamic port.

Automatically replace expired trial licenses with available regular licenses - Used to automatically assign a full license to a computer after the trial license expires.

Primary lookup key - Specifies the type of lookup key used to associate a new computer with a managed computer. The available options are Serial Number (SMBIOS), Asset Tag (SMBIOS), UUID (SMBIOS), or MAC Address (Default).

Domain Accounts

Select the **Domain Accounts tab** to display the available options.
Use this dialog to specify an account with the right to add computers you Domain.

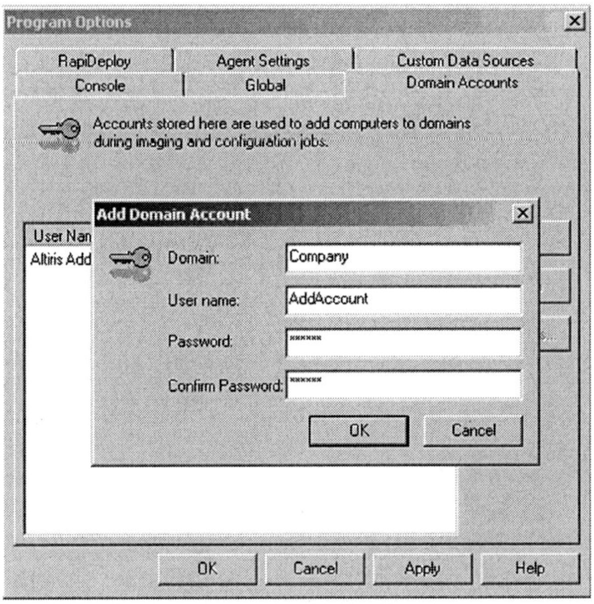

The account(s) added are used during imaging and change configuration jobs.

Click **Add** and enter the domain name and user credentials. Click **OK** to return to the Domain Accounts dialog. When all accounts have been added, click **OK**.

Configuring Altiris Express Server

On the Deployment Server, **open Control Panel** and **double click the Altiris Express Server icon**.

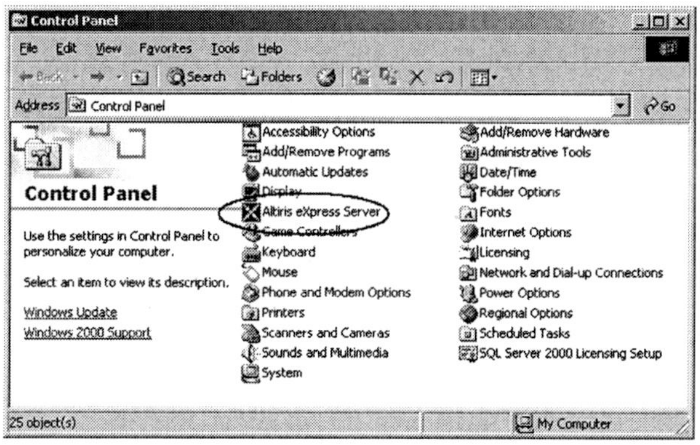

Select the **Options** button to display the Altiris Express Server options dialog.

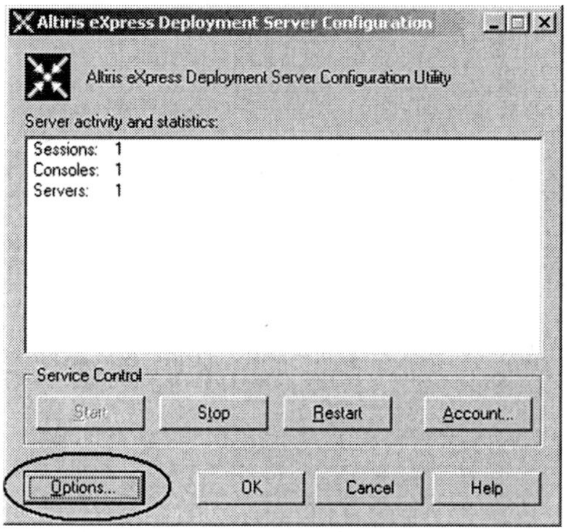

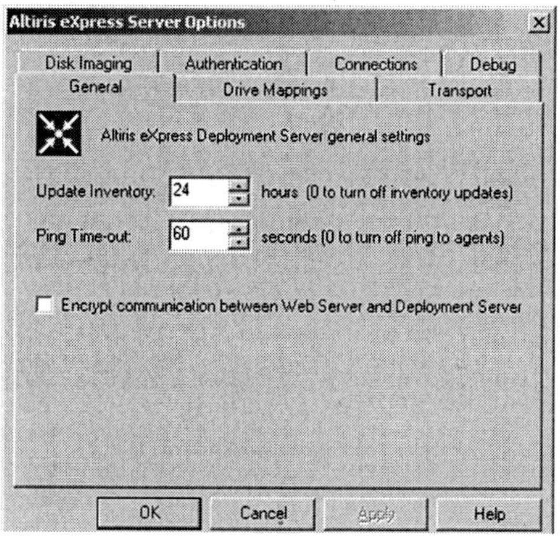

The **General tab** provides options to configure how frequently clients send inventory to the Deployment Server as well as timeout value when updating connections to clients.

An inventory is only executed when the Deployment Agent starts up on the computer. If a computer is not rebooted or restarted for a number of days, then inventory will not be taken during that time even though the update inventory value is set to 24 hours. When the computer is restarted and if the Update Inventory interval has elapsed, then an inventory will be run on the computer.

The **Drive Mappings tab** is used to add, delete and edit drive mappings used by the Deployment Server. Any drive mappings used to reference files need to be created within this dialog.

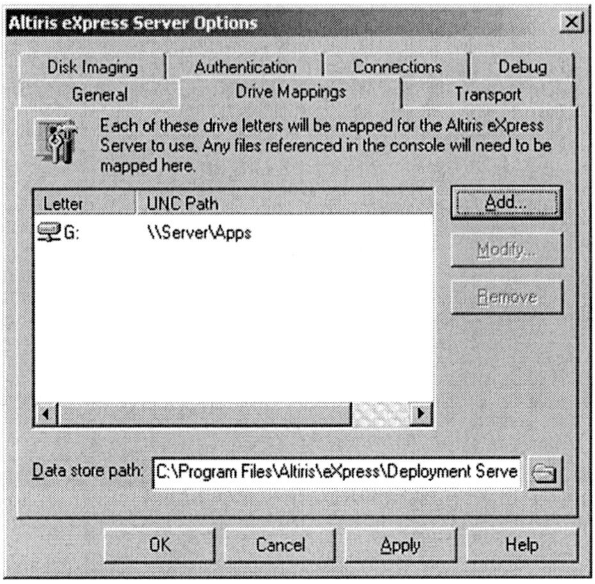

For example, if you create a task that distributes a software package from a drive on another file server using a mapped G: drive, then you will need to create the G: drive mapping on the Deployment Server using the drive mappings dialog.

The **Transport tab** allows you to specify transport protocols settings for the Deployment Server.

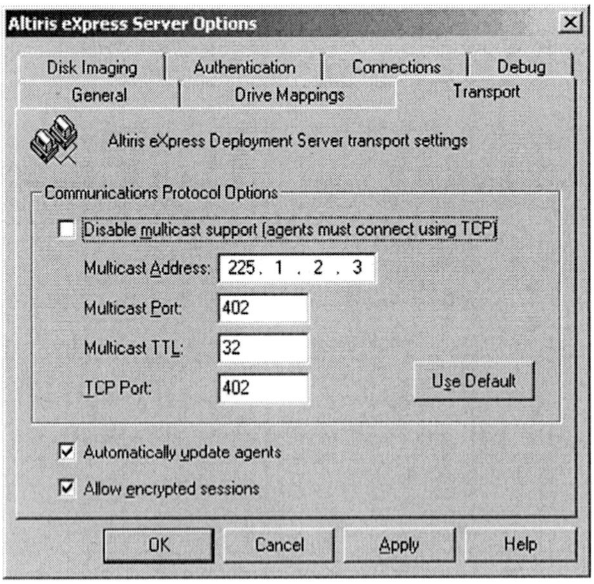

Disable multicast support (agents must connect using TCP) - This option disables multicast support, which means that clients must connect to the Deployment Server using TCP.

Automatically update Agents - If a client is running an older or newer version of the Agent than the version on the Deployment Server, the agent will automatically upgrade/down grade itself. Be careful with this option in a large environment. If a service pack or upgrade is applied to the Deployment Server and the agent version changes, all clients will automatically upgrade/down grade the installed agent.

Pre-boot Execution Environment (PXE)

Clients use PXE when uploading/downloading images, backing up and restoring the registry and running DOS scripts.

The following section provides an overview of the PXE process and instructions on basic PXE configuration but does not attempt to cover all options and scenarios.

How PXE works

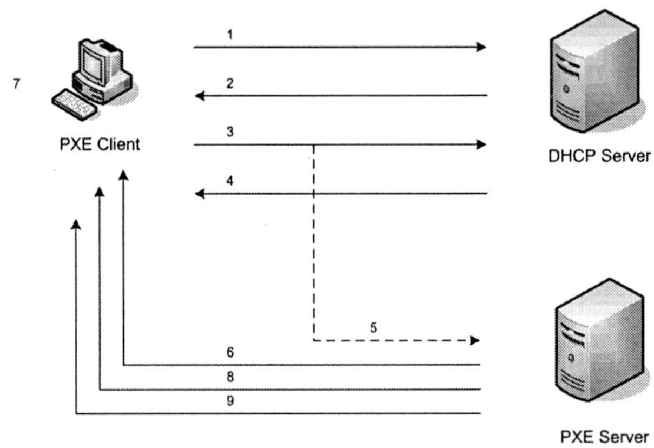

1. The PXE client is configured through its BIOS to boot using its network card. The client requires an IP address and so it broadcasts a DHCP Discover packet looking for a DHCP server.
2. The DHCP server responds with a DHCP offer.
3. The client broadcasts a DHCP Request and includes its MAC, IP of the chosen DHCP server and an option 60 to identify it as a PXE client.
4. The DHCP server supplies an acknowledgement packet (DHCPACK) to the client. If the DHCP server is also a PXE server then an option 60 is included in the acknowledgement packet.
5. During steps 1 to 4, the PXE server monitors the network for PXE clients requesting an IP address.
6. If a PXE server recognizes a PXE client DHCP request, the PXE server looks up the clients MAC address in the Deployment Server database for any pending jobs. If there are no jobs for the client, PXE boot is skipped. If there is a job for the client, then the PXE server broadcasts a DHCPACK packet containing only an option 60, which indicates that the packet is from a PXE server. At this point, the client receives an IP address from the DHCP server and it now knows the location of the PXE server.

7. The client requests a boot menu from the PXE server. The client is provided with a menu and the options on how the menu is to be displayed. Each item in the menu points back to the PXE server. If configured, a menu item will point to a set of boot files which the client can download and use.
8. When the client has determined whether a menu option has been selected, the agent requests the boot files for the selected menu item from the PXE server. There are two sets of boot files, one for new computers and one for existing managed computers. A PXE client that is new will receive the new computer boot files (newcomp.0) and a client that is already in the database with an assigned Job, will receive the managed set of boot files (managed.0).
9. The .0 boot files create a RAM disk on the client and then copy the corresponding .1 boot files (newcomp.1 and managed.1) to the RAM disk. The .1 files are effectively an image of a DOS boot floppy disk. The image contains the files required to perform a network boot. When the files execute, a NIC driver and protocol stack are loaded and a drive F is mapped to the express share on the Deployment Server using the credentials defined in the image. The client uses the F mapping to perform the requested operations.

An Overview of Configuring PXE

The following instructions guide you through the configuration of PXE for use with Altiris Deployment Server.

Step 1 - Boot Disk Creator

On the Deployment Server click **Start** and got to **Programs** > **Altiris** > **PXE Services** > **Boot Disk Creator.**

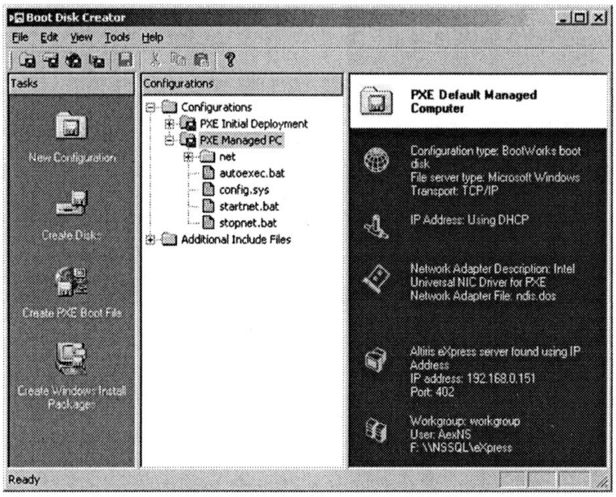

The installation of PXE during the Deployment Server installation created two boot disk packages. One package is for the initial deployment event (new computers) and the other package is for existing computers that have been assigned a Job (managed computers).

For the purposes of this exercise we will disable Initial Deployment and configure our own managed pc package from scratch.

Delete existing boot packages

In the Boot Disk Creator dialog, right click the PXE Managed PC package and choose delete from the shortcut menu. Click 'Yes' to confirm the delete.
Repeat the process for PXE Initial Deployment.
All packages are now removed.

Creating a New Managed PC Package

In the Boot Disk Creator dialog, click the New Configuration shortcut. This will launch the package creator.

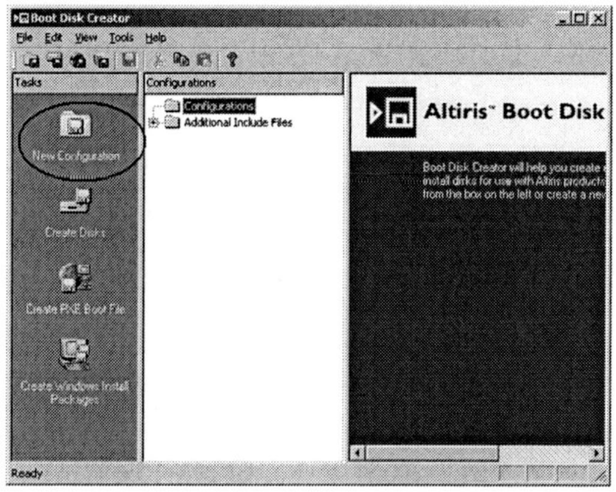

The Boot Disk Creator Wizard is launched.

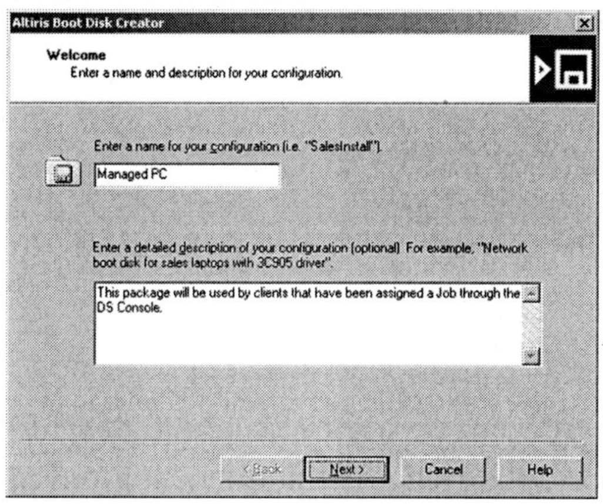

Enter the name and description for the new Managed PC package. Click **Next** to continue.

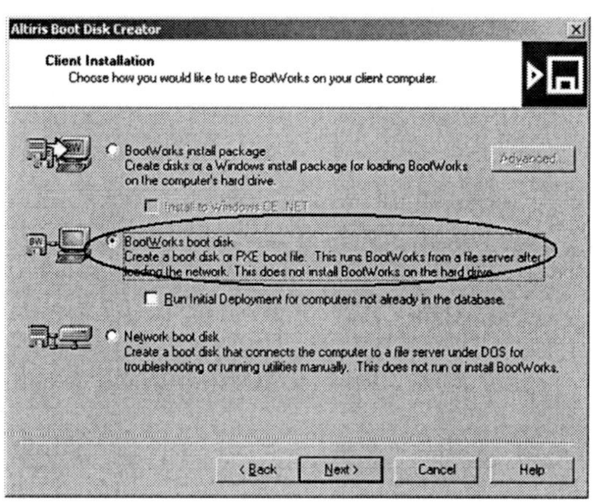

Select the option Bootworks Boot disk then click **Next**.

In the next step choose **Microsoft Windows** as the type of boot disk.

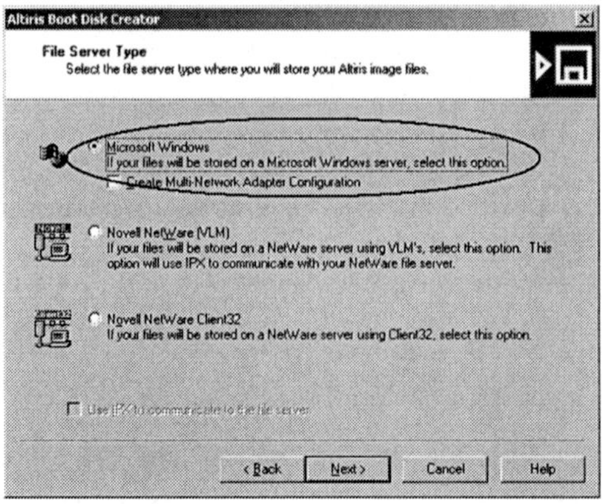

Click **Next** to continue.

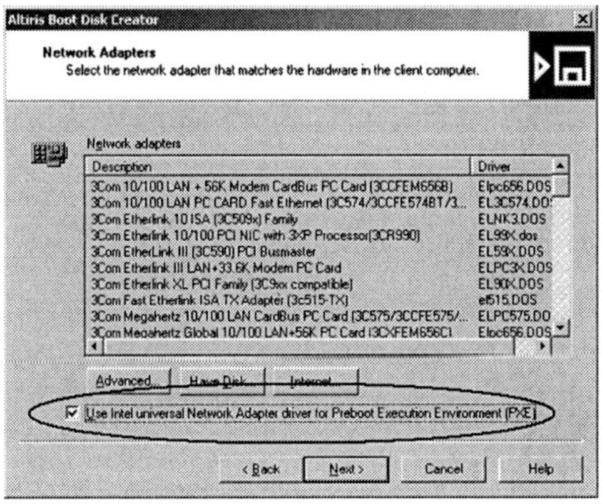

In the Network Adapters dialog choose a specific NIC driver to work with the clients that will use this boot disk or choose the Intel Undi driver. The Intel driver is a generic driver that works with most desktop and laptop machines.
Click **Next** to continue.

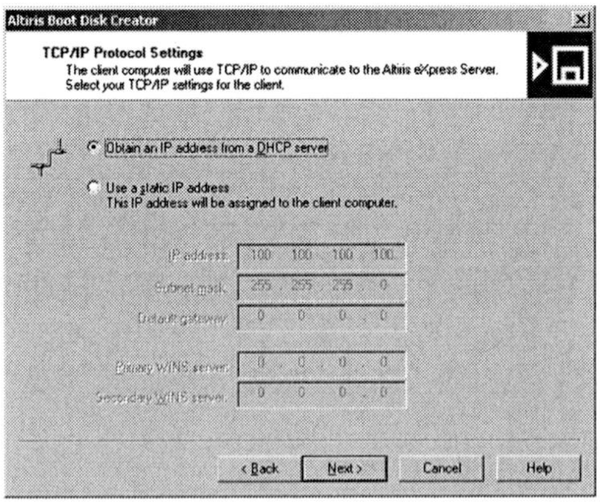

Choose the default option, obtain IP address from a DHCP server and click **Next** to continue.

In the Altiris Express Configuration dialog, enter the IP address and port for the Deployment Server.

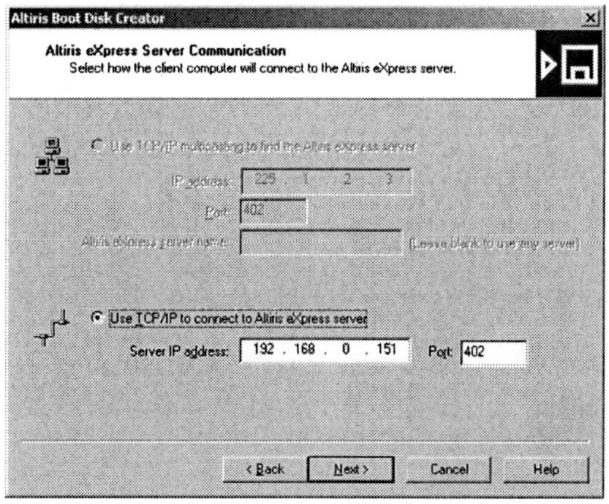

Click **Next** to continue.

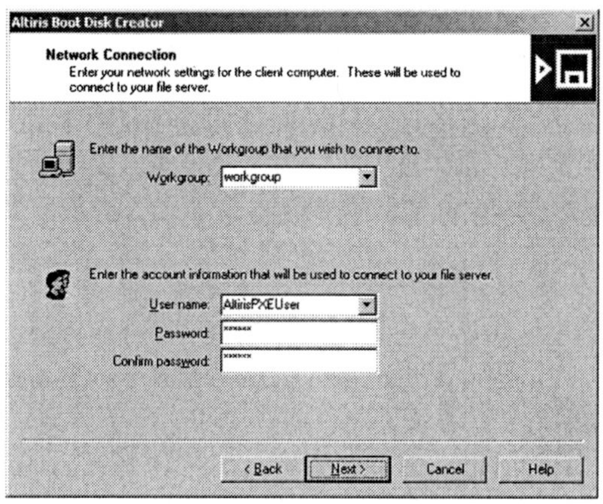

Enter the credentials that will be used by the PXE client to connect to the Deployment Server Express share. Click **Next** to continue.

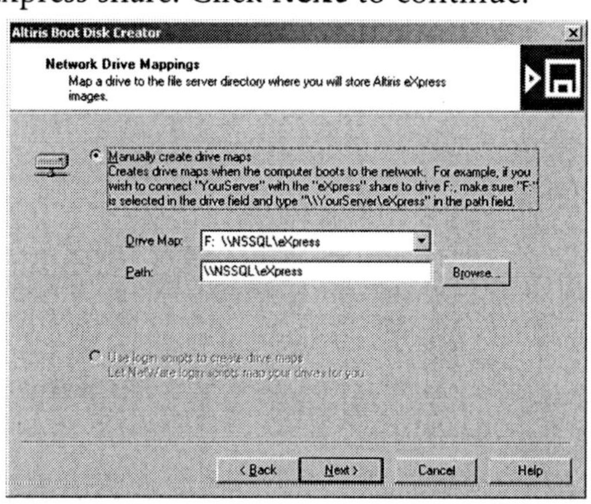

Add any extra drive mapping required when the PXE client maps drives. Drive F will be mapped to the Express share as default. Click **Next** to continue.

In the last dialog click **Finish** to complete the wizard.

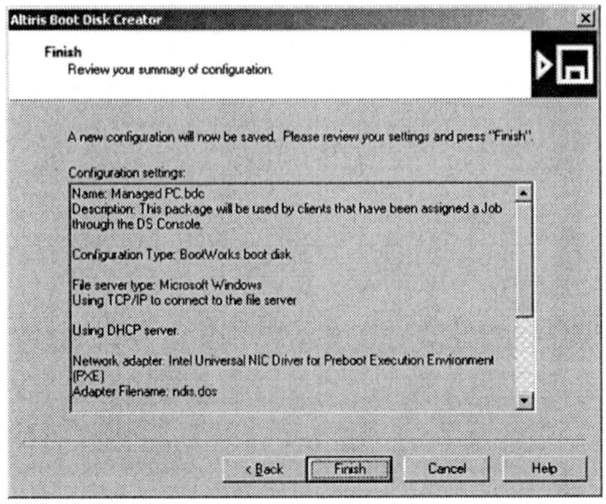

Click **OK** in the Boot disk Creator dialog to return to the main Boot Disk Creator dialog. The new Managed PC package will now be displayed.

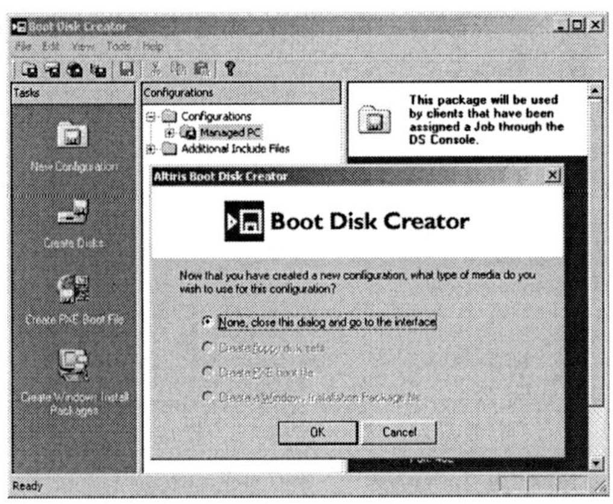

Now that the Managed files have been created, we need to link these files to the Managed PC menu item on the PXE server. **Close** the **Boot Disk Creator**.

From the Start menu on the Deployment Server go to **Programs > Altiris > PXE Services > PXE Configuration Utility**.

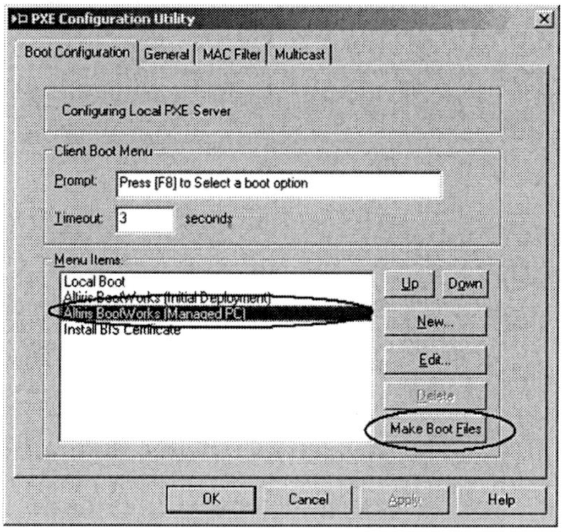

Select the menu item Altiris Bootworks (Managed PC) and click the Make Boot Files button. This launches the Boot Disk Creator application.

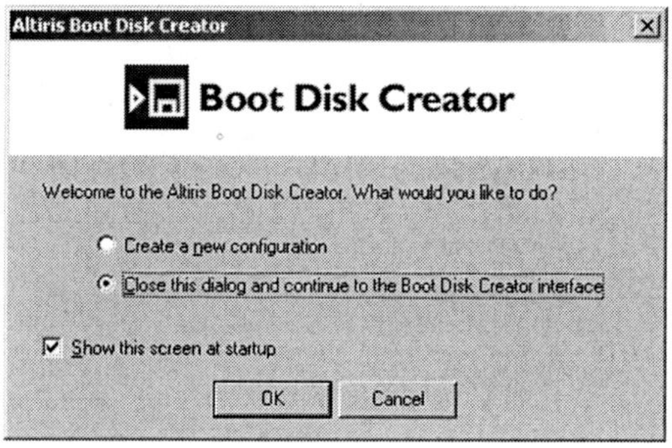

If the Welcome dialog appears click **Cancel**

In the Boot Disk Creator dialog, right click the Managed PC package created earlier and from the shortcut menu choose the **Create PXE Boot Files** command.

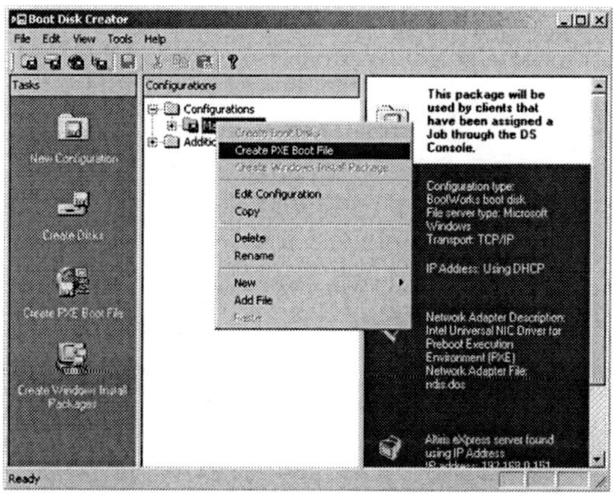

The Create a PXE Boot File dialog is displayed.

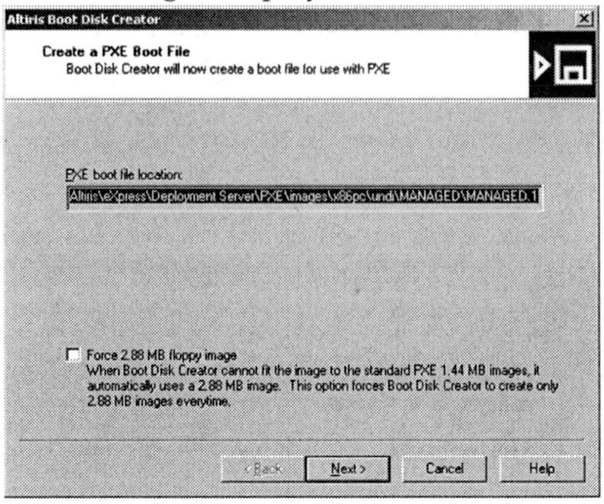

Click **Next** to continue.

When the PXE boot file creation is complete, the final dialog is displayed.

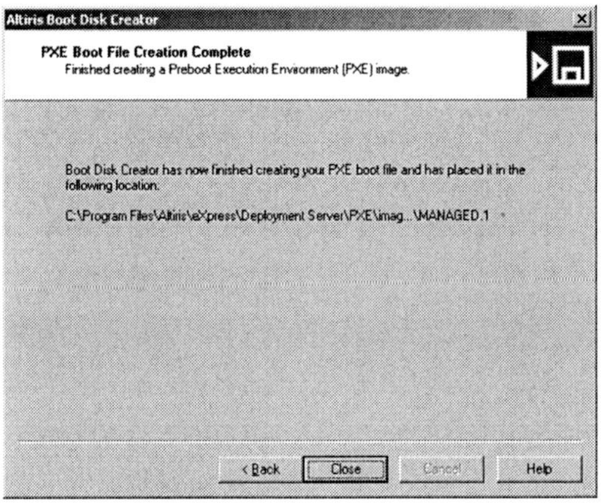

Click **Close** to return to the Boot Disk Creator dialog.

Important Close the Boot Disk Creator at this point to return to the PXE Configuration Utility.

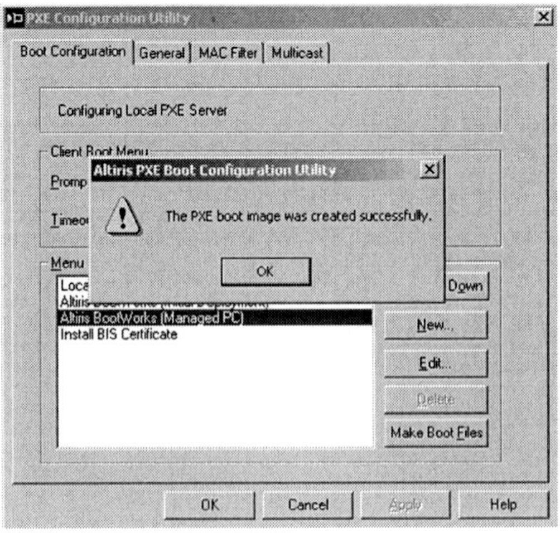

The configuration dialog displays a message box confirming that the Managed PC package has been linked to the Managed PC menu item.
Click **OK**.

This completes the configuration of the Managed PC files. When a client performs a DOS type Job, the necessary files and configuration are in place. It is also worth while disabling the Initial Deployment Menu item at this point.

Disabling Initial Deployment

The Initial Deployment Event is used to automatically assign a preconfigured event to run on new computers that perform a PXE boot. For example, Initial Deployment can be configured to deploy the corporate image to any new machines that perform a network PXE boot. This is useful in a factory type environment but rarely used in production.

To disable Initial Deployment, select the menu item Altiris Bootworks (Initial Deployment) in the PXE Configuration Utility.

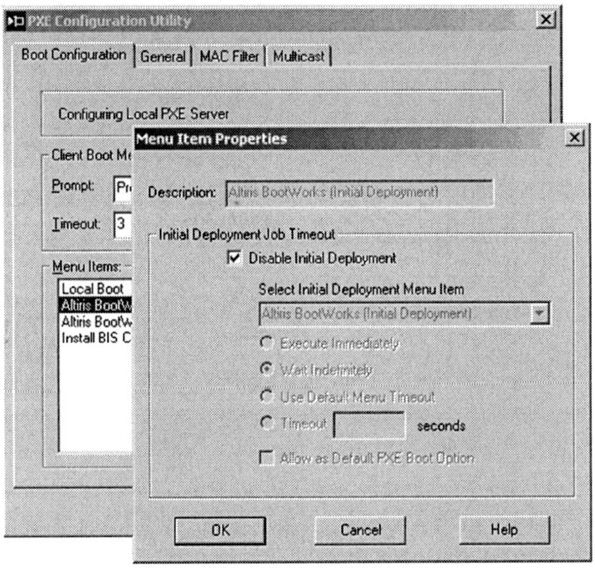

Click, the **Edit** button.

Disable Initial Deployment.

Click **OK** to exit the Initial Deployment dialog.

Click **OK** to exit the PXE Configuration Utility.

Configuring Console Security

Console security is used to secure access to the DS console. Security is based on defining groups of users and then configuring permissions on Computer and Job objects within the console using the defined Groups.

Groups can contain built-in users and or Active Directory users and be given general Deployment Server permissions and or specific access to perform actions on Groups of Computers and Jobs in the console.

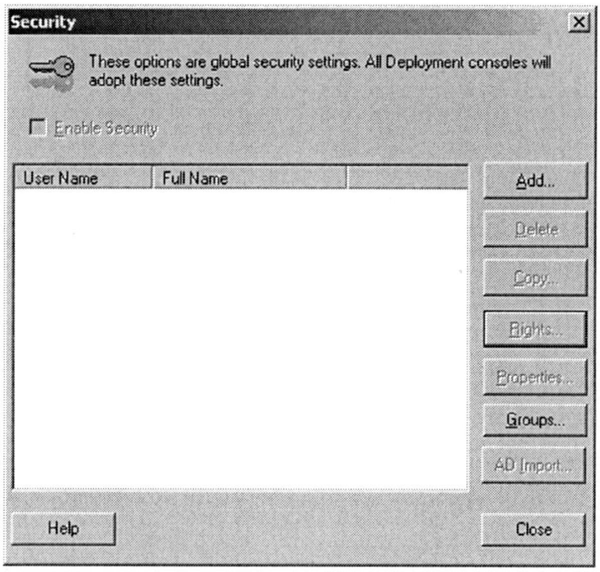

In practice you will have at least two Groups, one with full administrative rights and one with limited rights. For example you may have an Administrative Group with full access to the console and all objects and another Group that is permitted to access the console but only deploy images to desktop machines but not to Servers.

Creating a New Admin user

Two types of users can be added, a **built-in user** or an **Active Directory user**.

Adding a built-in user

To add a built-in user, **open** the **Win32 console** and from the **Tools menu** choose the **security** command.

When the Security dialog is displayed, click the **Add** button.

Enter a name, password, full name and description for the new user.

When the details have been entered, click **OK**.

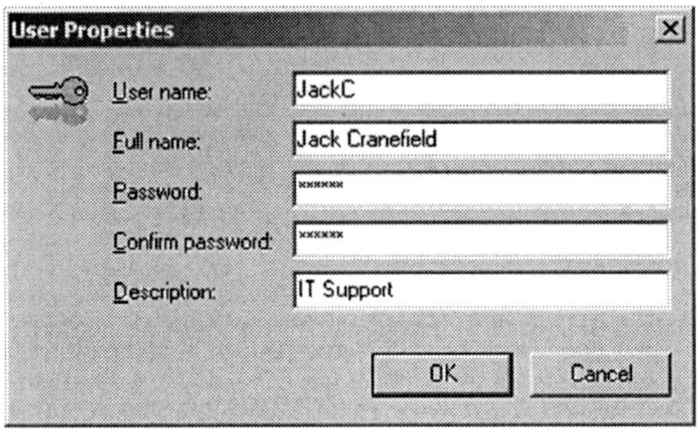

Adding a new Active Directory user

To add an Active Directory user, from the security dialog, click the **Add** button.

Enter the AD user in the form Domain\User. You'll notice that the password boxes become disabled.

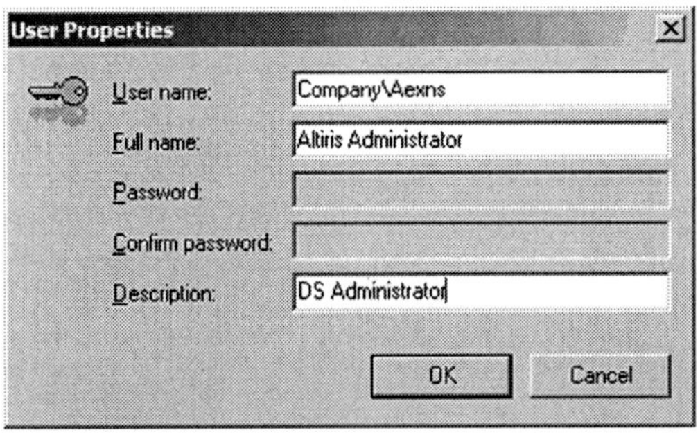

When the details have been entered, click **OK**.

Assigning the New User to the Administrators Group

In the security dialog **double click** the new user created previously.

In the Groups tab check to select the Administrators Group.

Select the **Rights Tab** to confirm that the Administration Right is checked.

Click **OK** to return to the main Security dialog.

When the first user is added, security is automatically enabled. Closing the security dialog you prompt you to login to the console.
Enter the new User ID created previously and click **OK**.

The next time you connect to the Deployment Server using any of the three Deployment Server consoles you'll be prompted to login.

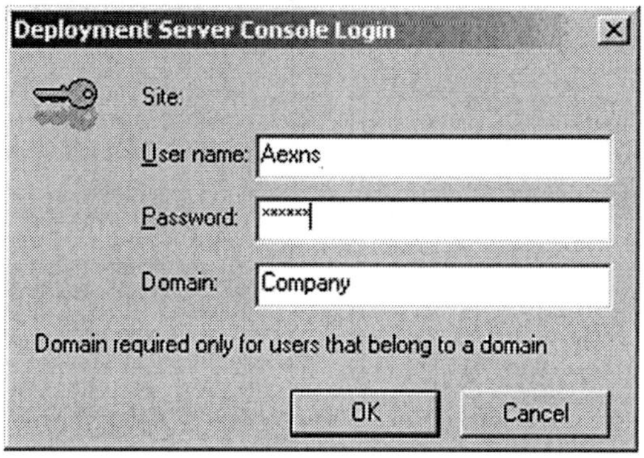

Enter the name, password and Domain if appropriate and click OK.

Creating a New Group

Open the Win32 console and from the **Tools menu** choose the **Security** command.

Security is based on a User being a member of a Group which has been assigned rights to objects such as Computers and Jobs within the Console.

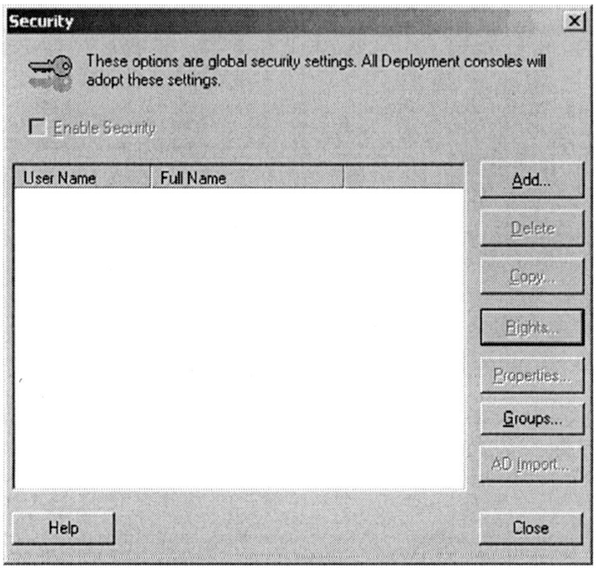

Click the **Groups** button in the Security dialog then click the **add** button to add a Group.

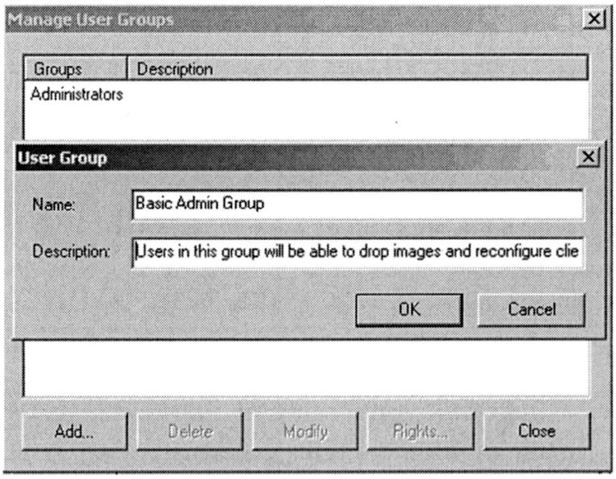

Enter a **name and description** for the Group then click **OK**.

The new Group is displayed.

Assigning rights to a Group

Select the new Group then click the Rights button.

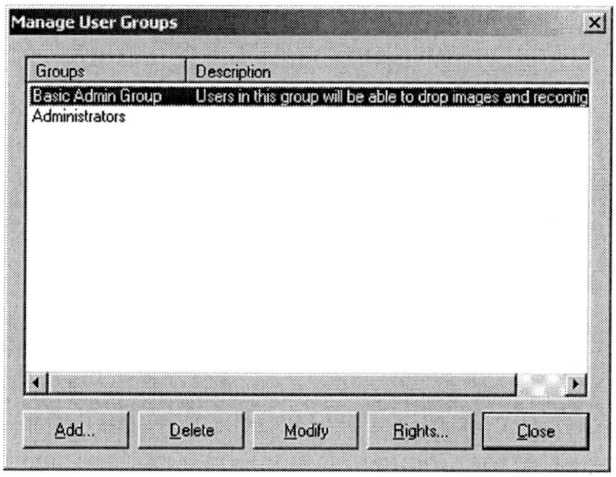

Console rights include the ability to modify general Deployment Server settings including the right to modify the Global and Security configuration of the Deployment Server.

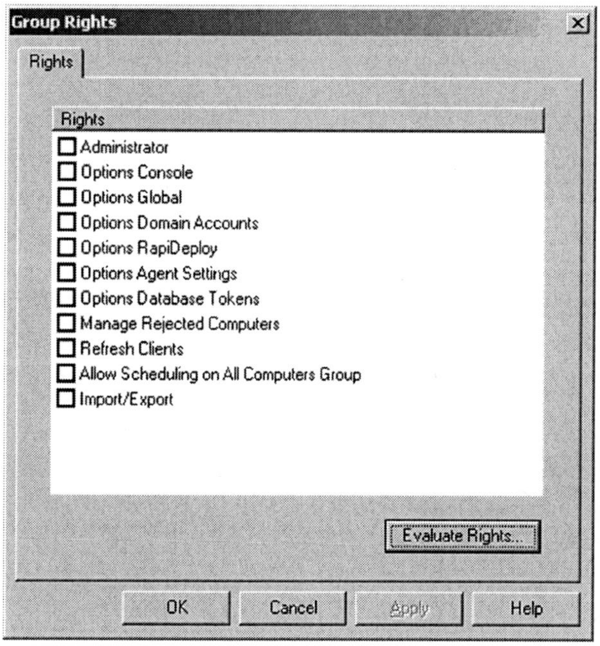

To give the Group a specific console right, check the appropriate right. If you just want to give a group of users access to Computers and Jobs in the console but not to advanced rights then don't check any of the rights.

When you have assigned general rights click **Close** to return to the Security dialog.

Creating a New non-Admin user

To add a built-in user, from the security dialog, click the Add button in the Security dialog.

Type a name for the user and enter a password, full name and description. Click **OK**.

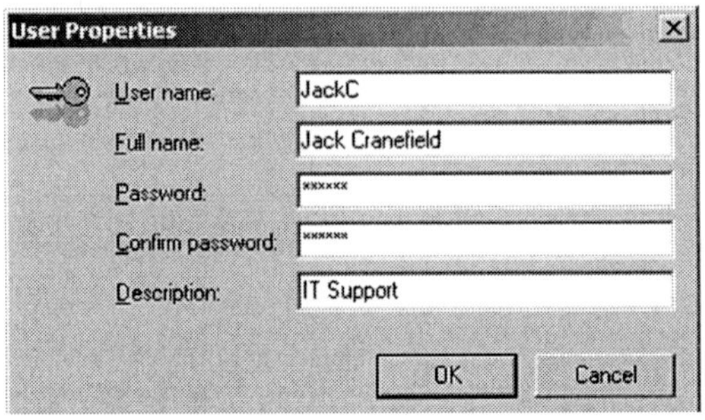

To add an Active Directory user, from the security dialog, click the **Add** button.

Enter the AD user in the form Domain\User. You'll notice that the password boxes become disabled.

Click **OK**.

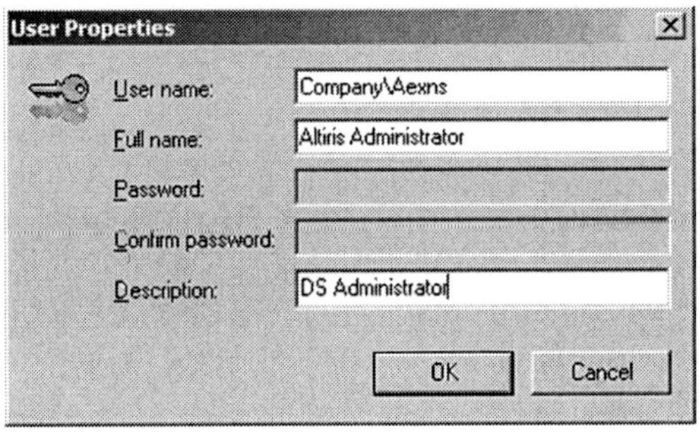

Assigning the New User to the New Group

In the security dialog **double click** the new **user** created previously.

Select the Group you want the selected user to be a member of, then click **Close**.

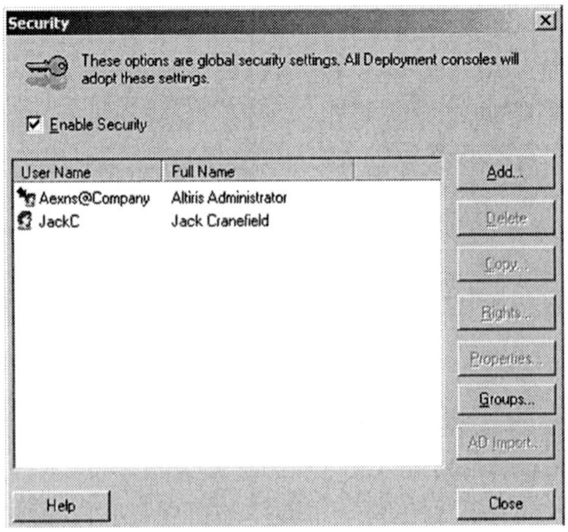

When the user has been assigned to the new group, enable Security and click **Close**.

Securing access to Computers and Jobs in the console

Now that you have added and configured users and groups to Security you can begin the process of locking down Computer and Job objects in the DS console.
Open the Win32 Deployment Server console and group your Computers and Jobs in to appropriate folders/groups. Grouping will make it easier to secure large numbers of computers and jobs.

Configuring Computer Group Access

Right click the Computer Group in the Computers pane to configure and choose Security from the bottom of the shortcut menu.
In the Object Security dialog select the Groups tab.

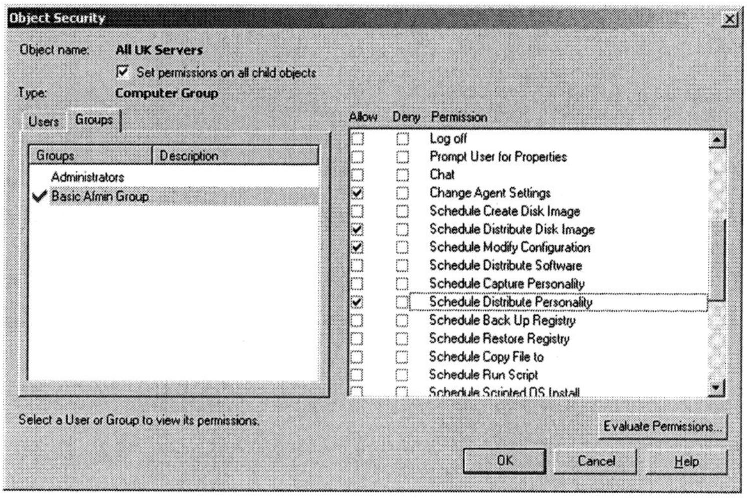

Select the appropriate Group(s).
Check Allow and Deny permissions as appropriate. (Members of the Administrators automatically have full access to all objects.)
If appropriate check the 'Set permissions on all child objects.
Use the Evaluate Permissions button to see the effective permissions for the selected Group. Click **OK** to finish.

Configuring Job Folder Access

Right click the Jobs folder in the Jobs pane and choose Security from the bottom of the shortcut menu.

In the Object Security dialog select the Groups tab.

Select the appropriate Group(s).

Check Allow and Deny permissions as appropriate. (Members of the Administrators automatically have full access to all objects.)

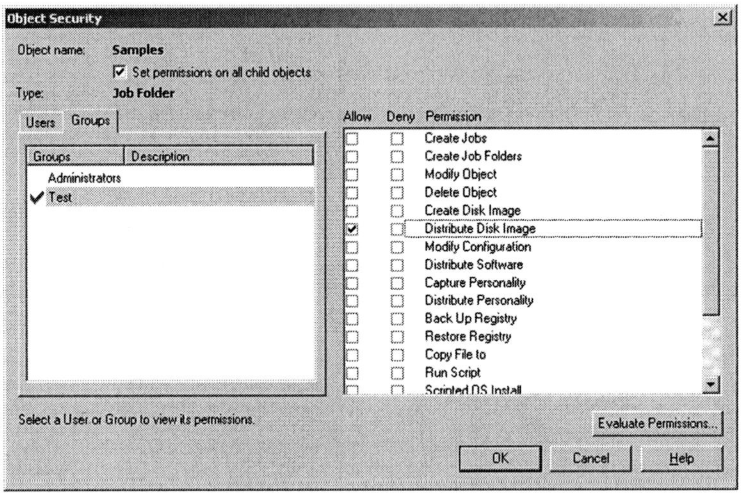

If appropriate check the 'Set permissions on all child objects.

Use the Evaluate Permissions button to see the effective permissions for the selected Group.

Click **OK** to finish.

Deploying the Deployment Server Aclient Agent

The Deployment Server Aclient Agent is the interface between the client and the Deployment Server. This agent is not a plug-in for the Altiris Agent but is a standalone product. This means that in an environment where Client Management Suite is used, a client will typically have two agents, one for Deployment Server and one for Notification Server.

The DS Aclient Agent can be installed on a client using several methods including:

- Included in a image
- Login script
- Pushed from the Win32 console
- Pushed from the Notification Server Web Console

Pushing the Deployment Server Aclient Agent from the Notification Server Web Console

If all machines that you want to install the agent too already have the Notification Server Altiris Agent, then you can use a Notification Server policy to push the agent.

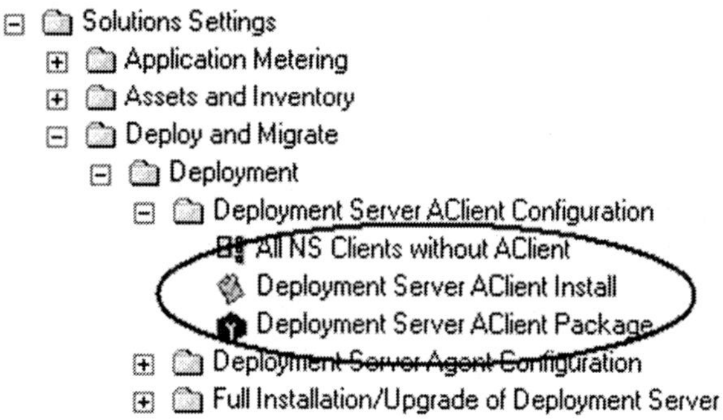

Open the Notification Server Web console and select the Configuration tab then navigate to **Solution Settings** > **Deploy and Migrate** > **Deployment** > **Deployment Server AClient Configuration** > **Deployment Server AClient Install**.

Enable the policy and click **Apply**.

The next time that machines in the targeted collection (All machines with the Altiris Agent) update their configuration they will download and install the Aclient Agent.

Pushing the Deployment Server Aclient from the Deployment Server Win32 Console

Step 1 -

Open the Win32 console and from the Tools menu choose Remote Agent Installer. In the first dialog, you are prompted for an account with administrative privileges on

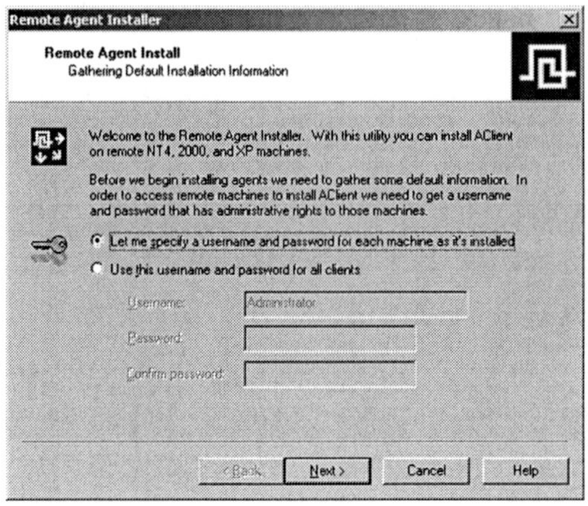

the machine(s) that the Deployment Server AClient will be pushed too. The credentials can be entered now or at a later stage in the wizard. Click **Next** to continue.

Step 2-

Enter the install path on the client. The options 'Enable this agent to use Sidgen and/or Microsoft Sysprep' can be enabled if you intend to create an image from the client. Don't check this box if you are just pushing the agent for management purposes only.

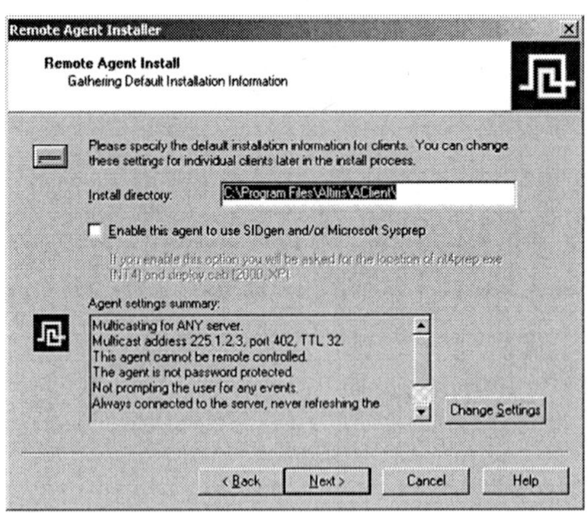

Click the **Change Settings** button to display the agent settings dialog.

Step 3 -

This dialog allows you to configure the Aclient settings for the machines that the agent is pushed too. For details on all of the options see the Deployment User guide. For the purposes of this exercise we will configure the Transport tab only. Click the

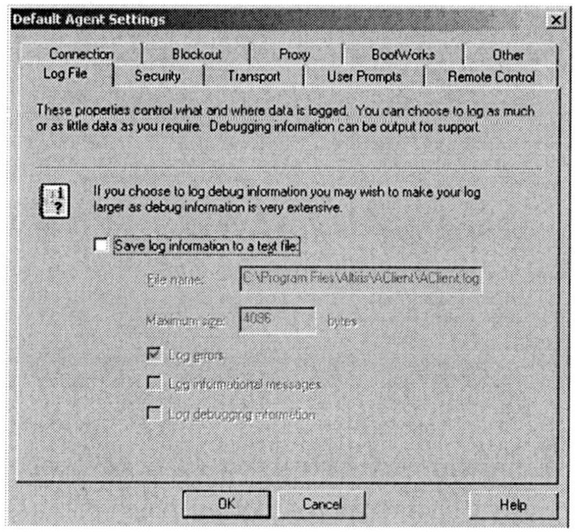

Transport tab to configure how the agent will communicate with the Deployment Server once it has been installed.

By default the agent uses TCP/IP port 402 to communicate with the Deployment Server. The client can use multicast or be configured to communicate with a specific Deployment Server. Using multicast means that a client will look on the network for a Deployment Server and communicate with the most responsive server found. This is fine if there is only one Deployment Server but it may lead to issues if there are more than one Deployment Servers within the client's multicast range.

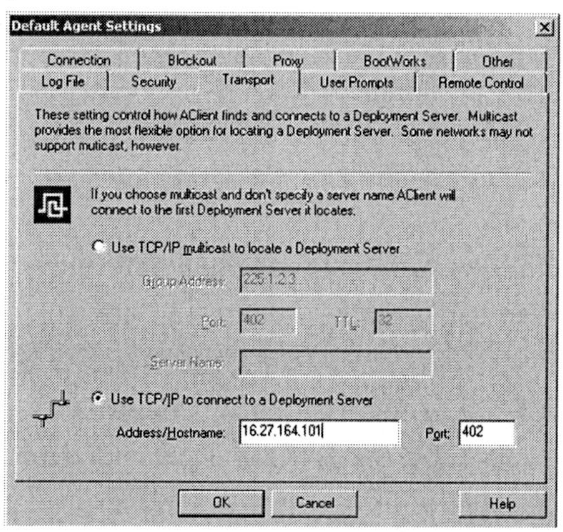

Choose the option **Use TCP/IP** to connect to a Deployment Server. Enter the name *(preferable)* or IP address of the Deployment Server you want your clients to communicate with. Click **OK** to return to the Remote Agent Installer dialog.

Click **Next** to continue to the next step.

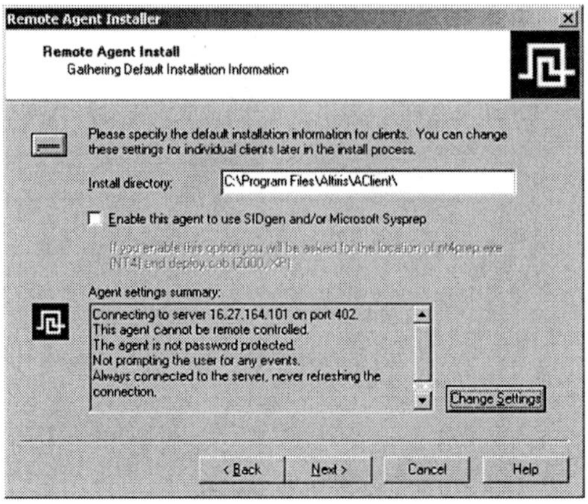

Step 4 -

In the Selecting Clients dialog you can either import a txt or xls file containing a list of machines or use the **Add button** to add individual machines. (Sample import files are in the samples folder on the root of the express share of the Deployment Server, they are ImportComputers55.txt and ImportComputers55.xls)

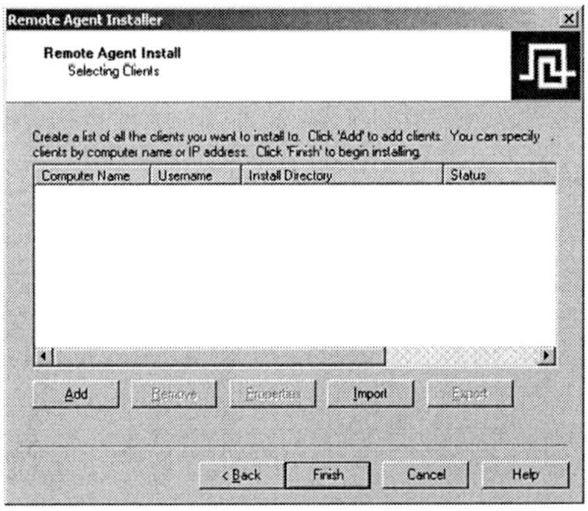

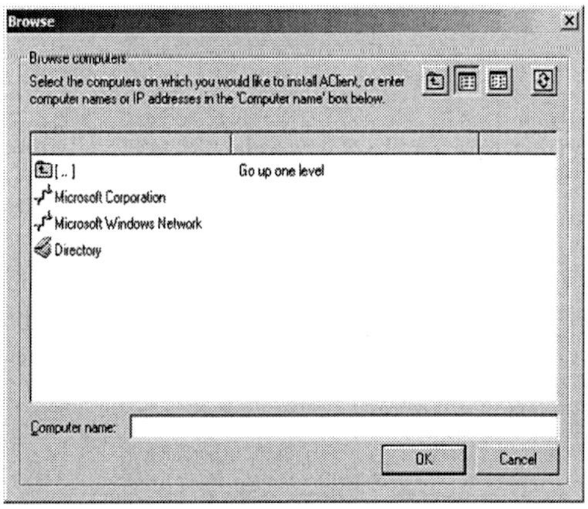

Using the **Add** button allows you to select individual computers from a browse list. Click **Add**. Select the target machines, using the control key to select multiple machines, and then click **OK**.

When all selected machines are displayed in the Selecting Clients dialog click **Finish** to begin the agent push.

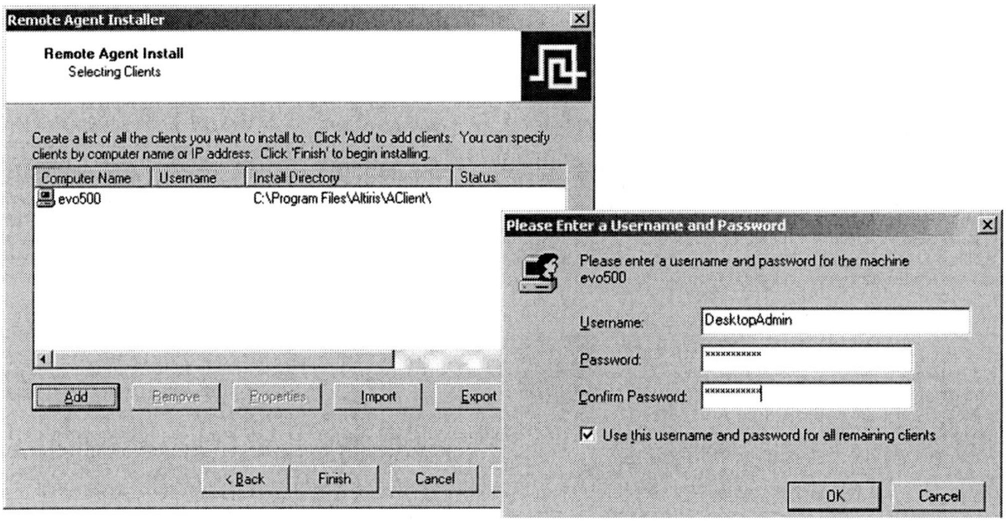

If the necessary administrative credentials were not supplied at the beginning of the wizard, enter them now and click **OK**.

Exit the Install Wizard once the agent has pushed successfully to the target machines.

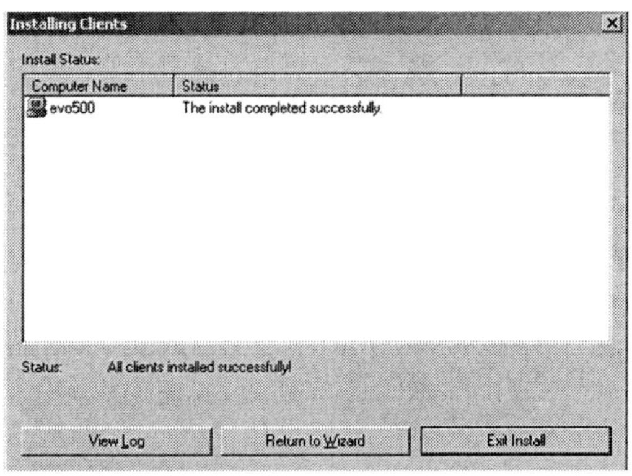

When the agent has been successfully installed on the target machine, it is added to the database of the configured Deployment Server and the client is displayed in the Deployment Server console.

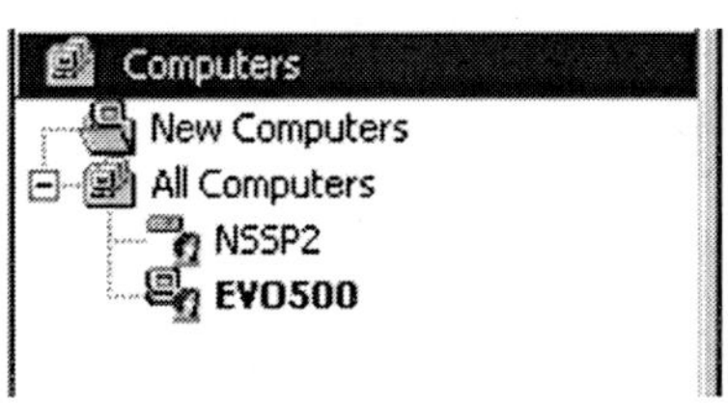

When the agent is first installed it sends inventory data to its configured Deployment Server.

Managing Deployment Server clients

The following section guides you through performing basic management tasks using the Deployment Server Win32 and Web consoles.

Viewing the properties of a client (Win32 console)

When a client has the Aclient installed it will send inventory information to its configured Deployment Server. To view the inventory and the properties of the client, open the Win32 console and double click the client, the properties are displayed.

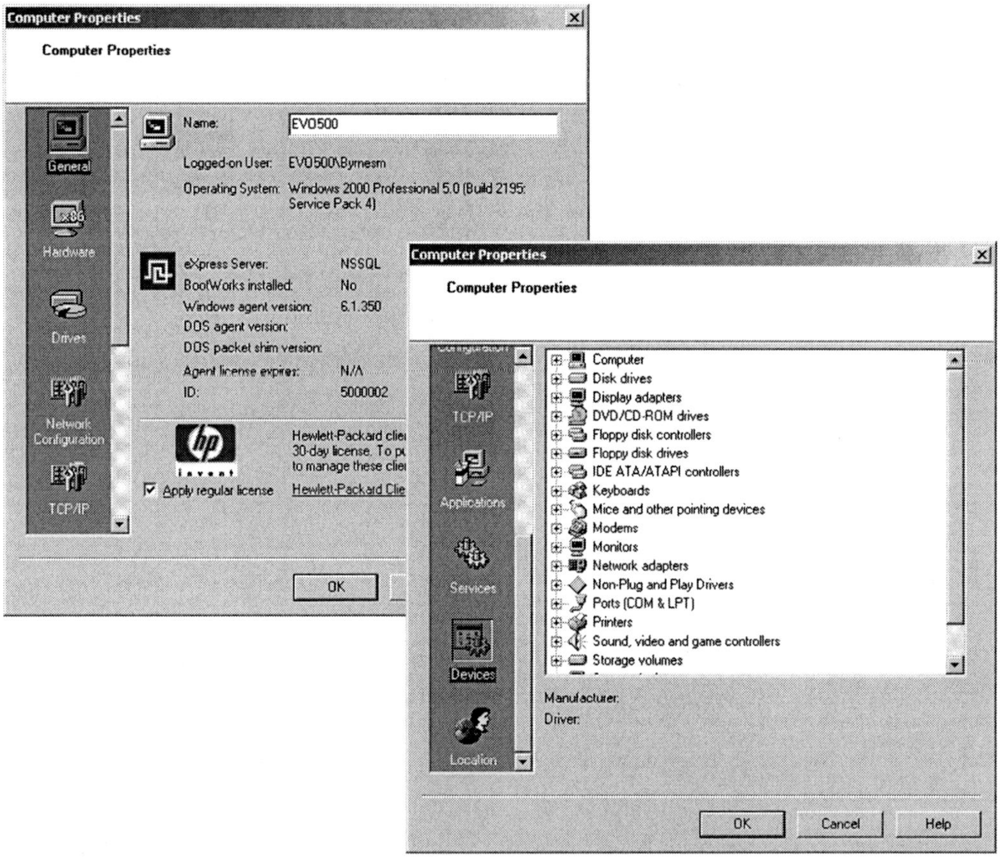

Viewing the properties of a client (NS Web Console)

Open the Web Console and click the Deployment tab. In the Computers pane click the required Deployment Server. The details pane displays the computers groups and any individual computers.

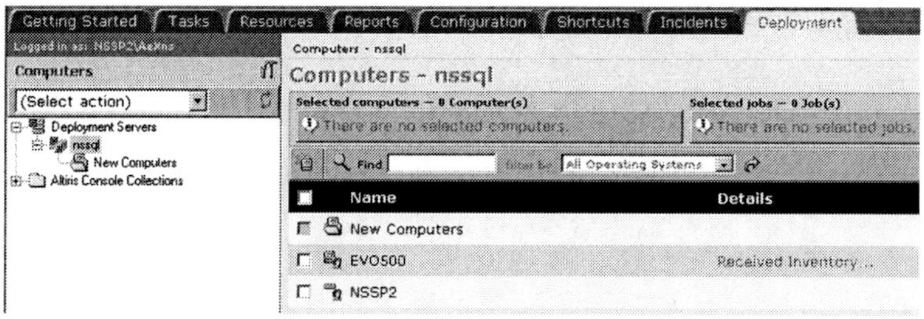

In the details pane click once on the computer name to display the properties.

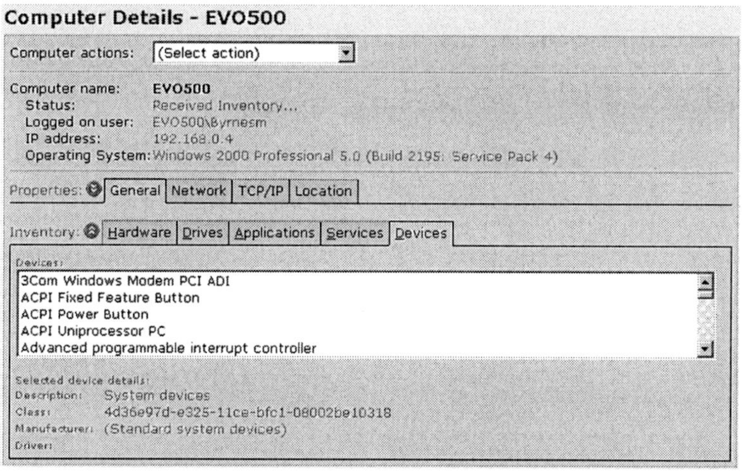

The format that the properties of a client are displayed in are different from the Win32 console but essentially the same detail.

Creating and assigning Jobs and Tasks (Win32 console)

Creating a New Job

Open the **Win32 Console** and **right click** in the Jobs pane.

Choose **New Job** from the shortcut menu.

Give the new Job a descriptive name and press **Enter**. The job is displayed.

Assigning Tasks to a Job

A job without associated Tasks is useless.

Select the Job in the jobs pane and from the Tasks pane click the **Add** button.

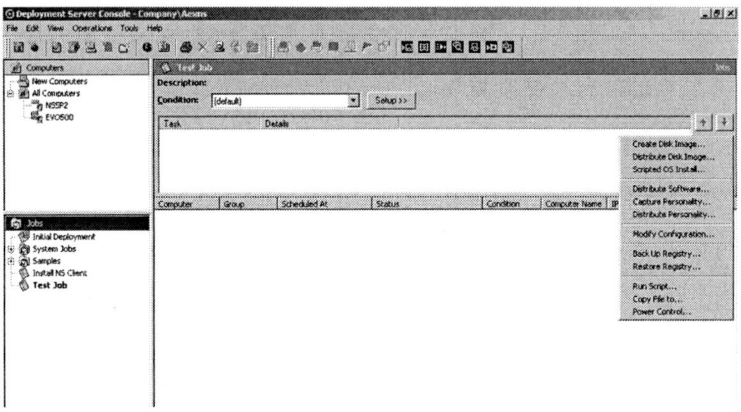

Choose a Task, for example the Copy File Task.

The dialog for that task opens.

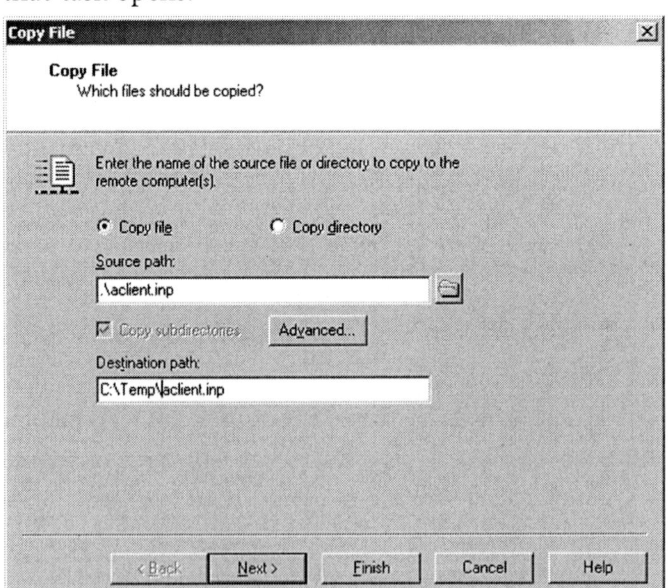

Configure all options and click **Finish**.

This Job now has a Task assigned to it and can be scheduled to run on one or more managed clients.

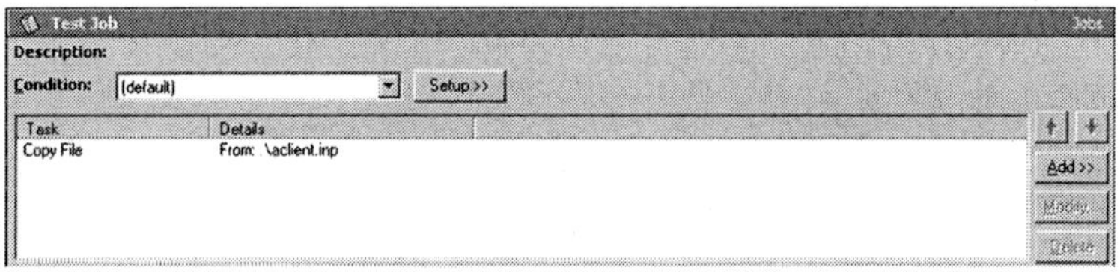

Assigning a Job to a Managed Client

Drag the Job from the Jobs pane on to one managed client in the Computers pane. Alternatively drag a computer from the Computers pane on to the Job.

In the schedule Job dialog, configure when the assigned Job will run on the managed client then click OK.

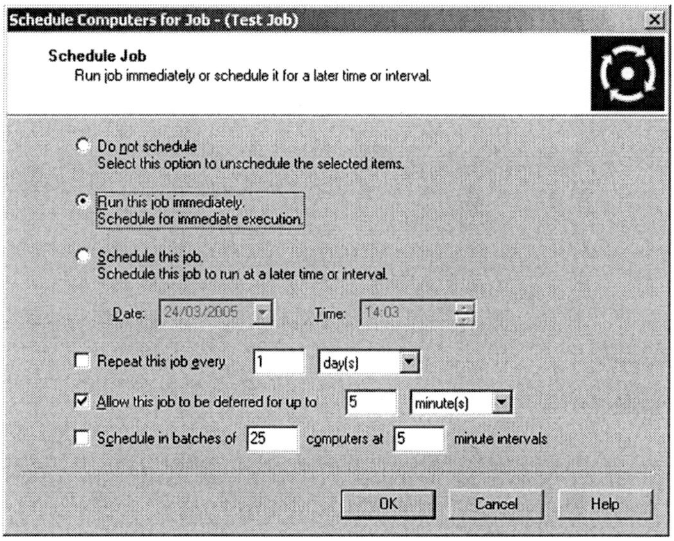

Assigning a Job to a group of Managed Clients

Drag the Job from the Jobs pane on to a group in the Computers pane.

Alternatively select several managed clients, using the control key, in the Computers pane and drag and drop them on to a Job in the Jobs pane.

In the schedule Job dialog, configure when the assigned Job will run on the managed client, then click **OK**.

Creating and assigning Jobs and Tasks (Web console)

In this section we will repeat the previous exercise but using the Notification Server Web Console.

Creating a New Job (Web console)

Open the Notification Server Web Console and select the Deployment tab.

In the Jobs pane click the name of your Deployment Server and then expand the tree.

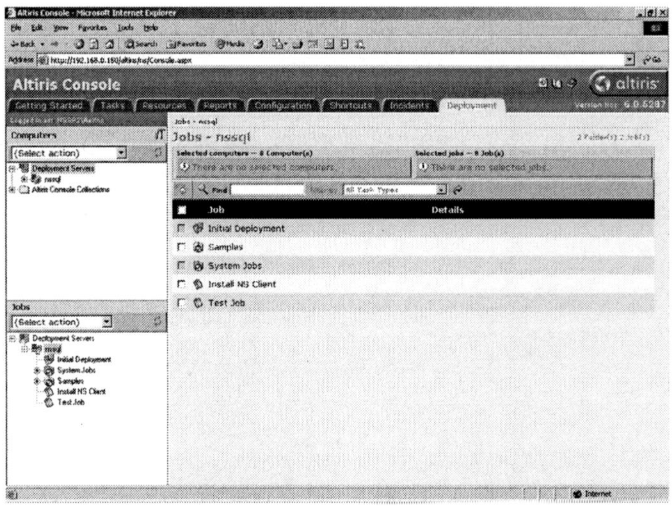

Click the **New Job** button or press **alt-n**.

Give the Job a name and description. The Job is now created but no tasks have yet been assigned. Click the **New Task** button or press **alt-n**.

In the Task Type dropdown select the Copy File Task.

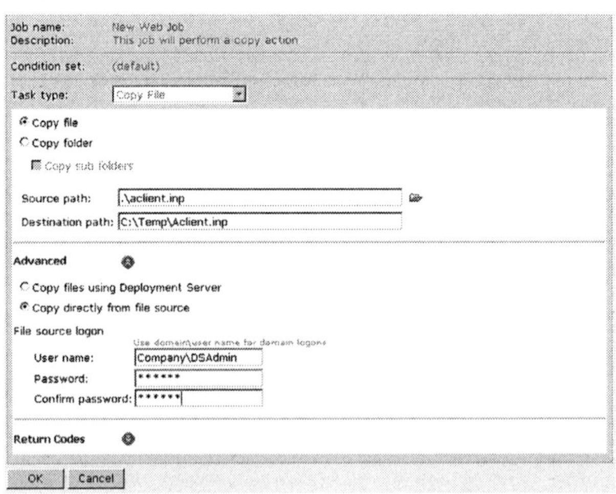

Configure the available options within the dialog then click **OK**. The new job has now been assigned a task.

To display the new job refresh the Jobs pane within the web console.

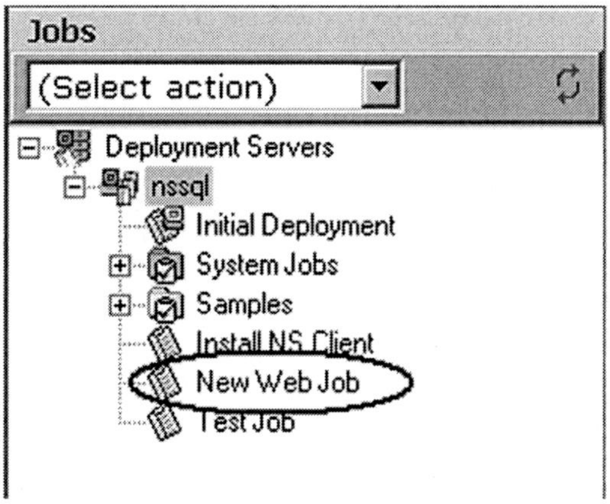

Assigning a Job to a Managed Client

In the Computers pane of the web console select the name of the Deployment Server so that the computers are displayed in the details pane.

Drag the Job from the Jobs pane on to one managed client in the details pane. The cursor will change to a small arrow when positioned correctly.

Alternatively drag a computer from the Computers pane on to the Job.

In the schedule Job dialog, configure when the assigned Job will run on the managed client then click **OK**.

Assigning a Job to a group of Managed Clients

Select the Job to schedule in the Jobs pane of the Web console.

In the Job Actions dropdown select 'Schedule Job'.

Select each computer that will be sent the selected Job by checking the select box to the left of each client.

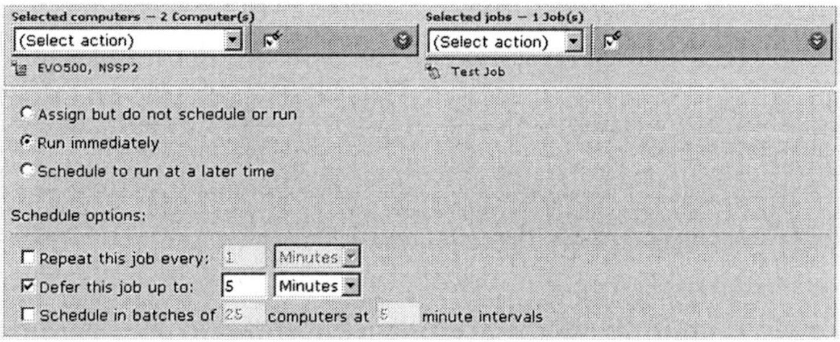

Click the Schedule button above the list of managed computers.

Configure the schedule dialog and click **OK**.

Running a command remotely on a client

Running a remote command (Win32 Console)

Open the Win32 console and right click the client in the computers pane.

Choose the Execute command.

Enter the path to the command.

Use the User button to configure the credentials the command should run under.

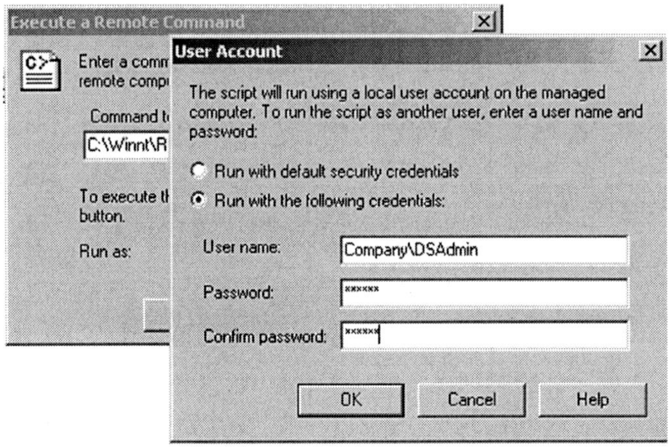

Click **OK**, then **OK** again.

The command is immediately run on the selected client.

Running a remote command (Web Console)

Open the Notification Server Console and click the Deployment Tab

In the Computers pane select the name of the Deployment Server to manage. This will display the list of managed devices for the selected Deployment Server in the details pane. Check the managed computers that will run the remote command.

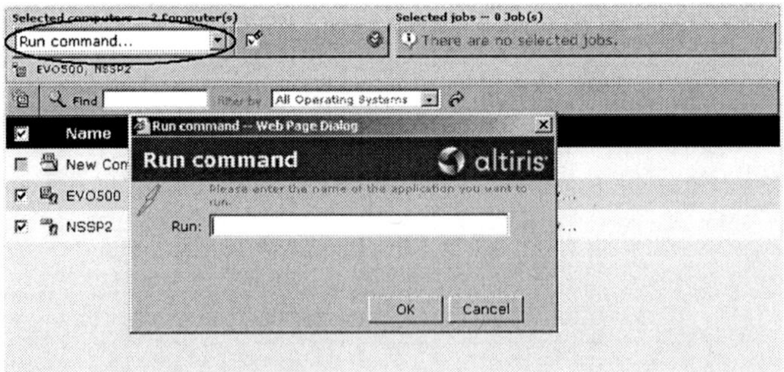

From the Select Action dropdown above the list of computers, select the action 'Run Command'. Enter the path and command line to run and click OK. For example *c:\tmp\setup.exe /q* or *\\server\apps\setup.exe /q*

Using Windows Scripts

Creating a Windows Script (Win32 Console)

Open the Win32 console and create a new Job in the Jobs pane.

Select the new Job and from the Tasks window use the **Add** button to add the Task 'Run Script'.

Select the type of script as a Windows script.

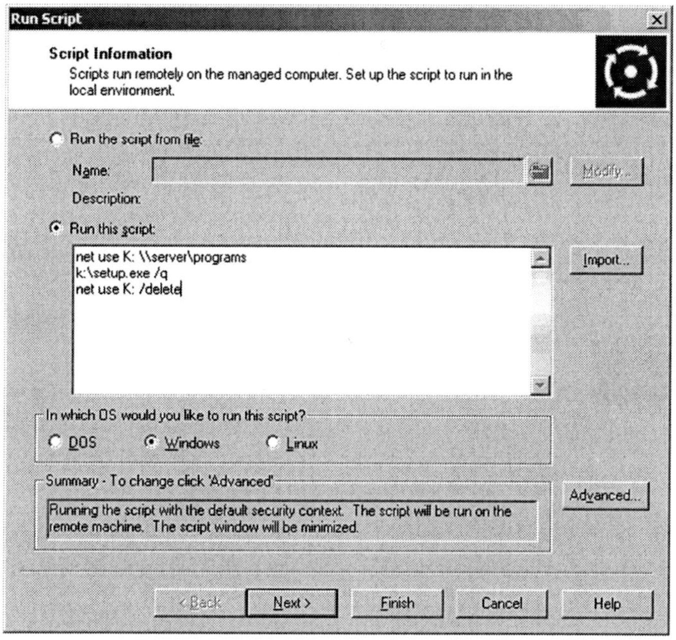

Enter the command line(s) to execute.

Use the Advanced button to configure the security context and execution location.

Click **Finish**.

Assigning a Windows Script Job to a managed client (Win32 Console)

In the Win32 console drag the Job from the Jobs window to the managed machine in the Computers pane.

Configure the schedule and click **OK**.

Creating a Windows Script (Web Console)

Open the Notification Server Web Console and select the Deployment Tab.

Select the name of the Deployment Server to manage in the Jobs pane and wait until the tree expands.

Create a new Job in the Jobs pane.

Once the Job is created, click the **New Task** button.

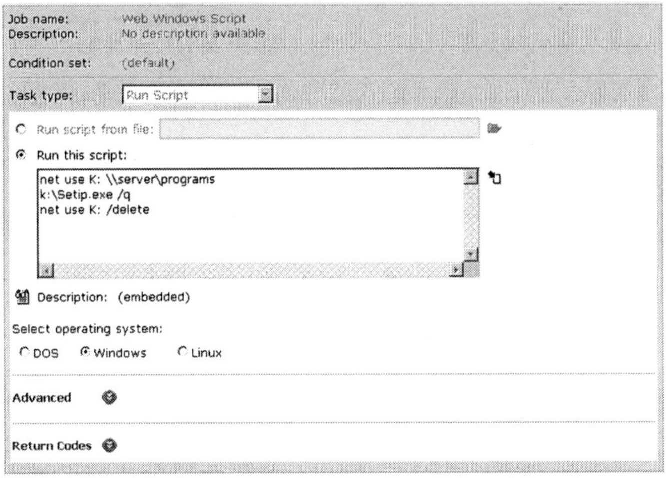

In the Tasks Type dropdown select the Task type of Run Script.

In the Task properties dialog choose Windows script.

Enter the command line(s) to execute.

Click **OK**.

The Job and Task have now been created.

Assigning a Windows Script Job to a managed client (Web Console)

Open the Notification Server Web Console and select the Deployment Tab.

Select the name of the Deployment Server to manage in the Computers pane and wait until the tree expands.

Select the name of the Deployment Server to manage in the Jobs pane and wait until the tree expands.

Drag the Windows Script Job from the Jobs pane on to a managed client in the details pane. The cursor will change to a small arrow when positioned correctly.

In the schedule Job dialog, configure when the assigned Job will run on the managed client then click **OK**.

Creating and deploying simple images

Imaging is used to take a snapshot of an entire hard disk or partition. The captured image can be used to restore a machine to the exact same state the system was in when the image was captured.

In a Windows network each machine must have its own unique name. In a Windows Domain environment each machine will not only have a unique name but also a unique Security Identifier (SID). Tools such as Microsoft Sysprep are used to ensure that when an image is deployed to a client, the name and SID of the machine are changed to something unique.

If a tool such as Sysprep is not used when deploying an image, then that image can only be deployed to the original machine the image was taken from or to a different machine providing the original machine has since been taken off the network.

The following actions will walk you through the process of creating and deploying a simple image, however the image captured can not be deployed to multiple machines.

Creating an image creation Job

The following Job and Task can be created using the Win32 or Web Console. In this example we will use the Win32 console.

Open the Deployment Server Win32 console and create a new Job in the Jobs pane. **Add** the Task, **Create Disk Image**.

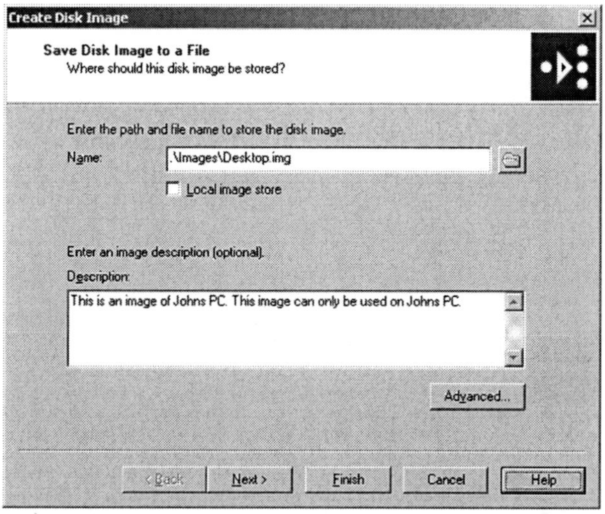

In the properties of the Task configure the name and the path where the image will be stored. The path must be under a shared folder.

Enter a description and click **Finish**.

Creating an image of a client

The following Job and Task can be assigned to a managed client using the Win32 or Web Console. In this example we will use the Win32 console.

In order to successfully create an image of a client without manual intervention, the client must be configured through its BIOS to boot to the network before booting to hard disk. PXE services must be configured and available to the client or Bootworks must be configured and installed on the client.

Open the Deployment Server Win32 console and drag the image creation Job, created previously, from the Jobs pane to a computer in the Computers pane. Configure the schedule and click **OK**.

At the scheduled time the assigned client will restart (or Wakeup depending on its state at the time and if WOL is supported) and perform a network boot.

During the network boot the client will connect to the PXE server and download the network card drivers and protocols that were configured for the Managed PC PXE menu item. Once the drivers and stack are loaded, the client maps a drive F to the eXpress share on the Deployment Server.

The client then uses the Rdeploy.exe on drive F to upload the image to the designated location. When the Job is finished, the client will reboot back to Windows.

Creating an image deployment Job (Win32 Console)

Open the Deployment Server Win32 console and create a new Job in the Jobs pane. Add the Task, Distribute Disk Image.

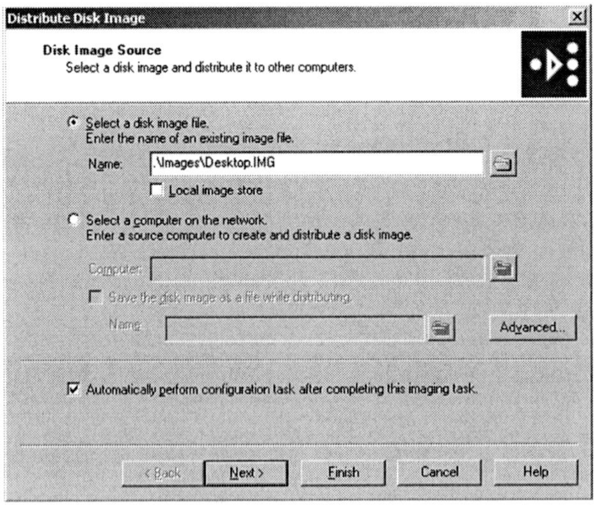

In the properties of the Task, configure the name and the path where the image is stored. The path must be under a shared folder. Click **Finish**.

Deploying an image to a client

The following Job and Task can be assigned to a managed client using the Win32 or Web Console. In this example we will use the Win32 console. In order to successfully deploy an image to a client, the client must be configured through its BIOS to boot to network before hard disk. PXE must be configured and available to the client or Bootworks must be configured and installed on the client.

Open the Deployment Server Win32 **console**.
Drag the image deployment **Job**, created previously, from the Jobs pane t**o a computer** in the Computers pane.
Configure the schedule and click **OK**.

At the scheduled time the assigned client will restart (or Wakeup depending on its state at the time and if WOL is supported) and perform a network boot.
During the network boot the client will connect to the PXE server and download the network card drivers and protocols that were configured for Managed PC on the PXE Server.
When the NIC driver and stack are loaded, the client maps a drive F to the eXpress share on the Deployment Server.
The client then uses the Rdeploy.exe imaging engine on drive F to download the image to the targeted client.
When the Job is finished, the client will reboot to the restored operating system.

An Overview of PC Transplant

PCT provides the ability to capture Desktop Settings, Application Settings, Printers, User Accounts and Files/folders. The settings captured by PCT are defined in a template. Once a template has been configured, a Deployment Server Task can be created and configured to use the defined template. When a target client runs the Task, it will gather the settings defined by the template and upload the captured data to the location specified within the Task properties.

Creating a PCT template

Step 1 - Start the Template Creation Wizard

From a desktop machine, connect to the express share on your Deployment Server and navigate to the PCT folder. The root of this folder contains the various applications that make up the PCT program. The Language subfolder, for example 'EN' contains the English configuration files for PCT.

Run the Template.exe file from the root of PCT by double clicking it. Click Next when the first dialog is displayed.

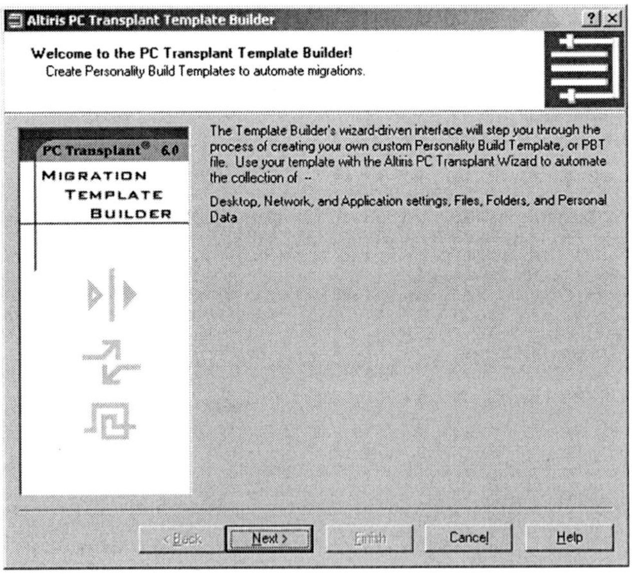

Step 2 - Create or Edit

In this step you will choose whether to, create or edit a template. Choose Create a New Template and click the Next button.

Step 3 - Desktop Settings

This dialog contains three tabs to configure Desktop, Network and Application capture settings. In the Desktop tab check and uncheck the desktop settings to capture. *(Checked means it will be captured)*

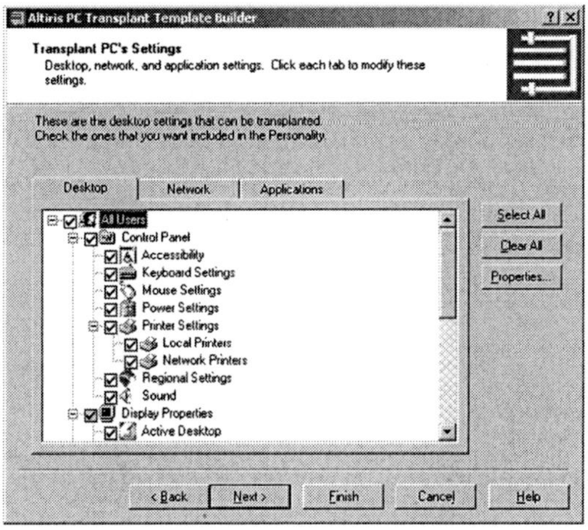

Keep in mind that this will capture the checked settings but not any files that are associated with the setting. For example if you decide to capture the Screensaver setting, the actual screensaver file(s) may also need to be captured. The available settings in this dialog are defined by the dsktp*.ini files in the PCT\Language subfolder.

Step 4 - Network Settings

The Network capture settings tab displays options for capturing network settings. Again check and uncheck as appropriate. The available settings in this dialog are

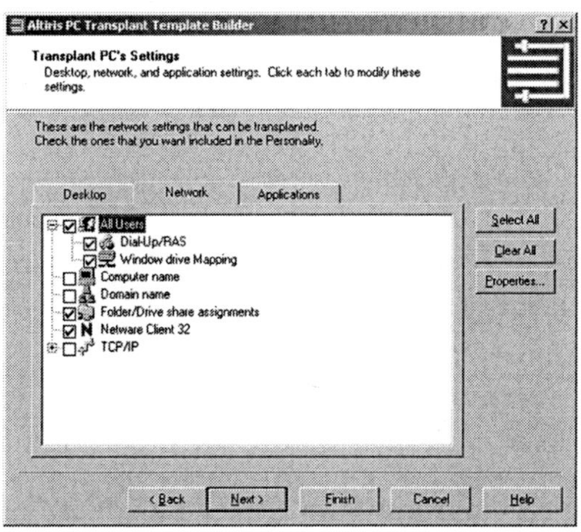

defined by the ntwrk*.ini files in the PCT\Language subfolder.

Step 5 - Application Settings

This dialog allows you to configure which application settings to capture. This does not capture the actual program/application, just the settings.

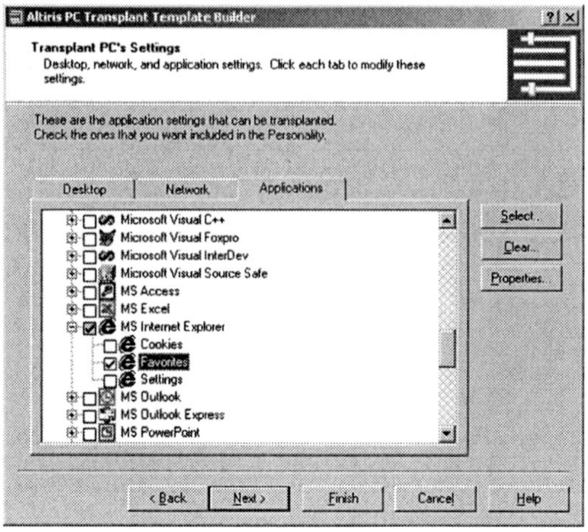

The available settings in this dialog are defined by the *.A2i files in the PCT\Language subfolder. *(The A2i builder can be used to add custom applications. See PCT documentation for more details.)*

Check and uncheck as appropriate. Click the **Next** button to continue.

Step 6 - Configure Install Applications

If any of the application capture settings were selected in the previous dialog, then the Transplant Install Application dialog displays the selected applications.

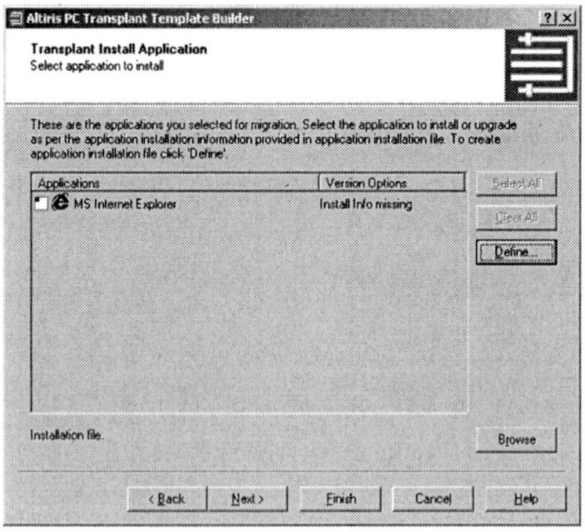

This dialog gives you the opportunity to define an application installation file that can be used to install an application prior to proceeding with a migration. *For more information on this option see the PCT documentation.*

Step 7 - Capture Files

The transplant files and folders dialog has three tabs which are used to configure the capture of files, folders and file types. The Files section lets you specify specific files to be captured.

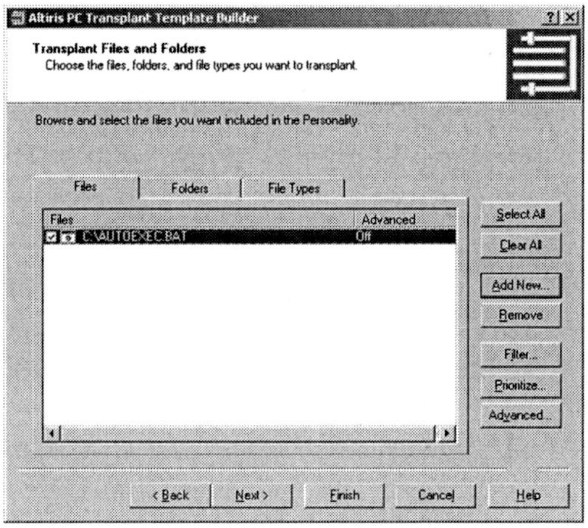

Use the **Add New** button to add a local file. Once a file has been added, use the **Advanced button** to define a different destination and more advanced capture criteria.

Step 8 - Capture Folders

Use the Folders section to define which folders if any to capture.

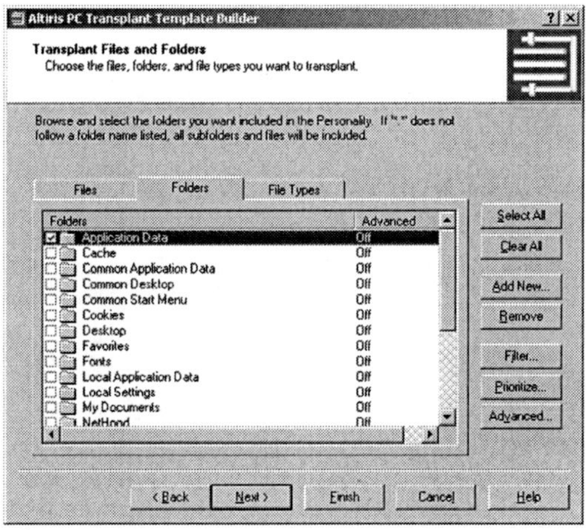

Use the **Advanced button** to define exclusions, advanced capture criteria and a different destination.

Step 9 - Capture File Types

The File Types section allows you to configure files of a specific extension to be captured.

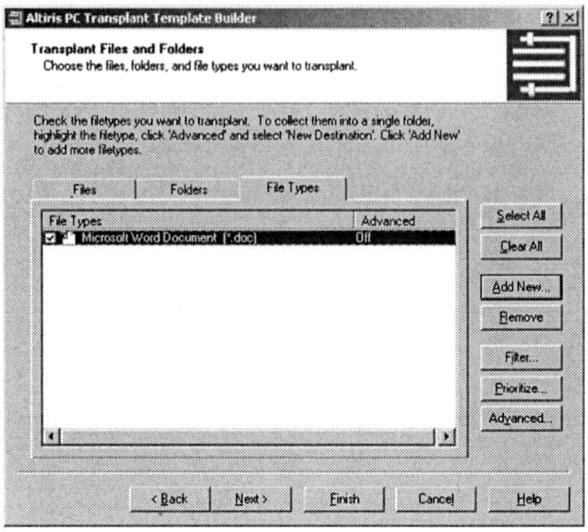

Check and **uncheck** the file types and use the **Advanced** button to define exclusions, advanced capture criteria and a different destination. A different destination is useful as it can be used to capture all files of a specific extension but ensure that during the migration the captured files are not restored to the original location but to a specific folder such as My Documents. Click **Next** when all three tabs have been configured.

Step 10 - Configure Options

This dialog contains the options used when captured data is restored to a machine. Options include tabs to configure Run (File Replace, Security, Undo and Reboot), Display (What to display on screen), Compression and Build (Package size spanning and Cleanup).

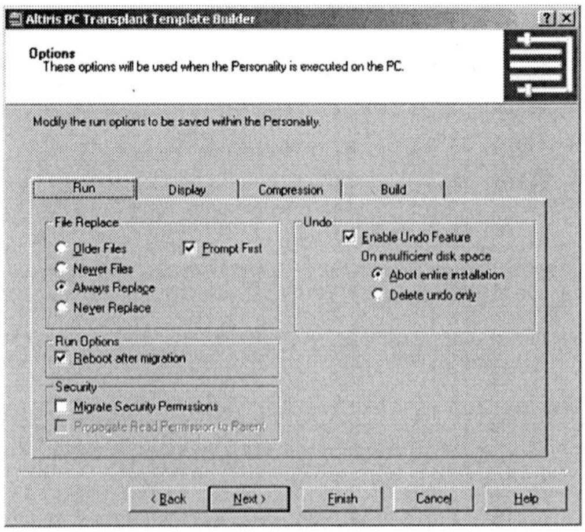

Configure all options and use **Finish** to continue.

Step 11 - Save the Template

In the last dialog specify the path to store the new template. I would suggest creating a Templates folder under the PCT folder on the Express share of the Deployment Server and saving it there.

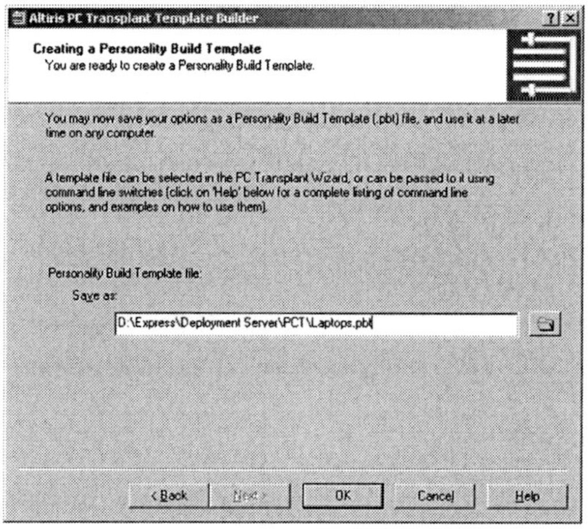

This template can now be used to capture and restore during a migration.

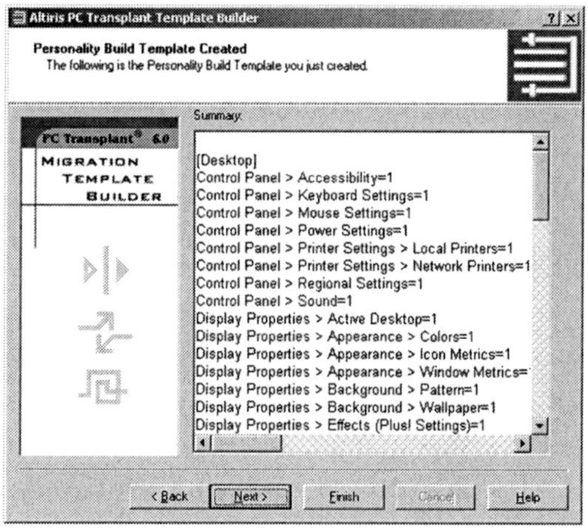

Capturing Settings using PCT

To capture settings on a machine(s), create a new Job in the Win32 or Web console with a Capture Personality Task. Specify the template to use and a destination path for the captured settings and files. When the task runs on a destination client, the following occurs:

- The client runs the PCT capture Task.
- The template specified in the Task properties is used to determine what is to be captured.
- The captured settings/files/folders are compressed in to one executable file.
- The file is given the same name as the captured computer name.
- The file is uploaded to the path specified in the Task properties.

Creating a capture PCT Job and Task

The following Job and Task can be created using the Win32 or Web Console. In this example we will use the Win32 console.

Create a Job by right-clicking in the Jobs pane of the Deployment Console and selecting **New Job**. Give the Job an appropriate name.
Select the Job then click the **Add button** in the Tasks window and select the Capture Personality Task.
The Capture Personality screen will appear.
Click the Browse button and select the template to use when capturing the personality.

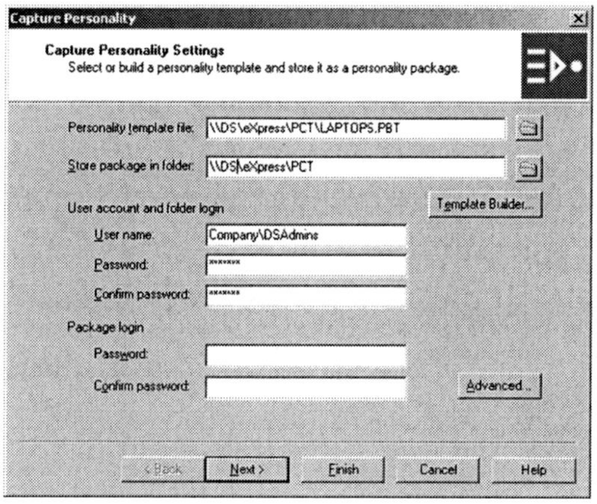

In the Store Package in folder box, specify where you want the Personality Package to be stored.
Enter a username and password with administrative rights on the target desktop(s).
Complete the Package Login and Advanced sections if desired. The Advanced button provides access to the Advanced dialog where you can specify which profiles are captured.
Click **Finish** to complete the Task creation.

The Job is now created and can be used to capture settings on one or more managed machines using either the Web or Win32 console.

Capturing Personality Settings (Win32 Console)

Open the Deployment Server Win32 console.

Drag the PCT capture Job from the Jobs pane to a computer in the Computers pane.

Configure the schedule and click **OK**.

The task will run based on the schedule and capture settings based on the configured template. A file with the same name as the NETBIOS computer name of the captured machine is then uploaded to the configured folder.

Capturing Personality Settings (Web Console)

Open the Notification Server Web Console and select the Deployment Tab.

Select the name of the Deployment Server to manage in the Computers pane and wait until the tree expands.

Select the name of the Deployment Server to manage in the Jobs pane and wait until the tree expands.

Drag the PCT Job from the Jobs pane on to a managed client in the details pane. The cursor will change to a small arrow when positioned correctly.

In the schedule Job dialog, configure when the assigned Job will run on the managed client then click **OK**.

The task will run based on the schedule and capture settings based on the configured template. A file with the same name as the NETBIOS computer name of the captured machine is then uploaded to the configured folder.

Deploying Captured Settings using PCT

To deploy captured settings to a machine(s), create a Job with a Deploy Personality Task. Specify the captured PCT exe file to use for deploying the captured settings and files. When the task runs on a destination client, the following occurs:

- The client runs the PCT deploy Task.
- The captured file specified in the Task properties is deployed to the targeted client(s).

Creating a deploy PCT Job and Task

The following Job and Task can be created using the Win32 or Web Console. In this example we will use the Win32 console.

Open the Deployment Server Win32 console and create a new Job in the Jobs pane.
Add a **Distribute Personality Task.**
In the Distribute Personality Task properties dialog, use the browse button to specify the name of the previously captured personality file (.exe)
Configure the Package distribution options and any additional command-line

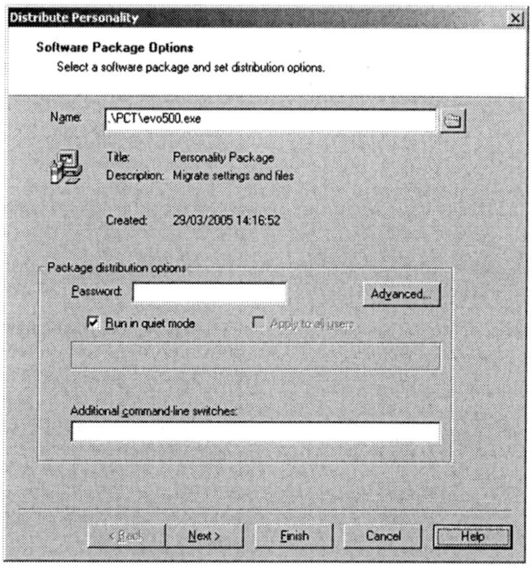

switches. Click **Finish.**

The Job is now created and can be used to deploy settings to one or more managed machines using either the web or Win32 console.

Deploying Personality Settings (Win32 Console)

Open the Deployment Server Win32 console.
Drag the PCT deploy Job from the Jobs pane to a computer in the Computers pane.
Configure the schedule and click **OK**.

The task will run based on the schedule and settings/files and folders contained within the captured file are restored.

Deploying Personality Settings (Web Console)

Open the Notification Server Web Console and select the Deployment Tab.
Select the name of the Deployment Server to manage in the Computers pane and wait until the tree expands.
Select the name of the Deployment Server to manage in the Jobs pane and wait until the tree expands.
Drag the PCT deploy Job from the Jobs pane on to a managed client in the details pane. The cursor will change to a small arrow when positioned correctly.
In the schedule Job dialog, configure when the assigned Job will run on the managed client then click **OK**.

The task will run based on the schedule and settings/files and folders contained within the captured file are restored.

Editing a PC Transplant Package

Open the Deployment Server Win32 console and from the **Tools** menu choose the command PC Transplant Editor.

In the PC Transplant editor dialog, select the File menu and choose the open command.

Browse to the captured package in the folder structure and click OK.

The editor allows you to view, add and remove files and registry settings that were captured.

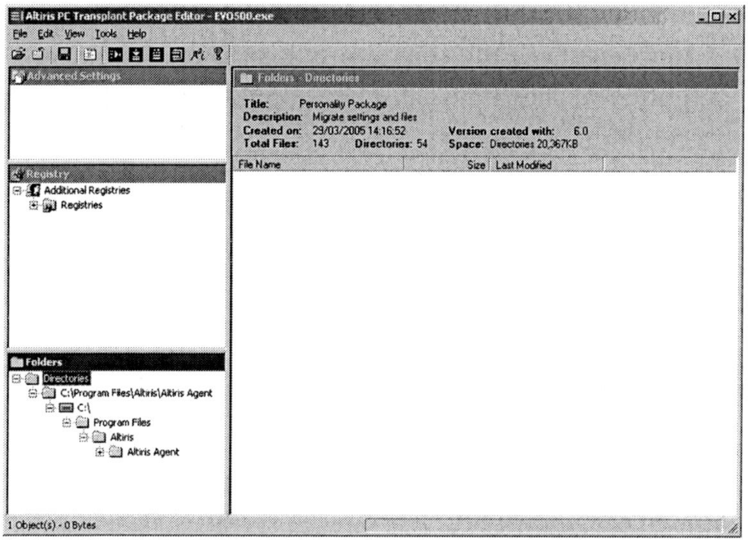

When all required changes have been made, save the file using a new name or an existing name.

An overview of RapidInstall

RapidInstall uses snapshot technology to create application packages. The basic principles for creating an application package are:

- Take a desktop/laptop machine and run RapidInstall to create an initial baseline snapshot.
- Install the application.
- Run RapidInstall again and create a second snapshot. RapidInstall will then create a package containing the differences between the first and second snapshots.
- The result is an executable file containing the changes to the registry and file structure. This file can be deployed using applications such as Altiris Software Delivery Solution or Deployment Server.

Creating an Application Package

Step 1 - Create your first baseline

From a desktop machine connect to the Deployment Server express share and navigate to the RInstall folder.

Close any open applications on the desktop then run the executable RapidInstall.exe.

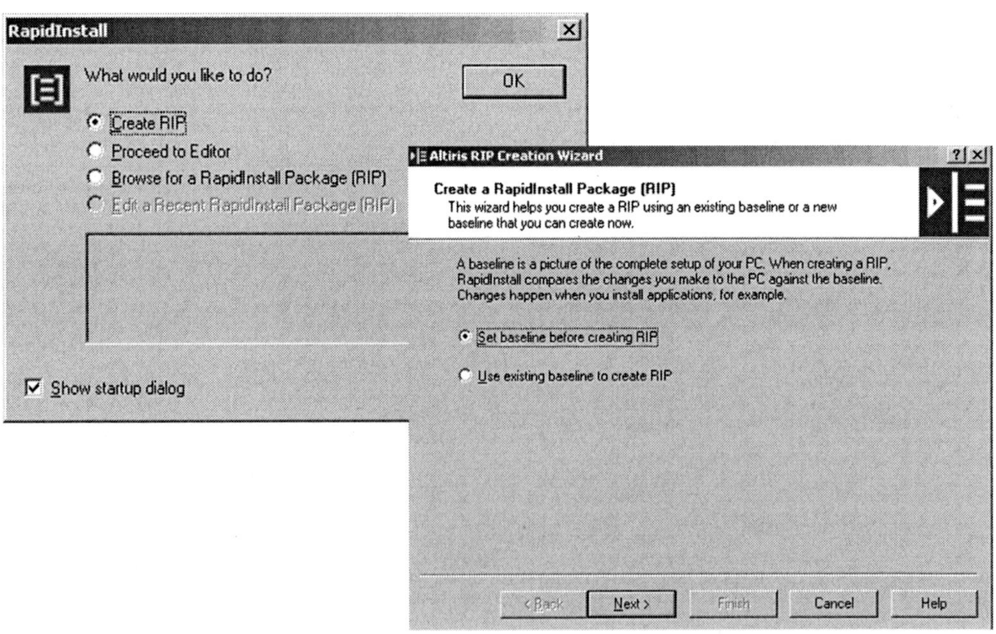

In the first dialog choose to create a RIP (Rapid Install Package) and click **OK**.

In the second dialog choose 'Set baseline before creating RIP'. Click **Next**.

In the third dialog enter the baseline details such as where to store the baseline and a name and description.

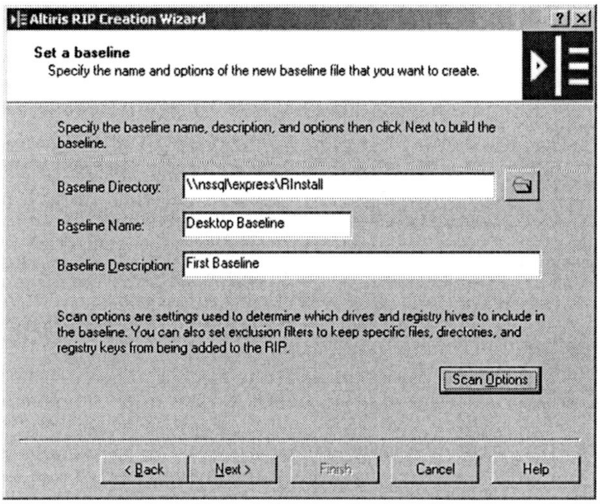

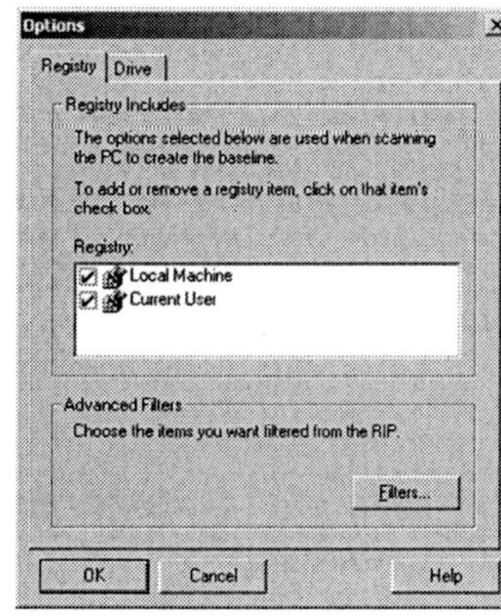

Use the **Scan Options** to configure which parts of the registry and file structure to scan (Default all). Click **Next** to continue.

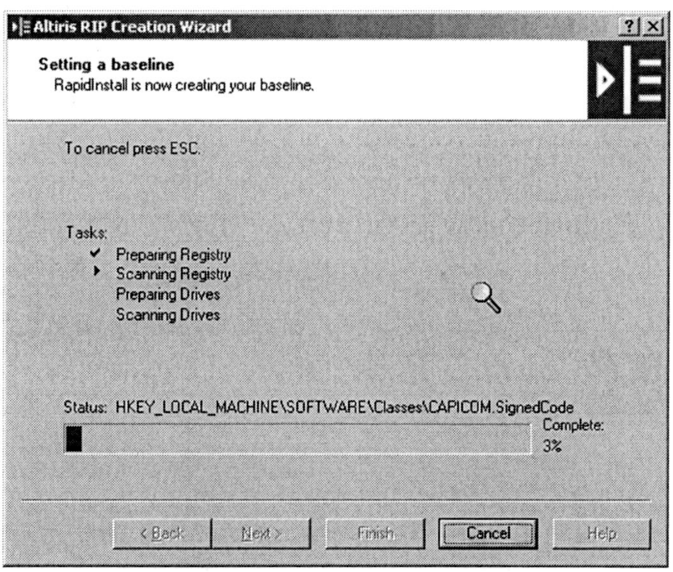

RapidInstall will begin scanning the registry and file structure at this point. This will take anywhere between ten minutes and several weeks (Joke) depending on the number of files and registry entries on the local machine. For best results perform the scan on a clean machine with few applications.

When the baseline is created, the Installing Applications dialog appears.

Step 2 - Install the application

The initial baseline is now created. Leave the RapidInstall dialog open and proceed with the installation of the application you want to create a RIP from. Once the application is installed, reboot if necessary but remember to login with the same credentials that were used when the baseline was run.

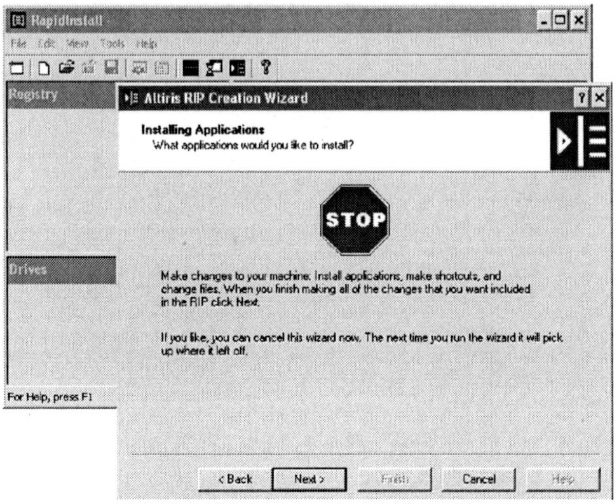

Step 3 - Create the RIP package

If the RapidInstall dialog is still visible then click **Next** to continue. If it isn't then run the RapidInstall.exe from express share of the Deployment Server. When the first dialog is displayed, choose 'Create RIP' and click **OK**. This should display the Installing Applications dialog as displayed above. Click **Next** to continue. (If the dialog isn't displayed then choose 'Use existing baseline to create RIP' and click Next).

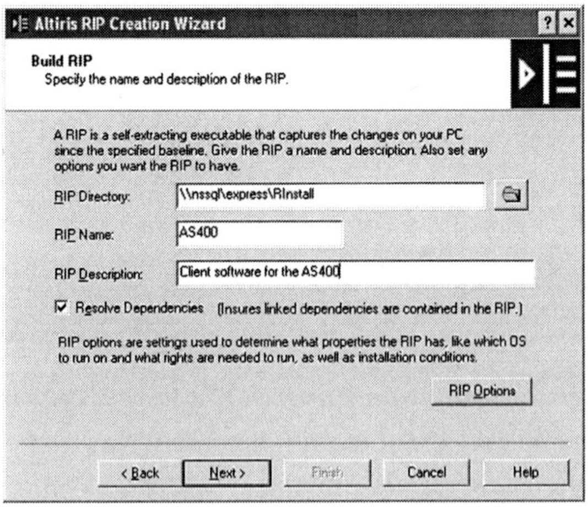

Specify a path, name and description for the new RIP. Use the **RIP options** button to define Options, Conditions and Visuals. Click **Next** to rescan the local PC for changes.

The changes found will be compressed in to an executable name as specified in the previous dialog.

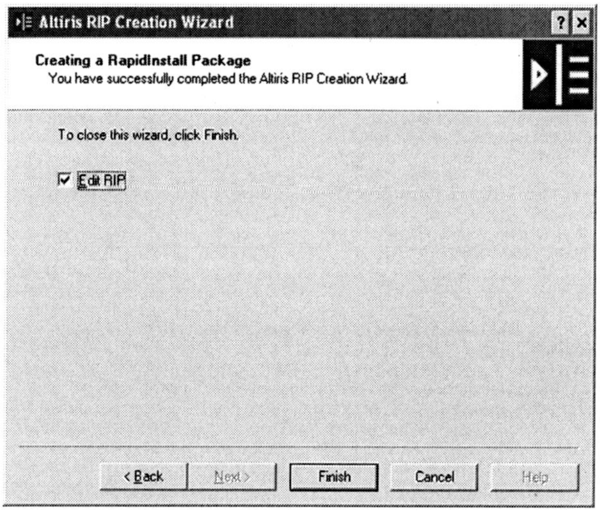

The last dialog in the wizard allows you to finish and indicate that you want to edit the RIP. Click **Finish**.

When the RIP editor dialog appears, it displays the Registry, Drives and details pane. Use the editor to add and remove entries from the RIP. I would suggest you save the package using a different name if you make changes, just in case.

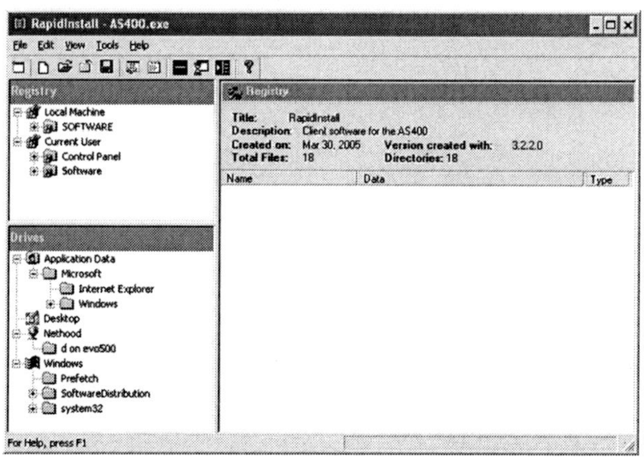

You may find that background tasks such as virus checkers add unnecessary registry or drive entries so remove them.

When all changes have been made within the editor, resave the file using a different name and exit the editor. The executable can now be deployed using your preferred mechanism (CD, Floppy, Login Script, Deployment Server, Software Delivery Solution, SMS, etc.

Deploying a RIP (Win32 Console)

To use Deployment Server to deploy the newly created RIP, create a new Job and assign a Distribute Software Task.

Configure the Task to use the newly created RIP.

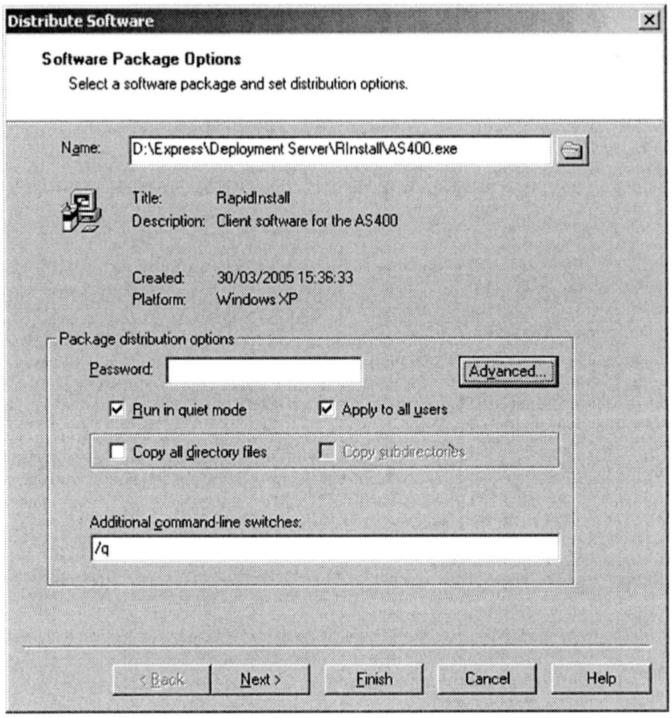

Deploy the software by dragging and dropping the Job to a machine or group of machines.

Deployment Server Replication

Deployment Server Replication falls in to three categories; Job, File Library and Database replication.

Replicating Jobs from the Notification Server to multiple Deployment Servers provides a means of ensuring that multiple Deployment Servers have a consistent set of Jobs.

Replicating a file library provides the ability to replicate applications and images from the Notification Server to Deployment Servers.

Database replication provides the ability to replicate part of a Deployment Server database (Express) from a Deployment Server to a Notification Server. This provides the ability to report on Job status information, Deployment Servers and Deployment Server clients.

Configuring Job/Task replication

To replicate a Job from the Notification Server to a Deployment Server, the Deployment Server must be running the Altiris Agent and be configured as a Package Server. For instructions installing the Altiris Agent and on adding a machine as a Package Server, see the chapters '*The Altiris Agent*' and '*Package Servers*' earlier in this book.

Step 1 - Export the Jobs to replicate

The first step is to take the Job(s) to replicate and export them to a .bin file. The .bin file will then be manually copied to the DSUtil folder on the Notification Server.

Open the Win32 console for the Deployment Server containing the Job(s) to export. Right click the Job or Jobs and choose the Export command from the shortcut menu.

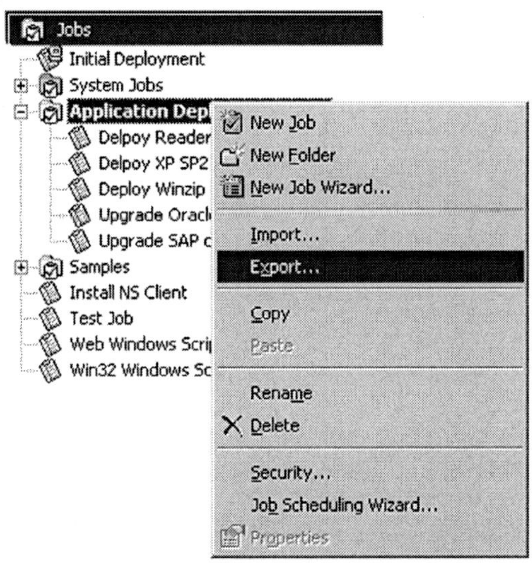

Export the Job to a file named Task.bin to the path:
\\nsserver\nscap\bin\win32\x86\DSutil where *nsserver* is the name of your Notification Serve.

Step 2 - Configure the DS Task Import Utility Package

The DS Task Import Utility Package is located on the Notification Server in the path *InstallPath\Altiris\Notification Server\NSCap\Bin\Win32\X86\DSUtil.* The package will now contain the Job import utility (Aximport.exe) and the exported Task.bin file created in the previous step.

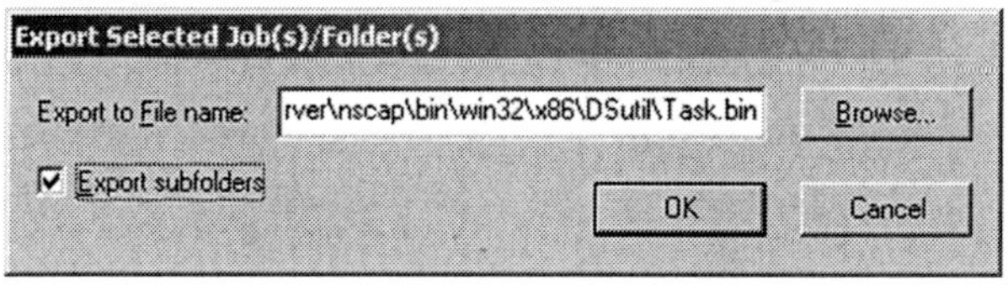

Open the Notification Server Web Console and select the Tasks tab then navigate to **Deploy and Migrate > Deployment > Deployment Server Replication**. Select the DS Task Import Utility Package (Blue box).

Configure the Package, Programs and Advanced configuration settings as appropriate then click **Apply**.

Click the **Update Distribution Points** button to update the package definition including the addition of the Task.bin file and any changes.

Allow the updated package to replicate to all Package Servers, particularly Package Servers that are also Deployment Servers.

Step 3 - Configure the DS Task Import Utility Policy

The Task Import Policy is used to configure when the Task.bin file is imported in to the Deployment Server.

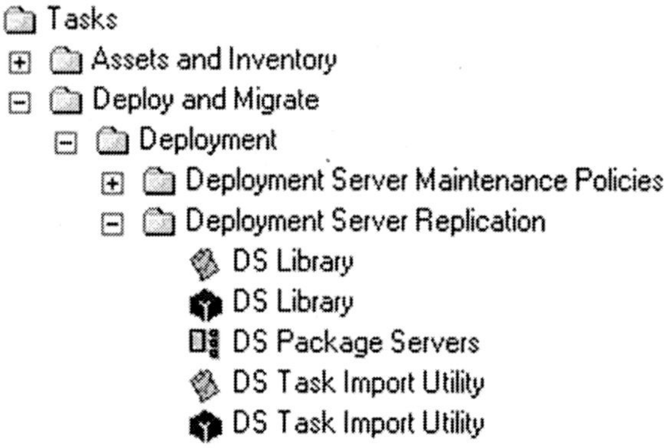

Open the Notification Server Web Console and select the Tasks tab then navigate to Deploy and Migrate > Deployment > Deployment Server Replication. Select the DS

Task Import Utility Policy.
In the details pane configure the schedule (Once or twice a week if there are many changes) and enable reporting (until you are confident that Job replication is working OK). Once all of the options have been configured enable the policy and click **Apply**.

The next time a Deployment Server requests a configuration update, it will see the import task and execute it based on the configured schedule. Jobs imported during the execution are displayed in the Win32 and Web Console.

Troubleshooting the Job import

Any import failures will normally be due to security. The first issue may be down to the credentials used to import the package (System default). To resolve this, modify the credentials specified in the Programs tab of the DSUtil package.
The second issue may be if security is enabled on the Deployment Server console. To resolve this issue add the /u and the /p switches to the command line shown in the Programs tab of the DSutil package. For example

Aximport.exe Task.bin /o /u SrvAdmin /p Adminpassword

Where /o overrides existing Jobs during the import
/u specifies a database user name
/p specifies the database user password

Configuring DS Library replication

Deployment Server library replication is used to replicate one folder and all of its subfolders from a reference server such as the Notification Server to all of your Deployment Servers. An alternative to using the Deployment Server Library is to use the replication functionality of Software Delivery Solution for Windows. (Using SWD offers the advantage of being able to replicate multiple packages.)

To replicate a package from the Notification Server to a Deployment Server, the Deployment Server must be running the Altiris Agent and be configured as a Package Server. For instructions installing the Altiris Agent and on adding a machine as a Package Server, see the chapters 'The Altiris Agent' and 'Package Servers' earlier in this book.

Using Software Delivery Solution instead of DS Library to replicate files and folders

Ensure that Software Delivery Solution for Windows is installed on your Notification Server. Create a replication reference point either on the Notification Server or on another server. Copy any application packages or images you want to replicate to your Deployment Servers to this path.

Open the Web Console and select the Resources tab, then navigate to **Resources > Software Management > Software Delivery Packages > Windows**.
Create a new package by right clicking the Windows folder and choosing New > Software Delivery Package from the shortcut menu. Name the package something like DS Replication data.
In the Package tab configure the package source and path for the replication reference point.
In the Advanced tab select to replicate the package to Selected Package Servers instead of All Package Servers. Only check/select the Package Servers that are Deployment Servers.
Configure the alternate destination path as \\%Computername%\express\library.
Click **Apply** then click the **Update Distribution Points** button.

The next time a Package Server that is also a Deployment Server requests a configuration update, it will see the DS Replication data package and pull the files to the local designated location.

Using DS Library to replicate files and folders

The default location for the DS Library package is on the Notification Server in the path *Installpath\Altiris\Notification Server\ Library*. This path can be changed by altering the properties of the DS Library package using the Notification Server Web Console.

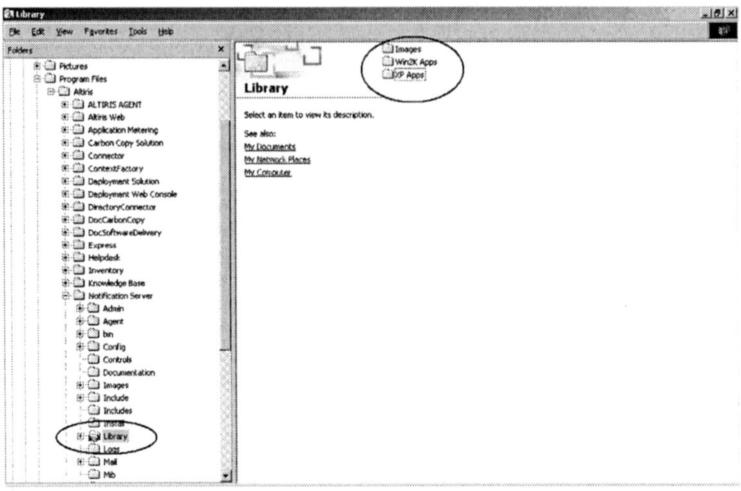

Copy any application packages or images you want to replicate to your Deployment Servers to the Library path.

Step 1 - Configure the DS Library Package

Open the Notification Server Web Console and select the Tasks tab then navigate to Deploy and Migrate > Deployment > Deployment Server Replication.

Select the DS Library Package.

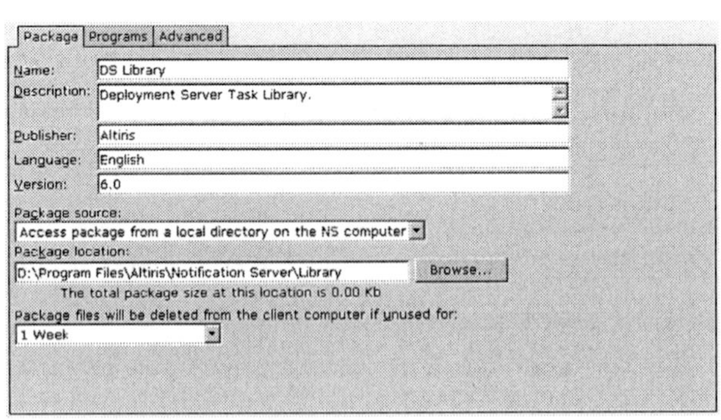

The package contains three tabs, Package, Programs and Advanced. For more detail on these configuration options see the chapter Software Delivery Solution earlier in this book.

Package configuration suggestions:

The combination of images and application packages can be quite large. If the Notification Server has limited space, host the DS Library package on a different drive on the Notification Server or on a different server. Modify the package source and location of the Library in the Package tab to change the location.

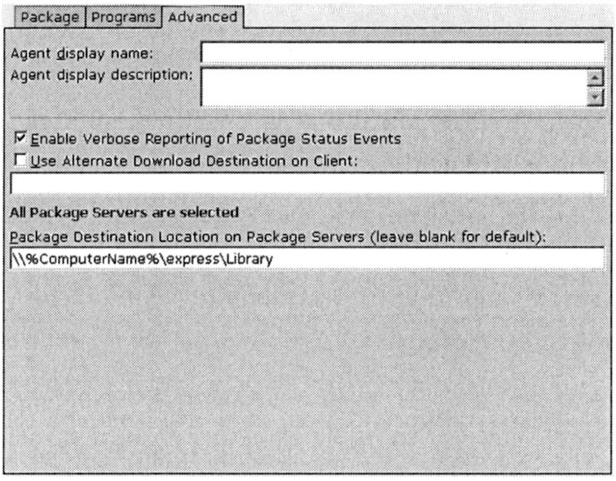

When the DS Library package replicates to a Deployment Server it is replicated to the default location (*Install Path\Altiris\Altiris Agent\Package Delivery*). To modify the default destination path to a more useful location, for example under the Express share of the Deployment Server, alter the Package Destination location option in the Advanced tab of the Library package.
Use the syntax *\\%computername%\Express\Library* to reconfigure the destination path to a Library folder under the Express share.

The next time a Deployment Server requests a configuration update, it will see the DS Library package and pull the files to the local designated location.

Configuring Database Replication

Database replication is used to replicate data such as Computers, Events and Jobs from the Deployment Server database to the Notification Server database. The replicated data is used when running many of the Deployment Server reports available within the Notification Server Reports tab.

Deploying the DS Agent

The DS Agent plugs-in to the Altiris Agent running on the Deployment Server controls the replication of data from the Deployment Server to the Notification Server.

To deploy the DS Agent, open the Altiris Web console and select the Configuration tab. Navigate to **Solution Settings** > **Deploy and Migrate** > **Deployment** > **Deployment Server Agent Configuration**.

Enable the Policy Deployment Server Agent Install/Upgrade.
This policy is configured to roll out to all Deployment Server machines. *(Notification Server knows which machines are Deployment Server based on the Basic Inventory sent by the Altiris Agent running on the Deployment Server).*

The next time Deployment Servers request an updated configuration, they will see the enabled policy and install the DS agent.

Configuring the DS Agent

The policy used to configure how often a Deployment Server sends data, is located at the **Configuration tab > Solution Settings > Deploy and Migrate > Deployment > Deployment Server Agent Configuration > Deployment Server Agent Configuration**.

The dropdown within the policy allows you to select different Deployment Servers or groups of Deployment Servers. The default is All Deployment Servers.

To configure all Deployment Servers with the same DS Agent settings use the default All Deployment Servers group when modifying the configuration.

Creating extra groups will allow you to use multiple Agent configurations to target different Deployment Server groups.

Before choosing polling intervals (10 minutes default), database logins or role user ID's for the policy, first choose the group of Deployment Servers to configure from the dropdown.

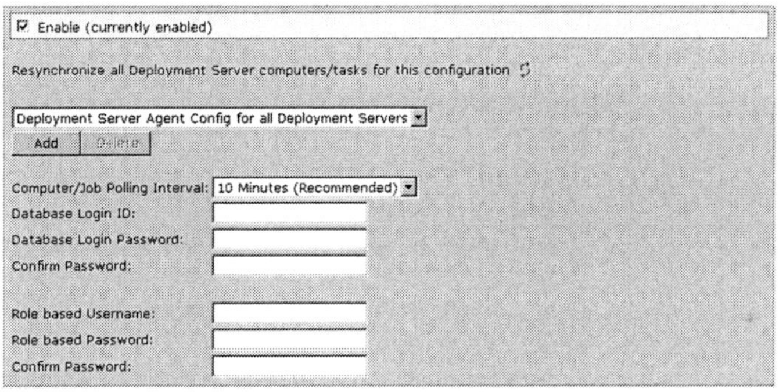

Once the selected group is displayed, configure the polling interval.

Enter the Deployment Server database login and password and if role based console security has been enabled, enter the user ID and password in that section also.

The next time Deployment Servers request an updated configuration, they will see the new polling interval and reconfigure the DS Agent accordingly.

Useful Deployment Server Reports

To view the following reports open the Web Console, select the Reports Tab then navigate to **Deploy and Migrate > Deployment**.

Total Deployment Servers and total managed computers

This report displays the total number of Deployment Servers that are being managed by this server, as well as the total number of client computers. Two further levels of drill down are also available.

Job Status by Deployment Server

This report displays job status (successful, failed and assigned) by Deployment Server. The drill down focuses on one particular job on the specified Deployment Server.

Jobs failed in last N days

This report displays a list of jobs that have failed on targeted managed computers in the last N days.

Overall event status by Deployment Server

This report displays overall job status by Deployment Server.

Count of managed computers by Deployment Server

This report displays a count of managed computers, grouped by managing Deployment Server.

List of managed computers by Deployment Server

This report displays a list of computers, grouped and filtered by the selected managing deployment server.

Please note that the above reports are only available if your Deployment Server(s) are configured to replicate data from the Deployment Server to the Notification Server using the DS Agent.

Summary

This chapter provided an overview of Deployment Solution design, the components, installation, Jobs & Tasks, PCT, Rapid Install and the integration of Deployment Server with Notification Server.

Altiris Deployment Solution is a collection of tools and components that offers operating system deployment, central management, remote control, imaging, configuration, computer "personality" migration and software deployment across hardware platforms and operating systems.

Deployment Server is the Windows component that provides the ability to deploy operating systems, remote control, application and script deployment, imaging and remote configuration.

Deployment Solution installed in to the Notification Server provides central management and replication.

Several tools come with Deployment Server including PCT and RapidInstall. PCT provides the ability to capture Desktop Settings, Application Settings, Printers and Files/folders. Rapid Install provides the ability to create application packages using snapshot technology.

Appendix

Appendix A - SQL Configuration Notes

Notification Server requires SQL 2000 or MSDE 2000 with at least service pack 3. MSDE should not be used in a production environment because of the lack of administrative tools, the 2GB DB size limitation and the concurrent connection limit, but it is useful for testing or lab purposes.

The database and the Notification Server do not have to be on the same server, however for obvious performance reasons it is better if they are on the same server. If the database is on a remote computer, there must be a fast connection between the database server and the Notification Server of at least 100MBps.

Be careful if using Anti-Virus software and real-time protection on the Notification Server. Real-time protection may slow down the console considerably.
To workaround this issue, configure the anti-virus software to exclude files with the ini extension.

When installing SQL use Windows Authentication and allocate approximately 60% of the available memory to SQL.

When upgrading from Notification Server 5.5 to 6.x, double the size of the database prior to upgrading.

SQL Memory Configuration

If SQL is installed on the same machine as the Notification Server the following applies:

On a server with less than 4 GB RAM limit SQL memory usage to 50% of available RAM.
On a server with 4 GB RAM or more, SQL memory usage can be left unrestricted.

Allow from .5MB to 1.5MB for each managed client.

Appendix B - Case Study - ABX Limited

Introduction

ABX is a large bakery and has 1150 employees located in one site in Dublin, Ireland. ABX requires a complete integrated solution that will help them to manage their desktop, laptops and servers. They have decided to use Altiris Client Management Suite. Certain aspects of CMS will not be used at this stage but will be implemented at a later date. For now, ABX have decided that they need to be able to gather inventory, deliver software packages and manage patch deployment to Windows machines. Inventory Solution, Patch Management Solution and Software Delivery Solution for Windows will be used. An analysis is done prior to implementation and the following information gathered.

Discovered Information:-

- There are two physical networks and one single Windows 2000 Domain.
- The main office is in site A with 75% of desktops and servers. Manufacturing is in site B and has the remaining desktops and servers.
- The WAN connection between the two sites is 2MB.
- Total number of workstations 910.
- Total number of laptops 170, all off-site.
- Total number of servers is 21 running Windows 2000 SP4.
- All desktops are running Windows 2000 Professional SP3 and all laptops are running Windows XP SP1.
- No-one has any idea what patch level clients are at.
- Laptop users dial in from home regularly but rarely visit the Dublin office and connect directly to the network.
- DNS is used for name resolution and DHCP is used for client TCP/IP settings.
- All servers have static IP addresses.
- In Site B the wide area connection and the local LAN are heavily used by manufacturing during the hours of 1:00 am and 12:00 pm.
- Some user's shutdown their machines when they leave work but others don't. Manufacturing machines should always be left on.
- Monitoring of RAS connections shows that laptop users dial in to the network in the morning and late afternoon.

Notification Server Configuration

It has been decided to purchase a new server, which will run Altiris Notification Server, Microsoft SQL 2000 and the chosen Solutions. A new server was chosen because even though several of the current application servers have spare capacity to run Notification Server, ABX are planning a takeover of a rival company. If the takeover goes ahead, it is expected that the number of users would rise to approximately 3,500.

The new server is installed with SQL 2000, Notification Server, Inventory Solution, Patch Management Solution and Software Delivery Solution. The server is placed in Site A where 75% of the users are located. This will help minimize WAN traffic.

Package Servers will be used for patch and software delivery, to minimize the load on the Notification Server and the WAN.
Two existing file and print servers will be used as Package Servers. There will be one Package Server in each site. Extra hard disks will be added to each server to accommodate package storage.

Four custom collections based on IP subnet and operating system type are created. The collections are:

- All desktops in IP subnet 10.10.0.67 (Site A).
- All servers excluding Package Servers in IP subnet 10.10.0.67 (Site A).
- All desktops in IP subnet 10.10.0.68 (Site B).
- All servers excluding Package Servers in IP subnet 10.10.0.68 (Site B).

The collections are created so that each site and OS type can have different Altiris Agent, Inventory scan and Software Update Agent settings.

It is important that the configuration accommodates the following:

- Servers in Site A are not rebooted during working hours by the Software Update Agent. (9:00 am to 5:30 pm)
- Servers in Site B are not rebooted during manufacturing hours by the Software Update Agent. (1:00 am to 12:00 pm)
- Desktops in Site B which are used by manufacturing are not rebooted between 1:00 am and 12:00 pm by the Software Update Agent.
- The network bandwidth between site A and B is not heavily utilized by Altiris traffic during the manufacturing hours of 1:00 am and 12:00 pm.
- Desktop, Servers, Laptops and Package Servers should get advertised patches as soon as possible.

Desktop Configuration

Inventory should be configured to minimize disruption and patch installation should happen within 14 hours of the patch being advertised to desktops.

Desktop configuration is default except:

Desktop Altiris Agent Site A

Basic Inventory is sent once every 7 days and configuration requested every 5 hours.
Bandwidth Throttling starts at 12:00 pm for 24 hours and uses 20% of bandwidth.
Disable communications after blockout and at start-up are configured for up to 1 hour.
Power Management is enabled and packages **will** always be downloaded and not run from the network.

Desktops in this site can download packages from the local Package Server or Notification Server at anytime. Throttling has been implemented but the fast connection within Site A will ensure that clients can quickly download packages.

Desktop Software Update Agent Site A

The 'All Windows Desktops Post SP2' policy is used to configure the update agent.
Apply software updates is every 10 minutes.
Reboot the computer is configured to reboot the desktop at 5:00 am every morning.
Reboot deferral is set to 0 minutes and notification is enabled.

If a patch requiring a reboot has been deployed to desktops in Site A, the desktops will reboot at 5:00 am the next day if the machines are powered on at that time. Work does not start until 9:00 am for office staff in Site A so a reboot will not have any impact on users.

Desktop Inventory Agent Site A

Inventory (Recreate Full Inventory) – This policy runs on all desktop machines in Site A at 11:30 am or as soon as possible after that, on the first day of every month.

Inventory (Recreate User Inventory) – This policy runs on all desktop machines in Site A at 11:00 am or as soon as possible after that, on the first day of every month.

Inventory (Hardware) – This policy runs on all desktop machines in Site A at 2:00 pm or as soon as possible after that, every Tuesday.

Inventory (Software) – This policy runs on all desktop machines in Site A at 3:00 pm or as soon as possible after that, every Sunday.

User Inventory – This policy runs on all desktop machines in Site A at 2:00 pm or as soon as possible after that, every day.

If a user's machine was powered off during the scheduled scan time, the scan will run soon after the user powers the machine on.

Desktop Altiris Agent Site B

Basic Inventory is sent once every 7 days and configuration requested every 7 hours.
Bandwidth Throttling starts at 1:00 pm for 12 hours and uses 20% of bandwidth.
Package blockout is configured from 1:00 am to 12:00 pm.
Disable communications after blockout and at start-up are configured for up to 1 hour.
Power Management is enabled and packages **will** always be downloaded and not run from the network.

Network bandwidth is limited between sites. All clients will request configuration information from the Notification Server and send status events over the WAN. All Packages will be downloaded from the local Package Server in site B. Because the network in site B is used heavily by production from 1:00 am to 12:00 pm it is important that clients do not download packages during this time, hence the blockout period. Disable communications has been configured for one hour after blockout. This means that after the block period all clients in Site B will pick a random number of minutes between 1 and 60 before starting communications.

Desktop Software Update Agent Site B

The 'All Windows Desktops Post SP2' policy is used to configure the update agent.
Apply software updates is every 10 minutes.
Reboot the computer is configured to reboot the desktop at 10:00 pm day.
Reboot deferral is set to 20 minutes and notification is enabled.

If a patch requiring a reboot has been deployed to desktops in Site B, the desktops will reboot at 10:00 pm that day if the machines are powered on at that time. It is important that machines are not rebooted during production hours.
Referral and notification have been enabled so that if the machine is being used, the user can defer for up to 20 minutes.

Desktop Inventory Agent Site B

Inventory (Recreate Full Inventory) – This policy runs on all desktop machines in Site B at 4:15 pm or as soon as possible after that, on the first day of every month.

Inventory (Recreate User Inventory) – This policy runs on all desktop machines in Site B at 4:00 pm or as soon as possible after that, on the first day of every month.

Inventory (Hardware) – This policy runs on all desktop machines in Site B at 3:00 pm or as soon as possible after that, every Tuesday.

Inventory (Software) – This policy runs on all desktop machines in Site B at 3:00 pm or as soon as possible after that, every Sunday.

User Inventory – This policy runs on all desktop machines in Site B at 2:00 pm or as soon as possible after that, every day.

The standard Inventory scans are used and configured to run during the day, out of production hours or as soon as possible after that. If a user's machine was powered off during the scheduled scan time, the scan will run soon after the user powers the machine on.

Laptop Configuration

Inventory should be configured to minimize disruption and patch installation should happen within a day of the patch being advertised to laptops.

Altiris Agent Laptop configuration is default except:
Basic Inventory is sent once every 7 days and configuration requested every 7 hours.
Bandwidth Throttling starts at 1:00 am for 24 hours and uses 50% of bandwidth.
Blockout is not configured.
Power Management is disabled and packages will always be downloaded and not run from the network.

Laptop users normally dial in over a 56k connection. Throttling has been used so that users are able to work normally (check e-mail etc.) while packages are downloaded by the Altiris Agent in the background.

Software Update Agent

The 'All Windows Desktops Post SP2' policy is used to configure the update agent.
Apply software updates is every 10 minutes.
Reboot the computer is configured to reboot the laptop at 5:00 am every morning.
Reboot deferral is set to 5 minutes and notification is enabled.

Laptops are normally shut down when users finish using it. If a laptop is not powered down after a patch requiring a reboot has been installed it will automatically reboot at 5:00 am.

Inventory Agent Laptop

Inventory (Recreate Full Inventory) – This policy runs on all laptops at 4:15 am or as soon as possible after that, on the first day of every month.

Inventory (Recreate User Inventory) – This policy runs on all laptops at 4:00 pm or as soon as possible after that, on the first day of every month.

Inventory (Hardware) – This policy runs on all laptops at 3:00 pm or as soon as possible after that, every day.

Inventory (Software) – This policy runs on all laptops at 3:00 pm or as soon as possible after that, every Sunday.

User Inventory – This policy runs on all laptops at 2:00 pm or as soon as possible after that, every day.

The standard Inventory scans are used and configured to run during the day or as soon as possible after that. If a user's machine is powered off during a scheduled scan time, the scan will run soon after the user powers the machine on. If the laptop is powered on but not connected to the network the scan will still run at the scheduled time, however the Altiris Agent will not be able to upload the inventory until the laptop is reconnected to the network.

Package Server Configuration

Two of the existing file & print servers in the organization will be used as Package Servers. Both servers will require additional hard disk space to store software packages.
Patch installation should happen within a couple of hours of the patch being advertised to Package Servers.

Altiris Agent Package Server configuration is default except:

Package Server Altiris Agent Site A

Basic Inventory is sent once every 7 days and configuration requested every hour.
Bandwidth Throttling starts at 1:00 am for 11 hours and uses 40% of bandwidth.
Bandwidth Throttling starts at 12:00 pm for 13 hours and uses 50% of bandwidth.
Power Management is disabled and packages will always be downloaded and not run from the network.

Package Servers, service package requests from clients and so it is important that Package Servers download new and modified packages before clients become aware of the advertised package. To achieve quick package availability, Package Servers in Site A, request configuration updates frequently and throttle at 40%.

Package Server Software Update Agent Site A

The 'All Windows Servers Post SP2' policy is used to configure the update agent.
Apply software updates is every 10 minutes.
Reboot the computer is configured to reboot the server every Friday at 10:00 pm.
Reboot deferral is set to 0 minutes and notification is disabled.

If a patch requiring a reboot has been deployed to a package Server in Site A, the Package Server will reboot automatically the following Friday at 10 pm. Package Servers in Site A are also used as file and print servers in Site A, so it is important not to reboot it during working hours.

Package Server Inventory Agent Site A

Inventory (Recreate Full Inventory) – This policy runs on Package Servers in Site A at 4:15 am or as soon as possible after that, on the first day of every month.

Inventory (Recreate User Inventory) – The Package Server will not run this policy.

Inventory (Hardware) – This policy runs on Package Servers in Site A at 3:00 am or as soon as possible after that, every day.

Inventory (Software) – This policy runs on Package Servers in Site A at 4:00 am or as soon as possible after that, every Sunday.

User Inventory – The Package Server will not run this policy.

Package Servers in Site A are configured to run Inventory scans out of normal working hours.

Package Server Altiris Agent Site B

Package Servers in Site B will use more throttling during production hours than outside of production hours. This minimizes the amount of traffic over the WAN.

Basic Inventory is sent once every 7 days and configuration requested every hour.
Bandwidth Throttling starts at 1:00 am for 11 hours and uses 15% of bandwidth.
Bandwidth Throttling starts at 1:00 pm for 13 hours and uses 20% of bandwidth.
Power Management is disabled and packages will always be downloaded and not run from the network.

Network bandwidth is limited between sites. The package Server will get packages across the WAN and so throttling has been used to minimize the amount of traffic. Allowing Package Servers to download during production hours with limited bandwidth will allow packages to be available sooner to clients in site B.

Package Server Software Update Agent Site B

The 'All Windows Servers Post SP2' policy is used to configure the update agent.
Apply software updates is every 10 minutes.
Reboot the computer is configured to reboot the server every Sunday at 3 pm.
Reboot deferral is set to 0 minutes and notification is disabled.

If a patch requiring a reboot has been deployed to a package Server in Site B, the Package Server will reboot automatically the following Sunday at 3 pm. Package Servers in Site B are also used as file and print servers, so it is important that these servers are not rebooted during manufacturing hours.

Package Server Inventory Agent Site B

Inventory (Recreate Full Inventory) – This policy runs on Package Servers in Site B at 4:15 pm or as soon as possible after that, on the first day of every month.

Inventory (Recreate User Inventory) – The Package Server will not run this policy.

Inventory (Hardware) – This policy runs on Package Servers in Site B at 3:00 pm or as soon as possible after that, every day.

Inventory (Software) – This policy runs on Package Servers in Site B at 3:00 pm or as soon as possible after that, every Sunday.

User Inventory – The Package Server will not run this policy.

Package Servers in Site B are configured to run Inventory scans out of normal manufacturing hours.

Server Configuration

It is important that servers excluding Package Servers in Site A are not rebooted between 9:00 am and 5:30 pm and that servers excluding Package Servers in Site B are not rebooted between 1:00 am and 12:00 pm.
Inventory should be configured to minimize disruption and patch installation should happen within a couple of hours of the patch being advertised to servers.

Altiris Agent Server configuration is default except:

Server Altiris Agent Site A

Basic Inventory is sent once every 7 days and configuration requested every hour.
Bandwidth Throttling starts at 1:00 am for 11 hours and uses 40% of bandwidth.
Bandwidth Throttling starts at 12:00 pm for 13 hours and uses 50% of bandwidth.
Power Management is disabled and packages will always be downloaded and not run from the network.

The Servers in Site A will get packages from the local Package Server in Site A. Allowing Servers to download during working hours with limited bandwidth will allow the Servers to receive updates quickly.

Server Software Update Agent Site A

The 'All Windows Servers Post SP2' policy is used to configure the update agent.
Apply software updates is every 10 minutes.
Reboot the computer is configured to reboot the server every Friday at 10:00 pm.
Reboot deferral is set to 0 minutes and notification is disabled.

If a patch requiring a reboot has been deployed to a Server in Site A, the Server will reboot automatically the following Friday at 10 pm. It is important not to reboot Servers in Site A during normal working hours.

Server Inventory Agent Site A

Inventory (Recreate Full Inventory) – This policy runs on Servers in Site A at 4:15 am or as soon as possible after that, on the first day of every month.

Inventory (Recreate User Inventory) – The Server will not run this policy.

Inventory (Hardware) – This policy runs on Servers in Site A at 3:00 am or as soon as possible after that, every day.

Inventory (Software) – This policy runs on Servers in Site A at 4:00 am or as soon as possible after that, every Sunday.

User Inventory – The Server will not run this policy.

Servers in Site A are configured to run Inventory scans out of normal working hours.

Server Altiris Agent Site B

Servers in Site B will use more throttling during production hours than outside of production hours. This minimizes the amount of traffic over the WAN.

Basic Inventory is sent once every 7 days and configuration requested every hour. Bandwidth Throttling starts at 1:00 am for 11 hours and uses 30% of bandwidth. Bandwidth Throttling starts at 1:00 pm for 13 hours and uses 40% of bandwidth. Power Management is disabled and packages will always be downloaded and not run from the network.

The Servers in Site B will get packages from the local Package Server in Site B. Allowing Servers to download during manufacturing hours with limited bandwidth will allow the Servers to receive updates quickly.

Server Software Update Agent Site B

The 'All Windows Servers Post SP2' policy is used to configure the update agent.
Apply software updates is every 10 minutes.
Reboot the computer is configured to reboot the server every Sunday at 3 pm.
Reboot deferral is set to 0 minutes and notification is disabled.

If a patch requiring a reboot has been deployed to a Server in Site B, the Server will reboot automatically the following Sunday at 3 pm. It is important that these servers are not rebooted during manufacturing hours.

Server Inventory Agent Site B

Inventory (Recreate Full Inventory) – This policy runs on Servers in Site B at 4:15 pm or as soon as possible after that, on the first day of every month.

Inventory (Recreate User Inventory) – The Server will not run this policy.

Inventory (Hardware) – This policy runs on Servers in Site B at 3:00 pm or as soon as possible after that, every day.

Inventory (Software) – This policy runs on Servers in Site B at 3:00 pm or as soon as possible after that, every Sunday.

User Inventory – The Server will not run this policy.

Servers in Site B are configured to run Inventory scans out of normal manufacturing hours.

Software & Patch Delivery in ABX Limited

With the configuration as documented in the previous pages the following should happen if an administrator advertises a software update to all machines in the network:

At 9:15 am the Administrator creates and deploys a Microsoft Software Update of 2MB to all machines in the network.

Site A

By 10:15 am, at the latest, the Package Server in Site A will be aware of the new package and start downloading it. The package should be made available by the Package Server to requesting clients by 10:30 am.

Servers will be aware of the package by 10:15 am, at the latest. Once the package is available on the local Package Server in Site A, the servers will download and install the patch based on the schedule. All servers in Site A will have the package by 11:00 am.

All desktops will be aware of the package by 2:15 pm at the latest. i.e. If a desktop updated configuration at 9:14 am it would not see the package, the next update for that desktop would be at 2:14 pm when it would see that there was a package to download.
Desktops that are aware of the package anytime after 9:15 am can download it once it is available on the local Package Server. All desktops will have the package by approximately 2:30 pm.

Site B

By 10:15 am, at the latest, the Package Server in Site B will be aware of the new package and start downloading it. The package should be made available by the Package Server to requesting clients by 11:00 am.
Servers will be aware of the package by 10:15 am, at latest. Once the package is available on the local Package Server in Site B, the servers will download and install the patch based on the schedule. All servers in Site B will have the package by 11:30 am.

Desktops will be aware of the patch anytime between 9:15 am and 4:15 pm, depending on their update cycle. Desktops in Site B will not be able to download the patch before 12:00 pm because of the Package Blockout configuration. Desktops in Site B will only be able to download the patch from their local Package Server after the block period. All desktops in Site B will have the package by 4:30 pm.

Laptops

A laptop user dials in to the network at 10:00 am and logs off at 10:15 am. The laptop will be aware of the patch but will be unable to download it from the Package Server in Site A because it is not yet available. At 2:00 pm the laptop user dials in for 5 minutes. The Altiris Agent starts the download but is unable to finish it. At 5:00 pm the laptop user dials in for 15 minutes. Because the Altiris Agent supports checkpoint recovery it can continue the download from where it last stopped. The Agent completes the download just before the user disconnects from the network. The patch is installed based on the schedule.

Future Expansion

If at a later date ABX acquires a competitor, package servers can be placed in the new sites and the Altiris Agent installed on machines that need to be managed. If the WAN connections between sites are unreliable or lacking in bandwidth, managed clients in the remote sites could be configured to use a high percentage of bandwidth throttling and a blockout period may also be considered.

Appendix C - Troubleshooting Custom Inventory

To troubleshoot Custom Inventory, start at the client and work up. Start by manually running the custom inventory scan from a client to ensure that there are no errors in the xml or ini files.

Manually run the custom Inventory

Copy the contents of the Inventory folder including the new custom inventory files from the Notification Server to the local temp folder on a client machine. Then use the Start-Run command to manually execute the inventory scan.

e.g. *C:\Temp\AexInvsoln.exe /s NewCustomInv.ini*

Notice that I left out the hidden switch so that I can see if the scan runs successfully. If the scan runs successfully, the local Inventory folder on the client will be populated with the new NSI file created by the scan.
This file will contain the actual data that will be sent to the Notification Server. The name of the NSI file is the name specified by the custom inventory ini file.

View the scan output

The Altiris Inventory viewer can be used to open the file. The viewer is a single exe located on the Notification Server under:
InstallPath\Notification Server\Nscap\Bin\Win32\x86.

Use the viewer to open the file. If an error is displayed when the file is viewed, then there is a mistake in the custom XML file. The most common issue is lack of a blank space after each line in the XML code. If the NSI file opens and shows a formatted table of inventory data, then the XML code is fine but there may be a problem transporting the data to Notification Server.

When the NSI file has been successfully created it is then transported by the Altiris Agent to the EvtInbox under the Nscap share on the Notification Server. Patience is necessary at this point as it may take a while for the Agent to transfer the data and for the various processes to add the data to the SQL database on the NS.

Check the database

If the custom inventory scan creates a new table in SQL, use a tool such as the SQL Admin tools to view the table names in the Altiris database. When the new name table appears that should indicate that the data has been added to the database.

View the Custom Inventory in the Web Console

Navigate a collection containing the machine used to run the manual scan.
Use Resource Manager to view the inventory data for the machine.
If the new data class and inventory do not appear, ensure that you have configured the new data class to appear. Read the 'Viewing Custom Inventory' section in the chapter 'Inventory Solution for Windows' for more information.
If the manual scan ran successfully and uploaded the data to the Notification Server database then the xml and ini for the custom inventory are fine. If the scan is still failing on clients, read on.

Check the Client

From a client that is part of the collection that the new Custom Inventory policy is configured to use, manually start a configuration update using the Altiris Agent GUI.

Check that the new custom ini and xml files have been downloaded by the client to its local Inventory Solution folder. In the local Altiris Agent folder look in the Software Delivery folder for GUID folders with a sub folder named cache. (GUID will be a long alpha numeric name.) Check each cache folder until you find the folder containing the Inventory Solution files.

There may be several reasons for this, including:

- The client may not be a member of the collection targeted by the Custom Inventory policy. *Check the collection membership in the Web Console.*
- The Notification Server may not yet have updated the distribution points with the added/amended inventory files. *From the Web Console select the Configuration tab and navigate to **Solution Settings > Assets and Inventory > Inventory > Windows > Inventory Agent Rollout** and select the Inventory Agent Package. In the details pane click the 'Update Distribution Points' button.*

Once the files are downloaded by the client either wait for the schedule to kick off the Custom Inventory or manually run it using the Altiris Agent UI. (Manually running the policy is only permitted if the option to let users run the policy manually is checked on the policy.)

As with manual testing, the Custom inventory will run and place the new NSI inventory data file in the local Inventory folder. The Altiris Agent will then transfer this data to the Notification Server.

If the scan fails to run, check the properties of the package and see if there is a command line or permissions issue. Use the properties of the Custom Scan Inventory policy in the Web Console to correct any issues.

Appendix D - NS File & Share Permissions

The following are the **minimum NTFS** and **Share** permissions that are needed for running Notification Server.

NTFS Permissions

Configure the local Administrators group with Full Control access and Everyone with Read access to the path: *install path\Altiris\Notification Server*

Configure the local system account and the local Administrators group with Full control access to the path: install path\Altiris\Notification Server\NSCap
Alternately, give full control permission to the Domain Administrators group.

The Internet Information Services user account IUSR_%computername% needs Full control of the following folders:
install path\Altiris\Notification Server\NSCap\EvtQFast
install path\Altiris\Notification Server\NSCap\EvtInbox
install path\Altiris\Notification Server\NSCap\EvtQueue

Share Permissions

Configure Everyone to Read access for the path:
install path\Altiris\Notification Server\NSCap

For standalone inventory, configure Everyone with Write access to the path:
install path\Altiris\Notification Server\NSCap\EvtInbox

Configure Everyone with No Access to the following paths:
install path\Altiris\Notification Server\NSCap\EvtQFast
install path\Altiris\Notification Server\NSCap\EvtQueue
install path\Altiris\Notification Server\NSCap\install

Appendix E - Windows XP SP2 Notes

Altiris Agent

For a push install from the console:

Make exceptions for TCP port 445, "Web Server (HTTP)".
Enable "File and Print Sharing".
Ensure XP Simple File Sharing is turned off
Admin$ share is not disabled.

For Altiris Agent Power Management (Tickle)
Open TCP ports 52028 and 52029.

Carbon Copy

Add an Exception for SHELLKER.EXE in the Carbon Copy install folder.

PC Transplant

Open Ports 41415 & 4949
Add PCTRTDestAgent.exe in the Exception list for Windows Firewall.
Add Port 80 or 'Web Server (HTTP)' to the Exception list and for SSL add Port 443 or check 'Secured Web Server (HTTPS)'.

Network discovery

Open ports for SNMP (UDP 161 and 162) and NETBIOS (TCP/UDP 137).

Web Administrator for Windows

Open TCP ports 445 and 135

DS Agent (Aclient.exe)

Remote push of Deployment Agent from the Console:

Make exceptions for TCP port 445, "Web Server (HTTP)".
Enable "File and Print Sharing".
Ensure XP Simple File Sharing is turned off
Enter an Exception in Windows Firewall for AClntUser.exe before installing the Deployment Agent

Other

If remain mostly disconnected from server is configured on the DS agent then open UDP port 402

Deployment Console

Make an Exception in Windows Firewall for eXpress.exe